# REMEMBER TO REMEMBER

HENRY MILLER

# REMEMBER TO REMEMBER

## HENRY MILLER

VOL. 2 OF THE AIR-CONDITIONED NIGHTMARE

A NEW DIRECTIONS BOOK

Library of Congress Catalog Card Number: 45-11390
(ISBN: 0-8112-0113-9)

ACKNOWLEDGEMENTS

Many chapters of this volume have already appeared in maga-zines, anthologies and pamphlets in this country. For permission to reprint we beg to thank the editors of the following:

*Circle; The Alicat Book Shop; Portfolio, Town & Country; Hemispheres; The Harvard Advocate;* and Bern Porter, Berkeley, California.

Manufactured in the United States of America.

First published as New Directions Paperbook 111 in 1961.

Published simultaneously in Canada
by McClelland and Stewart, Ltd.

New Directions Books are published for James Laughlin
by New Directions Publishing Corporation,
333 Sixth Avenue, New York 10014.

FIFTH PRINTING

# CONTENTS

## THE ILLUSTRATIONS

The portraits of Henry Miller and Varda were photographed by Johann Hagemeyer, and the portrait of Beauford DeLaney by Gjon Mili. Henry Miller's watercolor *The Honeymooners* was photographed by Rey Ruppel and is reproduced by courtesy of the Pat Wall Gallery, Monterey, California.

# PREFACE

In this volume are included a number of portraits of people to whom I wish to pay homage. The number could be extended easily, but that would entail the making of an album, which is not my purpose. In the space of six years, even if I did nothing but sit still, it was inevitable that I should meet a great number of people. With a few exceptions the meetings recorded were accidental. By that I mean that fate threw these people across my path.

My life seems to revolve about chance meetings. Most of the friendships I have formed were created in this way. Usually the people you long to meet are disappointing when you do catch up with them. There are people with whom you correspond whom you are destined never to meet, and it is generally better that way. I have met only a few celebrities in my life, but I have known quite a few men of genius, most of them still unheard of by the general public. Of neurotics and psychopaths I have had more than my fill; of bores and pests there seems literally no end. The people I like best are little people, the unknown ones.

When I left New York (in June 1942) I became the permanent guest of Margaret and Gilbert Neiman, at Beverly Glen, Los Angeles. My resources then were completely exhausted. The cabin at Beverly Glen, which is contiguous to the Bel Air Estates—the Gold Coast, so to speak—was a delightful place. When the Neimans left for Colorado I shared the cabin with John Dudley of Kenosha. It was a bad period for me in many ways, relieved only by the itch to paint. To go to Hollywood and Vine from the Glen was like making a journey to Alaska. To shop, I went to Westwood Village or to Beverly Hills, usually on foot. Twice I was offered the gift of a car but refused. Finally, largely because Dudley was lazy, I bought one for forty dollars. It lasted ten days and then we left it in a ditch beside the road.

The person I shall remember longest, in connection with this period, is Attilio Bowinkel of Westwood Village. It is not because of what he did for me, though that was considerable, but because of what he was. In appearance and in spirit he reminded me strongly of my father when the latter was Bowinkel's age. He had the same easy, indulgent ways as my father. He was born with a generous nature and a spirit of forbearance. I speak of him as if he were dead, but he is still very much alive. I miss him more than I miss any one whose acquaintance I made since returning to America.

To Jean Varda I owe a great debt—the discovery of the Big Sur

Site of an old convict camp at Anderson's Creek, Big Sur. Henry Miller lived here before he moved to his new home higher up the mountain side.

country where I have made my home since 1944. It seems, actually, as though I had been living here much longer, perhaps because for the first time in my life I have the feeling of being at home in America. If it was Varda who introduced me to the Big Sur it was Lynda Sargent who made it possible for me to live here. But Lynda is a character whose portrait I am reserving for a special volume.

A few months after arriving at Big Sur I was called East by my mother's illness. While East I visited Dartmouth College to see my friend Herbert West, professor of literature there. With him I saw some of New Hampshire and Vermont, a region I found charming and gracious. Herb West, also the son of a tailor, I discovered, was like a brother to me. Of all the professors I have met, in America or elsewhere, he is beyond a doubt the most human. It is easy to understand why he is a favorite with the students at Dartmouth.

I could not return to California without looking up Paul Weiss, then professor of philosophy at Bryn Mawr. He had been urging me for months, in his letters, to come East and meet Jasper Deeter of the Hedgerow Theatre at Moylan. He was so insistent about it that I almost passed Deeter up, which would have been a misfortune for me.

At Boulder, Colorado, I met Thomas George, a Greek who runs a candy store there. In the back of his shop one evening he treated a group of us to a meal such as I hadn't tasted since I left Athens. It was when we thought we had finished the main course that he opened the oven door and showed us the roast kid he had prepared for us. That meal stands out in my memory as the most lavish one I was ever invited to.

I think immediately of another Greek whom I used to visit now and then when I was in New York. He was the lavatory attendant in a famous hotel patronized by literary celebrities. He also shined shoes when you wanted him to. The first time I struck up a conversation with him he was eating his lunch, down there in the underground, in his glittering little realm where all the foul odors are concentrated. When I informed him that I had been in Greece once he immediately put aside the sandwich he was munching; his face lighted up as if I had pronounced a benediction. Every time I was in that neighborhood I would drop downstairs to visit him. Nothing more than a little chat, but it always set me up for the day. Through him, and despite the foul odors, I touched Greece, her sunny skies, her blue waters, her deep spiritual abundance. Many celebrities visit that toilet: I wonder if any of them ever takes notice of this emissary from the kingdom of light.

Always the interesting figures are found in obscure, unsuspected places. I remember a certain professor urging me once to pay a visit to Alfred North Whitehead. Perhaps I missed a great opportunity in not acting upon his suggestion. Nevertheless, I feel certain that Whitehead would not have interested me nearly so much as a certain dark-skinned man I used to chat with in Hollywood. This individual was none other than the bootblack in a barber shop on one of the main boulevards. I came upon him for the first time one evening after the barber shop was closed. He was sitting at a typewriter on the sidewalk, right next to the window. It was in this public spot that he wrote most of his novels. After a brief chat he invited me to call on him next day in order to show me his work. I glanced through several fat tomes of typescript, all full length novels, huge ones. The language employed in them was certainly not the Queen's English. I suppose it could best be called "African." It was, in any event, like nothing I had ever seen before. By this I don't mean to say that it was unintelligible. Quite the contrary. Compared to the novelistic prose of Aldous Huxley or of Evelyn Waugh it was rich, exalted language. No one could possibly fall asleep reading it. The plots were sensational, to say the least.

Frescoes rather than novels. I tried to think of a publisher who would have the courage to bring them out, but I couldn't think of one. Here was something unique in American literature—a black man's book done in an honest black man's way—something bad perhaps, atrociously bad, but exciting, a thousand times more exciting than the cheap novels which glut the market. Something bad only when viewed from the prejudiced standpoint of a literary esthete. So bad, in this sense, that it was refreshing, stimulating, superb in some cock-eyed way. Hollywood is a place where they are (supposedly) always looking for new talent. But they always look through a telescope to find the right man. This man is right there at their feet day in and day out, shining their shoes and brushing their coats—and nobody the wiser.

Wandering aimlessly about, one meets many strange, curious, and often forlorn, figures. Since the war was then on, I would pick up a soldier or a sailor now and then. Usually he was a deserter, or thinking of deserting. I never picked up a single man in uniform who believed in the war, believed that it was necessary and right for him to go to the front. None of them had their heart in it, a rather astounding fact, when you think of it. Most of them were simple lads—from mountain, prairie or village. Some were deserting because they missed their wives and children, some because they were worried about their livestock, some because they were just plain homesick for the land they grew up on. All good, honest fellows, the salt of the earth. How many of them, I often wondered, were shot or put in irons, or tortured by ignorant, vicious guards.

Once in Mississippi, in a saloon, I encountered a book salesman —he was handling the Encyclopaedia Britannica. It was almost like meeting my own ghost. There he was, getting himself plastered after a humiliating day's work, telling me all the things I knew by heart from bitter experience, boasting in his broken-hearted way of the money he was rolling up in commissions. I wondered why he didn't try to sell me an encyclopaedia. Perhaps he was too far gone to give a shit. When he staggered away from me at the corner I observed out of the corner of my eye a big black buck stalking his trail. I wondered if America really needed that extra book salesman—or did the Negro need the money more. And then I thought of an American author whom I met in the South somewhere, a man who was trying to entertain his guests one evening by relating his drunken exploits with a pugilist friend. Seems that just to amuse themselves they would walk down a dark street and, without provocation, without the slightest warning, go up to a darkie and knock him cold. The trick was, as he put it, to fell a big buck with one punch. (Negroes are supposed to have particularly thick skulls.) If that didn't work, then a kick in the guts or a bottle over the head. . . . Pretty story. You can imagine how bored an American writer must get sometimes.

Willie Fung, now, is a horse of another color. Willie Fung runs a saloon in Los Angeles; he also plays in the films now and then. That's how I recognized him when we walked in. Willie Fung is fond of music, any kind of music. He had three musicians, all Oakies; he had hired them more for his own entertainment, I suspect, than for that of his clients. His habit is to draw up a chair behind the piano player and sit with folded arms and the rapt expression of a devout Buddhist. Now and then he looked around to see if we were listening. When he smiled, a very broad smile, it was like the sun setting over Waikiki. It was a smile that seemed to say: "Music velly good, velly good." The piece over, Willie Fung rises and asks in a cordial, gracious tone of voice what we would like to drink. He wanted us to be happy; he didn't seem to care who bought the drinks, we or him. Just drink and listen to the music. Now and then the musicians drank with us. They were simple folk, doing the best they knew how. It seemed perfect that they should be the ones to play for Willie Fung. They belonged there.

I liked Willie Fung instanter. I liked him more and more as the evening wore on. He spoke only in choppy phrases, accompanied always by that ingratiating, inundating smile. I remembered vividly some of the roles he had played in the films, none of which had done him justice. I was on the point of telling him this several times but I wasn't certain he would understand me. So I just kept smiling at him the whole evening long, applauding the music, and saying to myself: "Music velly good, velly good. Willie Fung velly good too, velly good." I hope he understood.

Speaking of saloons. . . . I had been to Fortress Monroe one afternoon, a place I had always been hankering to see. Just had to have a look at Old Point Comfort—and that grand dilapidated hulk of a Chamberlain Hotel. For years I dreamt of spending a vacation here. And then, just a week before he committed suicide, I made the acquaintance of a cornet player who spent most of his life running from the hotel to the fortress. Anyway, that afternoon, after visiting Old Point Comfort, I found myself standing at the bar of a saloon in Phoebus. Abe Rattner was with me. We couldn't help but notice that the place was crowded with paintings. Some of them were not bad, not bad at all. It was the proprietor of the saloon, we soon discovered, who had painted them. Listening to his talk, I doubt if he had ever seen the work of a good painter. I doubt if he had ever set foot outside the precincts of little Phoebus. (Nor seen her steeds water at the spring.) Long, long ago he had ceased to paint. He was not even a Sunday painter now. I suppose it had never occurred to him that a man might go on painting, make it his life's work. He seemed to take it for granted that it was just a pastime. It occurred to me then how many thousands of men there are in America like him, men with talent who never knew they were artists. Failures. Failures because there was nothing in their environment to nourish them. Failures because they exist in a void—hear nothing, see nothing, know nothing. . . . So what by the clock? Nothing. Just that.

There are people and there are places. Have you ever driven all day and suddenly, towards dark, in the midst of nowhere, come upon a roadside inn, a bar, a café? Do you remember the feel of such places, that dreary emptiness, that end of the world ambiance? Maybe a lone figure at the end of the bar is talking to himself. In a corner, among the cobwebs, a battered old Moll is weeping or gnashing her teeth. What's the difference? The juke box will be going in a moment. That same old song which trailed you everywhere from the time you left home. Such melancholy warbling! Just the thing to cheer you up at the end of a day. You wish you could get drunk too, but you can't. You swallow your drink and push on. The next place is just as dreary, just as melancholy, and the juke box is giving forth the same weary plaint. So you give it up. You pick a hotel at random, a modest one, and you find yourself back in England, about the time of the Crusades. Then you wash up and look for a place to eat. The menu reads like an advertisement for indigestion. You go to bed and try to read. You blow your brains out . . . I mean you turn the light out . . . and lie awake all night recreating the American scene.

Places. . . . Well, take Main Street, Los Angeles. For all the weird, cock-eyed, down at the heel, unbelievable things, you always refer back to L. A.   Main Street Los Angeles is about the worst street in America, to my way of thinking. It hollers with ugliness. You walk along and glance at the figures sitting at the bars, and you shudder. A simian world. A simian world on high heels, rolling from stool to stool. I know foreigners who think it has atmosphere.

This is the raw, crude America, they think. Gimcrack. Everything gimcrack. They love it. To them it's quaint. Until one day some ugly bloke takes a poke at them—just for nothing. Because maybe he doesn't like the man's looks. That's America. And you don't have to go to the movies to discover it. Just walk up and down Main Street—any Main street.

America is full of places. Empty places. And all these empty places are crowded. Just jammed with empty souls. All at loose ends, all seeking diversion. As though the chief object of existence were to forget. Everyone seeking a nice, cosy little joint in which to be with his fellow-man and not with the problems which haunt him. Not ever finding such a place, but pretending that it does exist, if not here then elsewhere. Each one saying to himself, like a monomaniac: "It's nice here. A good joint. I'm happy here. I'm going to forget I'm lonely and miserable." And with that one gets really lonely, really miserable. And then you notice some one's talking to you. It's the middle of a beery monologue. This guy's not only lonely and miserable, he's cuckoo. Finally you get so desperate you decide to go home. To do this one has to be really desperate, because home is the last place on earth to go when you're in despair. Of course it's furnished with all the latest improvements—radio, frigidaire, washing machine, vacuum cleaner, Encyclopaedia Britannica, the funny papers, the telephone, steam heat, electric grill, shower bath, etc. All the comforts, so to speak. But never was a people more uncomfortable than the Americans at home. A sort of temperate, cheerless lunacy pervades the atmosphere. Sitting in your easy chair you have only to turn the knob and there comes to you over the ether waves the sound of that bland, especially chosen voice saying: *"The world looks to America!"* If only it could look deep into the heart of America, see what it's like in the bosom of the family! Maybe then the world would turn its face away. Maybe it would be a thousand times better for the world if it ceased to hope and believe in America. This is just a thought.

Of course there are other places beside home, sweet home. Nice, clean places, like the church, for instance. Could anything be nicer and cleaner than the inside of a church—a Protestant church, of course? Only a hospital or the morgue. The outsides of the churches are always a bit gaga, what with the bilious color scheme and the gloomy stained-glass windows, some showing sheep piercing the clouds or else that man Jesus, our Saviour, nailed to his cross. Inside, however, it's almost inviting. Pew after pew, and the psalters hidden away in the back pockets. Standing in the pulpit always one of those good, clean, upright men, a man of God, as they say. A pitcher of water in front of him, in case he gets hoarse or thirsty. How he loves his flock, the dear, good pastor! He loves every single one of them, just like he loves his dear Jesus. Such a good man. If only he wouldn't talk such shit all the time. If only he had a real message!

No, the church is not the place. Neither is the bowling alley, nor the cinema, nor the billiard parlor, nor the drug store, nor the military academy, nor the boarding school, nor the penitentiary, nor the deaf and dumb asylum, nor the bughouse. Each one more empty, more cheerless, more sinister than the other. Even to belong to the Moose or the Elks is no help. Perhaps you have to become a Communist to realize that there just ain't no place to go to. Yet just the other day, when I was visiting Jack London's old place in Glen Ellen, I thought to myself—"here is the nearest thing to Paradise I've ever seen in America." But Jack London didn't live there very much, I was informed. He was too restless. He made a Paradise for himself and then locked himself out.

They say that Pushkin, after he had laughed himself sick reading

*Dead Souls*, exclaimed: "What a sad place our Russia is!" That's what I keep saying to myself all the time about America. "What a sad place it is! What a fiasco!" The French, I see, are just beginning to discover this, thanks to the current vogue for American literature. They are amazed, apparently, that American authors have worse things to say about their own country than any foreigner. They admit now that Duhamel's book on America (*Scènes de la Vie Future*) is tame by comparison with the observations of such writers as Faulkner, Steinbeck, Caldwell, Dos Passos and others. They are felicitating our writers on their growing awareness.

That "future life" which Duhamel tried to warn his countrymen about is of course being lived already in Soviet Russia. There it seems to be taken for granted that there is no escape. The Russians are already in the New World, feet foremost. Here we try to pretend that it is possible to live in two worlds at once. Viewed from the Party line, our ablest writers are reactionary. They represent the tail-end of something. There is too much pessimism, too much disillusionment in these social satirists. An up and coming people are full of faith, full of courage, full of optimism.

It should be borne in mind, of course, that our ablest writers have but little influence upon the country at large. The masses will still vote the Republican and Democratic tickets, come what may. Russia is plunging ahead in full consciousness, plunging with boot and spur. We in America are lurching drunkenly in a semi-stupor. The men who enabled us to win the war were for the most part conservative men—professors and technicians, industrialists, inventors. They didn't want a new world; they wanted a return to the good old days. The Russians want a new world and will go to any lengths to get it. And, whether we want it or not, the new world is already in the making. It is a world, however, that nobody likes very much thus far. Even the Russians are not very comfortable in it. To be sure, it is the general expectation among those who believe in a new order that the common man will eventually inherit the fruits of all the inventions and discoveries now being made. But over whose dead body, I'd like to ask? No one seems able to give a convincing explanation of just how this miracle will come about. How will the common man inherit anything if he has no appetite, no taste for Paradise? How will a new order come about if the men who are to compose it have not grown new hearts, new consciences?

When I said a moment ago that America is a sad place, I meant just that. It is sad to think that a country which has the greatest advantages has so little to show for it. It is sad to think that scarcely anyone likes the job he is doing, that scarcely anyone believes in what he is doing, that almost no one, barring the professional optimists, sees any hope in the future. It is even more sad to observe that no real effort is made to do anything about anything. Yes, I know that the workers are constantly organizing, constantly striking or threatening to strike, in order to get better wages, better living conditions. But I also know that, at this rate, they will never get sufficient wages to meet the rising cost of living. The great bugaboo here in America is "the dictatorship of the proletariat." Looking at the rank and file, the so-called "masses," does any one honestly believe that these men and women will dictate the future of America? Can slaves become rulers overnight? These poor devils are begging to be led, and they are being led, but it's up a blind alley.

The war is over and, instead of the Four Freedoms, we have all kinds of tyrannies, all kinds of misery, all kinds of privation. The victors are divided, as always happens. Where are the leaders, who are they, who will make the new world, or help to usher it in? Can you call Stalin one, or President Truman, or de Gaulle, or the

Bank of England? Are these the men who incarnate the time spirit? Are these the men who will lead us out of the wilderness?

The new world is being born of necessity, in travail, as all things are born in this human realm. It is being born of forces which we only dimly recognize. The elements which will make the coming world comprise a whole which no political ideology can hope to embrace. Only a new mentality, a new consciousness, only a vision capable of embracing all the conflicting tendencies, of seeing around, beyond and above them, will permit men to adapt themselves to the order and the ambiance of this new world. Once men become imbued with the idea that the "age of plenitude" is inevitable, all the current world views, petty, destructive, mutually exclusive, will vanish like dust. There is not a single political leader to-day who can see beyond his nose, not a single scientist who can reckon with the forces which have already been unleashed, much less marshal or control them. We are only faintly beginning to realize that the world egg is truly shattered, that this happened a few centuries ago, and that in its wake is a staggering cosmos in which men will be forced to play the role of gods.

The atomic bomb is only the first little Christmas present, so to speak, from the blind forces which are shaping the new era. Does any one suppose that we are going to be content with just this one dazzling new toy? How antiquated already are the railroads, the steamships, the automobiles, the aeroplanes, the electrical dynamos! In a jiffy we can be in touch with China, India, Australia, darkest Africa; in a few hours (to-day, that is, but what about to-morrow?) we can be physically transported to any one of these distant places. And here we are lumbering along, millions and billions of us, as if paralyzed, as if deaf and dumb. With the proper will we in America could, almost overnight, supply the whole world with everything it needs. We don't need the support of any country. Everything exists here in superabundance—I mean the physical actuality. As for our potential, no man can estimate it. Wars give only a slight intimation of what this country can do when it feels the vital urge. We are in possession of secrets which, if revealed and exploited, would unleash incalculable power and energy. We could inspire such hope, such courage, such enthusiasm, that the passion of the French revolutionists would seem like a mere breeze. I am thinking now only of what we actually possess, what we actually know, what we can actually visualize, myopic as we are. I say nothing of the suppressed, frustrated dreams of our inventors, our scientists, our technologists, our poets, of what would happen were they encouraged and not discouraged. I say, taking stock of only that which we now know and possess, we could revolutionize life on this earth to an unthinkable degree, and in the space of a few short years. What Russia, for example, hopes to accomplish in the next twenty years would, from this viewpoint, appear childish. To the dreams of our wildest dreamers, I say—"Yes, entirely possible. Possible right now, to-morrow. Possible a thousand times over, and to an extent that not even the wildest dreamer imagines." The future is galloping towards us like a wild horse; we can feel her breath on our necks.

One does not have to belong to any party, any cult, any ism, to sense what lies ahead. One does not have to swear allegiance to this or that to make this new world feasible. If anything, we have to forego these allegiances—they have only been halters and crutches. Our allegiance is always given to dead things. What is alive does not demand allegiance; what is alive commands, whether one gives adherence or not. What is necessary is that we believe and recognize that which is asserting itself, that we put ourselves in rhythm with what is vital and creative.

To-day the world is bound, cramped, stifled by those existing forms of government known as the State. Does the State protect us or do we protect the State? Whatever form of tyranny exists to-day exists by our consent. No matter into what corner of the globe we cast our eye to-day, we see the spectre of tyranny. Perhaps the worst tyranny is that which is created for our own good. There can be no common good unless the individual is recognized first and foremost—and until the last, the weakest, of men is included. Everything proceeds from the living individual. The State is an abstraction, a bogey which can intimidate but never convince us, never win us over completely.

In every State there is an element, like some mortal disease, which works to destroy it. And eventually, through a process of undermining, it does destroy it. No State ever had humanity in mind, only the interests of the State. When will we forget about the State and think of humanity, of ourselves, since it is we, all of us, who make up humanity? When will we think of all instead of just "our own?"

A new world is always more inclusive than the old one. A decadent, dying world is always jealous and possessive in all its parts. Since it can no longer live as a complex organism it strives to live cellularly, atomistically. Birth means disruption. It means the abandonment of one temple for another, the relinquishing of the known and the proven for the adventure of freedom and creation. It means above all—release. Those who are saying No! those who are defending the old order (the sacred temple, the sacred cow), those who are dubious and disillusioned, these do not want release. They want to die in the womb. To every urge they say "but," "if," or—*"impossible!"* Their motto is always the same: "Proceed cautiously!" Their talk is always of concession and compromise, never of faith, trust, confidence.

If the Russians are going to think only of Russia, and Americans of America, the hidden forces which direct the world, the forces which represent *all* humanity, will sooner or later put them in open conflict, incite them to destroy one another. When they talk of disarmament do they not mean stacking arms? If they mean peace, why do they wish to retain their weapons, their arsenals, their spies, their provocateurs? Wherever there is the jealous urge to exclude there is the menace of extinction. I see no nation on earth at present which has an all-inclusive view of things. I say it is impossible for a nation, as such, to hold such a view. Every one will tell you that such a view would be suicidal. Yet it is as clear as the handwriting on the wall that the nations of this earth are finished, though they have not yet come to their end. The dissolving process may continue for a span, but the outcome is certain and definite. Nations will disappear. The human family does not need these water-tight compartments in which to breathe. There is nothing any longer which warrants the survival of the nations, since to be Russian, French, English or American means to be less than what one really is.

Let me digress for a moment on that suicidal policy which a humanitarian instead of a national view of the world is supposed to entrain. I cannot help but think of the fervor with which, during the final days of the war, the helpless nations looked to America or Russia, sometimes to both. Two mighty nations, prepared to make any sacrifice to win the war, dazzled the world by their ability to mobilize seemingly inexhaustible powers, both moral and material. The end accomplished, their miraculous resources, the spiritual ones especially, seem to be drained. More even than during the war, the helpless peoples of the earth need the aid of these two mighty powers. The winning of the war was only half the battle. But where now is the constructive energy to match the spirit of destruction? Mindful of that fervor which we inspired as warriors,

I ask myself if we could not inspire a thousand-fold greater fervor if we as a people, every man, woman and child, were to dedicate our lives to the relief and the rehabilitation of Europe and Asia. To protect our homes we were asked to make certain sacrifices. Could we not make the same sacrifices now? Could we not make even greater ones? Why did we destroy valuable stocks, valuable equipment, valuable material when the rest of the world had need of these things? (When even our own people had need of them!) How is it that we can make a surfeit of aeroplanes to destroy other peoples' homes and not make them now in even greater quantity to supply these miserable people with food, clothing and building materials? If we could disrupt our economy, as they say, to kill, maim and destroy, why can we not disrupt it still more to aid, nourish and protect? Are we not guilty now of making war on defenceless people? If we do not raise a hand to prevent people from dying of starvation it is not because we are unable to do so, as our politicians maintain, it is because we do not care to do so. It is because we lack the imagination to see that a people which sits with folded arms while the rest of the world agonizes is just as murderous at heart as the army which devastates their land. If every American considered it his solemn duty to do something for an unknown brother in Europe or Asia, if he regarded it as only right and natural that he share whatever comforts he enjoyed with those in dire need, if he did this as a private citizen, without regard for the policy or diplomacy of his government, if this became a burning issue with every American, do you suppose the present condition "over there" would not alter radically overnight? The mere fact that Americans had the courage—or shall I say "simple decency?"—to formulate such a project would in itself resuscitate millions who now regard themselves as doomed. We are told that we must take care of our own people first, provide them with those necessities and luxuries which they were denied during the war years. But if it had been necessary to continue the war another ten years, would we not have done without these indispensable necessities and luxuries? Would we not have accommodated ourselves to even greater privations? (After all, the war affected us least of all the warring nations, that is indisputable.) Moreover, we ought not to forget that the sacrifices which we make so much of were involuntary sacrifices. The sacrifice I am thinking of would be a voluntary one and its effect, consequently, would be far greater. There would be another difference discernible too, let me add—a people who of their own free will volunteered to sacrifice themselves would wax in joy and strength; they would not be diminished or exhausted as they were from the war effort. It is true, bearing in mind the arguments of wary politicians, that in the midst of such a devotional performance the American people could again be stabbed in the back by some jealous power. One could build up such a fancy—about the Russians, let us say—with considerable eloquence. But supposing we were helping Russia, our potential enemy, too? What answer is there to that, I wonder? And, whether we were stabbed in the back or not, what is more important now, this moment—that we watch the world die on our hands or make an effort to save it? Will we be able to live in a world filled with sick, starving, homeless, helpless people? Who will be our holy "customers?" Will we be forced to eat our own money? Is that the end of national economy?

It is almost foolish to talk about the emptiness of the slogans which were foisted upon the warring peoples of the world by the mouthpieces of universal guilt. It is dubious that any but a weak minority of the respective publics ever believed in these catch phrases. What then were we all fighting for? To win the war, obviously. To win the war and return to a so-called normal mode of existence. But what about this "normal mode of life?" How normal was it? Nobody believed much in the good, comfortable routine that we all longed to return to. In every country, rich or poor, Fascist or Democratic, the conditions were well-nigh intolerable. People may not always have admitted it openly, but it was so. In private conversation, in the bosom of the family, behind locked doors, the same plaint was going up everywhere. Men said to one another, to their wives, to their children: "This is no life. This must end." And then suddenly, in all these countries where this so-called "normal mode of life" prevailed, the citizens were warned that even this simulacrum of life was better than what the enemy threatened to impose; they were told that it were better to sacrifice their lives, their all, for this pseudo-life or there would be eternal hell, eternal slavery. And each of these fear-stricken countries sent its legions of able-bodied men (and women too, and sometimes children) to slaughter one another. With a little package dropped from the sky we Americans accomplished the trick which put an end to the war. We held the trump card. And finally we played it.

Many have wondered, and with justice, why it was that, holding such trumps, we did not carry on, did not put an end everywhere to tyranny and injustice, to misery and privation. We could have cleaned up on a grand scale, and not for our own aggrandisement but to establish a better, saner world. If we could wipe out whole urban populations in far off Japan we ought certainly, one would think, have been able to eliminate all the little Caesars whom we delight in smothering with scorn and ridicule. For that, however, we would have had to do some liquidating right at home, to say nothing of the punishment we would have had to inflict on our Allies. I am putting all this in very simple language—any one ought to be able to understand what I am saying. The question is, "Why didn't we do it?" And the next question is: "Who are *we*?" Immediately you perceive that *we* are not *it*. *We* are always just the people. *We* do not start wars, but the government. If we, the people, had intended to establish the Four Freedoms, what could have hindered us, assuming that *we* won the war, that *we* held those trump cards up our sleeve? No, *we* are never anything but cannon fodder. And so are those who call themselves "we Italians," "we Germans," "we Russians." We will do anything and everything to destroy one another and nothing to preserve ourselves. We elect representatives whom we know in our hearts will betray us. We permit others to regulate our lives for us, and we are amazed and bewildered when they ask us to surrender our lives.

In *The Joy of Man's Desiring*,[1] the peasant Jourdan says: "There is one thing that I do not believe; that is that any one deliberately wants us to be unhappy. I think that things were made so that everybody can be happy. I think that our unhappiness is a sort of disease which we create ourselves, with big chills-and-fever, with bad water, and with the evil that we catch from each other in breathing the same air. I think that if we knew how to live, perhaps we wouldn't be ill. With the habits we've gotten into now, all our life is a struggle; we strike out in the water, we fight, to keep from going under. Our whole life long. Whether it be your animals, whether it be your seeds, your plants, your trees, you've got to police against them all. What we want, it seems that the entire world does not want. They seem to do it on purpose. That must have given us a distaste for everything, in the end. That must have forced our bodies to produce any old way, how can we tell? . . . The world forces us to shed blood. Perhaps we are unconsciously creating a special kind of blood, a blood of distaste, and instead of there flowing through our bodies, everywhere—in our arms, in our thighs, in our hearts, in our stomachs, in our lungs—a blood of desire, our great pipe system washes us with a blood of disgust."

[1] By Jean Giono, Viking Press, N. Y. Edition exhausted.

I have hopes of some day adding a third volume to this *Night-mare*. In it I should like to speak only of what could be. I would like to take this country of ours and recreate it—in the image of the hope which it once inspired. I too believe "that things were made so that everybody can be happy." I see evidence of this truth constantly. Native of a land which has been richly blessed, I was imbued from infancy, I might almost say, with the conviction that we have the power to do well-nigh anything. My earliest recollections are of plenitude, of peace, of joy. I had a golden childhood amidst humble surroundings. My people were ordinary folk, gifted in no way. It is true, they were the product of immigrants—there was a certain advantage in that. But are we not all, in America, the products of immigrants at some point along the line? America was made entirely by foreigners. What makes us Americans, and not simply the sons and daughters of foreigners, is that we used to believe we could accomplish miracles. We were born in the middle of the horn of plenty. We had no enemies on our backs, unless it was "the mother country," England. We had the good-will of the world. We had no desire to take over the world and run it.

To-day all that is past. We have been forced to take a hand in the running of the world; we have been forced to share our treasures; we have been forced to make enemies and to fight them. In doing these things we have also been forced to take stock of ourselves. We have been obliged to ask ourselves whether we are a force for good or for evil. That we are a force we know, and the knowledge of it, the responsibility which it entails, frightens us. What many Americans are asking themselves is this: "What have we to give the world, now that we have succeeded in dismantling it? Can we put it together again?" Many of us wonder if we shall ever be able to disintoxicate ourselves—for we are drunk, drunk with a power beyond us. Despite all back-sliding, always we have stoutly maintained that we want only peace. But never have we been more ready, more willing, to engage in war. We seem to invite trouble. We stand like the big bully who has cleaned up the whole neighborhood, and we ask defiantly: "Who next?" I don't say we, the people, but we, the government of the United States. Like all governments, our government too pretends that it wishes to protect the interests of its citizens. As if every Tom, Dick and Harry had some foreign interests which he was eager to preserve. We are told about the oil wells in some distant region of the earth, and how important it is that this country or that should not get hold of them. (We talk about them as if they existed in a no-man's land, the public domain of King Nod.) We are warned that the next war will probably be started over the possession of these foreign oil fields. When the time is ripe for it, the common man in America, in Russia, in Great Britain, and in other places too, will be persuaded by the right propaganda that the most vital thing in his short life is for one of us countries to gain possession of those oil reserves. We will be told that "we" need them, that our very lives are dependent on the possession of these natural resources. By that time it is quite possible, indeed even most probable, that one of these progressive nations will have found the way to reach the moon, possibly other nearby planets. It is altogether conceivable, in view of the universal fear, distrust, panic and alarm, that these neighboring planets will be used as hide-outs for the monstrous new engines of war which will be invented. Anything is possible.

Fifty, or even twenty, years ago, the thought of being able to visit the moon seemed the most stupendous feat imaginable. And now, now that the moon is almost within reach, the probabilities are that we shall think of it only in terms of military strategy. Think to what an extent our fears can lead us! How tragic for the universe at large that our war-like spirit envisages the possibility of bursting its terrestrial bounds and seeks to fill the heavens with its thunder! To satisfy our lust for destruction we are ready to invade the stars, exploit the very heavens.

To some, of course, this will sound like the wildest fancy. But in ten years the wildest flights of fantasy may well become stark reality. We are moving with a pace which is electrifying. A return to a slower, easier rhythm is impossible. Acceleration, more and more acceleration, that is the key-note of this new epoch. The pace is set for us by our inventions. Each invention augments the magnitude of the gear, the gear of a vehicle whose form is not even discernible yet. Would you know where lies the seat of our heart's desire? Look to our great inventions. We pretend that we created them for our own use, but we are no longer the masters, we are the victims. We and our inventions are one. In every sense they answer to our deepest desires. When we yearned to be able to kill a man at long range we invented the rifle; when we yearned to communicate with a fellow mortal at a distance, we invented the telephone; when we yearned to turn night into day we invented the electric bulb; when we no longer yearned to have children we invented the contraceptive; when we became impatient with piece-meal destruction, we invented the high explosive. When we get ready to destroy the earth we shall doubtless have invented the means of migrating to another planet.

We in America are the most inventive people on earth. It is in our blood. Back of this mania for invention exists the delusion that we are making things easier for ourselves. Easier and better. Or else bigger and better. We despise work and yet we toil like slaves. We never think beforehand of the consequences which a new invention entails. Only now, now that we have invented the atomic bomb, do we begin to ponder about such things. (Nobel, the father of dynamite, foresaw the dilemma long ago.) Suddenly we have become acutely aware of the Janus-like quality of the atom bomb. That swords could be beaten into plough-shares, this is something we all knew from childhood, though none ever acted on it. But when it finally sunk into us that the world's most destructive weapon could be converted to the most expansive utilitarian ends, something like "a shock of recognition" swept the world. Indeed, at this particular moment, the world may be said to be vainly struggling to recover from a double shock, namely the recognition that it must choose between annihilation and paradise. That middle ground, to which the men of the old order so desperately cling, that in-between realm which we once regarded as human and which we characterized with appellations such as Culture and Civilization, has become like quicksand under our feet.

If it is possible for a mere novelist to present us with a picture of the future, such as Werfel gave us in *Star of the Unborn*, what is not possible in the next fifty years? I say this because reality has a way of catching up with the dreams of poets in short order. Werfel situated his fictive world in a time one hundred thousand years distant. The inciting imaginative challenge which Jules Verne made to the men of his generation, Werfel has made to our generation. Much that Werfel's phantasy prefigured could be actualized in less than five hundred years. One crawls on all fours for aeons, seemingly, but the moment one stands erect one can not only walk and run, but fly. One babbles until one has acquired a vocabulary; after that it does not take much to establish communication with God. We make machines which defy the laws of gravitation, but will the time not soon be here when gravitation itself will be exploited, as now we exploit that mysterious force called electricity? How long will we bother with cumbersome machines, with tools even of the finest precision? Is not the machine a rude model, a crude hieroglyph, if you like, of a language which, when understood, will give us a movable and inexhaustible alphabet enabling us to translate instantaneously from impulse to desire, from desire to thought, from thought to act, and from act to fulfillment?

We have entered a new magnetic field of energy, one which will condition us to live like gods. It will no longer be possible, as at present, to bury the clues to these mysterious forces in our patent offices; our children already inhabit an imaginative world more daring, more in keeping with the new age, than the mental world of the present-day adult. The sparks which have been kindled will grow into flames. We cannot put the brakes on this spirit of investigation and exploration. The earth is rushing onward, carrying us along like detritus.

When the desire to be in a distant place becomes greater than the physical means of getting there, we will most certainly discover how to be in that place *without the use of a conveyance.* If we truly want to hear and see what is going on in distant parts of the earth (or distant parts of the universe), it is not only possible but altogether probable that we will dispense with all our instruments. There can well come a moment of impatience, a moment of need, a moment of inspirational fervor so great that the way will be broken open—and we will perform those seeming miracles which have been spoken of in all ages. To open up a new realm of consciousness will be no more impossible than to make sound, light or heat issue from the end of a wire. Indeed, it will be absolutely necessary to attain this higher state of consciousness. At the present level the human intellect is unable to cope with the forces it has unleashed. The irrational world is rapidly gaining the ascendancy. There is no hope of achieving that harmonious unity of the psyche, now more than ever indispensable, with the intellect functioning like an adding machine. The mind and consciousness of man will have to expand to meet the demands of that soul which will reflect the new universal spirit. In our souls we know that the universe is not a haphazard affair. In our souls we know that nothing is impossible. In our souls we know that death is only a shadow which accompanies us. Our poverty-stricken, terrorized minds may tell us differently, but this mind which would keep us in fear and trembling is only the kernel of a greater mind. We are made of the same substance as the stars, the same substance as the gods. We are one with the universe, and we know it quietly in moments of crisis. It is for this reason we are able to sacrifice ourselves on occasion. We know that in some unknown accounting, by some bookkeeping which is beyond our comprehension, nothing is lost. Indeed, we know more, we know a better thing than that . . . we know that the more willing we are to lose everything the more certain we are to gain all. Weak man, shrewd men, sombre, worldly men, have tried to deny this. They have tried to make us believe that our lives are petty and vain, that we live to no end, counseling us at the same time to make the most of it while we can. But when a great issue arises, the influence of these men evaporates like sweat.

We are only gradually shaking off the tyranny of the Church. Now we face another tyranny, perhaps worse: the tyranny of the State. The State seeks to make of its citizens obedient instruments for its glorification. It promises them happiness—in some distant future—as once the Church held out the hope of reaching Paradise. To preserve its interests, the State is perpetually obliged to make war. The chief concern of a State is to be ready and fit for the next conflict. The important thing, which is the enjoyment of life, now, this moment, every moment, is constantly postponed because of the necessity to be prepared for war. Every new invention is appraised from this standpoint. The last thing which any State thinks of is how to make its citizens comfortable and joyous. The wages of the average man barely suffice, and often do not suffice at all, to meet the cost of living. I am speaking now of the richest country on earth—America. What conditions are like in the rest of the world beggars description. One can say to-day without fear of contradiction that never since the dawn of civilization has the world been in a worse state.

To aid our fellow sufferers throughout the world we are urged on the one hand to give all we can, and on the other hand we are informed that no matter how much we give it will be but a drop in the bucket. The despair which seizes the sensitive individual, confronted with this dilemma, is fathomless. One knows that there must be a way out, but who holds the answer? The way has to be created. There must be a desire, an overwhelming desire, to find a solution. To think for one moment that it will be found by the representatives of our various governments is the gravest delusion. These men are thinking only of saving their faces. Each one is pitted against the other, is obliged to win some sort of petty victory over the other, in order to maintain his position. While these mouth-pieces talk about peace and order, about freedom and justice, the men behind them, the men who support them and keep them up front, so to speak, are mobilizing all their forces to keep the world in a state of perpetual conflict. In China at this very moment America and Russia are playing the same game that was played in Spain a few years ago. There is no secret about it. Yet every day we are told through the newspapers and over the radio that America and Russia are seeking to understand one another, to live amicably in the same world.

It is not easy to see how the peoples of either of these great countries can liberate themselves. The American people are supine, the Russian people are acquiescent. In neither of them is there the slightest revolutionary ardor. In opportunities for self-development they are richer than any other people in the world. They could not only support themselves comfortably, they could between them assume the burdens of the starving nations of the earth.

And what is it they are worried about? Why are these two nations still at loggerheads? Because each is fearful of the other's influence upon the rest of the world. One of these countries represents itself as a Communist nation, the other as a Democratic nation. Neither of them are what they pretend to be. Russia is no more Communist than America is Democratic. The present Russian government is even more autocratic than that of the Czars. The present American government is more tyrannical than that of the British in the time of the thirteen Colonies. There is less freedom now in both these countries than there ever was. How will such peoples free the world? They do not seem to know the meaning of freedom.

It seems almost inevitable now that these two countries are determined to destroy, and will succeed in destroying, one another. And in the process of destroying each other they will destroy a large part of the civilized world. England is weak, France is helpless, Germany is prostrate, and Japan will be only too delighted to watch and wait, biding her time to make herself strong again. Of all the countries which participated in the war, Japan learned her lesson best. When the West is in ruins she will rise again, invade Europe, take it over.

"Nonsense! Ridiculous!" the critics will scream. And, burying their heads in the sand, they will whistle from their rear ends. For once, Democrats, Republicans, Fascists, Communists will agree. "Impossible!" they will shout. Well, this is a lone man's view. I have no axe to grind, no Party to sustain, no ism to further. All I clamor for is that freedom, that security, that peace and harmony which all these conflicting groups advocate and promise. I don't want it when I'm dead. I want it now. Everything I do is with that purpose in mind.

I ask no one to sacrifice himself in order to promote my ideas. I demand no allegiance, no taxes, no devotion. I say—free yourself to the best of your ability! The more freedom you obtain for yourself, the more you create for me, for every one. I would like you to have all that you desire, praying at the same time that you wish as much for the next man. I urge you to create and to share your creation with those less fortunate. If some one asks you to vote for him at the next election, ask him, I beg you, what he can do for you that you cannot do yourself. Ask him whom *he* is voting for. If he tells you the truth, then go to the polls and vote for yourself. Most any one who reads this could do a better job than the man now doing it. Why create these jobs? Why ask some one else to regulate your affairs? What are you doing that is so important? Does the man who asks for your vote find you your job, does he provide your family with food and shelter, does he put clothes on your back, does he provide the education you need . . . does he even bother to see that you get a decent burial? The only time he is concerned about you is when you can make money for him. No matter how little you make he wants part of it. He keeps you poor on the pretext that he is doing something for your benefit. And you are too lazy to protest, knowing full well that he thinks about no one but himself. From childhood you were taught that it is right and just to delegate your powers to some one else. You never questioned it because everything you are taught in school has one purpose: the glorification of your country. Somehow, though it is *your* country, you seem to have no part in it until the time comes to surrender your life. Your whole life is spent in trying to get a hearing. You're always on the door-step, never inside.

Wherever one goes in this civilized world one always finds the same set-up. The little man, the man who does the dirty work, *the producer,* is of no importance, receives no consideration, and is always being asked to make the greatest sacrifice. Yet everything depends on this forgotten man. Not a wheel could turn without his support and cooperation. It is this man, whose number is legion, who has no voice whatever in world affairs. These matters are beyond his grasp, supposedly. He has only to produce; the others, the politicians, they will run the world. One day this poor little man, this forgotten son, this nobody on whose toil and industry everything depends, will see through the farce. Uninstructed though he may be, he knows full well how rich is the earth, how little he needs to live happily. He knows, too, that it is not necessary to kill his fellow-man in order to live; he knows that he has been robbed and cheated from time immemorial; he knows that if he can't run his affairs properly, nobody else can. He is suffocated with all this bitter knowledge. He waits and waits, hoping that time will alter things. And slowly he realizes that time alters nothing, that with time things only grow worse. One day he will decide to act. "Wait!" he will be told. "Wait just a little longer." But he will refuse to wait another second.

When that day comes, watch out! When the little man all over the world becomes so desperate that he cannot wait another minute, another second, beware O world! Once he decides to act for himself, act on his own, there will be no putting him back in harness. There will be nothing you can promise him which will equal the joy of being free, being rid of the incubus. To-day he is still yours, still the pawn which can be shuffled about, but to-morrow there may be such a reversal of all precedent as to make your hearts quake. To-day you may still talk the absurd language of the Stone Age; to-day you may still coerce the young into preparedness for the next conflict; to-day you may still convince the blind and the ignorant that they should be content to do without the things you find indispensable; to-day you may still talk about your possessions, your colonies, your empires. But your days are numbered. You belong in the museum, with the dinosaur, the stone axe, the hieroglyph, the mummy. The new age will come into being with your disappearance from the face of the earth.

At the dawn of every age there is distinguishable a radiant figure in whom the new time spirit is embodied. He comes at the darkest hour, rises like a sun, and dispels the gloom and stagnation in which the world was gripped. Somewhere in the black folds which now enshroud us I am certain that another being is gestating, that he is but waiting for the zero hour to announce himself. Hope never dies, passion can never be utterly extinguished. The deadlock will be broken. Now we are sound asleep in the cocoon; it took centuries and centuries to spin this seeming web of death. It takes but a few moments to burst it asunder. Now we are out on a limb, suspended over the void. Should the tree give way, all creation vaults to its doom. But what is it that tells us to hasten the hour of birth? What is it that, at precisely the right moment, gives us the knowledge and the power to take wing, when heretofore we knew only how to crawl ignominiously on our bellies? If the caterpillar through sleep can metamorphose into a butterfly, surely man during his long night of travail must discover the knowledge and the power to redeem himself.

# REMEMBER TO REMEMBER

VARDA

# VARDA: THE MASTER BUILDER

THE TOWN of Monterey reminds one faintly, very faintly, of a picturesque fishing village in the South of France. To-day there is scarcely anything left of its original charm. It is like any other town, almost wholly lacking in color, distinction or validity. The one thing which would redeem it is color, vivid color. Monterey demands color, just as women of tawny complexion and barbaric features do. The one house on the whole peninsula which has character is the red barn at 320 Hawthorne Street, in New Monterey. Here is where Jean Varda and his wife Virginia live and work—*and play*.

It is one of Varda's theories that the most interesting architecture

3

in America is reserved for the stables. Immediately you think about it you realize how sound and accurate is this judgment. Often our stables and barns have the grace and purity so noticeable in the works of Italian Primitives. The home, on the other hand, too often reflects the unconscious sadism of our impotent architects who, despairing of ever realizing their cherished dreams, take pleasure in designing life-long prisons for their neighbors.

One of the first things Varda does on taking over a building is to break the walls down and let in the light. He is a Greek, of course, and for him light is what it is for the physicist—absolute. If he were permitted, I am certain he would do the same with the celebrated canvases of the old masters. "Masters of black and white" he calls them, and chief among his *bêtes-noir* are Rembrandt and da Vinci.

In the last ten years or so Varda has practically dispensed with the brush. He has two media now: the *collage* and the mosaic. I doubt if any artist has explored the possibilities of *collage* to the extent that Varda has. When one gets to know him, becomes acquainted with his theories of art and metaphysics (and their marriage), one realizes how completely and convincingly his ideas are set forth in this medium. For him the *collage* is no longer, as it was for Picasso and other French painters, an experiment or notation preparatory to the final attack. With Varda it has become the thing-in-itself, a creation, just as any other attempt at picturization would be. The materials employed, be they bits of colored paper, rags, or what not, are just as durable as pigment, as Picasso himself has said. There is no reason, therefore, since the *collage* is entirely a product of man's mind and hands, why it should not be approached with the same attention and reverence (if possible) as a painting. If anything, there is less opportunity to cheat in the *collage* than in oils. It also offers the advantage (before the pattern is finally glued

4

down) of shifting the material of the composition about at will. The use of the thumb tack saves a lot of scraping and worrying.

There is one thing which is anathema to Varda, and that is waste. It explains why he takes such delight in plundering the refuse heaps and from the plunder creating veritable mansions of light and joy. One of the first things I was instructed in, on coming to stay with him, was never to throw away tin cans or empty bottles—nor rags, nor paper, nor string, nor buttons, nor corks, nor even dollar bills. Not even garbage, for wherever Varda goes the birds and beasts follow, as with Giono's unforgettable character, Bobi. Like Bobi, Varda too has something of the *saltimbanque* in him. He does everything with ease, *everything*, no matter whether it be a menial task, a herculean feat of strength, or a difficult ballet step. I have watched him nurse his wife, when she was ill, and at the same time cook meals for a half dozen visitors, first running to the beach to get timber, then to the rocks for mussels, instructing and entertaining his guests while preparing the meals, laying out patterns for his next *collages* between times, hoisting and lowering beds from the balcony when it came time to put the guests up, reading passages from his favorite books, and so on and so forth, all with joy, ease, and the best will in the world.

No wonder that people love to visit his place. I have never met a man so plagued with visitors. They come like locusts, people from all walks of life, some of them the most insufferable bores too. They come in search of that mysterious elixir which no vitamin seems able to supply our people with: the joy of creation.

From the moment he gets out of bed Varda is not only alive and awake but vitally interested in everything. I doubt if he has ever known a dull moment in his whole life. He is alert and attentive *always*. He gives to exhaustion and revitalizes as easily as an animal. (He does *not* take vitamins!)

The secret of his exuberance, fertility and invention lies in his single-mindedness, which is another way of saying purity, I suppose. He is really a saint in disguise. He has weathered all temptations and is now, a man turned fifty, able to consecrate his energies entirely to creation. Just as in the red barn, which he remodeled according to the principle of joy (a house made entirely of refuse: bottles, tin boxes, rockers, lead and iron pipe, rope, dismantled hulls and masts of wrecked ships), so in his inner being Varda has left a hole into which he sweeps the waste matter that accumulates during the day. (Always merry and bright, because always fluid and solvent.)

The chief elements with which he brings all transformations about are fire and water. The ideal home, in his opinion, is one in which the blazing warmth of the hearth commingles with the odorous sound of the rain. Instead of the Scagliolic effect of pseudo-baronial halls with their tuxedo-like wainscotings, Varda's walls would be made of papier-maché soaked in colors that never fade. Through huge panes of glass one would enjoy the sight and fragrance of tropical growths made lush by the rains.

In the middle of the great room at Hawthorne Street (which is really a *salon des surprises*) is a circular fireplace with a huge drum and chimney. It derives from no anterior model, unless it be from the alchemist's laboratory. While drinking or conversing, showers of sparks rain on one like confetti, thus adding to the charm of fire hazards. The doorways are reminiscent of early Greek temples, both in color and material. The entablatures and architraves are studded with masks of audacious simplicity representing such Muses as Melpomene and Urania, the mythological figures of the Atlantean world, early Minoan gods and demons, and so on. The ogival effects of the windows were obtained by the use of rockers. The only materials employed for this animated décor were discarded bits of tin,

6

lead, glass, rope, pewter, wood and stone. On the walls are what I choose to call metaphysical mirrors, mirrors certainly which it has never occurred to our manufacturers to manufacture. They are of elegant simplicity, achieving their optimum through the airy, jewel-like quality of the frames which, like everything else in the Varda establishment, are composed entirely of discarded objects. Everything about the house testifies most eloquently to the absurdity of an economic order based upon chaos, waste, ugliness and misery.

In the cubicle which leads by a ladder to the solarium (surmounted by four heraldic pennants) I read, during the March gales, two marvelous books which Varda thrust upon me: Bédier's *Tristan et Iseult* and Chirico's *Hebdomeros*. The walls, a cold pigeon blue, were relieved by severe canvas window curtains on which Virginia had painted the symbolic configurations of their Neptunian adventures. Gazing between the rungs of the ladder I could see, as though floating in an ascending mist of vanishing egg-shells, that most enchanting of all Varda's *collages* (Women Reconstructing the World) which he recently bequeathed to Anais Nin. What marvelous fantasies the austere ambiance of this cell evoked as I reclined on my elbow, hypnotized by the calligraphic figures already engaged in altering the world. A little later I took to reading *Wuthering Heights*, marveling all the while that the human mind could have conceived a character as black and relentless as Heathcliff. When disturbing shafts of moonlight flooded the room from the solarium above I would get up and, drawing back the painted veils, gaze out upon the red house to which the red barn belonged. From the hay-loft of the building once set apart for the animals and their fodder everything seemed topsy-turvy. The red house in which the admirable and astounding octogenarian lay slumbering had now the aspect of a retreat for demented members of the Masonic Order. It belonged to no period of architecture that I

7

could recall; it had been conceived in a nightmare and executed during a time of drought and pestilence. The scabby shore line of the peninsula seemed etched by the hand of a melomaniac. Obscured by the fabulous red house lay a little park, a dreary, empty park which did not even boast of a comfort station. I felt as if I were back on Wuthering Heights listening to the howling of a creaky moon. Nothing in Monterey could possibly have drawn me to its precincts, except Varda. I thought of the constant round of visitors, their comments, their delight, their dismay, their astonishment, their perplexity. I thought of the Women at Point Sur and that lighthouse endlessly throwing out its revolving beams. Two poets living on the very edge of the Western World; one sombre, prophetical and keen as a hawk, the other gay, full of wisdom, and endlessly rearranging the world. In the big room, suspended from the rafters in the poise of a diver, her skin-tight garb bifurcated by two primary colors, her hands spread angel-wise, Phoebe the household Muse dispensed seraphic benediction. Except for the golden hair, which was real, she might have been an emanation from one of the *collages* that studded the walls. Often in the night the glass figures locked in cement stepped forth from their mosaic casements and held weird rounds with the gods that gleamed like rubies in the doorways of the temples.

To Varda women gravitate as naturally as bees to the flower. He enchants them, as Orpheus did of old. He clothes them in fitting raiment, tells them how to dress their hair, suggests the flower or the perfume they should use, teaches them the use of their limbs, what stance to take, and whether to bound like an antelope or canter like a palomino. He endows them with all the graces. He also instructs them obliquely how to listen, or how most effectively to resemble the various musical instruments which accumulate about him like weeds. For Varda the cardinal elements of every

8

picture are based on the boat, the musical instrument, and woman. In his daily life these elements, or principles, are faithfuly incorporated. In a gathering, which is always a "composition" *chez* Varda, he himself represents the watery principle. His guests, all palp and palimpsest, form the plasma of which he is always talking, because when Varda is not busy making a picture he is distilling the ingredients of one. Out of the Protean bosom of his amniotic seas there is always forming an island of repair, a nucleus of seeming immobility in the flux of interpenetrating waves of light. Light and dark, flux and reflux, solid-fluid, concave-convex, line-color, form-fancy, all the hermaphrodites of his contrapuntal world dance in orgiastic antiphony. At the peak of realization they reproduce the illusion of the frozen flutter which the ballet dancer illustrates unerringly when between two incredible bounds he suspends himself in mid-air and strums with fan-like fins on the invisible guitar of his ecstasy. It is at this point, or moment, that, like one of the countless characters in his endless reservoir of tales and anecdotes, Varda the moujik kneels before the retching hole of his foundering ship and mutters: *"besoin de faire l'amour,"* or *"besoin de mourir,"* or sometimes in petto simply: *"besoin de pisser."* It is here that his fatuous Arab, garbed in the mufti of Occidental gibberish, stands before the postcard picture of a moon-lit desert and mumbles grandiloquently: *"Vue genérale!"*

If I lapse into French it is because Varda is now shelling mussels; we are no longer in Monterey, but in Alexandria or Cassis; he is tired of speaking a Turkish which I do not understand. Georges Braque is coming up the road, dreaming of subtle, melodic grays and of the funeral pomp and splendor of his boyhood when the cadavers, freshly washed, reposed in the plush contours of their brocaded boxes soon to be consigned to the worms. What a life that was in Cassis, when for eight years the abode of Varda became the *carrefour* and caravansary of itinerant and indigent artists. Now and then the kind but absent-minded landlord (the host) would threaten to return. An Englishman, of course. Whereupon Varda, clapping his hands and running excitedly from wing to wing of the crumbling mansion, would shout: "He's coming! *Vamoose! Vamoose!*" I can see him standing there, wreathed in that most seductive sheepish smile of his (which appears also when he blushes over his own mythomania—the Zymole Trokey grin!), ready to greet his benefactor with the innocence of a school-boy. "Yes, your lordship, the zahlias have all been trimmed . . . the pigeons are moulting *most* beautifully," or whatever it may be that leaps to his mind in such embarrassing moments. Barely time to drown the cats, the guests meanwhile scurrying frantically for the caves, the wharves, the chandeliers, their fabulous names unrecognizable to the noble lord even were he not deaf and dumb.

At fourteen Varda, according to his fond mother, was a portrait painter worthy of hanging in the Louvre. Born in Smyrna and forced to a quick bloom in the *terrain à vendre* of Alexandria, he excelled with such facility that he committed suicide three times. (Varda never says, "I was on the point of committing suicide," but always *"I committed suicide."*) Before the first World War began he found himself adrift in Paris. There he was vaccinated by the now aging Dadaists and Surrealists of the time. Then England, where he dances in the ballet a few years, abandoning it because it becomes too professional a pursuit. For the last fifteen years or more he has had shows in London and Paris every year (New York also), each one a sell-out. He has been lionized by the snobs of the *mondaine* world who themselves live only on the fringe of the subliminal threshold. Always he has been a builder of boats—his first apprenticeship. Always a dancer. Always a superb chef. Always the nimblest raconteur. Always the last one to go home. Never tired, never irritable, never angry, never bored. Inventing new theories with the facility of a Buxtehude.

His defects? Well, there are some critical-minded souls who, unable to see a Kohinoor for the rubies and smaragds, pretend that Varda lives in a state of perpetual chaos. Nothing could be farther from the truth. Varda has an order all his own. In living it he corroborates Bergson's theory that disorder is only an unfamiliar or as yet uncategorized order. At any rate, all appearance of disorder chez Varda is thoroughly illusory. Never was there a man whose mind, heart and soul were more in order. Sometimes, however, to better illustrate his theories, it is obligatory for him to open many drawers of the inner mansion; in the enthusiasm of displaying the jewels so carefully stored away Varda now and then spills one of the drawers; or it may be that a guest arrives and demands to be fed, whereupon our alacritous host will begin peeling onions, carrots, garlic and other edibles with his two not altogether immaculate feet mired in the jewelled disarray. Frequently the guests arrive early, before he has even had time to rub the sand out of his eyes; they see with stupid astonishment a man clad in a woolen blanket striped like the Greek flag. Out of courtesy Varda now and then throws a buffalo robe over his shoulders, or dons a pair of strawberry-colored corduroys. Naturally he is unconscious of his garb. All light and innocence that he is, he changes like the chameleon. These sudden metamorphoses entail *malgré lui* a certain amount of what is termed "disorder." But when the guests depart, and I have witnessed the miracle with my own eyes, what a scavenger this sweet, mystic-looking zany doth become! Beds are thrown about like baskets of plums; garbage cans that would give the ordinary intellectual double hernia are handled with the ease of a French *démènageur*. With bucket and mop he swabs the decks fore and aft, not forgetting to feed the cats a few choice morsels, nor to pause a moment

11

at the back door and throw crumbs to the birds. All this whilst humming to himself in Turkish, Armenian, Greek or Arabic. Always wreathed in a cherubic smile. Ready to drop everything if you have a tooth-ache; ready to take you to the bus station or the beach at a moment's notice; making notes for the next picture between tasks; recommending three books which you must read without fail, *instantly*; illustrating the dance by a picture or a picture by the dance. Not for a moment overlooking the coming picnic for which he will be sure to devise a title on the spur of the moment—such as the Festival of the Iniquitous Baptism, or the Banquet of the Discordant Muses. All of which reminds him, whilst gathering the crumbs at your feet and mopping up the sink with blotting paper, that there is a passage in Origen which previsaged certain notations made by Picasso in this or that period. Always, between times, a little dithyramb about Picasso. Always an excursus on Bach, or one of his unfamiliar contemporaries. Or a soliloquy on the vegetable and ophidian qualities of Oriental art. Or back to Massine and the ocean of immobility punctuated by the flutter fins. (*And would you like me to get you some more Grape Nuts, Henry?*)

One day, he muses, we must visit his friend Graham who has a little farm on the outskirts of the town. We shall see there a certain goat, a fabulous goat, which Varda himself raised in the convicts' camp at Anderson Creek, where he lived for a time. There is something about the goat, he avers, and again I see that Zymole Trokey grin spreading, which surpasses all understanding. But we shall have to leave that until we come to Bucephalus, as the goat is called. "Graham is such a wonderful man," he adds. (And so he is—a dream of a man!—for eventually we did visit him.) But the thing to note is that Varda said *"wonderful man."* So characteristic of him to find people good, charming, *wonderful*. (In Greek, incidentally, the word for wonderful is a wonderful word. Even

12

more wonderful than *wunderbar*.) As I say, it is his special quality to see always the potential, and often quite invisible, nature of his friends. He sees them as only the saint or the guru sees human kind. Sees them thus because he himself is all these things, because in the gleam of his powerful, radiant light even the dull flesh of the most inconspicuous creature, be it human or animal, reflects his faith and ardor.

"How can people live without mirrors?" he exclaims one day. They are there, of course, everywhere, but not the "metaphysical" mirrors which are strewn throughout the barn. Only black and white mirrors—like the paintings of the dead masters. Varda knows only the prismatic mirrors of the rainbow. He never gazes into them; he creates them all about. His whole conversation is like the play of the spectrum. Never black and white. Never facts. To Varda a fact is an invisible nonentity of an opaque nature conceived by a gremlin in the flanks of a dead meteorite. "*C'est un mythomane*," the French would say of him. Yes, an atavistic sport spewed from some legendary womb; a freak of extraordinary inventiveness who is at home everywhere because, with the cunning and resignation of an archangel, he recognizes that "*il n'y a que le provisoire qui dure*." Each home he builds, and by this time he has surely founded a thousand, is made to last as long as joy lasts. They are made of the imperishable refuse which the squanderers leave in their wake. Imperishable because transmogrified by the master builder into mythomaniacal dwelling places. Who can imagine the death of Phoebe, for example? To begin with, it was never necessary for her to draw breath, as with other mortals. She was born immortal and bifurcated by the two great primaries. His cat, Melanesia, has not the proverbial nine lives but ten thousand lives, all of them intersecting one another like the planes of a good *nature morte*.

Once he dreamt of becoming a monk. He did not know then that

13

he was already a saint. He found a master and the master told him he must renounce everything. "Even painting?" asked Varda innocently. "Yes, *everything*," said the master. "Then I can never become a monk," said Varda sorrowfully, in that moment making (for him) the supreme renunciation. "But you *are* a monk," I say to him. This while Virginia is trying out her new gown made of dyed hemp and studded with Indra's thousand eyes all a-tinkle as she reels round and round before the blazing fire. "You are the monk of paint. With every picture you make you teach renunciation. You mint only what is pure. You are the metaphysician of space and color. You are an Origen without having suffered the calamity of self-inflicted castration. For you to go now to Mt. Athos would be a sin. It would be the supine resignation of a voluptuary. Your place is in the world, in the midst of chaos, ugliness and corruption. You must practise the nine virtues surrounded by every manifestation of vice."

Yes, Varda, I remember this conversation well. I remember too the beautiful meal you cooked for me. I remember your especially wonderful dithyramb that evening on Picasso, that great ship with gleaming eyes in her prow which bore down on you in the night and capsized all your fine theories about art. In that dream you really committed suicide. The other occasions when you committed suicide were only charming excursions on the ferry-boat of the English language.

BEAUFORD DELANEY

# THE AMAZING AND INVARIABLE
## BEAUFORD DeLANEY

YES, HE IS amazing and invariable, this Beauford. It has been storming now for forty-eight hours, here at Big Sur, and the house is leaking from every cement and stucco pore of its being. That is why my mind dwells on Beauford. How is he faring now in the winter of Manhattan where all is snow and frost? Here it is warm, despite the leaks, despite the gale. We have only one problem—to keep the wood dry. A few sticks of wood in the stove and the place is cozy. But at 181 Greene Street, on that top floor where Beauford works, dreams and eats his paintings, only a roaring furnace kept at a constant temperature of 120 degrees Centigrade can combat the chill of the grave which emanates from the dripping walls, floors and ceilings. And of course there will never be such a furnace at 181 Greene Street. Neither will the sun's warm rays ever penetrate the single room in which Beauford lives.

It was night when Harry first led me to Beauford's heavenly abode. I shall never forget the forlorn, dismal look of Greene Street as we stood across the way looking up at Beauford's windows to see if he was home. There are streets which seem commemorated to the pangs and frustrations of the artist; having nothing to do with art, shunned by all living as soon as the work of day is done, they are infested with the sinister shadows of crime and with prowling alley cats which thrive on the garbage and ordure that litter the gutters and pavements.

It was only the beginning of Fall. The air was mild outdoors. But in the studio Beauford had the fire going. He was wrapped in several layers of sweaters, a woolen scarf around his neck, and a thick, fuzzy skating cap pulled well down over his ears. In a few moments the fire died out—and remained dead for the rest of the evening. In about twenty minutes the floor became icy cold, the dead cold of cold storage in which cadavers are preserved in the morgue. We sat in our overcoats, collars turned up, hats pulled down over our ears, our hands stuffed deep in our pockets. Just the right atmosphere in which to produce masterpieces, I thought to myself. Rembrandt, Mozart, Beethoven—just the temperature for them! A little more heat and the world would have been the loser. A little more food, a little more kindness, and we would have had more chromos, more musical comedies. Logic, our crazy logic, dictates that the environment of the creative individual must be composed of all the ugly, painful, discordant and diseased elements of life. To prove his genius the artist must transform these elements into durable

16

symbols of beauty, goodness, truth and light. For reward he may, if he is lucky, expect a monument to his glory—a hundred years after his death. But while he is alive, while he is a man walking the earth, while he is a living creator dedicated to the highest pursuits, he must not hope to eat anything but offal, nor associate with any living creature other than beggars and alley cats. Above all he must not ask for creature comforts, for warmth and light, for soft music . . . not even for a glimpse of the sun through his barred windows.

When such an individual also happens to have a dark skin, when in a cosmopolitan city like New York only certain doors are open to him, the situation becomes even more complex. A poor white artist is a miserable sight, but a poor black artist is apt to be a ridiculous figure as well. And the better his work the more cold and indifferent the world becomes. If he were to make Christmas cards people could pity him and dole out scraps of food or cast-off garments, but to aspire to greatness, to make pictures which not even intelligent white people can appreciate, that puts him in the category of fools and fanatics. That makes him just another "crazy nigger."

Beauford was an artist from before birth; he was an artist in the womb, and even before that. He was an artist in Africa, long before the white men began raiding that dark continent for slaves. Africa is the home of the artist, the one continent on this planet which is soul-possessed. But in white North America, where even the spirit has become bleached and blanched until it resembles asbestos, a born artist has to produce his credentials, has to prove that he is not a hoax and a fraud, not a leper, not an enemy of society, especially not an enemy of our crazy society in which monuments are erected a hundred years too late.

This night I speak of Beauford showed us, I remember, some small canvases of street scenes. They were virulent, explosive paintings devoid of human figures. They were all Greene Street through and through, only invested with color, mad with color; they were full of remembrances too, and solitudes. In the empty street from which, by the way, there seemed no egress, a spirit of hunger swept with devastating force. It was a hunger born of remembrance, the hunger of a man alone with his medium in the cold storage world of North America. Here I sit in Greene Street, said the canvases, and I am invisible to all but the eye of God. I am the spirit of hunger for all that has been denied me, one with the street, one with the cold, dead walls. But I am not dead, neither am I cold, nor yet invisible. I am of darkest Africa a luminary, an aurora borealis, a son of a slave in whose veins courses the proudest white blood. I sit here in Greene Street and I paint what I am, my mysterious mixed bloods, my inscrutable mixed hungers, my elegant and most aristocratic solitudes, my labyrinthine pre-natal remembrances. Here there are no sun, moon or stars, no warmth, no light, no companionship. But in me, the amazing and invariable Beauford DeLaney, are all the lights, all the stars, all the constellations, all the angels for companions. I am Greene Street as it looks from the angle of eternity; I am a crazy nigger as he looks when the Angel Gabriel blows his horn; I am solitude playing the xylophone to make the rent come due.

We looked at only a few canvases that evening, the cold driving us out into the open street, but the impression which I carried away was one of being saturated with color and light. Poor in everything but pigment. With pigment he was as lavish as a millionaire. It was a new period for him I learned later. He was in revolt. Against what? Against the imprisonment of Greene Street, no doubt. Against the cold storage technique of the North American lapidaries. Of portraits there seemed to be an endless variety. One friend of his, a man named Dante, he had already painted several times.

"Do him again," I said, "he's a good subject for you."

"I intend to," said Beauford smilingly.

"Do him over and over," I said. "Do him until there's nothing left to do."

"That's just what I'm going to do," said Beauford.

As we descended the dark stairway in which a tiny taper swimming in oil was burning, I wondered if Beauford would have the courage to do Dante fifty or a hundred times. Supposing that for the next five years he were to do nothing but Dante? Why not? Some men paint the same landscape over and over again. Dante was a wonderful landscape for Beauford: he had cosmic proportions, and his skull though shorn of locks was full of mystery. A man studying his friend day in and day out for five years ought to arrive at some remarkable conclusions. With time Dante could become for Beauford what Oedipus became for Freud. But he could never become food and rent, that is certain. Nothing Beauford did with love could earn him anything but love. A sane North American white man would have ditched Dante and made patent medicine bottles or cans of delicious preserved fruits. Or he might have tried his hand at flower pots such as the Academies are stuffed with. He would certainly never elect to live on the top floor of 181 Greene Street and devote himself to painting the living spirit of a tried and true friend. That would be insanity.

Few artists, I hasten to add, have ever impressed me as being more sane than Beauford DeLaney. Beauford's sanity is something to dwell on: it occupies a niche of its own. There are some utterly sane individuals who create the impression that stark lunacy might be a highly desirable state; there are others who make sanity look like a counterfeit check, with God the loser. Beauford's sanity is the sort that one ascribes only to the angels. It never deserts him, even when he is sorely harassed. On the contrary, in crucial moments it grows more intense, more luminous. It never becomes diffracted into bitterness, envy or malice. He sees clearly in good weather and bad, and always warmly, compassionately, understandingly. He sees his own remarkable plight as if it were an object he intended to paint. And if it's sometimes too cold to paint that plight as he sees it, he simply curls up, pulls the blankets over him, and puts out the light. He has no dialectic up his sleeve, no headache powders, no sedatives, no panaceas. He lives in Greene Street, and his address is always 181, even when he is not there. Even in his dreams it is still 181 Greene Street, the amazing and invariable Beauford De-Laney dreaming, in a temperature just cool enough to keep a fresh corpse fresh.

In this unbelievable temperature Beauford retains the green vision of a world whose order and beauty, though divine, are within the conception of man. The more men murder one another, bugger one another, corrupt one another, the greener his vision becomes. When the heart of the world becomes blacked out Beauford becomes positively chlorophyllic. At his greenest he has the faculty of coming out of a deep sleep, say about three or four in the morning when the drunks who have been ejected from the night clubs rap at his door, and not once, no never in the long history of 181 Greene Street, attempting to throw them bodily down the stairs. He will admit them, light the stove if there is coal or wood, drink with them, play the guitar, dance, show his paintings (and explain them if necessary), listen to their maudlin stories, give them his bed if they are unable to use their hind legs, and promptly at 8:00 A. M. when the first feeble rays of light penetrate the studio, sit

20

down before his easel and resume work on the portrait of his friend Dante.

This ability to resume work after the most distracting interruptions is one of the great qualities of the artist. Beauford has it to an extraordinary degree. His whole life, one might say, has been a series of uninterrupted interruptions. To resume work is no task for him because for twenty-five years all he has demanded of the world is permission to paint. He has been at it unremittingly, in fair weather and foul, through droughts and famines, through heat waves and cold spells, through rent crises, wars, revolutions, strikes, riots, hunger, despair, denigration, ridicule, humiliation, chagrin and defeat. He paints to-day even more enthusiastically than when he began. He tackles each fresh canvas as though it were his first. He uses his pigments lavishly though he knows not where the next tube will come from. He blesses himself when he begins and says Amen when he is through. He never curses his lot because he has never for a moment questioned his fate. He assumes full responsibility for success or failure. Should death interrupt the program, he knows that he will resume work in the next incarnation. His people have waited for centuries to see justice rendered them. Beauford is no different from his ancestors: he can bide his time. Should this Beauford DeLaney fail there are other Beaufords, all endowed with the same spirit, the same endurance, the same integrity, the same faith.

It is when he talks that Beauford reveals the mysterious stamina of his race. He speaks a doxology of the blood. He balances the good with the bad, and the equation comes out positive. When he gets nebulous is when he is at his best. His talk then becomes a sort of leafing and budding, an incantation to growth. Often, in groping for word or image, he closes his eyes and sways to and fro. Some-

21

times he repeats the thought, in different words of course—often through oxymorons—spiraling round and round the thought as if to draw it up from the inchoate depths and give it light and form. In these flights he mints new words, adjectives and adverbs especially; bizarre as they sound at first, they are always accurate. Many of them are grand words such as only majestic beings know how to employ. And always, like heavy incense, there floats above them the aroma of the doxology—PRAISE GOD FROM WHOM ALL BLESSINGS FLOW!

He was at his best one evening after the fire had gone out and he had wrapped himself in sweaters, scarves and blankets. He was particularly exuberant on this occasion because he had completed a portrait in a very few sittings and with obvious success. It had been an experience for me to sit for this portrait: I had not only learned something about myself but a great deal about Beauford DeLaney. Or rather, I learned something about the artist, something which demands constant corroboration, even by an artist. Harry was there at the time, grinning like a Cheshire cat; he imagined that Beauford had gone off the deep end again. Beauford was talking of realization, of how on occasion a painting will literally grow out of one's hand. This led him to curious divagations about the source of power, the source of inspiration. He spoke of his struggles with the medium and of how, at long last, he felt that he was just beginning to understand what it was all about, just beginning to know what he wanted to do. I smiled. That same day I had heard almost exactly the same words from the lips of another artist, a man I considered to be a master. Many times I have heard artists speak this way, always, it seemed, when they had reached a moment of realization. It was vision which they were acclaiming, not power, not pride or arrogance. "I am only just beginning to see . . ." And with this there was always expressed the devout wish to be able to keep the vision open. "If only I may be permitted to live a few years longer! Now I am on the track of it. I am just beginning to express myself, my own true self." And so on.

Listening to Beauford I was once again made aware of how insignificant the other, physical struggle was. One was no longer conscious of the falling temperature or other discomforts; one thought only of this unfolding power of sight which would spur him on to greater efforts. One could visualize him shooting forward through a maze of productions like a bullet through the threaded barrel of a high-powered rifle. There was no thought of reward, nor even of recognition; his only concern was to create. Rapidly, as he rambled on, I reviewed the stages of his development, putting together as best I could the fragments of his life as he had revealed them from time to time. He had come a long way already, this amazing and invariable Beauford DeLaney. He had started from the deep South with absolutely nothing and, after twenty-five years of struggle with a hostile world, had emerged superior to the claims of the world. The great white world seemed to grow smaller and smaller as Beauford talked. It was not that he cursed or derided it—he ignored it. One would not know in what country he was living, to follow his speech. There was no black and white, no master or slave; there was just the endless stretch of vision in which the imagination of all men dwells. On a dark and lonely night Greene Street was just another specimen of dark and lonely nights everywhere. It was not America, not Manhattan Island, nor the dismal purlieus of Greenwich Village; it was a thoroughfare lined with grim façades through which the human soul wandered in various states of being at various stages of its evolution. It was a state of mind which one triumphed over on good days and succumbed to on bad days. If captured with the brush during a siege of exaltation it could arouse ridicule or indignation on the part of an unseeing beholder; it could also make a sensitive individual bleed with anguish. But it would never bring pocket money, nor heat nor light, nor even apple fritters. It would take its place eventually with all the other canvases hidden away in this unbelievable sarcophagus of a room; it would die from not being looked at; it would make camouflage material for the next war. But somewhere in the universe, despite all physical loss or damage, Greene Street, like Dante, like Beauford's beautiful mother, would live out its dream and in some imperceptible way affect the vision of all other dreamers living and walking through empty thoroughfares lined with grim, hostile walls.

---

Long before I met Beauford I had formed an image of him in my mind. It was about two o'clock in the morning at Beverly Glen —in the Green House, as we called it—that Harry Herschkowitz, sailor and steeplejack, first broached Beauford's name to me. Harry had come down from San Francisco to see me; it was winter and the rains had set in. For two whole days Harry had sat around waiting for a chance to have a heart to heart talk with me. Finally, about two in the morning he leaned over the typewriter at which I was working and commanded me to call a halt. "I want to talk to you," he said. "I'm leaving to-morrow morning." It was rather chilly in the Green House and Harry had his overcoat on, the collar turned up, his fedora hat tilted on the back of his head. I think of this because that's the way we sat around at 181 Greene Street when the three of us came together.

Among other things, Harry wanted to talk to me about money. He believes that money should always enter into the relations between good friends. "It forms a bond," was the way he put it. Harry is always borrowing or lending, I should add, even if there is no good reason for it. He has a passion for seeing money circulate. He also

24

has the idea that he knows best from whom it should be filched and to whom it should be given. He has become a sort of self-constituted, unauthorized Hermes.

It was just two days before Christmas and the talk of money seemed more than ever to gladden Harry's heart. He didn't need any for himself at the time, nor did I, strangely enough. But just the same, we made a transaction. It was a further bond between us, Harry observed. I remember that, to further cement the bond, we shared a huge slice of corn bread sprinkled with salt. I had just repaid Harry a small sum which he had loaned me. He held the money in his hand and, without looking at it, launched into a speech.

"It's about Beauford," he began. "I'm taking this because he's one person who needs it more than you or I. To-morrow I'll go to the telegraph office and send it to him. It'll make him happy." That's how he started. Then quickly he added: "To-morrow morning, before I go, I want you to sit down and write Beauford a letter. I'm going to tell you all about him in a minute, but before I get wound up I want you to remember this—*don't forget to write Beauford a letter!*"

Then he began about the Persian Gulf, his favorite jumping off point. It had nothing to do with Beauford but then, if it's a good yarn Harry wants to spin, he must start with the Persian Gulf. (And I must say right here that every time I hear about the Persian Gulf from his lips I become more enchanted, more intoxicated, more hallucinated . . . and ever more willing to accede to his fantastic ideas about bonds, whether of blood or money, especially if the ceremony is concluded with a good slice of buttered Jewish bread with a little salt sprinkled on it.) Every time Harry came back from sea, of course, he went to see Beauford. Sometimes he stayed at Beauford's place—that was before 181 Greene Street—and some-

25

times Beauford had to nurse him through a fever, because when you go up the Tigris or the Euphrates you always get some kind of ailment, a skin disease, dysentery, or fever, as I say, but not just ordinary fever, *fever*, the Persian Gulf variety. Usually, on returning from a trip, Harry had a bit of money with him as well as gifts for all his friends. When the money gave out Harry would return to sea. It was just like that, simple as could be. Once you had a taste of the sea you never thought of earning a living on land; you stayed ashore only long enough to spend your money, then you looked for another lousy, leaky ship with rotten grub and a crazy, sadistic captain.

Ashore, Harry had a boon companion named Larry King—Leib to his cronies. I believe it was Larry who had discovered Beauford. Anyway, when Harry was out to sea it was Larry who watched over Beauford. In those days Beauford had an even crazier abode than 181 Greene Street. It was in the very thick of Bohemia and Beauford, unable to say No to anyone, lived very much like a permanent guest in a flop house. He couldn't even go to the toilet alone. How he managed to work only a genius can say; the place was infested with hangers on . . . bums, cripples, phony artists, malingerers and derelicts. Regularly every month Beauford was threatened with eviction, and irregularly every month Beauford managed somehow to raise the meagre sum required. Larry would descend upon the joint at intervals and, like an angry emissary of the gods, sweep the place clean of human refuse.

At this point in his narrative Harry smiled and threw me a strange look. "I don't want you to get the idea that Beauford's helpless," he said. "No, not Beauford! He's really very shrewd, when you get down to it. But he needs watching over. Once in a while you have to give him a hand, else the harpies will sink their hooks into him. You'll know what I mean when you meet him. He's very

26

wise, very resourceful. He's also angelic. That's how people get fooled; they don't know what powers he has behind him . . . No, Beauford understands. He's nobody's fool, I'm telling you. The thing is, Beauford's tolerant. That's it, *tolerant*. He puts up with your lies and your nonsense, but he's never taken in. Not Beauford. When the situation gets critical Beauford always knows how to extricate himself. We *pretend* to help him, but Beauford isn't deceived. Actually it's Beauford who's helping *us*. If there were no Beauford the light would die out. Can you imagine what it would be like in America if there were no Beauford DeLaneys? Wait till you meet his friends . . . I mean his own people. That will be a treat for you. Beauford's got all kinds of friends—black, white, yellow, red, brown, and even some striped ones like the zebra . . . Once you know Beauford you never desert him. You can't. Your life is altered in some subtle way . . . everything takes on a different cast. Just why I can't say, but it's a fact. You become a different man after you meet Beauford. That's saying a good deal, but I mean every word of it." He paused a moment. "Beauford knows about you. I've written him about you in every letter. So when you sit down to write him, don't feel shy or delicate about it. Just begin: 'Dear Beauford . . .' and then put down whatever comes into your head. He'll appreciate it, believe me, and he'll answer you one day. You'll like his answer, too. He's not much on letter writing but when he takes it into his head to write he knows how to string the words out. A letter from Beauford is an event in your life. So don't forget, will you? Sit down to-morrow morning, before breakfast if you can, and write to him. I'll add a few words myself."

A few months later, obliged to make an unexpected trip East, I found myself one afternoon standing at the curb, on MacDougal Street, gazing at Beauford's paintings. There was an outdoor show on and Harry had suggested that I go to Beauford's stand; I was to creep up on him alone while Harry stood across the street and looked on. "He's very intuitive," said Harry. "He'll recognize you without your opening your mouth. You'll see." I did as Harry counseled. I got close to Beauford, whose back was half turned, and waited until he got through talking to the man who had engaged his attention. In the middle of a sentence Beauford halted abruptly, wheeled around, and with an expression of joy and absolute certitude, said: "Why, Henry Miller! You here? *How are you?*"

"How did you know it was me?" I exclaimed.

"Why, I'd have recognized you anywhere," said Beauford. "I just knew you were standing behind me."

Harry, who had been watching the scene from the other side of the street, came over with a broad grin. "What did I tell you?" he said.

Just then some college students came along and, spying one of the Dante portraits, began to make jokes about it.

"It must be tough," I said, "to stand here all day and listen to these stupid comments."

"Oh, I don't mind too much," said Beauford. "In fact, I rather enjoy it. It takes all kinds to make a world. They'll grow up one day. Time, time . . . give them time. You can't remain foolish forever."

.At this point a well-dressed man came out of an adjacent hotel. His car was parked behind Beauford's back. As he approached the car he greeted Beauford warmly. "I want to come to your studio some day," he said. He spoke with an accent. "What do you call that picture over there?" He pointed to one of the Greene Street paintings. Beauford gave the title. "And how much do you ask for it?"

I could hardly believe my ears. Was someone really going to buy one of Beauford's paintings? I moved away so as not to inject into their discussion the least aura of doubt or ambiguity. Whilst cooling my heels at the curb I offered up a quick and silent prayer: "Please God, make it a good sale this time!"

Soon more people came up. Everybody knows Beauford. Some were artists, I noticed, and these greeted Beauford with respect and admiration. Finally a garbage truck drew up and the Negro driver jumped down from his perch. They exchanged hearty greetings. I could see that the driver was somewhat nonplussed by Beauford's exhibition. Just the same, his remarks were not unintelligent. Beauford listened to his comments gravely and sympathetically; he was all gentleness and consideration. When the truck drew away Beauford told me in a few words about the sorrowful condition of the man's family. "He's having a hard time of it, poor devil!" The way he said this moved me. I knew that if he had sold a painting that day the money would go to his friend, the garbage collector.

---

## PRACTISING THE SEVENTH STAGE OF BUDDHA'S NOBLE PATH

"Sitting quietly with empty and tranquil mind, breathing gently, deliberately, evenly, slowly; realizing that however necessary the process of breathing is to the life of the organism, it is not the self, neither is it anything that a self can accomplish by volition or effort."

I am reading this out of a book while the storm rages. It has been raining steadily now for three days. I think of Beauford between times, during lulls in the storm when the ocean becomes visible and one can look out to sea, far, very far, almost to China. Beauford is not connected with the storm, but the storm has brought about an enforced peace and contentment, an acceptance, even if only an acceptance of the weather.

"Sitting quietly, breathing gently, deliberately, evenly, slowly;

realizing that the organism, if it is to become enlightened and brought to Buddhahood, requires something more than breathing, namely, it requires nutrition."

The papers have been telling of the great blizzard which has swept New York, of sleet and snow and ice, and of that sub-zero temperature which would chill even the heart of an Alaskan. It must be incredibly cold at 181 Greene Street, colder than Nome, colder than Iceland. Beauford comes of a warm climate, a warm race. He must be frozen to death by now. I want to send him a wire, but the telegraph office is fifty miles away. I wonder what he's doing, what he's thinking.

"Sitting quietly, breathing gently, deliberately, evenly, slowly; realizing that the organism, if it is to become enlightened and brought to Buddhahood, requires something more than nutrition, namely, it requires heat."

Passing one day through Beauford, S. C., I saw a Negro sitting on a two-wheeled cart driving a bullock slowly down the street. He seemed radiant with joy though poor and obviously despised. Beauford might just as well have been the man behind the bullock. And the man behind the bullock might just as well have been Thomas Carlyle, or Little Nemo, if you prefer that. Anyway, Beauford was named after the town I mention. Nobody will remember the town a hundred years from now. A hundred years from now Beauford's problems will be solved. The moral: Beware the bullock!

"Sitting quietly with humble and patient mind, with earnest and disciplined mind, waiting for the clouds of karma and defilements of the mind to clear away so that the pure brightness within may shine forth illumining the mind, revealing that self is nothing, that mind-essence is everything."

Is everyone happy? Is everyone sitting quietly, breathing gently, humming softly? Is this Beulah Land, with mashed potatoes, central heating, nutrition, intellection and conjunctivitis? Just for five minutes, won't everyone in the whole world please sit quietly and breathe gently, slowly, deliberately? For only five minutes. What a simple thing to do . . . and yet it can't be done. Not nohow. Not even with bullocks walking down the main street and Thomas Carlyle holding the whip. Does anyone on earth really want to become enlightened and brought to Buddhahood? I pick my nose while waiting for the answer.

Sitting quietly, realizing this universal emptiness and eternal silence.

ALL HAIL! THE BLISS-BODY OF BUDDHAHOOD!

---

And now the sun has burst forth and there is a radiant glow over the wet earth, that saturated smile of contentment, of Buddhic bliss and understanding, such as I have seen spread over the countenances of Beauford's real and only friends, the scattered remnants of a lost continent, a lost time, when all men were brothers and all alike, whether they had attained to unity, purity and peacefulness or not, worshiped the one and only God: the divine solar energy.

Strange that in these men of dark skin there is more light, more joy, more bliss, more contentment, more wisdom, more understanding, more compassion, more love than in the members of the great white race. Strange that from the men who have nothing, not even freedom, we receive gifts in abundance. Evidently the organism, when it is finally enlightened and brought to Buddhahood, so to speak, requires nothing more than is given—perhaps even less.

Sitting for the portrait, breathing evenly, gently, slowly, deliberately, I felt the black monarch opposite me imparting to the organism thirsting for enlightenment all the qualities which centuries of captivity, centuries of torture and humiliation, had failed to stamp out. Brother Beauford, poor and blessed, was painting a canticle to the sun. After he had limned the eyes, nose and lips, after he had put in the ears, came the aureole, the corolla, the corona, the nebula, the nova. On his shoulders sat two white birds, invisible but for their incandescent purity. Behind him were the barred windows and through the chinks one saw the factory hands across the way, hands without souls busy making buttons, busy making cigars, busy making boxes, busy, soul-less hands with warts and callouses, busy, busy, making innumerable nothings for non-entities living without grace, light, wisdom or compassion, organisms requiring only food, rent and movies, members of Local No. 56947½, free, white, doomed and driven to dross.

Sitting quietly, waiting for the clouds of karma and defilement to clear away, I watched Brother Beauford's hands as they plied the brush. Hands not busy but creative: disciplined hands formed to give joy to seeing eyes. Hands belonging to an ancient organism, not local but universal, the organism of the Brotherhood of Man. The only brotherhood which includes birds, beasts, flowers and stars— and whose members sing and dance.

Sitting quietly with the thermometer falling, the rent long due, and all that the organism requires seemingly absent, withheld or suppressed, I thought of the big white artists busy making medicine bottles, collars and neckties, furs, bracelets, sanitary napkins for sick white men and women riding back and forth under the ground looking for work or resting from work or dying from work; sometimes killing in order to work, or killing just for pleasure, but killing, killing, killing. The great white brotherhood of war and work, of rape and pillage, of starvation and taxes, of superstition and bigotry, of melancholy and misanthropy.

Breathing slowly, gently, evenly, deliberately, I thought of the Blessed One as he made the rounds. I saw him painting out all the blackness of the world, substituting light, grace, wisdom and compassion, until even Angulimala, the terror of the kingdom of Kosaia, Angulimala, the bandit and assassin, became conspicuous with virtue. Brother Beauford talks quietly as he mixes the pigments. He too is painting out the blackness of the world. Humming as he works, and blessing with every stroke of the brush, he covers the canvas with joy. Brother Beauford is making an image in heavenly colors, an image not of me nor of him, but of God. Painting out the blackness he also paints out the aboulia and apraxia of the world.

Yes, the amazing and invariable Beauford DeLaney, realizing that the organism, if it is to become enlightened and brought to Buddhahood, requires something more than food, heat and rent, throws caution to the winds and, with the recklessness of the innocent, adds to the divine image all the trappings of solar radiance together with the resplendent reflections of the most dazzling divine trappings. In his most amazing, most invariable state of beatitude, Brother Beauford is himself the summum and optimum of all the solar energies and radiances combined. He is like the mother of his own mother, the Veronica of St. Augustine . . . a vessel of light in the Nubian desert of night. He is also Alavaka the cannibal, Ugrasena the acrobat, Upali the barber, all converted by the Blessed One and made fit for enlightenment and Buddhahood. He is, in this exalted state, now fit to be memorized and repeated every day. He is the not this and the not that of the Upanishads, the it and the id, the quidem and the quondam.

And when he is through painting out the blackness what's to hinder us from going to the Italian restaurant on the corner of Bleecker Street and God knows where and filling our bellies with food and drink, stuffing our mouths with cigars, drowning our eyes in darkness? Nothing, nothing at all, because at six sharp Harry will arrive with another tale of the Persian Gulf and a pocketful of change. And at twelve ten midnight punctual as a March hare,

Leib will be standing outside the Miracle of Warsaw in civilian clothes with another pocketful of change and there will be more food and drink, more cigars, more darkness. By three A. M. the amazing and invariable one will be stretched out like a warm cadaver between the oil stoves in the sub-cellar at 530 East 13th Street, and when he is thoroughly thawed out he will be given a bubble bath by Larry and Harry, the Koenigsberg twins of Avenue A.

From this point on there is only repetition: food, rent, heat, light, pigment and lactation. As long as there is a white world there will be more karma and defilement, more Locals, more hangings, more work, more misery. The black man will drive the bullock and the bullock will bugger the white man, his mother, his sister, his children's children, even the rabbits in the field. As of a winter's night Orion sets the interstellar tune with her three diamond studs ablaze, so Beauford sitting at 181 Greene Street, breathing slowly, evenly, gently, deliberately, sets in motion the universal brotherhood of man, the white sisterhood of doves and angels, and the great serpentine constellation of birds, beasts and flowers, all caracoling towards the sun in color, peace and harmony.

# THE STAFF OF LIFE

BREAD: prime symbol. Try and find a good loaf. You can travel fifty thousand miles in America without once tasting a piece of good bread. Americans don't care about good bread. They are dying of inanition but they go on eating bread without substance, bread without flavor, bread without vitamins, bread without life. Why? Because the very core of life is contaminated. If they knew what good bread was they would not have such wonderful machines on which they lavish all their time, energy and affection. A plate of false teeth means much more to an American than a loaf of good bread. Here is the sequence: poor bread, bad teeth, indigestion, constipation, halitosis, sexual starvation, disease and accidents, the operating table, artificial limbs, spectacles, baldness, kidney and bladder trouble, neurosis, psychosis, schizophrenia, war and famine. Start with the American loaf of bread so beautifully wrapped in cellophane and you end on the scrap heap at forty-five. The only place to find a good loaf of bread is in the ghettos. Wherever there is a foreign quarter there is apt to be good bread. Wherever there is a Jewish grocer or delicatessen you are almost certain to find an excellent loaf of bread. The dark Russian bread, light in weight, found only rarely on this huge continent, is the best bread of all. No vitamins have been injected into it by laboratory specialists in conformance with the latest food regulations. The Russian just naturally likes good bread, because he also likes caviar and vodka and other good things. Americans are whiskey, gin and beer drinkers who long ago lost their taste for food. And losing that they have also lost their taste for life. For enjoyment. For good conversation. For everything worth while, to put it briefly.

What do I find wrong with America? Everything. I begin at the beginning, with the staff of life: bread. If the bread is bad the whole life is bad. Bad? Rotten, I should say. Like that piece of bread only twenty-four hours old which is good for nothing except perhaps to fill up a hole. Good for target practice maybe. Or shuttlecock and duffle board. Even soaked in urine it is unpalatable; even perverts shun it. Yet millions are wasted advertising it. Who are the men engaged in this wasteful pursuit? Drunkards and failures for the most part. Men who have prostituted their talents in order to help further the decay and dissolution of our once glorious Republic.

Here is one of the latest widely advertised products: Hollywood Bread. On the red, white and blue cellophane jacket in which it is wrapped, this last word in bread from the American bakeries, it reads as follows:

## BAKED WITH

whole wheat flour, clear wheat flour, water, non-diastatic malt, yeast, salt, honey, caramel, whole rye flour, yeast food, stone ground oatmeal, soya flour, gluten flour, barley flour, sesame seed, and a small quantity of dehydrated (water free) vegetables including celery, lettuce, pumpkin, cabbage, carrots, spinach, parsley, sea kelp, added for flavor only.

The only thing missing from this concoction is powdered diamonds. How does it taste? Much like any other American product. Of course, this is a reducing bread of which one should eat two slices a day three times a day and not ask how it tastes. Grow thin, as in Hollywood, and be thankful it doesn't taste worse. That's the idea. For several days now I have been trying to get a whiff of some of those ingredients—sea kelp especially—which were included "for flavor only." Why they were not added for health too I don't know. Naturally all these delicious-sounding items amount to about one ten-thousandth part of the loaf. And on the second day, stale, flat and unprofitable, this marvelous new bread is no more attractive to the palate or the stomach than any other loaf of American bread. On the second day it is good for replacing a missing tile on the roof. Or to make a scratchboard for the cat.

The second day! If the first is given to creation, to light, let us say, the second (in America) is given up to garbage. Every second day is garbage day in America. I know because I have had lots to do with garbage. I've hauled it, for pay, and I've eaten it upon necessity. I learned to distinguish between one kind of bread and another by salvaging dry crusts from the garbage can. I don't know which is worse—the day of creation, when everything turns to gas and bilge, with its concomitants dandruff, constipation, halitosis, false teeth, artificial limbs, psychic impotency, and so on, or the second day, given up to garbage, when all creation turns out to be nothing but a mirage and a disillusionment. It has been said, and I have no doubt it is true, that the garbage accumulated by one big American city would feed certain of the little countries of Europe handsomely. I know no quicker way to kill off the warring nations of Europe than to feed them our garbage. The pygmies might thrive on it, possibly even the Chinese coolie, who is supposed to thrive on anything, but I cannot see the Danes, the Swiss, the Swedes, the Greeks, the Albanians, or the Austrians thriving on it. No Sir. I would sooner feed them buzzards than the left-overs from the American table. Already, with our canned food products, our cold storage meat, our dehydrated vegetables, we have brought about a tremendous deterioration in these sturdy people of Europe. From these to the machine and thence to war is but a step. Then, famine, plague, pestilence, dung heaps. And monuments, of course. All sorts of monuments. Done by second or third rate artists.

The care and affection which once was bestowed on the human body now goes to the machines. The machines get the best food, the best attention. Machines are expensive; human lives are cheap. Never in the history of the world was life cheaper than it is to-day. (And no pyramids to show for it either.) How natural, then, that the staff of life should be utterly without value. I begin with bread and I shall end with bread. I say we make the foulest bread in all the world. We pass it off like fake diamonds. We advertise it and sterilize it and protect it from all the germs of life. We make a manure which we eat before we have had time to eliminate it. We not only have failed God, tricked Nature, debased Man, but we have cheated the birds of the air with our corrupt staff of life. Every-time I fling the stale bread over the cliff I beg forgiveness of the birds for offering them our American bread. Perhaps that is why they are not singing any more as they used to when I was a child. The birds are pining and drooping. It's not the war, for they have never participated in our carnages. It's the bread. The stale, flat, unprofitable bread of the second day. It shortens their wing-span, weakens their umbrella-ribs, reduces the scope of their swoop, blunts their beaks, deteriorates their vision, and finally—it kills their song! If you don't believe me, ask any ornithologist. It's a known fact. And how Americans love facts!

Another fact. . . . Food, when it is not enjoyed, kills. The best diet in the world is useless if the patient has no appetite, no gusto, no sensuality. On the whole, Americans eat without pleasure. They eat because the bell rings three times a day. (I omit mention of the clay eaters of the South and other poor whites who live on rats, snakes, and cow-dung.) They don't eat because they love food. To prove it you have only to shove a glass of whiskey before them. See which they reach for first! And now, with vitamins and all the other life-savers, food has become even less important. Why bother trying to squeeze a bit of life out of our worn-out products of the soil? Why pretend? Throw anything down the hatch to stop the gnawing and swallow a dozen vitamins. That way you'll make sure you've had your proper dose of the vital essentials. Should the vitamins fail, see a surgeon. From there to the sanitarium. And from there to the nut-house—or the dung heap. Be sure to get a Hollywood funeral. They're the loveliest, the duckiest, the most sanitary, the most inspiring. And no more expensive than ordinary ground burial. You can, if you like, have your dear lost one propped up in a natural reclining position, her cheeks rouged, a cigarette to her lips, and a phonograph record talking to you just as she once talked to you in life. The most wonderful fake imaginable. Jolly, what? O death, where is thy sting? What's more, she can be kept that way for an unspeakably long period; the cigarette is guaranteed not to rot away before the lips or the buttocks. You can come back and have a second, a third, a twenty-fifth look at the beloved. Still smoking a cigarette. Or you can have her reading a book, the *Iliad*, say, or the *Bhagavad Gita*—something uplifting like that.

I remember when I used to be served a slice of home-made bread with butter and sugar smeared over it. Glorious days! That bread really had a taste. *Schmecht gut, nichtwahr? Yah! Sehr gut. Wunderbar. Ausgezeichnet.* With a piece of bread like that I used to sit and read *Pinocchio* or *Alice Through the Looking Glass* or Hans Christian Andersen or *The Heart of a Boy.* Mothers had time in those days to make good bread with their own hands, and still do the thousand and one things which motherhood demands of a woman. To-day they haven't time to do anything, and hardly a bloody mother in the bloody land knows how to bake a loaf of bread. Mother gets up early now to work in an office or a factory. She's busy doing nothing all day, which is to say—earning a living. Earning a living has nothing to do with living. It's the belt line to the grave, without a transfer or a stopover. A one-way passage via the frying pan and the cookerless cooker. A child is an accident— bad rubber goods or else too much drink and recklessness. Any way, it's there and it has to be fed. You don't bake bread for accidents, do you? And why bother to produce milk from the breast when the cows are working over-time for the dairy companies of America?

Day by day the morons, epileptics and schizoids multiply. By accident, like everything else. Nothing is planned in America except improvements. And all improvements are for the machine. When a plenum is reached war is declared. Then the machine really gets going. War is a Roman Holiday for the machine. Man becomes even less than nothing then. The machine is well fed. The food products become plastics and plastics are what make the world go round. Better to have a good steering wheel than a good stomach. In the old days an army advanced on its stomach; now it advances in tanks or spitfires or super-fortresses. Civilians never advance.

40

Civilians always rot and help make insurance companies richer.

But bread. . . . Let's not forget, it's bread we want—and children that are not accidents brought about by defective rubber or bathtub gin. How to get it? Bread, I mean. By putting a monkey wrench in the machine. By going backwards on all fours, like giraffes with broken necks. By praying for life now and not hereafter. By exercising freedom and not inventing four, five or six freedoms won by the slaughter and starvation of twenty or thirty millions. Begin today by baking your own bread. First of all you need a stove. A wood or a coal stove. Not a gas range. Not an electric apparatus. Then let the flies in. Then roll your sleeves up and get your hands in the dough. Lick your fingers. Never mind if you lose your job. Eat your bread first, then maybe you won't want to work in an office or a factory. Life begins with bread. And a prayer. Not a begging prayer, but a prayer of thanks. Don't bless the block-busters. Bless God for his favors—air, water, sun, moon. God wants you to enjoy the bread of life. He never meant you to go out all day working at a job you loathe so that you can buy a loaf of store bread wrapped in cellophane. God gave us germs as well as air and water and sun. Germs attack only what is already rotting. Man is rotting in every fibre of his being: that is why he is a prey to germs. And that is why he is allergic to everything that is for his own good.

Before Communism was there was Communion and before that there was God and God said let there be light and there was light. And what a glorious light it was. It lasted for aeons, and then came the scientific age and darkness fell upon the land everywhere. Now everything can be proved backwards and out of existence and instead of soaring with our own wings or on the backs of our giant birds we make things of metal and plastics which spread havoc and destruction in their wake. We throw bones to the dogs and eat the dogs instead of the bones. Not one step has been taken towards improving the flow of milk from the mammary glands. Only mothers and wet nurses give milk, whereas with time and experimentation every one could give milk and the food problem would be solved for eternity. We wouldn't even need to sit down to eat: now and then a step-ladder might be necessary, but nothing more. Why hasn't any one thought of that? Is it so improbable? Ants have their milk cows—how did that happen? Anyway, with human milk the universal food, with manna falling from heaven, and nectar and ambrosia for dessert, think what a lot of work would be eliminated. Think too of the gratitude the animals would show, once they got on to the new scheme of things. All we would need, men and animals, would be one huge grass plot. No more dairy companies, no more containers, no more bottles, plates, knives and forks, spoons, pots, pans, stoves. The solution of the food problem would throw a monkey wrench into the entire economic and social system; our mores would change, our religions would disappear, our money become valueless. One can hardly imagine what the cause for war would then be, though doubtless a good excuse will always be found.

Outside of the foreign quarters, then, take it for granted that there is no good bread to be had. Every foreign group has introduced into our life some good substantial bread, even the Scandinavians. (Excepting the English, I should add, but then we hardly think of them as foreign, though why we shouldn't I don't know, for when you think of it the English are even less like us than the Poles or Latvians.) In a Jewish restaurant you usually have a basket filled with all kinds of bread from which to choose. In a typical American restaurant, should you ask for rye, whole wheat or any other kind of bread but the insidious, unwholesome, and unpalatable white, you get white bread. If you insist on rye bread you get whole wheat. If you insist on whole wheat you get graham bread. Once in a great while you come upon nut bread; this is always a sheer accident. Raisin bread is a sort of decoy to lure you into eating unpalatable, perfidious and debilitating white bread. When in doubt go to a Jewish restaurant or delicatessen; if necessary, stand up and eat a sandwich made of sour rye, sweet butter, pastrami and pickle. A Jewish sandwich contains more food value than an eighty-five cent meal in the ordinary American restaurant. With a glass of water to wash it down you can walk away feeling fit. Don't sit down and eat a Jewish meal, because the Jews are bad cooks despite their great concern about food, which amounts to a neurosis. It is curious, though, how the desire to survive has made the Jews keen about preserving the staff of life. It is even more curious that they are just as much riddled with disease as the other members of the community—more so, in fact, judging purely from personal observation. They not only have all the physical ailments which other white peoples are heir to but they have all the mental and nervous ailments. Often they have everything at once, and then they concentrate upon food with even greater acuity and despair. It is only when they become revolutionary that they begin to lose interest in food. The real American, on the other hand, though totally unrevolutionary at heart, seems born with an indifference to food. One can serve a white American food which would make an Igorote turn up his nose. Americans can eat garbage, provided you sprinkle it liberally with ketchup, mustard, chili sauce, tabasco sauce, cayenne pepper, or any other condiment which destroys the original flavor of the dish. On the other hand, olive oil which the French eschew when preparing salads because it has too strong a flavor, Americans hardly ever use in their salads. Nothing on God's earth is more uninviting, more anaemic, than the American salad. At its best it is like refined puke. The lettuce is a joke: even a canary would refuse to touch it. This concoction, mind you, is usually served before the meal, together with the coffee which is cold by the time you are ready to drink it. The moment you sit down at a table in the ordinary American restaurant, the moment you begin scanning the menu, the waitress asks you what you wish to drink. (If by chance you should say "cocoa," the whole kitchen would be thrown out of gear.) To this question I usually counter with another: "Do you have anything but white bread?" If the answer is not a flat No, it is: "We have whole wheat," or "We have graham bread." Whereupon I usually mumble under my breath: "You can stick that up your ass!" When she says; "What did you say?" I reply, "Do you have rye bread by any chance?" Then, before she can say no, I launch into an elaborate explanation of the fact that I don't mean by rye bread the ordinary rye bread, which is no better than white, graham, or whole wheat, but a succulent, tasty, dark, sour rye such as the Russians and the Jews serve. At the mention of these two suspect·nationalities a scowl spreads over her face. While she is saying in her most sarcastic voice that she is sorry but they do not have that kind of rye bread or any rye bread, for that matter, I begin asking about the fruit, what kinds of fruit, fresh fruit, they have on hand, knowing damned well that they haven't any. Nine times out of ten her answer will be: "We have apple pie, and peach pie." ("Stick it up your ass!") "I beg your pardon?" she says. "Yes, fruit . . . you know, the kind that grows on trees . . . apples, pears, bananas, plums, oranges . . . something with skin on it that you peel." Whereupon a light dawns and she hastens to interpolate: "Oh, but we have apple sauce!" ("Fuck your apple sauce!") "I beg pardon?" Here I look leisurely round the room, surveying the shelves, the counter, the pie plates. Finally, resting my gaze upon a bowl of artificial fruit, I exclaim with glee: "Like that over there, *only real!*"

44

Sometimes, upon scanning the menu and knowing that it will only give me a belly-ache, I ask immediately if they can serve me a large bowl of fresh fruit. Here, incidentally, let me call attention to the dishes of mixed fruit prepared early in the morning which stand rotting in disgusting sweet canned juices until lunch or dinner hour. In the Automat type of restaurant one sees the counter piled with these vile stews. These, like the salads mentioned a moment ago, and like the pies fabricated by the wholesale bakers (who are probably responsible for more deaths than all our wars put together), are peculiar to the American temperament. There is not the least food value in any of them. The salad is at its worst when served in one of those delightful little inns run by spinsters in villages of imaginary charm, such as one is supposed to find in Vermont, Maryland, or Connecticut. Here everything looks immaculate and is immaculate, and therefore without value, without flavor, without joy. One suddenly feels like a canary which has been castrated and can no longer warble or differentiate between seed and salad. Beginning with this obscene salad one just knows that the meal is going to end with a charming little dessert such as prune whip or vanilla ice cream. To ask for a grape or a herring in one of these places is like committing sacrilege. There are certain things you must never ask for in an American restaurant. Never. One is good sour rye such as the Russians and the Jews make. Another is a cup of strong coffee. (Exceptions: French and Italian restaurants, and Louisiana. In Louisiana you can get a cup of coffee that is like liquid dynamite. But it tastes good; it has chicory in it. And chicory is excellent, despite all opinion to the contrary.) A third is cheese. A fourth is grapes. A fifth is nuts. Never have I seen a bowl of assorted and uncracked nuts put on the table in an American restaurant. Now and then, rarely, very rarely, one sees nuts in an American home. Usually, however, they are there as decoration. The fruit likewise. Fruit and nuts belong on the side-board for the children, when there are any, to nibble at. The mixed fruit, or fruit salad, as they have the impudence to call it in America, reaches the height of abomination in the arm-chair Automat type of restaurant. Have you ever noticed the derelicts who frequent these eating places, sitting in the show window munching their lunch or dinner? Is there any more lugubrious sight on earth? (The corollary to it is the cheap traveling salesman type of hotel where all day long the weary commercial traveler sits in an enormous leather armchair staring vacantly out on the street. This is the type who gets orders for useless commodities which the American slave toils his ass off to accumulate, which he sells to his own kind and pretends thereby that he is earning an honest living. This is the type that votes the Democratic or Republican ticket year in and year out, in lean years and fat years, in war and in peace, and is always complaining that business is bad. This is the most traveled man in the world, and yet he knows nothing, absolutely nothing, and brags about it. This is the type who when you mention China says immediately—"coolies." If there is any more ignominious coolie than the traveling salesman I have yet to know him. The fact that he reads the "Digest" or some other compilation of facts gives him the illusion that he is informed and a useful member of society.)

But it's the pie that takes the cake. The pie is at its worst in the Greek restaurant, often called "New York Café," and encountered in every village and hamlet throughout the length and breadth of the land. In fact, everything is at its worst in this type of eating place. But it's here that the pie becomes positively obsessive. Often there is nothing to offer the weary traveler but pie. There they stand, row upon row of pie plates, all filled with gangrene and arsenic. The crust looks like scurf and is scurf, usually of the finest

46

rancid grease made by the Criscomaniacs of America. Here and there one can detect in a whole pie a piece of fruit, such as apple or peach; it is surrounded by a clot of phlegm swimming in a mess of undefinable paste. The piece of apple or peach is sourish, bilious, gaseous, having no more resemblance to the apple or peach in its native state than corn whiskey has to corn on the cob. The Greek proprietor delights in serving white Americans this unholy dish; he despises them for eating it, but, canny business man that he is, he believes in giving them what they ask for. He himself has a totally different cuisine, a damned good one, too, I must say, if you ever make a friend of him and get invited to his home. On his table you will see olives, real olives, okra, olive oil, fruits of all kinds, nuts, rice, vine leaves, the tenderest lamb imaginable, wines of all kind, including retsina, and cognac, Greek cognac, and other delicacies.

Let us digress here a moment. . . . How is it that Americans, composed of nothing but foreign nationalities, living amongst people accustomed to the most varied cuisines, people who have made an art of cooking from time immemorial, continue to be the worst cooks in the world, continue to open one foul restaurant after anther? Explain it, if you can. To me it's an enigma. The more mixed becomes the blood in our veins, the more American we become. And by American I mean the more set, crass, conservative, prejudiced, stupid, narrow-minded, unexperimental and unrevolutionary. In every big city we have Chinese, Italian, French, Hungarian, Russian, German, Swedish restaurants. Do we learn anything from these skilled restaurateurs? No, not a thing. We go our way, serving pies, mixed fruit salads, hamburgers, baked beans, steak and onions, vicious veal cutlets, whether breaded or unbreaded, and so on. Has any one ever had a good stew in an American restaurant? The peasants of Europe have thrived on stews for centuries. Here a stew means a couple of spoonfuls of superannuated meat swimming in a tiny pool of grease and bilge with bloated potatoes as a garniture. One hasn't begun to eat when the meal is over. It's an imaginary stew at the best. And the most imaginary part of it is the vegetables without which no stew is complete: leeks, carrots, turnips, onions, celery, parsley, and so on. If you find a tiny piece of any other vegetable than the potato you are indeed a lucky individual.

All right, steak then! Steak is the great American dish. Steak and onions. Fine. Nothing better, I say. Where can you get it? I mean without paying $2.50 per person! The first and only time I got the real flavor of steak was when I passed through Denver. Up till then I never knew what a real steak tasted like. The meat companies are for convincing us that meat from the refrigerator, meat that has been on ice several years, is the best meat of all. The whole world is being shipped and fed this cold storage meat, thanks to Armour & Co. and their subsidiary hog-butchers. In France I used to eat *filet de boeuf* practically every other day. It cost, for one person, a good portion, mind you, from twelve to eighteen cents, at the rate of exchange prevailing in the late thirties. It was delicious meat, and I knew how to prepare it. (Americans as a rule know only how to spoil a good piece of meat in cooking it.) When I came to America, in 1940, I went to the butcher one day and asked for my customary *filet de boeuf*. A piece for two people came to $1.10, so help me God. I couldn't believe my ears. And this was in a cheap butcher shop on Third Avenue, New York. Christ only knows what it would have cost in the Park Avenue neighborhood. I took it home and I fried it. I did everything just as I used to at the Villa Seurat. I had wine with it too, the best I could buy for $1.25 the bottle. I also had grapes and nuts, and a salad prepared with the best olive oil. I had several kinds of cheese, including roquefort and camembert.

48

Despite all precautions the meal didn't taste the same. There was something lacking. As a matter of fact, all the essentials were lacking. A piece of lettuce grown in America is like a piece of lettuce grown in France only in looks and name. American fruit, the most sensational looking fruit in the world (barring the tropics), is practically tasteless compared to the sicklier looking European fruits. American cheeses look delicious, and God knows the Kraft Brothers have tickled them up inordinately, but they do not have the flavor of the cheeses they are made to imitate. A stale piece of camembert in a dirty French restaurant is worth a whole box of beautiful looking fresh Camembert put out by the crafty cheese-makers of Wisconsin. The flat Dutch cheeses are of course still more flat and tasteless when you eat them in America, being as they are the product of the most pampered cows in all the world. Wines, even when they are good, and in the realm of ordinary table wines America makes some of the best, do not taste as good as in Europe, perhaps because the atmosphere, the violence, the tempo of American life destroys whatever blessings wine confers.

Wine with the meal, in America, produces the wrong result. What is required, when attempting to digest American food, is strong spirits—whiskey, gin, cocktails. The correct procedure is to get soused beforehand; this enables one to eat without noticing how vile the food is. It gets one flushed and excited, and the food is forgotten. It makes one argumentative, which aids in bringing on indigestion and dyspepsia, flatulence, constipation, hemorrhoids, and finally the operating table. Whichever road you take, in America, you always wind up at the surgeon's door. If you buy an automobile it's the surgeon you have to reckon with eventually. If you take a good-paying job, it's the surgeon who will bleed you to death. If you economize and eat in arm-chair restaurants, or the Greek restaurants (where American food is served—not the real Greek restaurant!), you meet the surgeon sooner or later, generally sooner. If you take to the soil and live the outdoor life, you first must have all your teeth pulled out and plates inserted. Farmers have about the worst teeth of all, even worse than factory workers. They have all the physical ailments, too, and are often as not undernourished. Farmers die of inanition in the midst of plenty. There isn't anything you can do, in America, by way of earning a living whereby you can escape dire taxation, disease, accident, misery and humiliation. At the end of every road stands the surgeon, who is for Americans what Nemesis was for the Greeks. The whole culture of America springs from two lunatics: the Marquis de Sade and Sacher Masoch. Justice, always retributive, is apotheosized by the surgeon. His henchmen are the dentists. If you have an ache or pain never mention it to the dentist, or he will immediately extract all your teeth. Nowadays even cowboys are proud of their false teeth. Scarcely any hard-working American, however splendid his physique, is without plates or bridges after forty. Hardly any normal American has a full head of hair after forty. Hardly any American over twenty-one, whether he works hard or takes it easy, is without eye-glasses. Almost every American suffers from hemorrhoids. Practically every American over forty has a bad heart. Cancer, syphilis, arthritis, tuberculosis, schizophrenia are so prevalent that we accept them as part of the bargain—i. e., the American way of life. Nearly every family boasts of one moron among its members, one lunatic, one drunkard, one pervert. All the food advertisements boast of the vitamin contents of their products. All the medicaments advertised boast of their cure for every thing under the sun. It is obvious that our foods lack the proper vitamins, just as it is obvious that in employing these health foods so rich in vitamins we nevertheless are afflicted with all the diseases known to man. We die young, mortgaged to the hilt, insolvent, despite all the insurance policies issued by all the insurance companies whose tentacles reach into every avenue of commercial and industrial life. It is also evident that, despite the fact that this is the land of opportunity where freedom reigns, where every one has the right to worship and the right to vote for the wrong candidate, that the zest for life is so low that less than one child per family is now produced, except among certain Indian tribes, certain religious communities, certain strata of poor whites, and among the Negroes as a whole. Even the Jews, known for their big families as well as their good bread, are beginning to have less children—in America. And when the Jew loses his desire to perpetuate his own kind there must indeed be something seriously wrong with the national life. In the poorest countries of Europe the Jew still remained fertile; here, with everything in his grasp, except recognition by the Gentiles, he withers away. Only among the American Indians, and there only in certain tribes, is the population on the increase. It is said that this is due in part to the practice of polygamy. And here we touch another tender subject, one almost as potent as bread. I mean the fear among native white Americans of indulging in any other form of marriage but that sponsored by the Christian churches. Why not polygamy? Why not polyandry? Why not any kind of marriage, including love marriages? With polygamy the Mormons were fast on the way to building an empire. Nobody can say that the Mormons are, or ever were, an undesirable element in the great American community. They were and still are one of the few communities in this country where poverty is relatively unknown. They produce less criminals than other parts of the country—and less morons, and less idiots, and less trouble of any nature. And God knows they were never, never more immoral than the other members of the community. On the contrary, they were not only more law-abiding, more peaceful, more prosperous, more social-minded

51

and far-visioned than the other communities of America, but they were absolutely more moral in the strictest sense of the word, that is, in the sense that they actually practised what they preached.

But to get back to bread . . . Today the mailman brought three kinds of bread: Italian bread, a milk loaf, and pumpernickel. (No sour rye, of course, no corn bread.) The bread comes from Monterey, the nearest town, which is fifty miles away. In Monterey there is no Jewish grocer or delicatessen, worse luck. In Monterey there are Mexicans, Portuguese and Filipinos, but who gives a damn what these poor devils eat? The Mexicans have their tortillas, the Portuguese their garlic, and the Filipinos . . . well, among other things they have all our bad habits. Nobody in Monterey has a good slice of bread to eat. Nor in Carmel either, unless it's Robinson Jeffers, and that would be a sacramental bread. Just outside of Carmel lives Edward Weston, the photographer. And that leads me to speak of another kind of bread: photographic bread. Have you ever noticed that even the photographic bread tastes poorly? Have you ever seen a piece of bread photographed by our advertising maniacs which you would like to bite into? I haven't. Edward Weston could undoubtedly make you the most wonderful photographic bread conceivable—*but could you eat it?* The bread you hang on your wall is not the bread you want to eat at table. Even a piece of bread by Man Ray would prove unpalatable, particularly if he just happened to be reading his favorite author, the Marquis de Sade. Sacher Masoch might have made a good bread, if he had lived long enough. It has a Kosher sound, *Sacher Masoch*. But in the long run I have a feeling it would make one morbid and introspective, this Sacher Masoch bread.

I have now found that the only way to eat our most unwholesome, unpalatable and unappetizing American bread, the staff of our unsavory and monotonous life, is to adopt the following procedure. This is a recipe, so please follow instructions to the letter.

To begin with, accept any loaf that is offered you without question, even if it is not wrapped in cellophane, even if it contains no kelp. Throw it in the back of the car with the oil can and the grease rags; if possible, bury it under a sack of coal, *bituminous coal.* As you climb up the road to your home, drop it in the mud a few times and dig your heels into it. If you have a dog with you, let him pee on it now and then. When you get to the house, and after you have prepared the other dishes, take a huge carving knife and rip the loaf from stem to stern. Then take one whole onion, peeled or unpeeled, one carrot, one stalk of celery, one huge piece of garlic, one sliced apple, a herring, a handful of anchovies, a sprig of parsley, and an old toothbrush and shove them into the disembowelled guts of the bread. Over these pour first a thimbleful of kerosene, a dash of Lavoris and just a wee bit of Clorox; then sprinkle guts liberally with the following—molasses, honey, orange marmalade, vanilla, soy bean sauce, tabasco sauce, ketchup and arnica. Over this add a layer of chopped nuts, assorted nuts, of course, a few bay leaves (whole), some marjoram, and a stick of licorice cut into fine pieces. Put the loaf in the oven for ten minutes and serve. If it is still lacking in taste whip up a chili con carne piping hot and mix bread with it until it becomes a thick gruel. If this fails, piss on it and throw it to the dog. But under no circumstances feed it to the birds. The birds of North America are already on the decline, as I pointed out earlier. Their beaks have become dull, their wing-span shortened; they are pining and drooping, moulting in season and out. Above all, they no longer sing as they used to; they make sour notes, they bleat instead of tweeting, and sometimes, when the fogs set in, they have even been heard to cackle and wheeze.

# A BODHISATTVA ARTIST

It was at the Café de Versailles, opposite the Gare Montparnasse, that I really became acquainted with Rattner. I remember that summer's evening well. The *terrasse* was fairly deserted. Now and then a few stragglers disappeared down the yawning mouth of the Metro. There was a mild breeze stirring, just sufficient to make the rug vendors buzz about us like horse flies. Now and then a *poule* tried to engage us in conversation across the tables but without conviction or animation. Under the arc lights the verdant foliage of the trees gleamed with a brilliance which made the chlorophyllic green of nature seem pale.

54

4 . its either that or
 utter stupidity

what for — ?
why ?

Life itself – just breathing
– eating – sleeping – walking
– sitting in the sun – or
at night – looking at the
sky . and doing nothing
about it all – but
absorbing everything .
even whatever reflections
in the mind that may
occur – just a kind of
a radio set that receives
all the waves in the air
without passing them on
and out

A page of Abe Rattner's handwriting.

Though I had known him for some time I had never heard Ratt-ner talk about himself. This evening, however, he was in a mood to unburden himself. We had been discussing the approaching war, a topic ever present in one's mind since the German occupa-tion of the Ruhr. Suddenly the other war erupted, like a shell burst-ing in the silence of the night.

It was in the second battle of the Marne, at Château Thierry, while directing the camouflage operations of the 75's, that Rattner was rendered *hors de combat* by a concussion which sent him fly-ing into a shell hole. The injury to his back which he then received he still suffers from. Transferred to Camp Souge (near Bordeaux) he took charge of the School of Camouflage which had just been started. All the camouflage work undertaken at the front, and at the experimental field near Nancy, had to do with the utter ab-sence of paint and painted color shapes (known as dazzle paint-ing.) His job was to construct actual concealments, structures made of poles, chickenwire netting, garlands of tinted burlap, trees, mud, plants, dummy cannons, and so on. Dazzle painting proved to be too limited a form of deception, ineffective because it did not con-ceal the basic structural shadow forms. The basis of camouflage was to fool the camera's eye.

I mention this phase of his war experience because, studying some of his earlier work, I had naively concluded that elements of the camouflage technique had crept into his painting. A quality which I often described as *"flou"* made these canvases contrast sharply with his later work in which the structural element is prom-inent. It was perhaps the prepossession with disturbing and often dislocating effects of light and shade which created the association. I am particularly fond of the work of this period in which it seems that his watery nature gains the ascendance, for Rattner is a strange mixture of fire and water. In these canvases the human figure blends with the patterns of nature in a sort of shadowy, translucent marine-scape. All is flow and movement, arabesques of infinite motifs. He seems to be feeling his way, but like a graceful swimmer rather than a tyro. Often the canvas seems like a mirror reflecting the evanescent shapes and movements of lazy clouds. The colors are vibrant but paled out, as if they had been filtered through a tank of sea water. There is a joyous, insouciant quality about them, a nature feeling which is transplanted direct to the canvas. They have the calligraphic quality of Cézanne's last water colors—not that they are unfinished or "unrealized," but that they suggest rather than embody. They are airy, incorporeal.

What I did not realize, in my first reactions to the work of this period, was that Rattner had already made bold advances in this direction when an architectural student at Washington, D. C. and while studying at the Corcoran School of Art. Even before entering the Pennsylvania Academy of Art his tendencies were cubistic rather than naturalistic or representational. Speaking of this period, and of his adventures in the realm of anatomy at the Georgetown Medical School, Rattner once made some observations which I think worth transcribing. He had been speaking of his search for the bigger principles of structure in works of art. These explorations, so he informed me, led to the question of the relation of structure to spirit. They revealed that the principles of structure were not limited to the physical merely, that there is also a structure to the things of the spirit. "Physical facts are not very important: a painting has to be impregnated with the artist's feeling, his love, his passion, his imagination—his soul, in short. I don't know what it is," he confessed, "but it is a quality or force pertaining to spirit which fuses all the plastic elements and makes it live as a unit."

I recall now that I was at first disconcerted when I saw Rattner's work. A little later, attempting to say something about this phase—

the "*flou*" period, as I call it—I used the expression "genesis of birth." I realize now how much more indicative of my own state such a phrase was than of his.

For it was through Rattner's eyes that I first began to see into modern painting. I remember with gratitude and affection the patience he displayed in listening to me and explaining what he was aiming at, what, in fact, all great painters aim at. There was never any arrogance or humbug about him; he was always open to criticism or suggestion, even from ignorant individuals like myself. Leaving him sometimes, after exhausting him probably with much talk, I would be at a loss to say which I admired the more in him, his perseverance or his humility. Every time I came away from his studio I felt inspired, not to paint or to write, though there was that too, but to reach that core of sincerity and integrity in myself which would match his. No one ever said of Rattner that he was clever, brilliant, or such like; people often left him with tears in their eyes, so moving, so convincing, was his earnestness. And what greater compliment can one pay an artist? Achievement is not everything; intention is something, and devotion or consecration still more. One feels in his presence that here is a man who lives paint, and living it, knows and touches all aspects of life, even the most remote.

But to come back to that evening at the Café de Versailles, which was so important to our eventual understanding of one another. . . . Like every one who knows him, I too had been impressed with his gentleness, his tenderness. He is one of those, you would say after a few minutes in his presence, who could never hurt a fly. He is so tender, in fact, that he actually melts. You not only feel his emotions, you can see them disintegrating and streaming away in rivulets at his feet. That is how he was then, and how he is to-day. How he will always be, for nothing on earth has the power to make

57

him hard and embittered. Imagine my surprise, then, when I heard him speaking about Philadelphia Jack O'Brien with whom he used to spar in the old days. Abe Rattner delivering a sock to the jaw? Incredible! But so it was. He had taken up the art of self defense in order to be equal to any emergency. He learned to give as well as to take. The ability to hit hard and straight is evident in his work. I have observed people recoil sometimes at what they called the brutality of his delineations. I have never shared this feeling, but I know what causes the reaction. In some paintings, especially when his sense of justice is involved, Rattner goes all out, as we say. Then he is like a slugger who dives into the fray with head down, using his arms like flails. In such moments his only thought is to give all he has, then retire in utter exhaustion. He is also, in such moments, a little like that other Honest Abe who said one day when watching slaves being auctioned off— "When I get the chance to hit that thing, I'm going to hit it hard."

So often in tender men there is a furious strength which reveals itself only in their work. Where does this violence come from, one asks? One might as well ask—Where do angels come from? In Rattner there is an inexhaustible energy manifesting itself in an endless recreation of the world. He is not merely rearranging the universe in his own terms, he is putting it to rights. There is a conviction of infallibility in all he does with the brush. He will be more amazed than any one, I am sure, to read this, for he certainly does not think of himself as a pope, even in the realm of paint. But every painting he turns out is another bull or edict. Each, in short, is a *fiat*. He is commanding that something be done about it. About what? About the way of looking at things. Each new canvas is an instigation to see and to act. I don't mean that each picture carries a moral—far from it! I mean that each picture is charged with the implication that there is a right and a wrong way of looking at things, or else a beautiful and an ugly way of seeing things. Naturally, even if he chooses what might be called an ugly subject, it is luminous with beauty. But that is only to say that the positive always wins out. Never would you say of his painting that it contained a negative note, not even if he were painting the destruction of the world. If to-morrow he were to take up the painting of ordure, rest assured that it would be a vital and beneficent ordure, an inspiring ordure. He is incapable of expressing himself except at the maximum. It is in this connection that one understands his violence better; it is like a sharp-faceted jewel, at once an implement, a weapon, and an adornment. There are times when he literally gouges out his subject, times when no milder treatment will do. It is a shock treatment which he gives the canvas, to awaken it to reality, as it were. In the great evolution which modern painting has undergone, the easel painting, as it is called, is subjected to a greater and greater test. In the same limited flat area, and despite the exhaustion of all subjects, all techniques, by the masters of old, the painter of to-day has to register things and effects which the painter of yesterday never dreamed of. On the surface, his whole work seems like a violation of the past. But it is only on the surface. Actually, the past and the future are both contained in the work of the outstanding canvases of the present. Rattner is no exception to the rule. He studied the old masters diligently, even before he went to the Pennsylvania Academy of Art. He appreciates them more now that he approaches them in spirit. His revolt was a healthy revolt, the purpose of which was to discover his own approach, his own discipline. The farther he moves from the beaten track the closer he comes to the great tradition of painting. He was never more like the old masters than he is to-day when he has become unique. His paintings can be hung beside the eminent ones of the past without jarring one's sense of continuity. He is as different from Leonardo, Uccello or Rembrandt as he is different from his contemporaries. He has earned his passport, and in the way that they earned theirs—by sweat and struggle, by unflinching devotion, by guarding the source of his inspiration.

---

The best day of his life was when he returned to France to lead the life of a painter. He remained almost twenty years, during which time he won the approval of the best French critics. I unfortunately did not get to know Rattner until he had left Montmartre and settled in his studio near the Sphinx on the Boulevard Edgar Quinet. I wish I had know him in the early days, when he lived near the Cimetière Montmartre, one of my favorite haunts after dark. It was there he met his wife Bettina who has been such a great help to him. In those days they were without visible means of support, but enjoying themselves, as who wouldn't in such a quarter. Later on the three of us used to go up that way occasionally to see a movie at the Studio 28. What a joy it was to stop off at the little bars which years ago had welcomed other then unknown painters, such as Utrillo, Van Gogh, Picasso, Marc Chagall—and that incredible poet, painter, wit, rogue and scallywag, Max Jacob. Figures come and go, façades are renovated, streets are widened, everything is changed—but Montmartre always remains the same. For a painter not to have spent a part of his youth there is a misfortune. The ground is hallowed by the struggles of so many celebrated painters and poets, all of whom underwent the fires of baptism there. Even to-day, though it has come to resemble Greenwich Village, the Place du Tertre is one of the most enchanting spots in Paris. It is a place which belongs to the artist, just as certain other spots belong to the monk and others still to the anchorite.

It was in the courtyard off the Boulevard Edgar Quinet that I first came in contact with Rattner's paintings. A railway bridge crosses the boulevard at this point; it is not a picturesque spot by any means. It was in this vicinity, if I am not mistaken, that Marc Chagall once had his studio. I mention Chagall because I feel a great tenderness towards him, because too, in reading his autobiography (*Ma Vie*) I felt that he had summarized the yearnings and the struggles of so many modern painters. In his simple, heart-rending narrative, Chagall tells how the one word which he never heard from any one's lips during his youth was "artist." Rattner gives me that same impression, that he too had never heard the word until he came to manhood. But if one had seen his handwriting, even at the age of twelve, one would have had no doubt about his choice of career. It is the most amazing, and perhaps the most incredible, handwriting imaginable. It tells the whole story, from the time of his conception to the day of his death, even if one knows nothing about graphology. Every time I open a letter from Rattner I get the same feeling—that I have received a message from the Angel Gabriel. He always writes on big sheets of paper in an immense scrawl, in India ink. What tool he uses to write with I do not know, perhaps the same sort of stylus which the Assyro-Babylonians used in their bold cuneiform. I can imagine no more decorative wall-paper than this arboreal interlinear of Rattner's. The thing which is most striking about his calligraphy, however, is the indelible message which it contains. His writing in itself is a proclamation, a manifesto of love, as precious and evocative as an illuminated missal. The language he uses is extremely simple; it is made of images largely, repeated in flowing arabesques, which give it the quality of a litany. In a way, it resembles the style of *douanier* Rousseau: it is made of individual leaves, boughs, twigs, branches, buds, roots, vines, creepers, flowers, fruits, creatures. This patient, love-drenched minutiae of detail which we find again in his painting, but there controlled and unified, expresses that caressing, em-

61

bracing gesture of his which is so eloquent and revelatory of the spirit.

I shall never forget one letter he wrote me in which he relates an anecdote about Van Gogh as told by Gauguin. It has to do with the sale of a picture for which Van Gogh received the ridiculous sum of *cent sous* (five francs). Rattner describes the incident in vivid detail, almost as if he were a witness of the sordid transaction. It is the winter of 1886, he writes, a cold December with snow on the ground, and Van Gogh is without a sou. He takes this now celebrated painting (*Les Crevettes Roses*) to a "*marchand de flèches sauvages, vieille ferraille, tableaux à huile à bon marché.*" In handing him the five francs the dealer explains: "My dear friend, I want to help you but to-day customers are hard to please. They even want Millets for very low prices—and your painting is not very gay." Van Gogh takes the money and as he is nearing his studio on the rue Lepic he is smiled upon by an unfortunate girl *désirant sa clientèle*. Van Gogh of course impulsively gives the girl his precious five francs. (Subsequently, Gauguin predicts, this painting will sell at auction for at least 500 francs—it was worth much more, he says. To-day it may be worth anywhere from fifty to a hundred thousand dollars.) "And to think," writes Rattner, "that in a letter to his brother Theo, just before he shot himself, Van Gogh says that painters are more and more *abois* (hopelessly desperate), that he senses more and more the futility of even trying to continue!"

The description of the scene, as Rattner gave it in his letter, was like one of Rouault's paintings—stark, grim, unforgettable. One felt the emotions which passed between the two derelicts translated into brilliant colors: the wine red of passion, the sap green of enthusiasm, the black of eternal despair. Their movements were registered in bold, direct strokes which suited the simplicity and dignity of the scene. For a long time I kept one page of this extraordinary letter on my wall. It seems that when he came to the heart of his story his calligraphy had changed with the telling; it had grown still larger and the spaces between the words were greater. It was as though he were writing it on the walls of your heart, in India ink, of course, and with the broad axe-stroke which he has patented. But there was another singular detail about this page which endeared it to me, and which was the reason for its being on the wall. That was the use of the word "that." I think I once counted eighteen thats on this single page. It began with the word that, two thats, in fact. . . . "that that day he. . . ." This that became a noun, an adjective, a conjunction, an adverb, a participle, an apostrophe, a caesura, a diuretic, an infundibulum, everything, in short, that *that*, when used eight times in succession, can still convey intelligibly. I am not trying to poke fun at his English. Not at all. I have a tremendous respect for that that. That that became for me a sort of talisman. Sometimes, when I was stumped for a way of expressing a thought, I would get up from the typewriter and go to the wall where this page was pinned, and I would study this page as if it contained the Open Sesame! If a painter, I would say to myself, can take a simple word like that and put it through such a performance, what can a writer with his enormous vocabulary not do! We need less words, not more, however. Shakespeare got along with ten to fifteen thousand words, whereas Woodrow Wilson used a hundred thousand or more.

The more I thought about that that, the more I began to see affinities between Rattner's use of simple words and his use of the simple colors of the spectrum. Red is one of the colors I associate most strongly with his paintings. What reds does he use? Just red. He may begin at the top left-hand corner, let us say, with a blob or speck of laque carmine. From here he travels downward or across, or diagonally through the canvas, with other blobs of red, which like that that I spoke of, become in turn crimson alizarin, vermilion, cadmium, Venetian red, Indian red, rose madder, rose Tyrien, and so on. From the most intense red he slides to the palest pink, with all the in-betweens of magenta, ruby, heliotrope, pomegranate and so on. Each red says "that" red. Red is redness. The tube may say "vermilion," but vermilion is only vermilion when placed in the right juxtaposition. That vermilion which that man Rattner uses in that certain way becomes that vermilion that only vermilion can become when it is truly vermilion. Is that clear? Well then, what I want to say is that this simple color red can become everything or nothing, according to the way a man sees red or doesn't see it. Red is the redness of things, capable of being expressed in a million variations and also capable of turning to the color of mud. But the man who can use it a hundred and one different ways on the one canvas must have a respect for the intrinsic value of red. He must, like Shakespeare, be able to express through the use of one simple attribute an infinitude of common experience. "When Shakespeare painted a horse, it was a horse for all time," a friend of mine once wrote me. He was a painter too, a painter who saw horses in Shakespeare.

Lest the reader get the impression, from this rather fantastic description, that Rattner simply daubs his canvas with blobs or specks of color, I must hasten to interpolate a word about his architectonics. Rattner paints with bone, muscle and sinew. His pictures are more durable, structurally, than the Empire State Building, for all the steel and concrete that went into its making. And now I must use another fantastic image to convey what I sense when I study this aspect of his work. It is—the impacted wisdom tooth. Think of a mouth full of nothing but wisdom teeth, all vieing with one another, struggling with one another, for egress through the gums. Some people never grow wisdom teeth at all. Now if you examine some of Rattner's paintings attentively, you will observe that architecturally an Olympian struggle is going on. The volcano spits forth lava which runs in molten rivers down the mountain side. But as time passes, as time works its way into the very seed of the inchoate, forms arise, and finally the mountain side takes on the character of an Oriental temple façade. My friend Varda speaks of this Oriental efflorescence as "vegetal," and holds it in loathing. I, on the contrary, find it overwhelmingly stimulating, no matter whether the forms are of the animal, plant or human world. Usually all three are interwoven, and so much the better, say I. There is something of this Oriental exuberance and excrescence in Rattner. But it is savagely subordinated to the Western dynamics. There is nothing remotely resembling a Tibetan scroll, for instance, in his canvases. Structurally, they are Western, American even more than European. He is a builder as well as a poet. Had he lived in the days of ancient Greece, his home would have been Corinth. (Corinth—that redness again! Corinth—a dream of elephantine splendor!)

Whereas the Hindus, in their caves and temples, spread all over the place, Rattner concentrates, crowds in. He may have begun as pure eruptive effluvium, as hot lava pouring down the mountain side, but when he lays the brush down the result is structural steel, stained glass, and perpetuum mobile. Within the narrow confines of a canvas his figures and objects elide and collide; some are crushed and distorted almost beyond recognition; some are imprinted in the rock, like ferns under pressure of geologic time; some squeeze out and threaten to dominate the ensemble, only to be pulled back by the mysterious intervention of another figure, another object, growing out of an unobserved area which may have begun outside the canvas. The general impression, as with high poetry, as with

65

the tragic chorus, is one of eurythmy. The whole picture sings and dances, not only in its ensemble but in its separate, multitudinous parts. There are echoes and reverberations from every angle. Above all, there is the attack. He attacks his subject with the fury and the tenderness of a moon-struck lover. He situates himself within and without the picture. Like Hitchcock, he is there somewhere in the crowd, directing the picture and participating in it. But you can never identify *him*, only his masterful touch. He is as mysteriously absent as Shakespeare. But his vocabulary remains, and even if it contained nothing but that simple word "that," it would suffice to create the universe which he moves in. That is his universe—that that which defies grammar and logic, which defies the whole dictionary and encyclopaedia of paint.

The efforts he made to unlearn what had been taught him in the art schools must have been prodigious. By the time I had caught up with him there was nothing in his canvases which showed signs of this tremendous struggle. Though he wrestles painfully with each new canvas, his work always gives the impression of ease and mastery. I never saw any of those awkward first pictures which every artist has to paint before he breaks through and establishes his own ground. When I first entered his studio it was during what I might describe as a green period. He seemed to rival nature itself in the variety of greens at his command. No matter whether it was a forest, a garden, a mountain, a sky, a lake, a boudoir, a still life, a figure or an apotheosis, everything was in terms of green. There must have been yellows and reds in those paintings too, of course, but I remember only the greens, the infinite shades of green. Then came a day when I saw nothing but reds. Again it seemed to me that there was nothing but red. But then there came the yellows and the blues, and I realized that he was exhausting the whole spectrum.

To-day, of course, it is acknowledged that Rattner is a colorist of the first magnitude. He has gone beyond Picasso, Matisse, Rouault, in this domain. He is all color, which is to say life incarnate. When we come to his crucifixions, his clowns and kings, his maniacs, we have all the colors of minerals, precious stones, of volcanic fires. He has ploughed up the spectrum and lavished its splendors with the prodigality of a maharajah. Never will I forget that sensation in the retina which assailed me when I stood on the threshold of the Rosenberg Gallery, New York, in October 1944 and glanced at the rear wall ablaze with his latest work. It was like the first glimpse of stained glass in the wall of an ancient cathedral. Instinctively I bared my head, instinctively I murmured a blessing. I was awe-struck. Nothing I had seen of his in the past had prepared me for this festive splendor. "You are a master now, Abe, my friend, and no one can deny it!" I whispered to myself. At the same moment a mild panic seized me, as I foolishly allowed myself to wonder if he had reached the peak of his production. I could not see, dazzled as I then was, how he could go beyond this point. He would indeed have to surpass himself, it seemed to me. It was a momentary fear, allayed as quickly as it had come. That very evening, looking at still more recent work on the walls of his studio, I realized that the collection at the Rosenberg Gallery represented *a* peak—not *the* peak. But what an evolution in the space of twenty years!

As a painter, Rattner is still a young man. He is only in his forties, which is youth as far as a painter's life goes. What he will do at sixty or seventy, or at ninety-five, is something we can only faintly imagine to-day. And, unless he meets with unexpected misfortune, Rattner is the type who will go on working until the very last day of his life, working with increasing clarity and vigor, increasing sincerity and honesty. Nothing can diminish his ardor, not even illness. He has given his best under the worst handicaps; he will continue, I am certain, to give his utmost under any conditions.

67

Neither wealth nor recognition will spoil him. He works indefatigably because he loves what he is doing. He would ask nothing better than that his working day be doubled. He gives to the point of exhaustion with each new canvas. Nothing can deflect him during working hours. Nothing can tempt him, unless it be to work more. Sometimes he rebels against his own furious energy. "I ought to take it easy for a while," he tells himself. And then perhaps he will take a trip to the country, only to find himself sketching, making notes for new pictures. This is the way of the true artist beyond all doubt, for the real artist is all creation, all energy, all impulse, all enthusiasm. He is a sun whose central fires never cease to blaze. He radiates warmth, courage, hope, because in himself he is the essence of these attributes.

---

When I got back to New York in 1940 I found Rattner working in a studio in one of those lugubrious buildings on the West side. It was a huge room with good light and a wonderful stove such as goes with a studio. I soon found myself visiting him a few times a week. He had graciously given me permission to fool with my water colors at his big table, while he worked at the easel. It was a wonderful period for me, though of too short duration. Rattner seemed to enjoy it too, perhaps because I talked and sang and whistled as I worked. Now and then a model, making the rounds of the building, would knock at the door. They were amazingly different from the models I had seen in Paris, especially with their clothes on. Rattner had no need for models but I used to urge him to let them come in just for the pleasure of looking at them and chatting a while. Most of them struck me as too intelligent for the kind of work they were doing. They all seemed to be well off, but I suppose everything they had was on their backs. The curious thing, though, was that none of them ever made a remark about his work. In

Paris a model, most any model, would have made a few interesting comments, often very acute comments. But the American model is strictly business: she has a beautiful bust to offer, or just the right pair of legs, or perhaps only her exquisitely modeled head. It is all one to her whether you are a good painter or a bad one. What you do is none of my business, that is her attitude.

It was during these visits that I came to appreciate some of those sterling qualities in Rattner which made him not only a good painter but a good teacher. The strong point was that he didn't teach, not directly, at least. He gave you paper, brushes and paint and urged you to enjoy yourself. Now and then he would leave his easel and steal a glance at the work in hand. He never said: "This is wrong," or "This is bad." Whatever he said was encouraging, stimulating. "Only be yourself!" he seemed to say. He made you feel that the important thing was not what you were doing at that moment, whether it turned out good or bad, *but that you were painting*. To be able to paint was a blessing, a gift, a therapy—that was what his attitude conveyed. It's not what *you* do, but what *it* does to you. He never said this in so many words, but that was what I sensed he meant. He was right, of course. The man who takes up painting, who pursues it with his whole heart and soul, *must* be a joyous individual. Myself I have always regarded it as the happiest medium to work in. It is a medium which seems to sharpen the psyche and restore the whole being. Compared with writers and musicians, painters impress me—the good ones, of course—as being more intelligent. They have a *life* intelligence, as Lawrence would say. They work with heart, head and hand, and their work is with symbols and images exclusively. In this sense they are more connected with the source of creation, it seems to me. When they converse they are aware of the relatedness of all things, and of the plasticity of ideas, which lends their words a more timeless quality

69

than the words of writers or musicians. Everything they handle is reduced to form, color, movement; the fluidity and the transmutative qualities of life are always preserved. Painters are usually better story tellers than writers, I have observed, and far better talkers, in any case. They are always *in* their subject, too, whereas the writer is often split. The writer who has a temptation to paint has to undergo a severe struggle with himself, for the temptation to paint is the temptation to enjoy oneself.

About the lessons . . . there is one little observation I must make because it seems to partake of universal law, and that is this: often, when I had finished a water color, or thought I had, and was discouraged about the results, Rattner would urge me not to abandon it. "Go back to it to-morrow," he would say. "You can still do something with it." His saying that always had the desired effect. The next day I would tackle it again, perhaps changing it utterly, and I would be amazed at myself, amazed at the apparently unlimited possibilities which unfolded. Often when I had done everything I could with it as a water color, I would use crayon or inks or chalk. In this way I sometimes made out of one picture a half dozen or more. The final result was no longer important, it was what happened along the way that counted. One could afford to ruin a good picture if in the process one learned something about painting. Speaking purely for myself, of course, I would say that the best pictures were always the ones which were ruined; they became incorporated in the blood stream in all their embryonic phases. It was these failures which went into the making of a more or less successful one. Had I given up earlier, hoping to hit it off right the next time, I would never have learned the lesson. The lesson is to persevere, even if you ruin the thing. It is not to be successful but to see more, see bigger, see better. The paintings which are realized, those successful ones which everybody acknowledges as good, are by-products. The real paintings, the ones in which you feel you are advancing, are the ones which go into the waste basket. It is not the same thing with writing, I feel. A script which undergoes many changes often ends by destroying all one's enthusiasm. The transmutations which a painting goes through should, in a piece of writing, be done beforehand, in the head. When one is ready to write one should write, and it should come off in a steady, even flow, like ink from the tip of a pen. Writing is liquid, not plastic. In painting the wrestling has to be done with and on the canvas; it is that which makes it a delight and an agony. A painting is a live thing, both in the process and in the final result, whereas a piece of writing, once it is done, is dead—for the writer, at any rate. It does not continue to live in his mind after it is written; it *was* alive during the period of gestation, but in the act of giving birth the child dies. Painters will insist, perhaps, that it is the same with painting, but no matter what they tell me I remain unconvinced. Undoubtedly it is because I am not enough of a painter that I see such a fundamental difference between the two mediums. All artists are convinced, to be sure, that with each creation they die another death. But that is another matter. What I am saying is that whatever pertains to thought is dead the moment it is born. And writing is above all else thought. It is in poetry that thought remains most alive, and precisely because it gets away from thought more than other forms of writing. Poetry deals in symbol and image, like painting, and these ingredients are durable. But I am rambling. Yet this is but an illustration of what I mean when I speak of the great stimulation which painters and paintings give me.

And now, at this point, I think it meet to render that special prayer of thanks to Abe Rattner which I have been storing up for so long. Two months ago, when I thought I was about to start writing of him, I got up one day and, before sitting down to the typewriter, went to the sink and carefully scrubbed my hands. It was only when I sat down to the typewriter that I wondered why I had performed this strange gesture. Immediately the answer came: *you are making yourself clean in order to pay him homage!* And then I allowed myself to be sidetracked. That was also strange, since I was burning to write about him. But that too became clear to me later, in the midst of the work I became engaged in. I realized that I had to do the other thing in order to prepare myself for the task of speaking the truth about Abe Rattner. I had to know why one man could deny his calling in order to appreciate to the maximum the man who has consecrated his life to his work. In short, Rimbaud became the demon and Rattner the angel, the angel of deliverance. In their work both men speak of crucifixion. The difference between the two is that Rattner accepts his crucifixion and makes it flower. Meditating frequently on his complete and unrestrained submission to his role, using him as a guide and model when my own frail spirit lags or wavers, I have gradually come to regard him as the Bodhisattva artist. By that I mean an artist who, having attained grace and freedom, having realized himself, elects to remain in the realm of painting in order to inspire other artists. This is a strange way of describing what I mean but it serves to indicate *a* way in which I would differentiate Rattner from other artists of our time. I see him as that special kind of artist who appears now and then, expressly, it would seem, to awaken other artists. He leads the same sort of life they do, and yet it is not the same at all. His life is all devotion, all consecration. It is a voluntary ordeal. He is a guardian of the flame, an inspiration to all those who know him.

———————

When I had my first show, in Hollywood, I wrote Rattner a letter about it. I explained to him how my good fortune was due entirely to the picture framer in Westwood Village, Attilio Bowinkel, who had supplied me generously with gifts of paper, brushes and pigment, who framed my water colors and exhibited them in his shop, all of his own accord and without hope of reward. Immediately Rattner wrote back saying that I must never forget this man. A wonderful letter it was. So characteristic of him to think first of the man who had helped me. Behind so many great painters there stands an Attilio Bowinkel. But who remembers these humble, helpful souls?

In digging out this letter I began to re-read some of his other letters. I was impressed all over again by the avalanche of his torrential spirit. The words stick out like spray-drenched boulders emerging from a rapids. Certain words appear over and over again; they are the key words which indicate the nature of a man's spirit. *Heart* is one of them, *enthusiasm* another, *illumination* another. He is always relating what just happened to him, where he was, what he saw, what he felt, and relating it to other episodes, events, circumstances, moods, cities, skies, personalities. Each letter is a fiesta, a carnival, reeking with color, dripping with perspiration, hot with passion. From the slaughterhouses in Chicago he moves almost without transition into the realm of the Chinese painter's technique. He tells about the strokes they categorized and defined: "axe-cuts, lotus-veins, bullock's hair, the folded belt stroke, hemp fibre, wrinkles for mountain forms; streams are flowing stream, foaming stream, hanging water-falls, hidden stream, folded stream . . . More strokes: iron wire, willow leaf, bamboo leaf, nail head and mouse tail, bending weeds, earth worms, water wrinkles, silk string . . . styles: without-bones style (wash). Four kind of brush-strokes—muscles, flesh, bones, spirit. Firm and straight—*bones*; rising and falling—*flesh*; short, uninterrupted—*muscles*; undefeatable lines—*spirit*."

In another letter he takes time out to write me about water colors, more precisely, what a water color means. "Keep up the work on water colors. They are the expression of your intense emotional outbursts. Your *joie de vivre* comes out in them. They become another facet of your imaginative soul and will become an integrated part of your story. I believe in you—and that you will do great ones. Stick to your child-like wonder over things that happen in them—and please do not try to 'know something' about so-called technique of water color. When the child gets 'knowledge' he generally loses *profondeur* of expression. The water color becomes a water color. It evolves. Starting as nothing, the process is a continuity of temptations which lead the artist into a series of adventures. The sum total ends an experience. It is less the record of an experience than it is the crystallization of the empathy of the artist for the excitations, pulsations, exaltations, elations, desperations over his courage and fear before the unknown. Therefore the water color becomes a living entity. It is an untamed spirit rearing to go off somewhere into the unexplored regions—demanding that whoever goes along must have the maximum of his sensitivities, taste, judgment, decision, selflessness, analytic mind, wits, wildness, wonder, etc. all co-ordinated with the precision of the matador, the good humor of a philosopher, and the ever-ready abandon of an ignorant but fearless lover, all these and more, right at the finger tip in full command. One display of weakness or lack of capacity to rise to a situation, and the artist is abandoned in derision by the water color. So it is not a question of some 5,000 water colors, but rather the doing of the 5,000th one the first time it is tried. And each time it is tried is THE FIRST TIME. There is no beginning. There is no end. That is a water color."

In closing this letter he adds these eloquent words: "I say it is by the grace of God, that's all. Yes, I pray each night before I close my eyes; I pray each morning upon opening my eyes, and talk to

74

God and ask for his guidance, direction, clarity, that I may be able to perceive and feel something of that which becomes Beauty. And so, confessing this to you, I ask you again—what is left for me to brag about?"

This same reverence and humility comes out whenever he examines the work of another artist. Somehow he always manages to find something good in what he looks at, some seed, some promise, and it is this he dwells on. Often the work presented for his attention made me feel embarrassed. How could he possibly say anything good about such a painting? I would exclaim to myself. But he could and did. And this because he sees more than the painting itself . . . he sees the effort that goes into it, the intention behind it, the desire for fulfillment which is in every artist great or small. It is to the potential creator that he addresses his words, words full of hope, confidence, encouragement. How much I learned of other things than art and aesthetics in listening to him appraise another man's work! What a splendid moral instruction!

On the battlefield at Gettysburg he was another individual. Having been a soldier, he could look at the scene with the sober eye of a military man. None of the topographical details escaped his attention. But he also saw with the eyes of the artist. Gettysburg still seems like a vast battleground. For Americans it is a most significant one. The place continues to exhale an atmosphere of tragedy. At the same time it has come to assume a grave charm. In Tennessee, standing on top of Missionary Ridge, where another bloody battle took place, one has again this impression of the awesome peace which only a blood-soaked ground can exude. Here the view is superb, the terrain exciting. One is in the heart of the South, and the South is beautiful, more beautiful, more full of melancholy tenderness and grace than the North. We visited many battlefields during the course of our trip. The battlefields, in fact, stand out in my mind more than any other phenomena we observed.

But it was at the Lincoln Memorial in Washington that I looked at Rattner with new eyes. I thought I would never be able to drag him away from the place. He read every word written into the walls; he read them aloud, like a man reading the Bible. They affected him so profoundly that I finally became ashamed of myself for my indifference. Here I realized how open, how exposed he always is. Reading Abe Lincoln's immortal words, Rattner was just like a child. He mouthed the words as if it were the first time he had ever run across them. It was this way with each event, each experience which confronted us. He was always stopping the car to get out and inspect things more closely. He must have been annoyed and irritated frequently with the speed with which I was dashing through the country. When I took the wheel he would sit beside me and make notes with brush and ink. He never asked me to slow down, he just went on making one notation after another as if we were standing still. Usually I held to a steady pace of about sixty miles an hour. One may indeed wonder what a painter can capture of a landscape traveling at that pace. (I can see the good old French painters turning over in their graves at the thought.) However, on arriving at our destination every evening, I would look over these sketches and sing out the names of the places. It was a game we played—to see how well we could remember these spots with such meagre, fleeting indications. What a pity, when I think of it now, that these could not be included in the book devoted to the journey. How illuminating those notes would be! I hope he has kept them—they would make a wonderful book in themselves.

Now and then I would allow myself to be persuaded to remain in a town several days. It was the very least I could do, for I had been rushing him to the grave. Thus once, during a spell of torrential rain, we stayed a few days at a tavern in Virginia. That was really an amusing interlude. We had not realized at first that the two charming spinsters who made it so comfortable for us, who cooked such delicious meals, were quietly offering their flesh to a select clientele during the late hours of the night. Because of the rain there had been no visitors the first two nights. Rattner and I, thinking to make things more cheerful for them, and never suspecting their calling, sat up playing cards with them, a feat which surprised both of us since neither of us gave a damn about cards. The Negro servant interested us both profoundly. Whenever we could we engaged him in private conversation. Like so many of his race, he had the gift of tongues. He could relate the simplest things enchantingly. He had all the charm and intelligence of a cultured man, yet there he was doing the chores, maintaining on his pittance a wife and child, but never complaining, never sullen or bitter. There were more like him, plenty more, as we traveled along. What a contrast to some of the white people who were our hosts!

When we got to Hampton, Virginia, we visited the famous Institute for the colored people. This was really the high-water mark of our trip. Never again, during the long journey, was I to experience the beauty and the fervor which the men and women of Hampton Institute inspired. When the soft evening came on, we walked through the grounds, accompanied by a youngster who had attached himself to us the moment we entered the grounds. There was the heavy scent of flowers in bloom, and there was peace and joy everywhere. From every window, it seemed, came bursts of song. And what voices! Later that evening we were invited to attend a rehearsal. Rattner and I sat there with tears rolling down our cheeks. These singers, men who were learning to become good carpenters, good plumbers, good bricklayers, possessed the voices of angels. They sang without accompaniment, direct from the heart.

They were men who were born to sing. Some of them will one day find themselves singing before the thrones of monarchs in remote parts of the world. They will sing just as they sang for us that night, as they would sing for their own brethren. These are the only people, the black folk, who really sing in America. We remarked that, Abe and I, as we moved from place to place. No singing going on anywhere—unless in the hills, among the poor white trash. Ordinary white folk have the phonograph, the radio, the movies; they don't need to sing any more, they let others do it for them. But Negroes *must* sing. They must sing or die of misery. Sometimes, when we found ourselves locked up in a crazy hotel, and there are more crazy, ramshackle, slap-board hotels in America than anywhere on God's earth, sometimes, I say, we used to raise our voices in sheer desperation. But it didn't make music. Not the kind of music which our black brothers make. No sir. Even our sadness was tainted. It was not the deep, spiritual sadness which is in the blood of the black man. Nor could we voice the deep joy which every black man is capable of giving expression to. Still, we sang now and then. We sang to drive the ghosts away. America is full of ghosts, do you know that, white man? Ghosts of people who were murdered; ghosts of people who were robbed, raped, degraded, and sold in chains. Not just black men and red men, but white men too. Everywhere we went there were things to remind us of the bloody, lawless past. Europe has her wars; we have our blood crimes. The land is stained with the blood of the innocent. Maybe that's one of the reasons why we don't sing so much or so well any more, why we have to hire others to sing for us.

Shortly after I said good-bye to Rattner—we parted in the heart of Louisiana—I found myself in Arkansas. There I heard singing again. Nothing grand or memorable about it, but it was some one singing with his own voice in his own way and happy he was singing. And from the looks of the shack whence the voice came the traveler would wonder what he had to be happy about. But it was Arkansas, and Arkansas is still a bit of the virginal America people dream about. There are good streams to fish in, good meadows to hunt in, good days to loaf through, good things to eat and drink, good clear skies and good pure mountains to elbow the sky. Driving through Arkansas I sometimes caught myself talking aloud. I had grown so used to Rattner being at my side that I forgot he was no longer with me. Even after I realized that I was to be alone for the rest of the trip I used to talk to him anyway. Passing a beautiful river I would say out loud: "Do you remember, Abe, when we stopped at the banks of the Suwanee River in Florida?" Or, passing a prison, I would exclaim: "Will you ever forget that visit we made to the Atlanta Penitentiary?" Here I would burst out laughing, for that experience had its comic as well as its grave side. Never will I forget the look on Rattner's face when I came out of the warden's office and found him sitting on the bench in the hall, in the same spot where I had left him. He looked up at me as if I were granting him his freedom.

———

In the outskirts of Atlanta we rested up a while. I remember the meals we took at a little restaurant, the conversations during and after the meals, when the proprietor sometimes chimed in. It was a little more like what we had been used to in Europe. After the meal we would stretch our legs a bit, though there was nothing to see, never anything to look at in the hundreds of towns, villages and cities we stopped at. Always just a few blocks of pavement, a clutter of houses, each house looking exactly like the previous one, and then dead end—the highway, route No. 169 or whatever it might be, and on the highways nobody ever walks, unless it be a Negro or a tramp or a crazy fool. Nothing could be more like the

**79**

Dark Ages than America to-day. Except for the electric lights, the lawn-mowers, the vacuum cleaners, the telephone, the radio, it is a complete blank, emptiness, dead end. There is no street life, no house life, no life of any kind. Men rush home from work, gobble down their food, fall asleep over the paper or while listening to the radio, and then it is morning, off to work in a rush, buried, lost in mill, factory, store. They are never where you look for them. Always absent. Now and then you hit a saloon in some dump like Phoebus, Virginia, where the walls are covered with paintings, and you find out that the owner painted them himself. But he is no longer interested in painting. He had to make a living for his wife and children. Wherever you meet an incipient poet, painter or musician you find a man terrified of the future. *How will I live?* that is always his first question. Wherever he lives he seems cut off; no one is interested in what he does. If he goes to New York or Chicago where art is rife, so to speak, he must first take a job. After ten years of trying to keep afloat he has lost all desire to write, paint or compose music. He is still terrified about the future, he is still in a void, he has accomplished nothing. He does not even earn a living. So what? Nothing. The same old story. It keeps cropping up wherever you go, wherever you turn. I remember one lad we met on a train down South. He wanted to be some kind of artist, I forget what now. He had made money on real estate, a quite unexpected, a quite handsome sum. Now he could paint or write, whatever it was he wanted to do. But no. He was afraid to start. He might lose his money and then where would he be? What was he doing on the train? Why, he was going to Detroit to pick up the car he had bought f.o.b. the factory and drive it home himself in order to save freight charges. And then? Then he would buy more real estate, sell it, make more money, bank it, wait another few years, and so on. What was he afraid of? *Life.* So it goes. We were dumbfounded at the number of young people who were terrified of life. They all had the psychology of old people, of sick people, of invalids. Only the old ones seemed to have vitality, to radiate hope, cheer and courage. The young ones, mind you, were not the sons of immigrants—they were the great-great-grandsons of the pioneers who settled America. In the space of just a few generations the sap had gone out of them. Incredible. Nothing like that had we ever observed in Europe. In Europe the artist usually had a much harder time of it, but he was never terrified. He was part of the grand old oak tree which had weathered every storm; he would go down when the tree fell, not before.[1]

These were the things we noticed, these were the things we talked about as we moved along from place to place. Always this comparison with Europe. It was inevitable. If we came to a stretch of road where there were trees, it reminded us of Europe; if we found a restaurant where the food was good and where we might linger after the meal, it reminded us of Europe; if we struck a home where there was no telephone, no radio, no refrigerator, just good food, good talk, good cheer, it reminded us of Europe; if we hit a place like Charleston, S. C., where it was a joy to roam the streets any hour of the day or night, where people had leisure, where money was not the dominant theme, it reminded us of Europe. In short, whenever there was a bit of life, a bit of leisure, a bit of real conversation, a bit of decent food, a glass of good wine, a moment of forgetfulness, of ease, cheer, tolerance and wisdom, we thought of Europe. But how often was that? Almost never. There was a time I can recall when it was all more like Europe than now. That was when I was a boy. And that is why, when I first got to Europe, I had that feeling of coming home. I was returning to the America I had known as a child. What a wonderful feeling that is! In those

[1] See *Artist and Public*, page 407.

wonderful old men of France whom I met in the provinces, those sturdy, immortal oaks with red apple cheeks and the gleam of youth in their eyes, I could see again what a young man my grandfather really was. I could see that he had always been younger than I would ever be, that all those old people of the Nineties who took us with them everywhere were young in spirit; I could see that they were not terrified of life; I can remember them singing, dancing, making jokes, eating, drinking, arguing, going for a picnic, going for a little walk, going for a bit of pipe tobacco, Long Tom preferably, or for a Sweet Caporal, going to the corner for a little nip, and in their hand a gold-knobbed cane, and slung across their beautiful vests a thick, heavy gold chain, and in their lapels a rose, a chrysanthemum or a sprig of shamrock.

*Do you ever see a man wearing a flower in his buttonhole to-day?*

Look at those pointilliste paintings by Seurat! If you've forgotten what Sunday means, take a good look at the *"Grande Jatte."* There they are, his men and women, pegged for eternity in the sun-splashed earth of a European Sunday. How beautiful those parasols! How lovely those old-fashioned costumes the women wore! If you don't care for Seurat, then look at Renoir. See how the women predominate, how they strew themselves around everywhere. How solidly those elbows rest on the tables where the boatsmen are taking refreshment! What good, frank, intelligent faces the men have! Do you see faces like that to-day? Do you meet people who enjoy life that way now? It isn't so long ago since these men and women existed, but there is a chasm between then and now. This is the beginning of a black cycle. The color is gray. The taste is neutral. Passion is dead. The future holds no promise except more war, more destruction, more catastrophe. Is it any wonder the young are terrified?

And in the midst of this we have a painter like Abe Rattner. It is

82

almost unbelievable. For there is no gray in him anywhere. No, nothing but color. Color and movement. Eruptions. Whence comes this flame, and why is it not stifled? Well, in every age, no matter how frightful the epoch, there are always a few who retain the spark of life, who *give* life. Rattner is one of these. He possesses that old-fashioned thing called a soul. He prays. When he comes to a place like Copper Hill, Tennessee, and looks at the terrain he is horrified. He stops the car, gets out, and treads the scarred earth; he takes his shoes off the better to feel the horror of it. If you glance at his face then you know that something has happened to him inwardly, something that will never be erased. He doesn't say much, sometimes not a word. But you feel the change in him. He changes with the country, with the terrain. He ages before your eyes. When he begins the next canvas something of Copper Hill will be in it. It probably will have nothing to do with Copper Hill, but it will be the spirit of Copper Hill as he experienced it in his soul. *That is painting*, as I understand the word. Not giving you Copper Hill, but giving what Copper Hill does to you. And that is what sometimes makes people jump back in fright when they come up against a painting they had not bargained for. "Why does he have to make those terrible faces?" you sometimes hear people exclaim. Or— "Couldn't he do something beautiful for a change?" (They say this, mind you, standing in front of Beauty itself, which, like Rimbaud, they have come to find *amer*.) Sometimes, standing behind these spectators, I feel like shouting: "Bring me flowers that are stars and I'll cram your gullets with them!" Of course they never take Beauty on their knees and fondle her. They stand off, don't you know, and if there's a lorgnette handy, so much the better. Beauty seen through the myopic lens of Erasmus. Beauty with kid gloves on and patent leather heels. Beauty at the department store, where jock straps flourish like hammocks. How beautiful is Nature!

The lovely flowers! But the traces marked by the hand of the moving soul are ugly to them.

Yes, everything which is a direct expression of the soul is shocking. In the little town of New Hope, where we stayed for a few days, there once lived a painter. His name was Pickett. He was what we call in our parlor language "a primitive." Or, to use another expression, "a popular master of reality." He was the only painter New Hope ever produced. He too was one of those who spoke direct. It was so direct that people took him for a lout, a booby. I have seen the work of a number of American primitives, all of them exciting, stimulating, all of them honest and true. Some of them vie with the work of the old masters in Europe, Persia, India, China, or with the work of those other masters of reality from Africa. The academies never turn out such masters. These "popular masters of reality" often wander about the country like itinerant peddlers. They are forgotten before they die. Then they are buried, and their work is jeered at by sophisticated jakes on Park Avenue and other places. Then some great artist comes along and recognizes these paintings as masterpieces. Then they are dusted off, auctioned, sold at fabulous prices, hung in museums, fenced off with barbed wire, numbered with little gilt *etiquettes*, and so on. And finally some art critic is persuaded to write a book about them; then all the smart, up to the minute folk talk about nothing but primitives. Like talking about debble-crabs, debble-crabs, debble-crabs . . . There are now 497½ art museums throughout the length and breadth of America, but there are only about 7¼ artists worth the name throughout this same length and breadth. The bulk of the great collections are either old masters from Europe, contemporary masters from Europe, or just bric-à-brac. And most of the bric-à-brac is from the good old U. S. A. But the real, honest to God bric-à-brac is in the National Gallery at Washington, D. C., where, to be hung,

84

a painter must first die. Here they hang—"all together," as Benjamin Franklin said—the fabulous-priced junk of Europe which the American gangster millionaires collected to while away the time and finally, in despair, wished on the National Gallery, which in turn wishes it on the public. When you read the biographies of these scoundrels you almost believe that they had a feeling for art. What sums they spent! What pains they took to gather these treasures! And did any of them ever help a living artist? Could an honest-to-God artist working in one of their mills or factories go to these connoisseurs and show him his work or get his working time reduced so that he could paint more? Can you imagine the look of horror on their faces should they discover that one of their employees was an artist? Seldom have I met a wealthy individual who was generous with his money where an artist was concerned. If you are desperate turn to the poorest man you know—he will help you. If I were a hungry painter I would never go to a millionaire, or to the director of a museum, or to the owner of a gallery. Never. All they ask of you, these individuals, is to die, and die quick. What a contrast, the lives of the painters and the lives of the men who collect paintings! The painters talk about food, clothes and rent, about the price of tubes and brushes and canvas; the collectors talk about art, how beautiful it is, what delicate strokes and nuances, what a sheen, what painstaking labor. Somehow the two never meet. They glide by each other, like ghosts stumbling about in a fog. Yet the streets are all lit up, signs everywhere pointing directions, clocks chiming the hour, calendars signaling the events, shows, exhibits, auctions, raffles, wrestling bouts, cock fights, executions. What's amiss? What hinders things? Why does the same story repeat itself endlessly? Why does one page of the paper feature in several columns the touching story of an artist dead a hundred years and at the bottom of another column devote a few

85

lines to the miserable death of an artist who lived in our midst, who painted our time, who begged our attention in vain? Why must the artist go to the wall and the helpless idiot be coddled by the State? If the idiot and the insane, who have nothing to offer society, can be nourished and protected, why not those who have everything to offer? Why does a fireman receive his wages regularly even if he never puts out a single fire? Does a policeman have to make arrests in order to be paid his wage? Why does . . . ? Excuse me, I thought I was still talking to Rattner on that long train ride from Charleston to Asheville. These were the sort of questions we were firing at one another. And then suddenly there were no more questions, just one long monologue, Abe Rattner speaking. It was the greatest monologue on art and the artist that I have ever listened to.* . . . But that is for another time. It would require a book to give the gist of this long discussion on the plight of the artist in the U. S. A.

\* See *Artist and Public*, page 407.

---

I keep thinking of *Les Crevettes Roses*. It's a beautiful title and it calls up a beautiful country. Wherever I go in my travels I am always reminded of Rattner. During my last days in France, wandering through the Dordogne region where the names of towns often end in "ac," I came one day upon the place where Rattner had spent some wonderful vacations. (Souliac). Immediately the whole countryside acquired a different look to me. Similarly I remember him returning one Summer from Brittainy loaded with sun-saturated canvases which made the walls of his studio glitter like mica. Just as we of another generation look back on the scenes of the Midi, Montmartre, the Ile de France with the eyes of Cézanne, Utrillo, Renoir, Van Gogh, Seurat, Bonnard, so the men of the next generation will look on the scenes of Rattner's wanderings, understanding the landscape better, sympathizing with its inhabitants, envying his joy, his vision, his enthusiasm for life. Even a place like Montauk Point receives a new lease of life, thanks to Rattner's visit.

How many homely things he has crowded into his canvases! In this respect he is like all the great painters. The clay pipe, the bowl of fruit, the battered hat, the work table, the mirror in the boudoir, the horse-haired sofa, all these common, every-day objects are incorporated into the galaxy of souvenirs, memories, longing which compose their work. The market places, the flower stalls, the kiosks, the gardens, the cathedrals, the butcher stalls, the *bistrots*, the boulevards, the factories and mills, the hungry ones and the vicious ones, all are remembered, recorded, and given new life, significant life. The sensitive observer, as he takes his daily stroll, will see these things not only with his own eyes, but with the eyes of those who went before; they will become a thousand times more precious, more meaningful to him, knowing how intently, how lovingly and discerningly, other painters looked at them. I know from my own experience how much more exciting were the walks I took in Paris, or in the Midi, or in other regions of France, because of the men who had looked upon these scenes before me. This is what one misses so much in America. People have not looked long or hard enough at things; they do not bear the impress of searching, loving eyes. France is man-made through and through. Every corner of the land has been looked at, studied, felt, fought over, watered with tears of joy and rivers of blood. How miserable we were during that American tour! Nothing but emptiness everywhere. Wherever man had passed there was the imprint of ugliness. Now and then an oasis, to be sure, but how few of them! A man like Jefferson had chosen for his home one of the fairest sites in all America. The mall which he designed for the University of Virginia is so distinctly and touchingly of another age that it makes one weep to behold. In the early part of the Nineteenth Century this country produced a flock of men who might truly be called cultured men. They were individuals, men of rounded vision, democrats in the real sense of the word. They were aristocratic spirits; they had links with the men of Europe. To-day they stand out as anomalies. To-day a man who remains an individual is looked upon as an eccentric, or an anachronism. Uniformity and conformity, these dominate the spirit of the present-day American. The words and the acts of their more robust forefathers now seem treasonable sometimes.

Wherever we went we seemed to be on the defensive; often we were put on the spot. And why? Because we dared to criticize the prevailing way of life. Sometimes merely because we spoke of the joy we had known in Europe. It was sinful to have gone away, to have chosen the good life, when those at home were left to grapple with the hydra of want, despair, and disillusionment. But why, if they had chosen to stay at home, had they not made a better life for themselves? we continually asked our friends. Many of the painters we met had given up painting. Why? Because there was no interest shown in their work. How is an artist living in a small town in America to make himself heard? Where will he show his canvases? If he wants to remain in that town he will surely die, as an artist. A small town in America may often be a place containing 300,000 souls. Can a place like Cleveland for example, be compared to a truly small town in France, Italy or Germany? On the other hand, what is there to compare a place like San Francisco with in Europe? San Francisco is a city, but can it be compared with Marseilles, for instance, or Naples, or Hamburg? For a new country with a wealth of natural resources what a host of dead cities we already have! I mention just a few at random—the reader can supply others. . . . Richmond, Milwaukee, Boston, Savannah, Balti-

88

more, Des Moines, Cleveland, San Francisco, Philadelphia, Cincinnati, St. Louis, New Orleans, Mobile, Portland, Detroit, Denver, Charleston, Chattanooga, Memphis, Seattle, Los Angeles, Santa Fé, Washington, D. C., Omaha, Butte, Louisville, Kansas City, Topeka. . . . So there remain only New York and Chicago, it would seem. And what is Chicago, after all? How does the name Chicago ring, culturally, compared with Leipzig, Florence, Cracow, Edinborough, Prague, or Copenhagen? New York has to be compared with Paris, London, Rome, Moscow. Well, *how does it compare?*

Poor Rattner! Why am I dragging you through these sink-holes? In Savannah I believe you touched the lowest depths. Savannah was a beautiful place once, no question about that. But to-day there is only the odor of decay and death there. In that little hotel room I knew you had come to the end of your exploration of America. I couldn't blame you. You stuck it out a little longer, just to please me. The last spot we saw together was, fortunately, a place of rare beauty—New Iberia, La., where Weeks Hall has his home. There we rested about ten days, and were, it seemed, out of the world. There we relived our days in France, protected by the high wall of the garden, invaded by the scent of jasmine, camellias and other rare blooms. What a beautiful house that was! Begun in the latter part of the Eighteenth Century, it is more beautiful to-day than the modern houses designed by our great architects. How is it that a country whose name is identified with progress can have deteriorated so much in the space of a hundred and fifty years? What happened to this beautiful America? Did the people suddenly grow old? Did they give up before they had properly started? It would almost seem so. Nothing that is of our time compares in beauty with the early American genre. Only the machine has burgeoned. This is our golden calf.

Now and then, I say, we came upon an oasis. An oasis is a spot in the desert where water, the water of life, has been introduced. An oasis lasts as long as man's courage and perseverance lasts. Water alone will not make things bloom. There has to be the touch of man's hand, the feel of his heart, the beauty of the eye that beholds paradise even in the bud. An oasis is virtually a well of desire. If we think of the oasis in these terms, then desire is almost extinct on this continent. Then we have to say that the American in general is not seeking beauty, peace, well-being; then we have to say that at heart he is very much like those men who first invaded the continent, a plunderer. Not only is he exploiting the country's natural resources, but he is also exploiting his fellow man.

What has all this to do with Abe Rattner? you ask. Well I am thinking that the day is soon coming when he will be hailed as one of America's great artists, when it will be told that he was born in such and such a town, (the town happens to be Poughkeepsie), and perhaps in that town they will erect a memorial to him. I ask now, how much has America contributed to his genius? Will it be remembered then that he got his inspiration, his training, his discipline, his very material, from France? To-day he is honored by the Academy where he once studied. They gave him a gold medal, I believe. But what is there in common between his work and the things which this Academy stands for? And what is a gold medal from an institution which one turned his back on twenty-five years ago? What meaning has it? Why did that Academy not provide for him in a foreign land during his years of struggle? It is easy to give medals, and it does not in the least mean that the academy in question endorses the spirit of the artist whom it honors. These medals come too late. The new Rattner, the one who is fretting and fuming in the precincts of that same Academy to-day, will also go unrecognized for twenty-five years. Belated recognition is forced recognition. Now the Academy, seeing that its pupil is about to enter the pantheon of the illustrious ones, comes forward to claim a share in his creation. These awards are saddening, discouraging. Give them to the young painters, the ones who need them! What will Rattner do with gold medals? Wear them on his lapel when he walks down Fifth Avenue? I respectfully urge the Academy in question to get back these medals, melt them down, and distribute the gold to the needy painters who have just left their grounds. Think about the coming Rattners, not about the arrived ones! Think forwards, not backwards!

Rattner is the last man on earth to talk about his own needs. When he talks about the condition of the artist, he means his fellow artist, not himself. He is at that point to-day where Utrillo and Bonnard are: he could cease giving his work to the world and surround himself with his own treasures. Recently these two veterans of other days were interviewed in their homes. What glowing pictures we get of them! They are still painting vigorously, still growing. But they no longer live in terror of the vultures who would grab their paintings still wet from the easel and sell them at a fat profit. Utrillo, a man of sorrows, deeply religious, still full of enthusiasm and love for his métier, is practically barricaded in his home. He has made a place of beauty and sanctity for himself in the midst of chaos. Bonnard, aging rapidly but gracefully, maintains his studio on the Riviera, works from dawn till sundown, takes his stroll down the hill to the seashore, quietly sips his *consommation*, then slowly winds his way up the hill to his home. Why should he part with his paintings? Why shouldn't he live with them himself? That is just what he is doing. Rattner could do likewise to-day. I almost wish he would. I would like to see him enter now a calm, serene period wherein he could enjoy his work to the full, never part with it, never struggle any more with the world of middlemen, critics and so on. He is truly above the fray now. He is in sure possession of all his faculties and free of envy, rivalry, jealousy or the need for fame. Already the young painters examine his work with the same eagerness and reverence that they give to a Rembrandt, a da Vinci, a Giotto. I have spent entrancing evenings with painters who had nothing in their hands but reproductions of his work. But they could see, even in the feeble reflections of a reproduction, the mastery of Rattner's hand. Meanwhile the public at large lags behind, the vast majority ignorant even of his name. Fifty years from now they will begin to talk about him, begin to perceive what it was he was aiming at. It takes just about that length of time for the public to know about a man's work. And then it only knows *about*. It takes another fifty years to understand the man's work, to even begin to appreciate his mighty spirit. There are exceptions, of course. To-day, thanks to the sensational treatment of their works by those who pretend to keep us *au courant*, the American public, or at least a fair portion of it, uses the names of living painters, such as Picasso, Chagall, Rouault, Utrillo, Léger, Klee, Kandinsky, Miro and others freely. Most of these painters are well advanced in years. When they were making history, so to speak, their names were unknown to us. Even to-day, talking to college professors, art teachers, critics and the like, I have heard these names, all so indisputably attested now, treated with contempt and ridicule. I have heard Cézanne and Van Gogh spoken of as though they were *"les fauves,"* as though indeed the whole modern movement in art was an illness and an eye-sore. I have also met presidents of colleges and universities who had never heard most of these names and were not the least bit interested in learning about their work. And what goes for the painters of course goes for writers, sculptors, musicians. In the halls of learning the men who are contributing most to the spirit of the age are the least known.

---

How it would have gladdened Rattner's heart, or any painter's, for that matter, could he have listened in on the midnight talk festivals which John Dudley and I conducted from bed to bed at Beverly Glen. Often we would attempt to retire about midnight, each in his own room with a book. We would read a bit, then suddenly one of us would shout to the other: "Are you still awake?"

"Why?"

"I want to read you something."

Or else, "I just thought of something. . . ."

Then it would begin. By the time an hour had passed we would be so hungry that we would get out of bed and fix a meal. As we hopped into bed again, the last words would be about painting.

There were three names about which these talks always revolved: Ramakrishna, Rimbaud, Rattner. Often as a sort of leit-motif, there would accompany these three other figures: Etzel Andergast, Waremme, and Doctor Kerkhoven. In a strange way, now that I think about it, these last three were very definitely related to the other three; they were the planets which revolved about the suns.

What strange music we wrung from these figures! It was sufficient to say "Abyssinia," and we were off. . . . The key words in these conversations were: ecstasy, crucifixion, hallucination, hysteria. Over the door leading to the kitchen Dudley had written in flaming chalk letters: *"When I hear the word Culture, I reach for my revolver."* That expresses eloquently the tenor of our discussions.

At the borderline of Culture we reined our galloping steeds. The high peaks came as we filled our bellies. Dudley was always illustrating some point with the stub of a pencil, usually on the back of an envelope or on a paper napkin. Almost invariably it would be necessary for him at some moment of the conversation to get up and search for the reproduction of Rattner's painting called Darkness Fell Over All The Land. With this in his paws he could elucidate the most knotty problems.

Sometimes we were visited at odd hours by Knud Merrild, the Danish painter. Then the tune would change—to D. H. Lawrence principally. But by midnight we would be back to the holy trinity: Ramakrishna, Rimbaud and Rattner. All three of them light bringers. The first bringing the light of illumination; the second bringing the light of inspiration; the third bringing the light of devotion. Ramakrishna, in his trances, experienced colors such as no man ever saw; Rimbaud, in his visions, described colors in a totally new way; Rattner, in his explorations, translated colors to the canvas as if they were unknown languages. The first was crucified by joy, the second by ennui. And Rattner is now crucifying himself through consecration. In Wasserman's brilliant trilogy which begins with *The Maurizius Case* the shadows of these flaming spirits fall athwart the pages. Waremme is like the dead moon of ecstasy, a Titanic figure shouting across the mocking void of an empty planet. Little Etzel Andergast is the living continuation of the youthful Rimbaud; his behavior is a caricature of the poet's visionary theories, his whole pattern a shadow play directed by an evil genius. Doctor Kerkhoven echoes the deeds of the consecrated ones. His is a fugitive spirit seeking blindly a way of expressing himself which will not lead to martyrdom. There is no sensuous element in his life whatever; he is a healer, an experimental healer whose energies are completely drained by his superhuman labors. He could be anything except an artist, and only through art would he have found salvation.

We did not discuss these figures in this light at all, I must make clear. This is the residue which I find now at the bottom of the glass as I shake it. What we talked about were incidents and events, correspondences, passages that lead from one realm to another. Their names came up because of the problems which confronted us each day. They were our points of reference, just as in the Middle Ages men fell back on Aristotle and Plato. It is utterly impossible for me to recall now how we glided from one name to another. They were glissandos, that is all I can say. But it is a wonderful thing to be shut

94

up in a cabin with another man, a man who is interested in the same things you are. It is even more wonderful that the pith and core of such dissertations should be a trinity as inspiring as Ramakrishna, Rimbaud and Rattner, that all three should be just as alive for you as if they were occupying the same room.

But of this subject there is no end . . . Let us go back to the Bible. Rattner is a sort of Bible in paint, I often think. He is not just the Old Testament or the New Testament but both, with Revelation, Apocrypha and Apocalypse thrown in. He paints figures as though they were cities sometimes, and landscapes like prawns or leprechauns; he paints the sun and the rain, paints heat and electricity, climates, hallucinations and crucifixions, leaves like awnings and now and then a goddess curled up on a leaf, like a butterfly emerging from the cocoon. He paints rocks and sea, women meditating like Buddhas, houris at their boudoir mirrors, judges who look like reptilians, their lips of sulphur and verdigris protruding like vulvas; he paints the monarchs among men as well as the rabble, brides who seem to have stepped out of *The Dybbuk*, card-players and musicians, vegetables and meats, as well as the bread of life. He has painted about everything imaginable which breathes, crawls, moves, speaks or cries; he has also painted the inanimate world, with due respect and attention to the hierarchies which divide it. He can paint air just as artfully as he can a bird's wing or a clay pipe. He can paint a thought even.

In all this teeming diversity of life's manifestations he does not neglect so much as a twig. He exhausts the content of whatever he makes the object of his study. Once he has painted it, it goes back to the button moulder. And in all this tormented beauty, this riot of energy and imagination, there is a gaunt, stern quality such as the prophets of old displayed. A terrible veracity, a truth beyond truth: something that sears and scalds. The more he enriches his paintings

95

the more naked the truth of them becomes. That is why I mentioned the Bible. There is everything in his canvases, but what shines through, what burns, glows, illumines and excoriates is the spirit. His is a fiery spirit, unchastened in the beginning, unmatched in the end. He is always unleashing the full quiver of bolts, like a god. He discharges his full strength, then gallops full speed over the battlefield, strewing gems as he rides the wind. To have painted just three or four of these canvases would have exhausted the ordinary painter. Rattner seems refreshed after each prodigal effort. He has set himself the task of illustrating the wonders of life. There is no end to wonder. Life may end, but never the wonder that produced it. That is Abe Rattner, the wonder of life painting the wonder of life.

---

One day some one will make a geodetic survey of this Rattner terrain, catch the dormant Rattner, Rattner *le rêveur*, Rattner *devant la création du monde*. Once upon a time he wondered if he ought not to change his name, it is such a homely one. But Moses is a homely name, and so are Job and Elijah. How could we change these names? Could anything represent more adequately all that it stands for than Abraham Rattner? A man with a name like Schicklgruber may have had reason to seek another moniker. Not a Rattner. Not a Hokusai nor a Utamaro, not a Uccello or a Giotto, not a della Francasca, not a Marc Chagall nor a Pablo Picasso. How wonderful are the names of artists! Often I lull myself to sleep repeating them. The best names in every sense, the ones the tongue loves to caress, are the painters' names. And I think there must be a profound reason for this. No matter how illustrious such names as Dante, Homer, Shakespeare, Rabelais, Goethe, or even Pico della Mirandola, they have not the power of evocation, the splendor, the piquancy, the aroma or the aura which many of the painters' names have. They seem forthright by comparison: they speak at once of ideation, of thought which is gray, or of morals. With the painters' names we see and hear rever-berations, plangent melodies, sun-splattered figures, cities, plains, forests of breathing creatures, fabrics of wondrous weave, patterns of unforgettable hue and line. We can remember some merely by a wave, a mountain, a rock, a tree, a nude. Think how the fragments of Botticelli's or della Francesca's work live on in memory, like eter-nal entities. Plato talks of the immortality, of the precedence of Idea, but who retains these pale eidolons, these phantastikons? Uccello immortalizes perspective itself; the Chinese artists immor-talize Nature; Picasso immortalizes invention; Rouault immortalizes man's sorrow; Utrillo immortalizes Suburbia; Rubens immortalizes flesh, and so on. If I were asked to say what Rattner immortalizes I should say Color, the color of the rose which blossoms on the cross. When he gives to a painting the title Darkness Fell Over All The Land he is not painting darkness, he is painting the light which shines through the darkness, the light in the soul of man which, no matter how deep the fall, remains inextinguishable. To paint man's suffering he has to give it the color of suffering, and God knows but suffering is multicolored. Melancholy he never paints. Melancholia belongs to the domain of black and white, to lithographs and wood-cuts, to the sombre world of despair. Sorrow is different; sorrow is black, but a black which is compounded of all the colors of life. Sorrow punctuates, sorrow accents; it impresses on every manifesta-tion of life the mark of the source, original chaos. How black Manet seems to-day! A dead black! The black of Rouault, on the other hand, is alive; it gleams, it lives like sorrow itself. Even in the work of that gay spirit from America, John Marin, there came a day when black had to manifest itself.

In speaking of the volume and diversity of Rattner's creation, even in referring to it as a Bible, I feel that I may not have given strongly enough the impression of religiousness which it conveys. I have hinted at the moral quality underlying his work; this, of course, is not the dominant note, but rather the sub-dominant. What I have failed to stress, I find, is the mystical overtone that accompanies everything he touches. Like the great artists in other fields, Rattner is a man pre-eminently of his time. But, in giving full expression to the times, he also foreshadows the future. He is highly aware that something new is in the offing, and that this new element is of the spirit, a quickening force and not a death-dealing one. Many of his subjects express the anguish and perplexity of modern man. But there is something in all his paintings which blossoms like a germ, and that is the future man, the future scene. If he is saddened by the knowledge that this is an end period, he is not dismayed or disheartened. He is a man who believes, a man of faith, *and his faith is in man.*

In my spare time recently I have been reading Egon Friedell's *Cultural History of the Modern Age.* Speaking of the final days of the Middle Ages, I see that he makes a comparison between the time of the Plague and our period of World Wars. In a passage on "the oversoul" I come across this:—

"Materialism and nihilism may stand for two antagonistic forces in the double soul of these centuries, but here it is a question of something more like an oversoul, which hovered calmly and mysteriously in blissful secrecy over the age. This something was *mysticism.* To all appearances the Devil ruled the world in those days; men believed it to be so, and we ourselves can hardly escape the same feeling. But it was not so: the truth is that he never has ruled and never does rule the world. God was not dead any more than now. He lived as powerfully as at any time in the souls of straying, seeking mankind. A whole new wild and fervent piety burst from the depths of the human soul just at that time . . . All the religious phenomena of that age arose out of one basic common will, the will to find the way

98

back to God—not to the Church's God, hidden under a thousand outward ceremonies and obscured by a maze of intricate syllogisms, but to the deep, pure, serene source itself from which all life flows . . ."

It is this deep urge towards God which I find in Rattner's work, and that is why, also, I think the element of color is so vital, so significant. With his vivid, vibrant colors he is singing God's praises all the while. He is in a perpetual state of grace, so to speak, and he uses his pigments in the same way that a devout monk would sing his orisons.

In speaking of Cusanus, Suso, Meister Eckhart, Ruysbroeck and the anonymous Frankforter, author of *The Little Book of the Perfect Life*, which he says "was really and truly written by God," Friedell suddenly launches into an account of the part which the great painters of that epoch played in spreading the new religion. I cite the passage in full because it emphasizes my own belief in the immense contribution which the painters make, a contribution which is seldom recognized in full.

"Now, there is a very remarkable relationship between this mystical speculation and the painting of the period. We shall frequently notice, and at a later stage examine more closely, the fact that the arts of form, and, above all, painting, are nearly always first in the field with the expression of new symptoms that are dawning in the soul of the age. Painting is at any moment—not always, but nearly always—the most modern of artistic forms of expression. The present case is an instance of this. The lonely individual thinkers visualized linkages which were far in advance of contemporary humanity's power of comprehension, and the pictures of the great German and Flemish masters are painted mysticism. Of course, the materialism and diabolism of the age made a strong impression on painting. In portraits, every tiny wrinkle in the face, every tiny hair in the fur, every thread of the coat, is registered with minute and often pedantic literalness. It not infrequently happens that we are strangely moved and alarmed by the positively gallows-bird physiognomies, full of fiendish perversion and devilish perfidy, and the coarse gestures, full of brutality and covetousness, which meet our eye, not merely in pictures where the subject would call for them (as in scenes of peasant life or martyrdom), but in some entirely unsuspected context. For instance, in the Adoration of the Child by Hugo van der Goes, the praying shepherds give the impression of convicts taken to Sunday service. Hans Multscher of Ulm was a masterly portrayer of exciting, vivid scenes of grotesque infamy and brutality. In his panels of the Passion he managed to get together whole ant-heaps of callous ruffians and tricky foot-pads. The engravings of the anonymous "Master of the Amsterdam Cabinet," again, are a complete zoology of monstrous Calibans. There is no trace of humanity left in his brawling peasants, sneaking pimps, ragged vagabonds, and gaping libertines, with their stupid bird faces and vile and degraded pig or tapir snouts. Even in serious and dignified subjects the figures are often strikingly ugly. Jan van Eyck's Eve in the Ghent "Adoration of the Lamb" is anything but idealized; with her sloping shoulders and feeble extremities, her hanging bosom and protruding abdomen, she is the worthy ancestress of the then existing race of man. But it is not the realistic creations that are either the great or the representative works of the age. The real highlights are those works in which the world of Eckhart, Ruysbroeck, and Suso turn into color. . . ."

The author then goes on to speak of the great "psychologist" painters of the time: the elder van Eyck, Roger van der Weyden, Stefan Lochner, Hans Memling. After describing the effects they were capable of producing, he adds: "But there is a secondary effect more mysterious than this. Occasionally (in early spring, about midday in summer, after prolonged watching or fasting, or even, maybe, without any visible cause) people and things and we ourselves appear to us as *intangible*, as if surrounded by an inexplicable isolating aura. Nothing can get through to us; everything, even our own body, seems to have forfeited its own oppressive reality, its claim to acceptance by the senses, and to have become weightless and immaterial. It is into this spiritual climate that we are transplanted by the pictures of the Flemish and Cologne schools. These lean, serious men, these austere and delicate women, with their slim, sad hands and their frightened up-all-night faces, all live in an imaginary world: far-away creatures, wrapped in their pensive melancholy and yet supported by a blessed eternal assurance. They grip us, these figures compounded of deep confidence in an all-pervading divine presence and constant fear before the deceptive hostile uncertainty of all earthly things. They are paralyzed in the fearful presence of a life which persistently torments every creature; they look out into existence with questioning, faltering, incredibly astonished eyes and cannot see where they stand for the inarticulate and indefinite terror that is in them. 'So that is the world?' they ask. In their child-like helplessness and angelic lucidity they are citizens of a loftier realm of dreams, which strikes us as distant and strange and yet, again, as like our own home. The world—the world of things and deeds—is not completely put away or deliberately ignored; it is there, but simply outside. It shines in through the high windows in ravishing landscape forms, in mountains, cities, and castles, rivers, mills and ships, but always as if seen through a telescope—not belonging, as it were. It flutters round the soul only like an unreal vision or a shadowy memory; but the soul, untrammeled by space, rests in God, though still on earth. Time seems to stand still, too. Past and future are one with the present; in God's eyes, they are not moving at all. 'And behold,' says Meister Eckhart, 'everything is one Now!' "

101

In reading this passage so many things reminded me of Abe Rattner. That is why I have given it in full. There are two phrases which I single out to dwell on. The first is: *"So that is the world?"* How many times, in talking to him, have I remarked that expression in his eyes. He listens so much with his eyes and so often these eyes reply: *"So that is the world?"* Remarking it to yourself, you know that he will go right back to his studio and prove on his canvas that it is *not* the world, the world is *this* or the world is *that*, the world is something hidden from the eyes of men, something infinitely greater, something infinitely more wondrous, more meaningful, more mysterious. "Yes, if you want that thing you were speaking of I will give it to you," he seems to say with his brush. "Here it is, just as you told me it was, but this is how I see it!" Whereupon he gives you your picture of the world, just as you described it, but sunk beneath his own splendorous vision. Your world is like a ship-wreck, a mass of floating debris: it is a world that is sinking to the bottom, there to lie in the mud, to disintegrate and nevermore be. His world rises from the wreckage, gleams phosphorescently, forces you to bow your head, to dream, to pray, to hope, to believe. *"This is the true world!"* it says. "This is the eternal, the unchanging."

The second phrase is: *"Everything is one Now!"* That is why I spoke of his having reached a state of grace. When one attains to this state everything *must* be one. And with Rattner everything *is* one. That is why, too, there can be in his paintings the ugly, discordant elements and yet the impression left be one of supreme beauty. Walking the streets of New York or any large American city, the man with an eye sees the same evil, repulsive physiognomies which the painters of the Middle Ages and of the Renaissance caught. The painter of to-day is also impressed with the wealth of man's surroundings, with the colossal dimensions of the creations that hem in the modern man. He expresses all this luxury o detail in more abstract terms, in dynamic movement rather than microscopic detail. He crowds his canvas with rhythms, with vibrations, with pigment. Behind the modern man one does not see those serene, godlike landscapes which the men of old used to give their figures depth, stature and significance. The landscape (as setting) has vanished in modern painting. Man is no longer in the landscape. What *is* in the picture, and very much to the foreground, is man's turmoil, man's anguish, man's dilemma in face of the world he has brought into being. This is registered in a thousand different ways, but one of the most essential features of this predicament is the use of ugliness. Life has become ugly, that is an inescapable fact registered by every great artist of our time. It is testified to by the poet, the sculptor, the musician as well as the painter. But if the painter is all conscious of the omnipresent ugliness of contemporary life, if he incorporates it in his work, it is not his sole obsession, as some imagine. His real obsession is, as with the men of old, the truth of life eternal. It is through the use of color that the modern painter asserts the validity of life and the supremacy of the inner vision. Everything can be one now as before. Everything is one, if only one has eyes to see. The division is not in nature, not in the world about, but in man, in the soul of man.

---

There is one curious blank in my remembrance of Rattner's paintings which I think worthy of observing, though my memory may be faulty, and that is the absence of self-portraits. Undoubtedly some exist, but why do I not remember them? I am keen about self-portraits; usually I remember them if I forget everything else. There are some painters, on the other hand, of whom I do not expect self-portraits, such as Léger, Vlaminck, de Ségonzac, Dufy. We never think, for example, of nudes or portraits in connection with

Utrillo, yet the other day a writer visiting him reported that he had seen in Utrillo's home quite a wonderful collection of portraits. I mention this hiatus *chez* Rattner because he has a remarkable face, one that should be known to future generations. On my wall, beside those of Krishnamurti, Keyserling, the Duse, Anaïs Nin, Katsimbalis, Sikelianos, Rimbaud and others, I have a photograph of Rattner done by Alfredo Valente of New York. I look at it frequently, I study it feature by feature in moments of distraction. It means a great deal to me, this portrait. I might say that it comforts me. Often I compare it with other faces which remain in my memory, such as Hans Reichel's, Blaise Cendrar's, Alfred Stieglitz's, John Marin's, D. H. Lawrence's, Rabindranath Tagore's. I like to know what the men I love and admire look like. Everybody does, I guess. Most men do not look at all like what you expect. But after you look at them a while you usually succeed in uniting them to their work. Some go far beyond their work, it seems. Some look out at you from the jaws of eternity. Faces I remember vividly, though I have not gazed at their portraits for years, are those of Strindberg, Dostoievski, D'Annunzio, Romain Rolland, Oscar Wilde, Nietzsche, Baudelaire. Cover your walls with the faces of the men whose work inspires you and they will talk to you, guide you, answer your prayers. The greatest face of all, perhaps because it was registered in ecstasy, is that of Ramakrishna. Take one good look at this face and you will understand why men of God are joyous men. The eyes are everything. All holy men have clear, spherical, untroubled eyes. Often they are like the eyes of a doe. They look out at you from the depths of the soul; full and liquescent, they inspire absolute confidence. Rattner has such eyes. You lose yourself in gazing into them; you fall into deep pools of self-forgetfulness. . . . There is another thing about Rattner which is unforgettable, and that is his hair. It is a mop of glistening black swamp grass, tangled like snakes, and oozing immense vitality. Seldom does one see a crop like this on the head of a Western man.

It gives him a wild appearance at times, especially when he dons one of his screamingly colorful shirts of which he seems to have a good stock. This is the hair his forefathers were blessed with. They were men of the desert, endowed with the gift of prophecy and the power to work miracles. They were men who never retreated before the enemy, gentle men filled with the wrath of the righteous. Let no one imagine for a moment, because I have spoken at length of Rattner's tenderness, humility and forbearance, that he is a meek individual. I have seen him in anger just a few times, sufficient to convince me that I would prefer to deal with a mountain lion. Abe Rattner irate is a flame and a sword, a scourge, if ever there was one.

Speaking of this face which I have studied so intimately, I suddenly recall another failing memory: *When and where did I first meet him?* I have searched my mind in vain. That moment in time is gone, buried, and it amazes me no end. The only explanation I can make is that "he was always there," that I had only to discover his presence among the others. I would almost say of him that, had I never met him, I would have had to invent him. There could not be a world for me without Abe Rattner. And when I say this I think of the tuning fork which my old music teacher always carried with him: this instrument was indispensable. In the same way Rattner too is indispensable. You use him to get the proper pitch. In his presence there can be no wrong, no sour, notes. He is always sounding the diapason. Whenever I meet him in a gathering, watch him moving towards me, it is as though he were parting the waters. Others beat circles around you in their enthusiasm; some do the corn dance, or the horn-pipe. But Rattner always moves straight towards you, direct to the heart, and nothing can deflect him. He walks right into your being, installs himself, and sets up his easel. Yes, just that. He never stops painting, not even when he has taken a place in your very vitals. It is just the same when you visit him. First he has to move things around, because when he works everything gradually is shifted to the wrong (the right wrong) place. To open the door it takes time; the impedimenta have to be moved here and there. But gradually you are in, and he is in with you, and the paintings are in too, and all the pots, brushes, trays, rulers, pencils, bottles, sponges, and what not. And while you are gazing about he is gazing too, reaching back of him for something, for a brush, the arm of the easel, a stretch of canvas, anything, but please go on talking, yes, that's right, now, hold it, just a minute, won't you, that's it, yes, I enjoyed it immensely, wonderful, could you move your head just a trifle, and so on. Sometimes he doesn't say a word, but you hear him doing these things just the same. He is listening all right, and answering too, good answers, not absent-minded (though sometimes he is absent-minded, very absent-minded), but usually all there, very much there, there and nowhere else, even if he has forgotten something, because what does it matter to forget for an instant, he has an eternity ahead of him, and so have you, so has every one, only most of us forget this, but not he . . . no, he may forget his hat in the restaurant or his camera forty miles out of Tucumcari, but never eternity, never the easel, never the joy of painting, or that to paint you must pray first, and the last thing on earth is to remember *who* painted it, because it is God who signs his name, not you, not even Abraham Rattner. And he will always ask you if you have eaten, or if you would like something to drink first. And while he goes for the food or reaches for the bottle, his hand seems to stretch out to infinity, touching first all those things he loves and was storing up to talk to you about;

106

when it comes to you, the food or drink, via that long unending arm of his, it comes with jewels, with parables, with outlandish French phrases which are just right because not thought out beforehand but fresh from the oven, fresh from France and the days of Montmartre, fresh from Souliac or Peyrac or Armagnac or Rocamadour, fresh from the Knights Templars and the mosques of Jerusalem, fresh from the tents of the Bedouins or the lips of men who sailed the Bosphorus. He has not been everywhere yet, he is too busy painting, but as he draws his chair up closer, as you draw closer to him, he is drawing the whole world into his net and offering it to you with the food and drink.

Many painters are like this, writers almost never, but none are quite like Abe Rattner in the doing of it. He is always with you, even when he becomes rapt or absent-minded, as they say. Because when he wanders off he is taking you along with him: he doesn't think of you as sitting there in the studio foolishly waiting for his return. He has simply wandered off to have a look at God's heaven, to see if all is well with the angels, and if you would only follow suit you would hear him talking, hear him explaining things to you—the color of white, the white that is more than white, like angels' wings, like the divine mercy, like the incorruptible core of men's hearts. He will point out to you what he would like to be able to paint some day, what he is painting already, in fact, only it requires the brush and the canvas to make it manifest. He forgets that he has painted everything twice. He forgets that he really does not have to paint everything, that he has done it all before. But he is a painter first and foremost, and so he must paint, paint, paint. If he is asked upon entering the pearly gates what he desires, a throne or a harp, he will say "an easel." Not a new easel, not a heavenly easel, but that old cumbersome one which he used at the

107

Boulevard Edgar Quinet studio, the one that requires effort to push around, the one that takes up valuable room, the one that could be made into a crucifix.

———————

And now it is time to bring this to an end. I feel as though I were about to begin another journey, because every time I was making ready to leave for somewhere I would have to say good-bye to Abe Rattner first. And every time I said good-bye I knew I would be saying hello to him again. You don't part from a man like Rattner forever. If you go to Abyssinia he follows you with that long arm. That's the arm he's always painting on his figures, if you notice. It's the long arm of coincidence, "the coincidence of opposites," as Nicolaus Cusanus said. It can reach right up to the doors of heaven, or into the depths of hell. It's an arm that brings everything back to its proper place, back into the circle of brotherhood. It was one of the first things I noticed when I made acquaintance with his work. It's the thing I remember now as I part with him again. More power to that arm, Abe! Let go the brush, if need be, but keep that arm!

# JASPER DEETER AND THE HEDGEROW THEATRE

JASPER DEETER, the director and animating genius of the Hedge-row Theatre in Moylan, Pa., is the type of American whom I like to think of as being a true representative of the New World, a sort of forerunner to the democratic man of whom Whitman sang. He is, of course, much more than a type; he is a unique individual. Like certain Shakespearean characters who, while being universal have lost nothing of their uniqueness, Deeter epitomizes certain rare qualities which have come to be regarded as purely American.

It is curious that the qualities which Americans have idealized, and exemplified only in rare instances, to be sure, are those which tend to exalt the common man. Despite all our failings, the world persists in believing that it is out of the American race, if we may use the term, that the new man will one day emerge. What fosters this hope is the appearance now and then of an American who is not at all distinguished for his brilliance or inventiveness, but for his simplicity, directness and humility, for that gentleness of soul which marks the chosen ones. One feels about such individuals that they are worthy of our complete trust.

I feel certain that I have not dreamed up such a type. That he exists in the flesh I have had proved to me on a number of occasions. Usually they were anonymous beings, which is thoroughly in keeping with their character. One of them, for example, was a barber in a small town in Arizona; another was a horse thief from Montana, and another was an ex-convict from San Quentin.

The outside world has come to recognize this type of individual through the movies. Gary Cooper comes nearer to personifying this sort of American than any one I can think of, especially in certain roles which he has made famous. He has that thin, lanky build of the pioneer, the naïvete and resourcefulness of the lone individual, the sensitivity of the artist, and the child-like trust which is often mistaken for immaturity. There is also a look in his eyes which we associate with the animal world, the look of pain and bewilderment which is more than human, and which we observe in dogs and simians. The city man never has this look, neither does the peasant; it appears only in those who possess the gift of letting the soul shine through.

I attach great importance to this expression. To define it as the mark of the soul is not enough: it is rather the look of a soul in space. I am not thinking of the eyes of the wanderer, for his is a lost look. Rather, the eyes of a being in whom the angel has gained ascendancy. The eyes of one accustomed to interstellar spaces, of one who is himself a cosmos.

In the Middle Ages, and again in the Renaissance, the painters have made known to us striking physiognomies the like of which we no longer see. The most outstanding feature of these portraits, taken as a whole, is the immense gamut which they run; in them we can study at leisure a galaxy of character and temperament ranging from the demonic to the sublime. The soul and the intellect vied with each other throughout this long period of what now seems like an extraordinarily *human* epoch. Sun and moon were strong; antagonisms were clear-cut and vital; male and female were distinct and separate; there were marriages in every realm. There was war and there was peace; there was black and there was white; surrounding the human figure there was a halo or nimbus, surrounding men's deeds an aura, and surrounding world events an ambiance or atmosphere as unmistakable as climate.

How gray, how neutral, seems the modern world! Our great figures are neither sublime nor evil in appearance; more often than not they look like exaggerated nobodies. If they burn at all it is with a cold, malignant fire. The splendor of the Old World has vanished from men's countenances; soul and intellect are obliterated. In the American this absence of inner contour, so to speak, reaches the limits of nullity. We have developed the man whose physiognomy is practically featureless. Nothing is registered, absolutely nothing, unless it be the ravages of disease upon the physical organism.

Nevertheless, it is among the Americans that a special type emerges, one utterly unlike anything which has preceded us in Europe. In this new product one perceives the common man freeing himself of the chrysalis, taking unto himself a distinct personality. Lawrence pointed out somewhere that, unlike other creatures, other species, man alone is untrue to type. Man has glorified God

111

and glorified Satan, but he has never glorified his humanity, which alone distinguishes him from the rest of creation. Man is par excellence the divided being, cut off not only from the superior and inferior worlds, cut off not only from other animate creatures which share the earth with him, but, most unfortunate of all, cut off from his fellow man—and consequently forever removed from the source of his own being.

In that strange expression of the eyes, which I spoke of a moment ago, something is conveyed to us of the feeling of brotherhood which, at some obscure point in our evolution, was lost. This awareness of a kinship with all that lives and breathes is nothing which can be recaptured by social or political amelioratives, however drastic or far-reaching. The fervor of the social revolutionary, however genuine, however inspired, is but a pale reflection of this anterior state of being and feeling. What is struggling for expression, in the great common man to come, is a recrudescence of our lost humanity. Society has organized itself, crudely and awkwardly, at the cost of suppressing man's real nature. The structural fabric of society serves only to imprison man; he is in the service of an exteriorized skeleton whose value was never more than armor plate.

———————

If we can imagine a new type of common man, one who is unique and inspired, then Jasper Deeter is a worthy forerunner. Everything about the Hedgerow group, which is his creation, bespeaks self-sufficiency. Entering their domain one enters the kingdom of the human family. No task is too menial for any member of the group to perform. The cooking, dish-washing, cleaning, laundering, mending, repairing, are tasks which demand the assistance of all the members. Everything which goes into the making of a play is done within the group. The one thing they do not attempt, and it is a pity they do not, is to write their own plays.

Such a procedure, one realizes immediately, is the very opposite of that followed by the commercial theatre. Naturally they do not have stars. Any one of the group may at any time be called upon to assume the principal role. The whole concern of each member is to enter so thoroughly and deeply into the life of the theatre that whatever he is called upon to do he will do with his whole being. Each play is lived through in all its manifold aspects. Each one supports the other, no matter how seemingly insignificant the task assigned to him. Whatever rivalry exists is skilfully used to increment the morale of the group. In a word, what we have here is a vital organism, a little cosmos.

To see Jasper Deeter at work is to understand that his great gift is the ability to inspire others. There is no moment of his life which is not given to his work. His rhythm is the most natural one imaginable; it begins the moment he opens his eyes. At breakfast, which he takes in the common room with the others, a room incidentally in which the rehearsals take place, he is already in the atmosphere of the theatre. There are no distractions, no temptations, no impingement of the outside world. A small library, quite eclectic, fills one whole wall of the room. The furniture is crude, homely, unobtrusive. Nothing could be more simple, more adaptable to their needs, than this common room in which most of the activities of the group takes place.

It was in this room that I spent my first evening with the group. It was one of the happiest evenings I ever spent in America. We had come from the playhouse, a most interesting edifice situated some distance from the other buildings, where they had given a public performance. It was towards midnight and I had supposed that they would all be ready to retire shortly. To my surprise a buffet supper awaited us, and beer was served from the keg. After a time Deeter went over to the shabby upright piano, struck a few mellow chords, and then launched into a popular ditty which was immediately taken up in chorus. For an hour or two the singing continued, good, hearty, joyous singing, such as I hadn't heard for years. After a lull my host, Paul Weiss, asked if they would favor us with a single act from one of their favorite plays. It must have been almost two o'clock by this time; I felt somewhat embarrassed that the request had been made for my benefit. I was even more embarrassed by the alacrity with which they consented to honor us.

About five in the morning we took leave. They had performed two long acts from one of Susan Glaspell's plays. The performance, unlike anything I had ever witnessed before, electrified me from the moment it began. There were no settings, no lighting effects, no costumes. Just a table and a few chairs by way of props. It was naked and intensely real. One could reach out and touch the participants. Every quiver of the facial muscles registered as vividly as if the noon-day sun were lighting up the room. No glamour except that which the earnestness of the actors created. Now and then some one forgot his lines. A slight pause, sufficient for the actor to collect himself, and the play proceeded. For me these interruptions had no disturbing effect whatever. On the contrary, I had the exquisite sensation which I sometimes get when in studying a painting I suddenly become aware of the artist's false starts. When smoothness and perfection are sacrificed for sincerity nothing is lost thereby.

The intimacy of the performance gave me the illusion of assisting, more indeed, it gave me the illusion of being in the very plasm of the medium, as much a part of it as the furniture, the actors themselves, the lines they were mouthing. When an actor walked off stage he did not retire from sight but stood in a corner, sometimes stretching himself, unlimbering his neck and shoulder muscles. All this synchronized with the acting going on in the center of the room, an enhancing rather than a jarring note. Sometimes an actor would stop abruptly and beg permission to start afresh. Such a moment was most exciting, every one being on his mettle, the spectators as well as the accompanying players, all endeavoring to aid the one who was attempting to strike the right stance, the right tone, the right gesture. Deeter was especially wonderful, I thought, when interrupting his own performance. He gave then the impression of being an instrument which knew how to tune itself up, an instrument which could, if needs be, carry on with a single string.

It was some weeks later, when I returned to Moylan to stay a few days with the group, that I had the privilege of observing Deeter at close range. One of the first things which impressed me was the quiet way in which his authority communicated itself. He did not assume authority, he was it. Years of self-discipline had moulded him into a fluid embodiment of freedom and ease. He made no visible efforts to enforce this discipline upon the other members of the group. He seemed to make no demands whatever of any one: his mere presence and example were sufficient to inspire the others to lift themselves to their own highest level. There was no aloofness about him, no detaching a part of his being in order to assume the role of critic, instructor or director. He mingled with the others as one of them, as student and worker, as seeker and experimenter, but principally as a devotee of the theatre. With all his knowledge and experience he was the last one to be bored or fatigued. At each rehearsal he displayed the same enthusiasm, the same curiosity, as if it were his first attempt at acting. Above all, he seemed to know better than any one I had ever met how to relax. His equanimity was preserved effortlessly. He had patience, infinite patience. And tolerance and forbearance.

---

In Deeter humility and certitude go hand in hand. It is a combination which inspires reverence. He is a very great teacher, Jasper Deeter, one of those who lives what he believes, who practises without preaching. He breathes confidence. Nothing negative or dubious about him. Like all the great teachers, he believes in putting his knowledge, or wisdom, to the test. He has no need to compromise because there is nothing in him which could be attracted out of the gravitational sphere of his integrity. He is all of a piece, as firmly held together as an atom or a star.

What he knows about the theatre constitutes a living truth. He lives this truth from moment to moment, not merely to demonstrate it but to share it. It is not the theatre which interests him but life manifesting itself as drama. To convert thought into action, to make each and every act eloquent, that is the essence and the function of drama. A group such as the Hedgerow players, whose daily life revolves about this principle, seems to be constantly enacting the drama of purification. To hold the mirror up to life is one thing; to render back the truth of life is another. However excellent the performance, unless the play is lived first it will never yield the truth which animates it. It is this hidden core of truth which Deeter and his associates strive to reveal in all they do. I do not wish to pretend that Deeter talks about such things consciously; I never heard him formulate any theories about life and theatre during my stay at Moylan. His talk was always so direct that one was never conscious of anything but the immediate truth he was uttering. I find it impossible to think of him as a man of theory at all. He was all flame and intuition, a man who tested everything with his whole being.

I shall never forget my first glimpse of him as he stood in the lobby of the playhouse, leaning against the big table. A man with-

116

out dross, I thought to myself. A man who has been through the fires. Rather tall, gaunt, unkempt. The man of altitudes. So direct, yet never disconcerting. Giving himself completely, yet inexhaustible. No artifice, no conventionality, no histrionics. Naked, truthful, sincere, communicating through his beautiful brown eyes a magnetic ray which bathed one in an electric effluvium. Beside him others looked made up—like actors. He, the supreme actor, was wholly natural—"a natural," as we say. A live, warm, spontaneous being functioning from the vital center always. A vitality in perfect equilibrium, that might express it better. Capable, it seemed, of inexhaustible transformations, lightning-like transformations. Always at your service, so to say, because adept at every hold, every fall, every stance. A spiritual athlete.

Looking at those about him, shifting one's gaze ever so slightly, one became aware of flabbiness, laziness, reticence, constriction. Deeter dancing perpetually, an inner dance, a fire dance, his movements always in rhythm with the external pattern. So alert, so ready, so beautifully timed and geared, that the answer was forthcoming before you had even formulated the question. Tremendously aware, tremendously alert—like an angel poised to gather up a disembodied soul. In this manner freeing one of the need for question and answer, theory and principle. Giving wings instead of argument or discussion. Giving the illusion that even the dead may be fleet, sure-footed, buoyant, resilient.

Of such a man one demands no proofs, no explanations. His medium is so definitely the miraculous that one believes implicitly. The most difficult way—he convinces you of this without words or persuasion of any sort—is the easiest. The norm is perfection. Anything less than mastery is out. What is it you wish to do? Do it! Do it now!

---

Looking over the repertory of the Hedgerow Theatre, which begins with the year 1923, one is impressed by the variety of their dramatic fare. George Bernard Shaw is the most heavily represented, followed by O'Neill, Shakespeare, Ibsen, Susan Glaspell. Andreyev and O'Casey are listed several times. In 1930 they produced that everlasting masterpiece of the Irish theatre—"The Playboy of the Western World." In 1934 they produced an adaptation of "Winesburg, Ohio," followed the next year by Piscator's adaptation of "An American Tragedy." There are several titles which are worth signaling, such as "The Yellow Jacket," "Ten Nights in a Bar Room," "The Old Homestead," "Love and Geography" (by Bjornson).

One realizes, in scanning this repertoire, how much the theatre has deteriorated since 1923. It is only from the Little Theatre that one can hope to receive anything like the stimulation which the stage play uniquely provides. A year or two before the first World War I heard Emma Goldman lecture in San Diego on the European drama. I have written elsewhere of what a decisive moment this was in my life. Most of the dramatists whose works she was then making known to the American public I had never heard of. For about a decade shortly after the war it was possible to see some of these European plays performed. Then came a lull followed by a slump. To-day the theatre, in America, is about at nadir. There are, of course, little groups here and there throughout the country, but not in proportion to the need. Moreover, their influence on the vast public is almost nil. What chance, for instance, has a man living in that vast and empty region called the Far West to see the play of his choice—or to see any play, for that matter? One would have to own an airplane, be ready to fly a thousand miles or more, in order to enjoy a seat at the theatre. There is no good reason why a town of ten thousand inhabitants, let us say, could not support

118

one good theatre group. But how many cities of even 50,000 or more can boast of a theatre?

A theatre such as the Hedgerow serves a wide area. People come from New York, and even farther away, to attend the performances. Still, one cannot say that it is a theatre known far and wide. Millions of Americans have never heard the name, I am sure, though we have more newspapers, more radios, more telephones, more publicity hounds than any country in the world. The law seems to be that with increasing means of communication less and less gets known. What Broadway does is heralded all over the world. The same goes for Hollywood, and for the radio jabberwocky. But the work of a serious group of artists who for over twenty years have devoted themselves to good theatre is almost unknown.

Now and then the Hedgerow players take their productions to New York, which is a sort of acid test, I suppose. I doubt if these ventures are attended with much success. The sophisticated metropolitan audience is conditioned by the meretricious standards of the Broadway producers. What the New York theatre goer expects in return for the exorbitant price he pays for his seat is a slick performance with a glitter of big names, sleazy settings and sensational hullabaloo. True, now and then the cosmopolite is given the opportunity to witness a performance by some eminent foreign group, but how often and in what proportion to the garbage being dished up week in and week out? And what comes of these foreign invasions, these blood transfusions? Do we suddenly find a crop of repertory theatres springing up all over the land? Do Chicago, Boston, San Francisco, New Orleans suddenly burgeon with native drama, native talent? Were I suddenly to find myself marooned for a night in Detroit, Cleveland, Des Moines, Tulsa, Little Rock, Portland, Butte, Jersey City, Harrisburg, Washington, D. C., Memphis, Atlanta, to name but a few fairly large cities, do you suppose that I could have the hotel clerk phone and get me a seat for a performance of any good drama, European or domestic, ancient or contemporary? One chance in a million. Perhaps the great event would be "Abie's Irish Rose."

I am not imagining this situation, it exists. I have been in most of the cities mentioned and have had the experience. All my life I have been hungry for good theatre. I know what the New York bill of fare is like. I was raised on it. If to-morrow I should find myself back there I am certain I could see all the good plays there are to be seen in less than a week.

---

In the old days I used to enjoy going to the Provincetown Theatre and the Neighborhood Playhouse, on Grand Street. I even enjoyed the Theatre Guild in the early days. It seemed to me that the theatre was very much alive then. There was a feeling of hope, at least. All sorts of groups were springing up throughout the land. Perhaps in Europe too there was greater interest in the theatre then than now.

It has been said that the cinema and the radio are responsible for the great change. Possibly. But it need not have been so. It certainly need not be true now. As medium, the theatre is more necessary to the public, from a purely cultural standpoint, than the cinema or the radio. It is not an outworn vehicle of expression, like the opera. The theatre will exist as long as there is drama in our lives. And there is no better way of expressing drama than over the footlights. The cinema does not make actors, it kills them. No good artist in the cinema world is satisfied with the artistic demands made upon him by the screen. They are all bored with their roles, bored with the rigid limitations imposed upon them by mercurial directors and producers. Bored most of all with the public which idolizes them. Bored with themselves too, since they enjoy neither the identity of the genuine artist nor the identity of a natural human being.

The contrast between the life at Moylan and the life on Broadway or on the Hollywood lot speaks for itself. The one is a picture of the human family in an atmosphere of creation; the other is a picture of lost souls revolving about the dollar sign. The Hedgerow players are desperately poor, desperately earnest. They are sustained only by a common urge to make the theatre their life. Everything they undertake is done with passion and faith. Can one use such terms as passion and faith in connection with Broadway or Hollywood? Mr. Mercedes-Silverbled-Pompadour has his finger, supposedly, on the public pulse. The slightest tremor and it registers —in solid box office receipts. When his sclerotic triune majesty pushes a button a veritable army of collaborating specialists step into action. Money is poured out like grated cheese. From all parts of the globe talents are commandeered overnight. Forests may have to be cut down in Yucatan or Malaya. The wires are kept buzzing from Labrador to Patagonia. Every trivial word emanating from the sanctuary of the silver-leafed czar is licked up by the daily press as if it were honey and treacle. The whole world is set agog waiting for that next great picture which is to reveal the amazing talents of those well-known sods, whoever they are, whom we are so tired of looking at that we get the creeps when we see their names blazoned on the marquees. The great picture, of course, will be adapted from the script of that unknown drip whose cute little story created such a success in the Saturday Evening Post, or was it Collier's? It will create epoch-making reverberations—because Mr. Mercedes-Silverbled-Pompadour or his brother-in-law, or some drunk at a poker game, willed it thus. It will be yesterday's shit wrapped in cellophane and labeled STUPENDOUS. And, to tell the truth, it will be stupendous—stupendously vile, stupendously nauseating,

121

stupendously boring. It will be so stupendously stupendous that even a vacuum will seem like a crowded place.

---

In the common room where the Hedgerow Players have their being I had that remarkable feeling of being restored to the folds of the family. There was something almost Biblical about the setting. One always feels this wherever a few are gathered together in sincerity and devotion. The man in the street senses it even more quickly than the intellectual. It makes sense, it has meaning. Something is communicated which addresses itself to you and you alone. No desire here to rock the world or shatter the egg. The play is the thing, not the sensation which it may create. It is an old, old thing, the play. Something that goes on forever, with or without costumes, with or without lighting effects. It can take place in the heart of a family or in a lonely place. It is something which has to do only with the heart and the changes which come over it.

Jasper Deeter is a man who lives from the heart out. At a rehearsal the whole room becomes a living heart. I said he aired no theories when I was with him. That is true. He doesn't store things in the mind, he acts his impulses out. He changes with the changing pattern. Changes not from expediency but in obedience to the deeper rhythm which is life's. He is a man of a thousand holds, as they once said of Earl Caddock. A good image. Suggests plasticity, flexibility, alertness. Deeter always knows when and where to throw his weight, when to yield—and how to slip out of a strangle-hold. He presses no buttons to obtain effects; he has merely to change the register or intonation of his voice.

We have come to think of a good performance as something dependent on material support, material arrangements. Actually the theatre can, if necessary, do with bare boards. What it requires, what it cannot do without, is collaboration. This collaboration is not something which has to be whipped up, it is a thoroughly natural tendency in the human being. It exists even in the animal world, as Kropotkin long ago pointed out in *Mutual Aid*. Human beings, as well as forces and things, function only in relationship, in rhythm with their surroundings. A truly isolated being is unthinkable. Isolation is only in the mind.

To-day, when society seems more than ever to be composed of nothing but atomistic entities, loose aggregates of nobodies, the events which shake the world take place in a void. We behave as if detached, as if these events were astronomical happenings. Unwilling participants, we can read only chaos and futility in them. The moment, however, that we become conscious of our part in them, the moment we feel the impulse to act, our lives take on meaning—and we find new life, even in the act of perishing.

To reawaken the sense of drama, passion and faith have to be rekindled. Individuals have to become again conscious of their importance, their unquestionable vast importance, even as nobodies. People have to learn to believe that what they do counts, and that what they fail to do or refuse to do counts even more. To-day we have plenty of action but no individual acts. One has only to think of the acts of the apostles, the high drama staged by little people, people acting on faith, to be aware of the difference between our world of action and that world of moving deeds.

Whenever we use the word theatre, and it is used loosely in many ways, we think of a place where vital action is localized. The spotlight always shines on the theatre of action, which is the focal center, the place where life is at white heat. Wherever the drama erupts, no matter in what realm, the rest of the world assumes the role of audience. In a world thoroughly alive the roles, passive or active, are reversible or interchangeable at a moment's notice. The spotlight shifts rapidly, the stage revolves, the players leap into their parts. The theatre, of course, is not such a world; it is a very shabby, very feeble, imitation of the world in action. If the theatre became alive it would adapt itself immediately to the rhythm and the purport of the external drama. It would not need plays already written out, it would improvise, it would act out events spontaneously, inspired by world events and not following behind like a funeral procession. Indeed, were it fully alive and geared to our needs, it would be ahead of world events, it would shape them, direct their course. The stage would then be the living script of things to come.

I come back once again to the common room at Moylan. I come back to it because, if things are ever going to be done on a big scale they must first take place on a small scale. That room, what went on in it, gave me a fertile inspiration. My eyes beheld the living nucleus, the cell which is the seed of growth.

Long ago Confucius gave the recipe for good government. "Their hearts being rectified, their own selves were cultivated; their own lives being cultivated, their families were regulated; their families being regulated, then states were rightly governed; their states being rightly governed, the whole empire was made tranquil and happy."

Always we are led back to the heart. It is there that everything is determined. A community must be organized around the heart, otherwise, no matter how rational the theory, how stout the principle, it will fall apart. This is the true theatre of operations: the heart. What happens outside, in the world, as they say, is only the echo of the passion play which goes on in the soul of every individual.

The vital factor in the Hedgerow experiment is the living and working together in the atmosphere of play. This is something which is lost sight of in all schemes of better government—that the end should be joy. We hear constantly of duty, sacrifice, obedience, loyalty, but the purpose of all discipline is the furtherance of creation, which is the only form of liberation. I speak of the Hedgerow group as a little self-governing community because it is just that—and seldom do we see self-government.

The human family, using the term in the broadest sense, has always stifled itself in the effort to establish an abstract, artificial organism by which it hopes to govern itself. It has never flourished on the level of inspiration. It does not view itself as a performing body but as a loose collection of mutually destructive organisms. Imagine what would happen to an individual if the heart, liver, stomach, spleen and kidneys were constantly at war with one another. We know that where there is no fear, no hate, no jealousy, no doubt, no suspicion, the individual is practically immune. The reality of the liberated being is one of boundless freedom; there is a harmony between inner and outer worlds, a correspondence seemingly miraculous. This is the natural climate of the human family, the one it would establish did it but believe in its own humanity. On this level all the world would indeed be a stage and each would have his part. One would not question if he had more or less than the other fellow, he would not question whether he stood full in the spotlight or waited in the wings. The play would be the thing, and the play would be life eternal. And the audience? God.

That is how I see the human family. A great world aggregate moving in unison and sustaining itself through sheer inspiration. The fact that any group, no matter where, no matter how small, can give the illusion of such an ultimate, means to me that it is possible to realize this condition of the human family on a universal scale. If any theatre anywhere in the world can inspire such hopes then the theatre is not dead nor even moribund.

# MURDER THE MURDERER

## Part I: AN OPEN LETTER TO PRIVATE FRED PERLES [1]

(Written in 1941—never sent)

DEAR FRED,

I am writing this from New York, summoned home by a telegram announcing the imminent death of my father. The message caught me at Natchez, Miss., with insufficient funds, as usual. I ar-

[1] *In a little flower there is a living power hidden in beauty, which is more potent than a Maxim gun. I believe that in the bird's notes Nature expresses herself with a force which is greater than that revealed in the deafening roar of the can-*

rived in New York just two hours too late. My father died alone in a Jewish hospital during a peaceful sleep. A few hours after his death he had already been embalmed and was lying in the parlor of our home wrapped in a bed sheet. The expression on his face was one of utter serenity, due in part no doubt to the undertaker's art. It was while the undertaker was clothing my father's body in a pair of woolen underwear which I had brought from Greece that I first stole a glance at your letter. It happened that in the same mail I received a huge letter from Moricand, who is still in Paris, and one from Durrell, who was then in Athens. It was a strange moment in which to open these precious letters, which I must confess I had to read surreptitiously; in the midst of the reading I was interrupted twice, once by the undertaker who wanted to know if we had found the lower set of my father's false teeth, and another time by my mother who insisted that I run to the Chinese laundry and have my father's white shirt re-laundered. When I came back from the laundry the friends and relatives began to arrive, and from that moment until the day after the funeral I had no time to look at the letters again.

I have just returned from the cemetery where I went to have another look at the grave. It is bleak and wintry there, and the flowers which are heaped in profusion over his grave look desolate. My mother informs me that there is a place reserved for me in the same lot, but something tells me that I shall never occupy it. I have the sure conviction that I shall die in a foreign land, in a very very re-

_nonade. I believe that there is an ideal hovering over the earth—an ideal of that Paradise which is not the mere outcome of imagination, but the ultimate reality towards which all things are moving. I believe that this vision of Paradise is to be seen in the sunlight, in the beauty of the spring-time, and the repose of a winter morning. Everywhere in this earth the spirit of Paradise is awake and sending forth its voice. We are deaf to its call; we forget it; but the voice of eternity wells up like a mighty organ and touches the inner core of our being with its music._
From Tagore's speech in Tokio.

mote spot, and that my remains will never be found. And this brings me back to your letter, to that phrase first of all in which you mention my having embarked on a nation-wide trip for the avowed purpose of writing a travel book. I must say a word or two about this before getting to the heart of your letter.

You will recall, perhaps, that whenever we spoke about America I always told you that if I were ever obliged to return I knew I would not remain for long. This trip, which I had planned several years back, was to be, as I often told you, in the nature of a last look at my native land. I tried to make it clear to you and to others that I knew I could never resume my life in America, that it was definitely finished, and that my face was set towards the Orient. When I arrived in Greece I knew that I was also finished with Europe—I believe I told you so in my letters. The fact that I obtained a contract to write a book of my impressions of America is of secondary importance. I would have made the trip and written the book even if I had not received the publisher's offer. You no doubt will remember that I had outlined the title and contents of the book at least three years ago, even before the Munich affair. It is part of the story of my life which I shall never stop writing, I suppose. Why it is so important for me to make this pilgrimage is something which I myself do not wholly understand, but it is certainly not a lark, not a pleasure trip. It is something which I feel compelled to do, something connected with the pattern of my destiny.

All this I have no doubt you understand, but that I should see fit to go through with it now, at this moment, when the whole world is divided and up in arms, is something you deplore. You criticize my "detachment," confound it with the detachment of the indifferent ones. You should know me better than to make such a judgment. The detachment which you condemn, rightly enough, is not really detachment but a deliberate refusal to look things in the face.

With it the individual usually nourishes the forlorn hope that he will be spared the fate of those about him. It is significant in itself that he speaks of *fate* and not of destiny. In my case, whether my detachment be considered censurable or not, one thing is certain: I have never refused to look facts in the face. As a matter of fact, like other intelligent persons who gave serious thought to the world situation, I foresaw the debacle years ago. I remember occasions in Paris when you used to ridicule me, and more particularly Fraenkel, for dwelling so extravagantly on "the death of the Western World." I could never have written the sort of books I did had I not been imbued with the absolute conviction of the imminence of the end. In what way the collapse of our world would affect me individually I of course could not foresee, but you may remember that I often expressed the thought that, even if it were the end of a period or an epoch, or even a whole culture or civilization, it would not be the end of *me*. I had long ceased to identify myself with any group or nation or cause or ideology—in a word, with this very civilization which is now going to pots before our eyes. I want you to know that I am writing you not as a citizen of that "half-hearted America" which has at last aroused your scorn, but simply as a human being, more than which I have never wanted to be. And as one human being to another, I wish to add immediately that I have nothing but admiration for the role which you have adopted. Each man has his own role to play, and in saying this I mean to include the criminal, the tyrant, the demented one and the evil one. Fortunately or unfortunately, the above types of individual occupy but a small place in the world: the vast majority of mankind is either ignorant or deluded, or both. The great sin, I think you will agree, is ignorance. And that which produces tragedy, always disguised as Fate, is, as you yourself point out, inertia. At this particular moment in the great drama which is being staged it is difficult, almost impos-

129

sible in fact, for most people, that is to say those who are always *forced* to act one way or another, to see any virtue or wisdom in inaction. Those who live under democratic rule to-day have as little freedom of choice, in this matter of acting or not acting, as those living under the Communist or Fascist yoke. In the name of freedom every one is being coerced to toe the line; the assumption is that when we have won the war (we are only dimly beginning to realize that we are already in it) we will be restored our freedom, a freedom, incidentally, which we never truly possessed.

Now I have always doggedly maintained the notion that if freedom can not be had in times of peace there is little chance of obtaining it by going to war. I have always thought of freedom, moreover, as something that one earns rather than as something conferred upon one by a benevolent government. Once again we are being told that freedom and liberty are at stake, threatened this time by those monsters, Hitler and Mussolini. Those who have the audacity or foolhardiness to voice their dissent with this view of things are confronted with the loss of what little liberty they possess. The difference between being out of step with a dictator and being out of step with the democratic majority is practically negligible. The important thing is to be in step. You know me well enough to realize that I have always been out of step, even with those who agree with me.

You admit somewhere in your letter that you have never been fond of war, though at present reconciled to it. The truth is that nobody is really fond of war, not even the military-minded. And yet, throughout the short history of the human race, there have been only a few breathing spells of peace. What are we to conclude from this seeming paradox? My own conclusion is the simple, obvious one that, though fearing war, men have never truly and ardently desired peace. I do earnestly desire peace, and what intelligence I have tells me that peace is not attained by fighting but by acting peaceably. If one were to make this statement to the draft board, on being called to the colors, one would be clapped in jail. Such a statement would not be considered bona fide unless one happened to be a Quaker or a member of some other religious sect recognized as being sincere in the belief that men should not kill one another. Yet, as you know, all the Christian sects throughout the world have incorporated in their doctrine the Mosaic law which says, "Thou shalt not kill!" To confront our Christian libertarians with this particular Biblical commandment at this time is to enrage them, curiously enough. This is no time for hair-splitting, they say. But nothing could be less hair-splitting than these brief unequivocal words.

To come back to that word "detachment," which you define only negatively when you say that "it is the one thing that cripples the soul irremediably." The figures who have most influenced the world all practised detachment: I mean men like Laotse, Gautama the Buddha, Jesus the Christ, St. Francis of Assisi, and such like. They did not remove themselves from the world, nor did they deny life; what they did was to lift themselves out of the vicious circle of every day life which leads nowhere, unless to confusion, sorrow and death. They reaffirmed the spiritual values of life. None of them advocated war to uphold their beliefs. In an earlier letter, which you wrote me from London, you quoted your friend Stein as saying— "an idea which is true needs only to be voiced, it does not require propaganda." To this I should like to add that, once the truth has been perceived, it cannot help but be acted upon. Men of truth are men of action, single-minded and invincible. The drama which their lives symbolize, and which therefore has for us the quality of the eternal, consists in acting out the truth. The pattern of their lives is as clear cut as a jewel; our lives describe only endless confusion. I noticed that, in that same letter to which I referred a moment ago,[1] your friend Stein also said: "War or no war, the world must be reformed before 1942. 1942 is the deadline. After that, if nothing is done, there can only be chaos." I must confess that I haven't the slightest hope of witnessing a world-wide reformation by 1942. In fact, the trend is quite the contrary. With each day we live, a greater area of the world is engulfed in the madness of war. War is the most hideous expression of inner conflict. We know from previous experience that all the nations now engaged in this war will emerge from it defeated. We are not even clear as to the issue involved, though it is said, as so often in the past, that it is civilization which is at stake. You know as well as I that this is not true. However much we may detest the German way of life, as exemplified by the Nazi regime, we cannot in all honesty pretend that ours is the only true way of civilization. The whole civilized world, from one end of the globe to the other, is rotten and must fall apart either now or later. I don't believe in bolstering up something which is falling apart. I don't believe that the preservation of the British Empire or any other empire, or any present system of government, for that matter, involves the preservation of humanity. The forces which brought about the war are bound up in the erroneous doctrines and beliefs which animate all members of civilized society. Civilization itself is in question. But the Germans, the Italians, the Japanese are just as much a part of this civilization as the English, the French, the Americans et alia. To prove by force of arms that one side or the other of these civilized nations now aligned in conflict is right or wrong will contribute nothing to the understanding of the meaning of civilization. Whether it be true or not, civilization has come to stand for something in the nature of a continuous advance, something ineradicable in the human

[1] Aller Sans Retour Londres—unpublished manuscript by Alfred Perlès.

scheme of things underlying the ephemeral birth and death of cultures. Is this advance maintained by war? If not, why should one take up arms, even though the aggressor be obviously in the wrong? Are those of us who believe in the efficacy of truth to be treated as cowards and traitors because we refuse to act except in accordance with the dictates of our conscience? Are we to pretend, for the sake of convenience, that we are willing to put the voice of a government above the voice of our own conscience?

I have nothing to say to those who believe in fighting for their rights. For one like yourself, who has come to a decision on his own and voluntarily elected to sacrifice his life, there are ten thousand who are incapable of making a decision, and ten thousand more who will abide by any decision so long as it is not of their own making. To say nothing of those who, realizing the misery of their plight, demand that the rest of the world keep them company. Nations make war upon one another on the assumption that the views of the people and those who govern them are one. The moment war is declared it is impossible to dissent. The man who yesterday might have been regarded as the greatest single contributor to the nation's happiness may find himself in disgrace, if not in jail, should he happen not to believe in making war. He may have declared his stand on this subject his whole life long, but that will make no difference. He is regarded as an enemy of society just as much as the lowest criminal, more of an enemy in fact than the man who stays at home and makes a fortune selling the instruments of destruction. People are almost never unanimously in favor of making war, especially in modern times. It is the minority which sponsors war, and this minority always represents the vested interests. No government ever has the courage or the honesty to put the question of war up to the people. Nor is there ever the remotest possibility of establishing a situation whereby those in favor of war

133

go to war and those not in favor remain passive. The unanimity of a nation, in times of war, is brought about by coercion pure and simple. You are one of the rare few in this present conflict who enjoyed the privilege of deciding your own fate. You had to be a man without a country in order to have this privilege. An ironical situation!

At the same time I have to point out another ironical fact. The country for which you volunteer to fight, in the name of freedom, denies the rights of freedom to a subject nation of over 300,000,000 souls. Even now, when England is threatened with extinction, when the good-will and the aid of the Indian peoples would be an invaluable asset, the government which has enlisted your sympathies refuses to make the slightest concession or compromise with the acknowledged leaders of India. It seems to me that even practical wisdom would have dictated a less stern and rigid attitude. No doubt you will say that you are not fighting for the British government but for humanity. Well, if sheer numbers mean anything, then it seems to me that it would be more humanitarian to fight for the liberation of 300,000,000 Hindus than for 40,000,000 English. Besides, we know very well that the British Empire is not controlled by, nor does it belong to, the forty million British citizens. We know that it is a mere handful of men, in England as in other parts of the world, who control the destinies of millions. In England itself, engaged as she is in a life and death struggle, we read that there is still a great number of unemployed. Such statements, if true, and I have good reason to believe they are, are incredibly fantastic. The man who has still a choice of entering, or not entering, the war may well pause to ask himself for what or whom is he supposed to fight. At present it is assumed that Hitler is bent on conquering the world, if not by force of arms, then morally or ideologically. Curiously enough, it is never taken for granted that the

134

democratic peoples of the world might be immune to the insidious propaganda of Fascism. Who would think, for example, of trying to seduce a holy man by tempting him with the pleasures or rewards of the material world? The idea is unthinkable. But the democratic peoples go into a veritable panic at the mere thought of allowing themselves to be subjected to Fascist influences. Where then is their faith and integrity? What about the democratic influence—is it so feeble that it can only be maintained by going into a huddle?

I have never been able to understand this fear and hysteria about the introduction of alien ideas. I have always tried to discover and assimilate what is valuable in the ideas of others. Now and then, you will notice, it is admitted here and there that certain ideas which the Fascists have made use of were not without value, but then, it is immediately urged, it is not against these we are fighting but against the evil doctrines of Fascism. And about our own evil doctrines—who are there who will even admit the existence of wrong, or error, in our democratic way of life? Moreover, it is not as though the political doctrines of Fascism were espoused by a handful of demonic individuals bent on destroying the world. To-day over 150,000,000 people have rallied together under this banner. In Russia another vast group of people practise a still different philosophy. It boils down to this, practically, that right or wrong, we have decided to defend our way of life. How? By vanquishing those who disagree with us.

There is one great fallacy in this logic of violence. We forget that the conquerers are always conquered by the defeated. The surest way to defeat Hitler would, in my opinion, be for Europe to surrender willingly. I go farther—I say let him have the whole world. Can you see what would happen to his grandiose ideas if there were no resistance? Hitler, or any one who seeks power, is only a force so long as he is opposed. Let him play God and he would fall apart. Imagine the whole world submitting to the will of this little man; imagine laying the problems of all the world before him and granting him the freedom to solve them! The man would die of brain fever overnight.

Let us talk sensibly. What brought Hitler into power? The humiliation and injustice wreaked upon the German people by the Treaty of Versailles. Who was responsible for this idiocy? You and I, or the millions who fought to make the world safe for democracy? Hardly. In a sense yes, we are all guilty, for, even if the error was that of a few short-sighted politicians, there was plenty of time before the rise of Hitler to right the mistakes of the war-time leaders. Much has been said about the futile policy of appeasement, about Hitler's insatiability, but it should be remembered that the desire to make concessions on the part of the Allies came too late, that they were made through fear and not out of generosity.

I remember well the long discussions we had in Paris about the economic condition of the world. Even such non-politically-minded people as you and I could see that a drastic change had to come about, that there could be no talk of peace until there was real equality, real brotherhood. The war would seem to have killed that hope for a long time. Yet, who can say that the war may not serve a greater purpose than is now apparent? Beneath the reluctance and hesitancy of the democracies to wage war lies the fear of unloosing a more devastating evil: world-wide revolution. That most likely will be the result of the present conflict, and in bringing it about, the Germans, the Italians, the Japanese are playing just as important and valuable a role as the Allies. When nations resort to war they blind themselves to the real forces at work; by opposing one another they make themselves the instruments of a force which is superior to their antagonistic aims. They stage a drama for an invisible audience—the men and women of the future. The participants of the drama receive their reward in suffering, not in realization. Conflict engenders conflict, war creates war, ad infinitum. Even if to-morrow world revolution is ushered in, the conflict will not cease. But without going too far afield, what I wish to point out is that the result of the war will probably be quite different than the hopes or desires of either side. Though outwardly enemies, both sides are blindly collaborating to bring about a new world order. I do not say a better world order. I say merely a necessary one. We have outlived the present pattern and we have not had the wisdom to create a new one peaceably. We learn through suffering. War is not necessary; it is an expression of our crude and stupid way of seeking experience. It comes as a blow of fate because we refuse to pursue our own destinies. The hatred that has been engendered brings together in a death-lock those who were sundered; admiration, sympathy, love follow in the wake of death. When the supreme sacrifice has been made there comes the moment of understanding, of recognition. Wisdom, however, does not demand such bloody heroism; nor does it entail the disillusioning aftermath which makes these sacrifices appear hollow. Wisdom consists in perceiving the real trend of the world and living one's life in accordance with it. When the whole world blindly rushes to arms it may be well that a few men remain aloof to guide those to come with a clear mind. For, one thing is certain—the men who are directing this war will not be at the helm when peace is declared.

To come back to the purely personal, for I am not going to attempt to make answer for the American people, whom I neither represent nor sympathize with. The American people, incidentally,

137

like the English and the French once were, are divided. Until war is actually declared this condition will probably persist. Because of my age I, like yourself, have the privilege of taking a stand. My stand is to keep clear of the conflict, so long as it lies within my power to do so. Until the Munich crisis I was actually afraid of war: I was a physical coward. But those few days in Bordeaux, when I thought I was trapped, somehow cured me of this fear. Later, on returning to Paris, I had reconciled myself to the idea of staying on at the Villa Seurat, if war should suddenly break out. When still later I found myself in Greece—it was at Corfu that I learned that war had been declared—I had another experience which convinced me that I had overcome my fears. In company with the Durrells and other friends, as I relate in the Greek book,[1] I took the boat for Athens. I was reluctant to leave, but my bags had been packed and a ticket bought for me. The panic that ensued at the dock because of the boat's delay in arriving, and because of the fear that there might not be room for all (it was the last boat for Athens), filled me with a terrific disgust and contempt for these wretches who were running for safety. As I said in the book, I almost wished that the Italians would sink our boat. I not only had no more fear, I was more serene and at peace with the world than I had ever been before. A week or two later I returned to Corfu alone, determined to have the vacation which I had promised myself on leaving Paris.

Of course the visit to Greece fortified me inwardly to a degree beyond anything I had ever known before. You had your awakening in London; I had mine in Greece. Mine was not due to the war; if anything it was the fruit of solitude. In Greece I came to grips with myself and made my peace with the world. I think it is significant of the change that came over me there that, having at last found the spot on earth which suited me ideally, I was able to

[1] The Colossus of Maroussi.

138

renounce it cheerfully when the summons came to return. In the Hamlet correspondence with Fraenkel [1] I have explained how my panic at the first threat of war was due to my attachment to a place, to the Villa Seurat, which had become my home. That experience taught me that it was absurd to be attached to anything, even to such a tenuous home as was the Villa Seurat. In Greece I think I succeeded in detaching myself completely; though I made no vow of any kind, what really happened was that I finally became a citizen of the world. To ask me now to become a patriot, or a supporter of the Allies, or even a militant pacifist, is to wish me to become something less than I am; it would mean regression. I can say truly now that I am prepared to do anything which may be demanded of me in the service of humanity—except to kill. Even if I were able to succeed in killing dispassionately, I should refuse to do so. I have said it before and I repeat it solemnly: if it comes to a test I am willing to be killed rather than to kill. I have said over and over again that I can understand a man committing murder in passion; if I were a judge I would condone such crimes. But I cannot bring myself to believe that killing indiscriminately in cold blood, which is what war entails, is justifiable. As for killing an idea by killing the man who cherishes it, that to me is simply too preposterous for words.

People often say, it's all very well to talk this way but what would you do if you were obliged to live under the Nazi rule? Frankly, I don't know at this moment what I would do under such circumstances. I don't believe in crossing bridges beforehand. But there is one thing I do know, in connection with this question, and that is that I am not terrified of the idea. Some say even more pointedly: you know that you would never be allowed to write as you do if you were living under a Nazi regime. No doubt I wouldn't. But then

[1] Hamlet (2 volumes) by Michael Fraenkel and Henry Miller.

neither am I allowed to write such books in England or America. I was allowed to in France because my books were in English; as soon as my books were translated into French they were rejected by the French publishers, or else the manuscripts were allowed to rot on the shelves. The only country which had the courage to publish me in translation was Czechoslovakia, and since I can't read Czech I have no way of knowing whether the translation of *Tropic of Cancer* was a faithful one or not. In short, the English-speaking countries have never appeared to me as a haven of liberty, where freedom of speech reigns.

I am not, it seems, precisely a desirable type either in the Democratic world or in the Communist-Fascist world. I fit in nowhere, as things stand to-day. In actual life I get by because I don't make a nuisance of myself, but the moment I express myself in writing I find all sorts of barriers erected about me. Even when I write an innocent and beautiful book of my impressions of a foreign land, such as *The Colossus of Maroussi*, they find me unacceptable. Before the Greeks entered the war the publishers, in rejecting it, said that nobody was interested in Greece (though the sale of Will Durant's huge study of Greece had already proved the contrary). Now they simply say—"Can't you give us a book on America?"

All this, to be sure, is of little moment. I cite these instances merely to show that in all that truly matters I am still, as I have always been, *persona non grata* in this world. If I think of France with love and gratitude, it is because there I was at least *tolerated*. Here they are waiting for me to submit. The moment I show signs of compromising the doors will be opened to me. Meanwhile they pursue the usual tactics of starving me out.

Soon they will be getting the book on America which they are all asking me for. I can tell you in advance what their attitude will be: they will deluge me with insults, they will say that I am warped and twisted, that my ideas are subversive, that I am a traitor and a renegade. When I say "they" I mean, of course, the critics and reviewers, the army of hired prostitutes who blow as the wind blows. Only to-day I learned from a friend of mine that Giono's book which I sent you recently—*The Joy of Man's Desiring* [1]—has been remaindered. That means that less than a thousand copies were sold at the established price. I can't tell you what a shock it was to me to hear this piece of news. No matter how well aware I am of the steady and rapid decline in the reading public's taste, each new corroboration of my judgment gives me a renewed feeling of despair. That the man who, to me, seems the most promising writer in France cannot find a thousand readers among the 140,000,000 Americans who make up this land strikes me as incredible and incomprehensible. Giono was the last Frenchman I tried to see on leaving for Greece. I made a pilgrimage to his home in company with his friend and translator, Henri Fluchère. Unfortunately he was away at the time, but I was privileged to wander through his house, to meet his mother who is blind, and his wife's mother, to whom he seems to be equally devoted. Later I wandered through the town, where he was born, saw the places which he describes so touchingly in *Jean le Bleu*. That visit stands out in my mind as a fitting and beautiful close to my ten years in France. When I learned a little later, in Greece, that he had been thrown in prison for "refusal to obey," I felt that a great crime had been committed. And then one day there came the news that he had been released, through American intervention. My joy was unbounded. I said to myself—"Good! Giono's freedom is more important than the safety of France." That is saying a good deal, I know, but I meant it, and I am still of the same opinion to-day. To me Giono represents what is best in France, what is alive and flowering, the very

[1] Viking Press, New York.

substance of the future. Americans know scarcely anything about that France; they welcome men like Jules Romains and André Maurois, and pay handsomely to listen to such men deliver verbal autopsies on the dead body of France. Meanwhile Frenchmen of value, trying to escape from their hideous prison, are subjected to stupid and vicious cross-examination because it is feared that their influence here may be pernicious. The situation is much the same as a few months ago when there was talk of rescuing the British children. Some vile would-be saviours had the audacity to demand pedigrees of their expected wards. The same attitude prevails towards the refugees: the first and most important question is—*have they any money?* Though we have room enough here to accommodate the entire population of Europe, though we produce a surplus sufficient to feed the starving peoples of all Europe, we are unable to provide for our own meagre population. A third of the American people, it is admitted, are living below the level of normal subsistence. Despite the number of men already drafted, despite the frantic and gigantic efforts to mobilize for defense, millions of men are still unemployed. What a colossal farce! Eventually, of course, the majority of these unfortunate creatures will be taken off the dole and put to useful work, i. e., creating the instruments of their own destruction. Some of them are even now at work preparing materials which are being shipped directly or indirectly to the "enemy." Laws have first to be enacted before such suicidal traffic can be stopped. No one stops instinctively, or out of a feeling of patriotism. As for the defender of our liberty, England, over whom we are shedding crocodile tears at the moment, it seems to many of our good citizens that England ought to be separated from some of her huge possessions in exchange for the help we are ready to give. This is our chance, don't you know! England has had her day —now it is our turn. And throughout all the confusion, chicanery, envy, greed and betrayal there runs, like a leit-motif, the cry: "Keep us out of war!" From the president on down, the politicians are blithely promising the people that they will not be led into war. They do not admit that we are already at war. They are afraid to tell the truth, to say openly: "We will do everything within our power to defeat the Axis powers!" If there was ever a time to declare war it was months ago—years ago, in fact—assuming as they do that Germany and Italy were guilty of international crimes in all their aggressive moves. But no, like others before us, we waited and waited—and we are still waiting—just as Hitler predicted. Even to-day we are still hoping and praying that we will be spared the necessity of going to war. That is, those who have any illusions left, are. The vast majority of people know deep down that the day is drawing near. They are not enthusiastic about the prospect, as you might think people would be who had decided to enlist in a great cause. No, they are dumb and silent, more or less reconciled to their lot because it seems inevitable. The truth is they are not passionate about the prospect of imminent war; they lack the hatred and the fear which possess the European peoples. But the radio and newspaper poisoners are gradually whipping them up to the proper state of frenzy required to launch a nation into war. Soon the band will strike up and our gay crusaders will be off to rid the world of the forces of evil. When they sail away they will be hailed as heroes; when they return, those who are lucky, they will have to pawn their medals and stand in the bread line. Unless in the meantime the forces of evil on this side of the water have been vanquished too. Perhaps it is the fear of this which has kept our politicians, usually so ready and lavish with other people's blood and money, from declaring themselves sooner. This time the war won't end with the mere dissolution of Fascism and Nazism. The real war only begins at this point—that's what they fear. What will Russia do once

Hitler and Mussolini are vanquished? What is Russia's game? Of course, like Hitler and Mussolini, the Russians too have been telling the world all along what they intend to do, but because it isn't nice, what they say, we pretend not to listen. We just can't and won't understand why they refuse to play the democratic game.

It isn't nice either to think what India might do should the victorious Allies emerge from the war exhausted. It may be that India will step out of the British Empire without asking permission of his Imperial Majesty, the King of England. India may go thoroughly democratic and decide to govern herself. How the defenders of freedom and civilization can honestly object to such a procedure is beyond my powers of logic. Nor do I see how an after-war Europe, determined to become really democratic, can be coerced by these same crusaders into accepting a make-believe form of democracy, such as we enjoy to-day. We read every day of the efforts being made to force Churchill to avow his true aims. Aside from the fact that the question is a little premature, it is also, it seems to me, somewhat indelicate to ask a leader who is trying to save his country from extinction to say what he is really fighting for. But it is characteristic of Americans, when drawn into something distasteful, to disguise or ennoble their behavior by giving it an idealistic motive. We could never admit to ourselves that we have decided to kill the Germans off because we are incapable of convincing them that our way is the better way—no, we must first believe that they are not only wrong but evil, a menace to the world. Then we can kill with impunity. Naturally I do not share this attitude. Even if I prefer this way of life, with all its evils and disadvantages, to that of the Russian, Japanese, German or Italian way, I would never think to defend it by force of arms. It seems to me that the principles of freedom and justice must have been sadly demonstrated by us if they have had so little effect upon our neighbors as to make them scorn us and jeer at us. If there be such undeniable truth behind our principles of faith as to make us willing to sacrifice our lives for them, then why have they not been more convincing? Why are other nations ready to die for *their* principles? Is it because they too believe them to have the authority and sanction of truth?

I don't wish to quibble. I know as well as you that the plain, common people who make up the members of the Axis group are not passionate and fanatical about the political beliefs of their leaders. But I say that neither are we, neither were the French, neither were the English, until long after the war began. The plain, common people of the world are not passionate, normally, about anything, unless it be food and drink, and shelter and raiment. They are obstinately determined, as we well know, to be left in peace as long as possible. It has been dinned into them for thousands of years that the civilized way of life is the best and only life for them. And civilization has always been represented to them as a peaceful, industrious and pleasurable mode of life. To get people to fight it has become obligatory to make them denounce one another as "barbarians." But people who have been regarded as civilized by the other civilized nations of the world can't possibly become barbarians overnight. That is a charge which is conveniently trumped up when all logic fails. That is simply a wish which we project on to our opponent. As soon as peace is declared the barbarian is taken back into the fold; he may even be honored and respected for having been a "valiant enemy."

As a matter of fact, to pursue this idea further, one of the hopeful aspects about the present world situation is the fact that there no longer are any barbarians in the offing. Civilization, such as it is, holds sway over the entire planet, except for the primitive peoples from whom we have nothing to fear. There are no longer any Vandals, Huns, Goths or Visigoths to threaten the might of the

145

present contending empires. This time a solution has to be found from within or else the whole planet relapses into a night deeper than any ever known. There is no fresh, vigorous race of barbarians on the horizon. The war-makers are all civilized peoples, all relatively old. If they cannot find the wisdom to establish life on a more sane and equitable basis than that which has obtained for the last ten thousand years, if they are unwilling to make the great experiment, then all the trials of humanity throughout the ages will go for nought.

Frankly, I don't believe that the human race can regress in this manner. I believe that when the crucial moment arrives, a leader greater than any we have known in the past will arise to lead us out of the present impasse. But in order for such a figure to come into being humanity will have to go through an ordeal beyond anything heretofore known; we will have to reach a point of such profound despair that we will be willing at long last to assume the full responsibilities of manhood. That means to live for one another in the absolute religious meaning of the phrase: we will have to become planetary citizens of the earth, connected with one another not by country, race, class, religion, profession or ideology, but by a common, instinctive rhythm of the heart. So far civilization has been the story of repeated failure. We have had civilizations, but no civilization. We have seen and read of the emergence of great world-cities, epitomizing in their brief span of life the flowering of one culture after another; with their extinction the life of a whole people, or peoples, has withered and vanished. In our short lifetime we have seen the death-blow dealt to Vienna, Prague, Copenhagen, Amsterdam, Budapest, Paris, Shanghai, St. Petersburg. It is quite possible that before we die we shall see the others go too— Moscow, Berlin, Tokio, Rome, London, New York, Athens. But this time the fall of these great cities does not necessarily mean the end of another civilization. On the contrary, there is good reason to believe that not until these cities perish (and with them all that they represent) will we really begin to have what people dream of when they use the word civilization.

There is another term which is being increasingly used, to replace the older one which is falling into disrepute, and that is *community*. The fundamental difference underlying these symbolic terms is that the new one carries with it the idea of inclusiveness. It carries with it the assumption that there can be no viable civilized effort until the organism embodying the ideal becomes world-wide. Which is tantamount to saying that the human race can make no real advance until every member of the race is acknowledged as a vital and indispensable element of the greater organism. The fact that we are all alike before God has to be demonstrated in practise. The crisis through which we are going, and which is admitted everywhere to be of a different order than similar crises in the past, is rooted in the fact that we all hold beliefs contrary to our behavior. We are actually being forced to admit that we have been deluding ourselves for thousands of years. Either we square our practises with our beliefs or we perish. We have to *will* our salvation as a mass; we cannot hope to be saved again simply by *believing*. To achieve this step it is inevitable that the whole world be involved in the struggle. But mark me well, that struggle has not yet begun. That struggle only commences, if it ever does, when the present opposing forces have rendered one another prostrate. In the present conflict there are no issues worth fighting about—yet.

It is a cruel law, perhaps, but experience confirms it again and again, that the innocent, because of their ignorance, are doomed to perish with the guilty. Millions are doomed who do not even know why they are doomed. Nobody can alter that ineluctable law. But out of the suffering created by these millions of deaths may come the realization that a new way of life is possible, and that its inauguration rests with the living. We must get rid of the false notion that the creative spirit, which underlies all cultures and civilizations, needs to be defended by force. Spirit is never defended by recourse to violence. People try to defend only that which is already dead; when these futile efforts seem almost on the point of succeeding, when the very spirit of life is walled in and the status quo apparently secure, then you have what is called revolution. The present war, like all other wars, is merely the manifestation in ugly terms of a disease which was hidden. It is not a divine visitation, nor the mere result of the diabolical machinations of a clique of evil geniuses. Hitler and Mussolini are simply instruments of fate; I can detect no more evil in them than in Churchill or Roosevelt, or any other of the democratic leaders. No man, in my opinion, has the right to demand the sacrifice of human lives. We throw up our hands in horror when we read of the sacrificial rites of the Aztecs, but we see nothing ignoble in the periodic sacrifice of millions of lives in the name of country, God, Democracy, or civilization. What monstrous things can these be in whose name these horrible sacrifices are demanded? Who is it that makes these demands? No one has the courage to assume the responsibility; each one points the finger accusingly at the other. This attitude is in itself the most flagrant admission of the evil of war. We exonerate ourselves by saying that we are merely defending ourselves. With this half-truth on our lips we make ready to commit the most dastardly crimes. First we absolve ourselves of all guilt, then we go to it with a vengeance. So long as the onus is conveniently shifted to the enemy, it matters not how we behave. That is how wars are made to-day—quite differently, you must admit, than in olden times. We have a bad conscience about it, but, as is always the case when there is a bad conscience, we go about our sinful ways just

148

the same. Nobody in the midst of a war suddenly throws away his rifle, and shouts: "This thing is wicked; I refuse to continue the fight!" To act thus would be to invite the strait-jacket or a bullet through the back of the head. Any other form of insanity, mind you, might be dealt with sympathetically—but not this one. This insanity is called treason. Yet there was never a man whom the world venerated as a holy man (with the possible exception of Mahomet) who was not also a traitor, in this sense. In the most profound sense these men were also traitors to the human race, I might add. They were all implacably set against the current order; they were precursors of a higher type of man. Hence their martyrdom, in most instances—in the West more particularly. For I might say, in passing, that in that benighted India where the British have long held sway in order to plunder and enlighten, in that India where over 300,000,000 souls ask nothing more of their benefactors than the freedom which was taken from them, it has been the custom for centuries to permit any and all religious doctrines to be expounded and practised. It is the one country in the world, I believe, where there has truly been religious freedom. It is the one country where non-resistance is openly practised. "Resist not evil," said the Christian Saviour. The Christians have seldom, if ever, taken these words seriously. But they were meant to be taken literally and seriously. It is the very core of Christ's teaching.

I would like to contrast all this with the newspaper headline this evening: "*No Peace Now—Roosevelt.*" Who is Roosevelt to say, "No peace Now!"? Is he the special emissary of the Almighty? Is he to tell us whether we should kill or not kill? The whole world rises in pious protest when Hitler orders his minions to prepare for war. It foams at the mouth when, after openly preparing for war, he keeps his promise and goes to war. This sort of behavior is looked upon by our realistic-minded fellow-citizens as deep, dark treachery.

149

And what did the opponents of Hitler do? Did they in loving kindness throw down their arms and say, "Strike if you will, we will not resist because we do not believe in meeting evil with evil"? Do you think there could have been a war had Hitler's threats met with such a response? Do you think the German people would have blood-thirstily girded themselves and fallen upon us with lust and vengeance since we had made ourselves defenseless against them? No matter if, in effect, Hitler said in his book that those who had not the courage to defend themselves must be eliminated—Hitler was not arming himself against the weak nations of Europe. His enemies were those who had vanquished Germany before and who relied for their strength on keeping Germany weak. Even, I say, if he had had the courage to enslave the weak he would not have had the courage to enslave the strong, especially if the strong had demonstrated their superiority by refusing to match arms with him. He would not have had the strength to continue his program if there had been even a modest show of generosity on the part of his opponents. After all, he was not dealing with altruists; the men who represented France and England at the Munich conference may have been Christian gentlemen, whatever that may mean, but they were certainly not brave and generous souls. If anything, they were more like frightened, reformed bandits; they had come, in answer to his summons, to save what they could of the swag which they had illegitimately confiscated. And as one bandit to another they talked it over, made compromises and concessions, tried to save their faces. We have all been made aware since then that Hitler is no gentleman, whatever else he may be in the eyes of his people. He was not only positively rude, he was authoritative. He very probably told the quaking representatives of the Democratic countries that he had no fear of them whatever, that he would go on exposing them despite their compromises and concessions. I am out to get what belongs to me, he must have told them, and if I don't get it peacefully then I will get it by force of arms. And they, knowing that, knowing that they were ill-prepared, made still further concessions and compromises while hastily endeavoring to put their houses in order. To put one's house in order, in the language of these gentlemen, means to make ready for war. And, by a curious logic, while making ready to meet the enemy with his own weapons, gentleman-like they furnished for a little cash some of the very weapons they so sorely needed to the enemy. In the last war, as you well know, these gentlemanly transactions were carried on while they were at one another's throats. *Gentlemen*, I must say. Fine Christian gentlemen. Even now, as I write, we are still selling materials to the Russians and Japanese which we know are being used against our allies and will soon be used against us. As gentlemen they legislate the question before the traffic can be halted.

"No peace now" is the edict from the White House. And we have not even declared war! We stand here on the other side of the ocean, and in our high and mighty aloofness we cry out: "Keep it up! Come to a military decision first, then we will talk about peace!" In other words, not until one side has been beaten to its knees can we dare to allow such a blasphemous word as peace to cross our lips. Roosevelt, or Churchill, or Hitler, if you like, versus Christ. First prove that you are strong as a gorilla, then act like a dove: that seems to be the logic. To me it doesn't make sense. If I am a gorilla I want to remain a gorilla. If I am a dove strong words will never make me a gorilla.

There are all sorts and conditions of men making up this vast, composite civilization. The majority of them, I honestly believe, think that they are against making war. That they are only deluding themselves one cannot hold against them. One has to pity them for their ignorance. If any one doubts that this is so, let him think

151

back to the Munich crisis and try to recall the delirious manifestation of joy which swept over the peoples of Europe, Germany included, when the peace of the world was saved, if only for a time, as even then every one feared. Some there are who read into these manifestations cowardice. Even if cowardice be the dominant motive (which I doubt, for only a few months later these same cowards proved themselves to be heroes on the battlefield), still it remains a fact that the people show more enthusiasm for peace than for war. Militant monster though he is said to be, Hitler was not less idolized by the Germans when he kept them out of war. His popularity did not increase, even among this war-like people, because he made war on Europe. Oddly and ironically enough, it is in the Democratic countries that a leader becomes more popular with the declaration of war. This is often cited as an example of the greater unity among the people of a Democratic nation. It provides us with the paradox of a man like Lincoln being reviled while peaceably proclaiming his ideals and venerated as "the great leader" after precipitating the most bloody internecine strife that ever a nation participated in. It is interesting to remark here that, though he is now labeled the Great Emancipator, he is still not a hero to the South. We have never convinced the South that we were in the right; we merely subdued them. As for the emancipation of the slaves, which we pretend was the real issue of the War between the States, the chief result of it, as I see it, has been the enslavement of the whites as well as the blacks. We came out of the great Civil War shorn of some of the very liberties we had fought to defend. By saving the Union, to please the industrialists of the North, we put our own white brothers in a position of serfdom even more rigid than our black brothers had known. To-day no man is free except he who has money or who owns the machines we work with. At least 80% of the world's gold is buried in the earth, in our own

Kentucky. England, whose empire covers almost two-thirds of the globe, has to ask America to lend her money to continue the war. And these two great nations, the wealthiest in the world (though never so per capita) are obliged to squeeze from the poor by taxation sums of money which, had these same poor demanded them of their government in peace times for food and shelter, would have been given them in the form of bullets.

It has been said that the first World War cost the nations engaging in it a sum approximating $250,000,000,000.00. "With this staggering sum," says the author of this statement (who was not a Bolshevik, by the way, but an American ace), "we could have built homes costing $2,500.00 each on 5-acre lots costing $100.00 an acre. We could have equipped each of those homes with a thousand dollars' worth of furniture and given such a home to every family in Russia, Italy, France, Belgium, Germany, Wales, Scotland, Ireland, England, Australia, Holland and the U. S. A." What do the war-leaders say? Better to lose everything we cherish and keep our liberty than surrender to the enemy! But what kind of liberty is this which thrives on the loss of the most elemental needs of man? Liberty for whom? Liberty for those who retain the upper hand, for those who will live in comfort even though the country is ruined? I would have nothing to say if the men who urge us to war were the first to strip themselves bare, the first to go over the top, the first to be carried back wounded and broken. I would have nothing to say against military discipline if the officers were the first to bear the shock of assault. I would have still less to say if the generals and admirals fought it out among themselves exclusively. I would be absolutely silenced if the leaders of the warring countries offered themselves up as sacrifices. I have nothing to say to the man who volunteers to fight for his country, or for a principle which he believes is the right one. Such a man may be a hero or a fool, or

153

both. But what I protest against, and what I will never admit to be right, is forcing a man against his will and his conscience to sacrifice his life for a cause which he does not believe in. It does not matter to me if he is one in a million—he is still to be defended. To question the sincerity of such a man, as is done to-day by recruiting officers, is to my way of thinking not only stupid and irrelevant but dastardly. It is extremely obvious that the sense of duty which is supposed to animate all good citizens of the Republic is regarded as being too low to rely upon. We dare not ask each and every man whether he is willing to do his duty or not. The answer would be, in the majority of cases, NO! In this matter of duty those above us, who should have inculcated the faculty by example, have shown themselves deplorably deficient. Duty, service, sacrifice—these are words which are always thrown at the dogs. If we had had at the top men of duty, men of service, men willing to sacrifice themselves, there would be no need to demand these qualities of the under-dog. But those in power have shown only the opposite qualities: greed, fear, selfishness. Now, when their security is threatened, they trot out these noble terms, they ram it down the throats of the oppressed. What would I do if my mother were attacked? That is my own private affair, and whatever I might do, I must say that it has no bearing in this matter of going to war or not going to war. Where were you, I might ask my interlocutor, when my mother was without food and shelter, when she could find no means of supporting her starving children, when she could not find a bed to die in because she had no money? Where were you when the very bread that was offered her was robbed of its vital substance? Where were you when she was dispossessed and thrown into the street? Where were you when, demanding the right to a living wage, she was clubbed by the police, sprinkled with tear gas, thrown in jail like a criminal? One might go on *ad nauseam*. Duty is wonderful when it is spontaneously and silently rendered; when it is demanded of us by thieves and blackguards it stinks. I would rather see a man evade his duty than force it from him by threats and blows. My duty concerns my own behavior, not that of my neighbor. My duty is to treat him as a fellow-man and not to sit in judgment upon him. If I perform my duties properly, the chances are he will perform his also. There is nothing like example to inspire right conduct. And the most ignominious behavior that I can think of is to preach duty and shirk it oneself.

Apropos of duty, I recall vividly now the reaction of French audiences when the news reels gave them a glimpse of the Germans goose-stepping before their Fuehrer, or when Mussolini appeared on the balcony to address his feverish followers. The reaction of the audience, I remember, varied considerably with the quarter in which the picture was shown. Around the Champs-Elysées there was always a violent outburst of rage, a prolonged jeering, hissing and cat-calling; in the poor quarters, though there were sporadic outbursts, the attitude in general was one of gloom and silence. Now and then you would hear some one say—"he must be crazy, that guy," meaning Hitler or Mussolini. Often, when I left the cinema of an evening, I had the feeling of living in a strangely unreal world; even if I had not read *Mein Kampf*, even if I had not followed the papers, the evidence which I had seen with my own eyes was so convincing that it seemed to me only dreamers could avoid the obvious conclusion thereof. If the subject came up one would inevitably hear that the French were by no means asleep, that it was simply not in their nature to make such brutal demonstrations. "When the time comes they will find us ready!" That was the usual answer. What the military men were doing I could not tell, but, as far as the rank and file were concerned, I could see with my own eyes that there was no radical change in their behavior. Everybody went about his business as usual, grumbling, to be sure, that business had gone to pots. As for the situation across the border, well, the government was tending to that. And the government, as you know, changed hands so many times that nobody could say who or what the government was. This is the condition that prevailed almost everywhere beyond the domain of the Axis powers until the outbreak of the war. It is the condition which prevails right now in this country, despite the huge defense program which is under way. We are preparing for war and at the same time trying to do business as usual. People who sit through the anti-Hitler movies, and fervidly demonstrate their disapproval of him, go quietly to bed and patiently resume their hum-drum lives as usual the next morning. They groan when the taxes are increased; they go into a panic when they are called for the draft. They want Hitler and Mussolini suppressed, but they would rather give England the money and materials to do the job than volunteer themselves. Every aid short of war, was the cry until a few weeks ago. Now it is—we will go to war if necessary. *If necessary!* As though by all logic it hadn't been necessary before.

I wonder sometimes what would happen if the people ever became really enthusiastic about making war against Hitler. Supposing some silver-tongued orator succeeded in so inflaming the whole country that the people took the situation in hand themselves. Supposing the menace to their freedom became such a vivid reality that they could do nothing but concentrate their entire energies upon defeating the enemy. Can you imagine what would happen overnight here? In the first place the existing government would be ousted; the present war-leaders would be kicked out, the generals and admirals deposed, the Senators and Congressmen thrown into jail. The banks would be cleaned out, the insurance companies abolished, the leaders of industry executed. There would

156

be no business any more except the business of making war. There would be no need of money any more because there would be no profits to be made, no wages to be paid, no savings to be tapped. The surplus stocks of food, clothing and other necessities of life would be distributed among the needy. Everybody would have to work for freedom, and consequently every one would have to be fed and clothed. One man would be as important as the next man, no matter what his task. The schools would be closed and the children would also be impressed into service. I can hear the Generalissimo saying—"we need the help of every man, woman and child; we need the help of the aged, the infirm, the insane, the criminalminded." The sick would be looked upon suspiciously, as malignerers, and the criminals would be treated as sick or pathological. But all would be forced to work, even the paralytics, even the bedridden. If we needed 50,000 aeroplanes we would make 500,000; if we needed 500 battleships we would make 5,000. There would be a perfect frenzy of activity, because not only freedom but life itself would be at stake. If such a picture seems preposterous, we have only to think of the miraculous sweep of the Crusaders, or the conquests of Mahomet, or the exploits of Tamerlane. If life and freedom are to be defended by the sword, then it is our duty to forge the most miraculous sword ever man wielded. If this be the way out, then let us become the scourge of the earth. Let us not stop until every man, woman and child who believes differently from us is annihilated. That is my idea of the way war should be made, if war it is to be. No half-way measures, no dillydallying, no sportsmanship, no give and take, no quarter. If those opposing us are threatening the very foundations of existence, then God have mercy on them, for we shall exterminate them until the last man. That is my idea of an all-out war. No prisoners, no Red Cross nurses, no Salvation Army, no Y. M. C. A. Complete devotion, sacrifice and

157

consecration to the task—nothing more, nothing less. No retreating, no surrender. If arms are lacking, fight on with tooth and nail. Don't bury the dead: let them rot and sow pestilence. Risk everything, because there is only one goal; if that is not reached then nothing is worth saving. If Mr. Roosevelt or any other man in authority can say, "No Peace Now!", then he ought to be able to go the whole hog. Nay, it is his duty to do so, because every delay, every compromise, every half-hearted effort, every man, woman and child not actively and fanatically engaged in the pursuit of victory, brings the shadow of ultimate defeat a step nearer. By the logic of war defeat is the one thing that cannot be tolerated or envisioned. If our defeat means the end of life, liberty and happiness for the world, if that idea should become firmly lodged in the minds of the American people, not merely as idea but as flaming reality, then nothing is too fantastic to expect of us. If Hitler accomplished his miracles in seven or eight years, then we can accomplish even greater miracles in one or two years. Provided, as I say, the idea becomes a reality.

Personally I do not believe it will happen. I believe it will take a few more wars, each more terrible and devastating than the other, before such a change of heart can come about. There will have to be less and less to hope for with the cessation of each new war. When the last illusion is shattered then perhaps the miracle will come about. And then perhaps the miracle will assume a guise totally different from that which I have just described. For the only miracle that man can honestly hope for is that he will change, that he will know peace and cherish it above everything else.

That a change in this direction *is* possible we have the barest indications of already. Perhaps the most hopeful sign, even though it is expressed in negative terms and usually hypocritically, is, as I remarked before, the fact that no government to-day is capable of eliciting the support of its people in undertaking an offensive war. Every war nowadays is justified as a defensive war. How long it will take the people of the world to realize that nothing can be defended by war it is impossible to predict, but even now, among the English people themselves, there is an element enlightened enough to protest against waging war merely to defend the British Empire. Slowly but surely men *must* recognize the fact that the only empire worth fighting for is the Empire of Man, which is the earth itself and *all her inhabitants.* To defend that empire it is useless to destroy one another, because the only enemy of man is himself. Already, I repeat, a serious breach has been made in the hypocritical position which the Democratic peoples, who for the most part are Christians, have put themselves in these last two thousand years. Only the other night I saw a news reel showing conscientious objectors who, because they belong to a particular branch of the Christian Church which literally obeys the commandment "Thou Shalt Not Kill!", were exempted from taking up arms. Various kinds of non-combatant service are offered them, including the giving of aid to the wounded on the battlefield. Supposing now that in the years to come, even if only for the base (?) motive of escaping the duties of a soldier, more and more people become members of these admittedly legitimate groups objecting to war— what then? What will happen when there are more stretcher-bearers than soldiers? For many centuries in China the only armies which could be raised to defend the country against the invader were mercenary ones. In India there was a long period of peace established when a certain war-like ruler, after having conquered over all his enemies, finally conquered his own war-like nature. It *is* possible for people to live in peace—it has been proved again and again throughout history. But there is a difference between the Pax Romana (which the Germans are reviving) or the British Empire sort of peace, with its skillful double-dealing divide and rule strategy, or the American-Russian isolationist policy, and the peace of a people who are too peaceful at heart to fight no matter what the reason may be. To the question, "what would you do if your country were attacked?", there might one day be the answer—"we would like to know *why* our country is being attacked." (In the case of America at this moment, let me interject, *nobody* has as yet attacked her. We are being given the specious examples of countries such as Austria, Finland, Czechoslovakia, Poland, Norway, Denmark, Holland, Belgium, et alia, as though to say—our turn is next! Twenty years from now, when all the white papers have been issued, there will be a different tune to sing with regard to these wanton attacks.) The vast majority of people in the world to-day not only believe but know the sole reason for war, in this day and age, is economic rivalry. And knowing this, they still allow themselves to be swept headlong into war by cheap and vicious slogans which disguise the issue. I say they allow themselves: I should modify this to say— *they are helpless to do otherwise!* They are innocent and guilty at the same time. By giving every day of their lives their mute assent to a way of life which is false and disastrous they bring about their own cruel dilemma.

I am only forty-nine years of age, yet how many wars and revolutions have occurred in that brief period! And we are supposed to have lived in an enlightened era! When we look backward over the brief span of civilization we see how one war engendered another. That this present one grew out of the last one nobody has any doubt about. And to-morrow then—will there not be another one born of this? What is achieved, if, no matter how noble and valiant the effort, the result is always war, war, war? When I think of the situation in this light I am reminded of that story by Blaise Cendrars in *La Vie Dangéreuse*, wherein he tells of the simple little French soldier whose body was so horribly torn and mutilated that it took hours to dress his terrible wounds. I think of it because the drama which centered about this screaming bundle of human flesh is so symbolic of the eternal drama of man. You may recall that, in spite of his pleas to be put out of the way, the victim was kept alive by the superhuman efforts of the Mother Superior. And then one day the Grand Medico of the French Army, who had come to inspect the work of his butchers, insisted on demonstrating his skill on the helpless, screaming little soldier who was swinging from the ceiling in his aerial bed-basket. Quickly and ruthlessly he opened up each and every wound, of which there were hundreds, the little fellow so crazed with pain that he lay there like a demented oyster ploughed with red hot prongs. An hour after the great surgeon had demonstrated the success of his new method the little fellow was dead. The prolonged superhuman efforts of the Mother Superior had gone for nought. The victim's prayers had been answered: he was dispatched by the butcher-in-chief in the name of progress and surgical advance. And that is the way of the war mongers. They take the bloody, quivering, agonized body of humanity and, in the name of progress and advancement, they plough open the wounds; when the body is cold and dead, when it no longer quivers with pain and fright, they pronounce the experiment a success. *Every military success sets the world back a million years*. The merciful work of the angels is like the fluttering of wings in the dark to a man who is dying. We have scarcely time to open our eyes and look upward before we are stabbed with a thousand swords. The compassionate Mother Superior in Cendrars' story had given her last ounce of strength to comfort the sufferer who was doomed. She knew that her efforts would not save the man, but she persisted just the same. And then came the medico, who cared not whether the man lived or died, but who was animated by one thought only—to establish the success of his method. The example is perfect. Those who sponsor war, though they do so in the name of the Most Holy, at heart care nothing for the sufferings of their fellow-men. They talk of the future blindly, caring nothing for the lessons of the past. They close their eyes, shut their ears, harden their hearts—in order to perform their duty. To me the screams of one agonizing individual rings louder and more imperious than all the exhortations of the righteous. I would rather be called a coward and a traitor than neglect the plea of that helpless individual. If we could see into the conflict more profoundly we would see that it makes no difference from which side of the battle ground the cry for mercy goes up. We are lying on both sides, we are victor and vanquished simultaneously. A little interval of time and the cry must go up on one side or the other. Why wait until the horror of it stays the sword? Have we no imagination? Can we not look ahead a few moments and see ourselves fraternizing with the enemy? *Why not peace now, this very moment?* Is the sword thinking for us? Is the sword alone capable of solving our problems? Do we reckon in dead alone, or can we reckon with living men also? Is the idea of right and wrong more important than life itself? Or do ideas grow out of life? And if we are right and dead, right and broken in spirit, what good is it then to be right? Who can be certain that he is absolutely right, so right that he can exact the death of his fellow-man? We the people who make up this continent almost annihilated the Indians from whom we robbed this land. To-day we, the descendants of the men who robbed, burned, raped, plundered, murdered, poisoned our enemy, the American Indian, now honor him and try in vain to make amends for the wrongs we perpetrated against him. It is now our proudest boast to say that we have Indian blood in our veins. What irony! What mockery! In the bloodiest Civil War that was ever fought we, the people of the

162

North, subdued by fire and sword our own brothers of the South. To-day, when the picture called *Gone With the Wind* is shown in the North, we hiss and boo our own Northern soldiers, we join with the South in loathing and execrating the name of the general who dealt the South a mortal blow. We act thus out of a sense of shame and guilt, in acknowledgment of the grievous wrongs we committed against our own brothers. We learn fifty, a hundred, five hundred years too late. We learn how to behave in the past, but never how to behave in the future. *Learn now*, I say. The future is in our hands. We are making it by our acts this day. The men who urge us to kill do not belong to the world of the future; they belong to the past.

I do not say that the men who believe in war as a last resort are necessarily evil, necessarily worse than other men; I say they are stupid, they lack vision, magnanimity, wisdom. When they speak of war as being the last resort can we be certain that they have tried every other means of preserving peace? I am afraid not. I am afraid that even such a sorry figure of an appeaser as Chamberlain had done very little to avert the inevitable. What merit is there in pretending to save the peace of the world when one is unwilling to yield the very things which are the cause of the conflict? It is easy to say we want peace when we are the stronger, when we have the necessities for which the other is hungering. Naturally the one who is desperate enough to risk an open conflict is not playing the game according to our rules. *Naturally* he is the disturber of the peace. *But what made him disturb the peace?* Sheer malice? Sheer diabolical greed, envy, hatred? Even if one has to admit that the Germans are poisoned with hatred, one has also to admit that we who oppose them are not precisely suffused with radiant love. Men do not become poisoned with hatred in a vacuum, nor when surrounded by loving, sympathetic neighbors. No great mystery surrounds the psychosis of the German people. Neither is there any mystery attached to the unwillingness of the British imperialists to part with their illegitimate possessions. Nor is there anything mysterious about the reluctance of the American people to enter a war which concerns the fate of an empire which has always been hostile to our best interests . . .

MY DEAR FRED, *it's a good three years since I wrote the fore-going. The war is still on and nobody knows when it will end or how. Just the other day I had a letter from our friend Claude Houghton, in which he said: "I have two feelings about the war (you can't think about it, of course). One is, that its end will be something unimagined; the other is, that it is an incident in an event wholly outside our most inspired guess."*

*You may wonder why I have waited so long to make public my answer to your letter. I waited deliberately until the outcome of the war seemed certain. With victory in sight people will again think about peace. What kind of peace? Everlasting peace? The war leaders are already busy formulating peace plans: they are going to underwrite a new peace policy. The only thing I am certain of, in connection with this insurance policy, is that it will be the most expensive one ever devised. That it will be effective only until the next war goes without saying. So, until the next war, peace be with you!*

HENRY.

*June 25, 1944.*

## Part II: MURDER THE MURDERER

A PERIOD of darkness has set in. The world seems determined to resolve its problems by force. No single individual can stem the

164

tide of hate. We are in the grip of cosmic forces and each one does what he can, or must.

To each man the conflict assumes a different face. Millions of men and women will sacrifice their lives; millions more will be maimed and mutilated. The innocent will suffer with the guilty, the wise with the foolish. It is beyond control now; we are in the hands of Fate.

Useless to say now that it need not have happened. It is not for us to question what happens; it is for us to accept. But there are a thousand ways of accepting the inevitable. In the way we accept lies our ability to transform a situation. No disaster is irremediable. The whole meaning of life is contained in the word suffering. That all the world can be suffering at one time is a fact of tremendous significance.[1] It never has happened before. It is an opportunity which we can reject or use to advantage.

Since I am having my say, I want to reveal what I sincerely believe this opportunity may be. We, the American people, having resisted war to the very last, have now thrown ourselves into the universal conflict. Whether we admit it to ourselves or not, whether or not we have lived up to that faith which the other peoples of the world have in us, *we are the hope of the world*. That is the rock on which America was founded. Let it be our rock now!

Are we at war to extend our empire, to increase our possessions, to gain ascendancy over the other nations of this earth? I believe the great body of American people would answer NO! Like other peoples, we have been misguided. Above all, we had grown callous and indifferent. That was our crime. To-day we are ready to accept our share of suffering, along with the righteous and the unrighteous. Moreover, we are determined to endure what we have never endured before. That was evident the day war was declared.

[1] Not quite the whole world!—the "civilized" peoples mostly.

165

What can we as a people do beyond anything our allies may expect of us? We can be magnanimous and far-sighted, we can be patient and full of understanding; we can be hard as steel, yet wise and full of tenderness when the time is ripe. We can be all these things because we are the favored people of the earth. Our forefathers, when first they came to this country, were hailed as gods. To our disgrace they behaved as demons. They asked for gold instead of grace. To-day their sins are visited upon us. We are paying now for the crimes committed by our ancestors. They fled their self-imposed prisons because they had a vision of Paradise. Had they acted as the gods they were mistaken for by the aborigines of this continent they could have realized the Paradise which they were seeking. But they were only men and they were weak, and because they were weak the dream of Paradise was forgotten. Dreams are hard to kill; they linger on even when the memory of them is faded. The dream of golden opportunity still clings to the name America no matter what part of the world you may go to. It is regrettable that we, the American people, have fostered a false interpretation of that dream and thereby helped to further poison the world. We have given the impression that America was a place in which to grow rich. We have emphasized gold instead of opportunity. Out of greed we killed the goose that laid the golden egg. Yet, despite the tragic error, we all know that there *was* a golden goose. We are now at the point where we are obliged to interpret the fable intelligently.

What *was* the golden opportunity which was offered the American pilgrim? The opportunity to serve the world, the opportunity to bring about enlightenment and justice. Since the inception of this republic we had no enemies save the mother country, England. We were surrounded by friends. The only great struggle we had was an internal one. Then, in the last war, we were dragged into a world-wide conflict whose significance we only partially understood. The war over, we tried to take refuge again in our comfortable shell, unwilling to accept the responsibilities we had assumed as participants of that great conflict. We refused to sit at the Hague Tribunal and assist in the first crude attempt to establish some kind of international law and order. We refused for years to recognize the one government which had taken the lesson of the war to heart and was endeavoring to bring about a more intelligent and equitable order of human society. With the emergence of the dictators we sat by and watched one little nation after the other swallowed up and enslaved. When France fell we were full of bitterness. We cried "Shame!" though we hadn't lifted a finger to help her. We would have suffered England to undergo the same fate, but the English were made of different stuff. Until the treacherous attack by Japan, which we should have anticipated, considering all the lessons we had been given, we were undecided what course to pursue. Now suddenly we are united and, as in the last war, we are pretending that we are fighting to free the world. The newspapers are doing their best to make the American people believe this beautiful legend, knowing well that the psychology of the American people is based on a sense of utter unreality, that only when we visualize ourselves as saviours and crusaders can we kill with fury and efficiency. "Now at last," I read in to-day's paper, "a single devotion inspires the nation, a great moment has touched us and America has fallen in step to heroic music. We have renounced triviality, indifference and fear, we have taken up the responsibilities of our position in the world, we have turned as one man toward a shining star." [1] It goes on like that, soaring, skyrocketing, to end with the phrase "without compromise—to win."

It is unthinkable that we shall lose. But what do we hope to win?

[1] New York Post, December 13, 1941.

167

Or better, what do we hope to win to? That is the question which the editorial gentry cleverly evade by grandiloquent phrases such as "ridding the world forever of the Nazi pestilence," and so on. Are we microbe hunters and bug exterminators? Are we merely going to preserve the *tomb* of Christ from the desecrating paw of the infidel? For two thousand years the world has been squabbling over the dead body of Christ. The Christians themselves will admit that God sent his son, a *living* Christ, to redeem the world. He didn't send us a corpse to fight over. In effect, however, that is what the Christian world has done: it has welcomed every excuse to fight in the name of Christ who came to bring peace on earth. There can be no end to this repetitious pattern until each and every one of us become as Christ, until belief and devotion transform our words into deeds and thus make of myth reality.

"To War—and Beyond" reads the caption of the editorial I just cited. We are all interested in what lies beyond the war. Nobody is any longer interested in war for the sake of war. But what comes after the war depends altogether on the spirit in which we wage war. We will accomplish exactly what we aim to accomplish, and no more. In this respect war is no different from peace. The fact that we are desperate instead of lethargic means nothing, if we are not clear as to what we wish to attain. To defeat Hitler and his gang is not a particularly brilliant goal to set oneself. Hitler and his gang could have been defeated without war had we possessed the intelligence, the will, and the purity to undertake the task. Wherever there is indecision, confusion, dalliance and an atmosphere of unreality, you have Hitler. Just as Judas was necessary in order for Christ to enact the drama which was ordained, so Hitler was necessary for this age in order that the world might enact the drama of unification and regeneration. Christ chose Judas to betray him; we have chosen Hitler. All the intermediary figures, the supernumeraries, so to speak, good, honest gentlemen though they be, are dwarfed by this Satanic figure which looms across the horizon. Churchill, Roosevelt, Stalin, none of these is big enough to cope with the monster alone. It is fortunate that they are not, for now it devolves upon the little men, the poor anonymous figures who make up the great mass of humanity, to answer the challenge. Christ chose twelve little men to do his work—not great world figures.

I come back to that idea which America has always inspired in the minds of other peoples, the idea that the lowest man may rise and "make his place" in the world. (It would have been better had we inspired the idea of "finding one's place" in the world.) I repeat that the behavior of the American people has brought about a distortion of that idea. We have shown in ways too numerous to specify that we have reduced the conception of freedom and service to mankind to a poverty-stricken notion of power and riches. Power and riches, not for *all* Americans—that would be bad enough!—but for the few. Our democracy has been the worst democracy that has ever been tried out. It has never had anything to do with freedom, has never been anything more than a name. Put to the test, it explodes, as was demonstrated in the War between the States. It will explode again when the pressure becomes great enough, because it is not founded upon a respect for the individual, for the sacred human individual who in aggregate makes a democracy and in the ultimate will make divinity. We have been democratic in the crassest political way, but at bottom we have never been deceived about it. Our jokesters, our cartoonists, our caricaturists reveal only too clearly the conscious and unconscious disillusionment of the people.

What can the people of America do then in this great world crisis—beyond the intention of their dubiously disinterested leaders? How can they win a war which they had no desire to participate in and which very conceivably the peoples they oppose had no desire to initiate? I think of the film called *Juarez*, of that moment when Juarez confronts the assembled representatives of the European governments and tells them what the people of Mexico suffered from the "civilization" of the Europeans. How like jackals they looked, the assembled plenipotentiaries of Europe, in their pomp and persiflage! From time immemorial the dignitaries of Church and State have looked this way. And from time immemorial the people have looked on dumb and impassive, always shackled and manacled by their own spokesmen. We see the same thing happening to-day in the Labor movement. A Lincoln, a Lenin, a Juarez are not to be had every day. We have had only one Buddha, one Christ, one Mohammed, one Ramakrishna. We have had only one American who was capable of saying: "While there is a lower class I am in it; while there is a criminal element I am of it; while there is a soul in prison, I am not free." Can the American people endorse these simple, Christ-like words? *Will* they? If not, then some other people will assume the leadership. The Russians are already far beyond us in the realization of their aims. To-morrow it will be China and India perhaps. We no longer lead the procession; we are being dragged along by the scalp.

What is our role? How shall we act? What example can we give?

To begin with, let us begin at the beginning. Put on your hat and go into the street. Stroll quietly down the avenue and look into the shop windows. Take a pad and pencil and list all the objects— clothes, food, furniture, drugs, jewelry, gadgets, knick-knacks— which you consider unnecessary to produce now that we are at war. Send the list to President Roosevelt and mark it "Personal."

That's the first step. The second is to go home, sit down quietly and meditate. Try to picture what the world would look like if these useless things were eliminated. Ask yourself if you could get along with the bare necessities of life. Assume that the President will give serious attention to your suggestions.

The next step is to think about wages. Do you think you are entitled to more than the man in uniform who no longer has the right to vote and who is asked to sacrifice his life in order to protect you? Can you see any logical reason why a sergeant should receive higher pay than a private or a second lieutenant more than a sergeant? Can you see any reason why the president of the United States should receive *money* for the privilege of leading his people to victory? Can you see any reason why anybody should think about money when the government which represents us has in its power the means to provide us with the necessities of life? We are no longer on the gold standard; we buried our gold in the earth, where it belongs. But we have bright coins such as would please a savage, and little bits of paper expressing our confidence in God and in one another. To-morrow, if the government chooses, these objects can be made meaningless. There is nothing sacred about these monetary symbols. In themselves they have no value: they are merely relics of an ancient way of thinking.

What is a panic? It is anything but a manifestation of loss of confidence? A panic is engendered by the realization that something we thought was there is gone. To-day there is a panic on all fronts. *This is what war means: a complete loss of confidence on all sides.* Lacking faith, intelligence, good-will, we move in with big guns, tanks, battleships, bombers, high explosives and try to fill the breach. Even a child can understand the futility of trying to instill faith and confidence with bullets and poison gas. The theory behind the philosophy of war is that the enemy must be made to come to terms—*our terms*. Then and only then can we talk turkey.

To-day this idea, like other atavistic notions, is very much in

171

question. People are getting fed up with the idea of talking turkey only after wasteful slaughter and destruction. If there weren't such a strict taboo on the eating of human flesh it might not be so bad; one could eat a fresh corpse and live to fight another day. But making manure of human flesh and blood is a rather expensive method of fertilizing the earth. There are better things to be accomplished with the human body—at least some people think so.

Let's go back a bit. We were questioning the practicability of retaining little round pieces of metal and little oblong pieces of paper. Metals are scarce now and so is paper. And since they are only symbols of our mutual confidence, these relics of the past, why not scrap them and convert them into war materials?

*And how will I buy a ham sandwich to-morrow?*

Very simple. There will be no buying or selling to-morrow; there will be only give and take. If you have a bigger stomach than I you will eat three ham sandwiches to my one. And if you want twenty ham sandwiches at one sitting why you will have to take the consequences imposed by the laws of nature. The man who insists on having three overcoats, five hats and seven pairs of shoes will have to wear them all at once, otherwise he forfeits them. Whatever superfluous possessions you have will be redistributed among the needy. In war-time we can't have people bothering about needless possessions—it's too distracting. What we want, if we are going to rid the world of useless vermin (that's to say Germans, Japs, Italians, Hungarians, Roumanians—the inventory isn't quite made up yet), are men and women united in a single purpose: *to exterminate the enemy.* We can't have fighters who are thinking of stocks and bonds, high or low wages, profits and losses, perfumes, patent medicines, toilet water, platinum settings, monkey furs, silk bathrobes, collars, ties and alarm clocks. Especially not alarm clocks! We want an army of men and women, soldiers and workers, killers

172

and producers, who will wake up without an alarm—people who can't sleep any more because they're itching to rid the world of human lice. People so restless, so wild with excitement, so full of ardor and devotion, that when they get through exterminating the foreign vermin they will go after their own. People who will exterminate one another, until there are no vermin left in the world. Isn't that it? Or have I exaggerated the case?

*A people wild with excitement* . . .

For example: supposing that to-morrow, owing to the most expert propaganda, there would be such a fever to enlist in all branches of the service that every able-bodied worker from ten to seventy-five years of age, including the eight or nine million unemployed, would descend upon the recruiting bureaus and demand the right to fight. A grand chaos ensues, with the result that everybody is ordered back to work. Good. They return to their jobs, still feverish, still rearing to go, still itching to serve in some vital, splendorous way. Then a wave of disgust, as they realize more and more each day that they are being asked to produce non-essentials. Supposing they take it into their heads to stop wasting time. Supposing they go on strike, fired with the exalted idea of producing only what will keep the war machine humming. They win, let us say. Nothing being produced now but the vital necessities. A new thing happens: the workingman becomes delirious with enthusiasm. He asks nothing better than to work and work and work. And so, instead of six or eight hours a day, the workers of America work twelve, sixteen, twenty hours a day; they drag the children out of school and the criminals out of jail and the insane out of the asylums. Everybody is put to work, without exception. They work night and day, day in and day out; no Sundays, no holidays, no rest periods. They work themselves to the bone, obsessed with a single idea: to bring about a speedy victory. In the meantime they ransack the patent offices and the secret archives of those whose interest it serves to withhold new inventions. They create new machines which provide an incalculable release of energies natural, human and divine. They invent, create and produce in five months what formerly it required five years to accomplish. And still they refuse to rest. They form suicide brigades of workers and producers. They drive their former slave-drivers to a quick death; they drive the sick and the aged to the grave; they force the children to mature, as blossoms are forced in the hot-house. "Work! More work!" they cry. The President is for caution, but the pace increases. Faster, faster. Fast and furiously, without let, without cess. A mania for work such as was never heard of on any planet in the memory of God. The President, bewildered by this inexplicable access of zeal, continues feebly to abjure and protest. "I beg you, my good fellow-citizens, don't work yourselves to death!" But it's in the blood now, they can't stop. God Almighty couldn't put a stop to it, so virulent and deep-seated has the mania become.

It becomes necessary to remove the President from office—he is regarded as a slacker. The Vice-President takes over. In forty-eight hours he's demoted too. A new party arises, calling themselves "The Bees and Ants." There is no opposition—just one unanimous Party now. A new President is chosen, the hardest, fastest worker in the United States. He is to serve until he drops from exhaustion.

In the midst of this incredible toil and bubble new inventions are being turned out by the hour. Finally the great invention of the ages is ushered in—a sort of human Flit. A device which destroys the enemy everywhere instantaneously. Something so ingenious, so simple too, that it needs only to be stamped with a single word, such as *Japanese, German, Bulgarian, Italian,* and it goes directly to the mark, annihilating its victim. Total annihilation of the enemy everywhere! Think of the effect which this produces! At last

174

the ideal victory. Something indeed which the men of this scientific age might well be proud of! Power! Absolute power! No need for Peace Conferences henceforth. No need to ball things up through compromise, chicanery and intrigue, as in the past. All our enemies are dead. Annihilated. The power to rule the world in our own hands. Who now will dare to rise up against us? Magnificent, *what?*

There are those, of course, who will immediately cry "Absurd! Fantastic! Impossible!" A *human Flit?* . . . tsch, tsch, tsch! How many years ago is it that the same was said against the steamboat, the railroad, the aeroplane, the telegraph, the telephone, the electric light, the X-ray? Is it necessary to reel off the whole list of what was once absurd, impossible and fantastic, to say nothing of impracticable, unprofitable, demonic and diabolical? *Whatever man sets his mind on accomplishing he accomplishes*. That is the beautiful and terrible thing about man, that he has within himself the power and the ability to make his dreams come true.

Nature too has certain powers which man, despite his superiority, is sometimes helpless to combat. Now and then man has to acknowledge that there are powers beyond his. For four long centuries there raged in Europe, and even beyond the confines of Europe, the plague known as the Black Death. Not one man living in that dark period was capable of finding a means to stem the avalanche of death. Death ruled like a demented monarch, turning everything topsy-turvy, including legal and moral codes. It seems almost incredible to-day. But it was so. It did happen. Only when Nature herself grew weary, and provided the antidote, did the Black Death cease to be the Supreme Master of Europe.

Will we take the cue from Nature? Will we, weary of shedding blood, create an anti-toxin to self-destruction? Perhaps, when we have had our fill of slaughter. Not before. We must kill and kill until we hit upon the means of killing without effort and without

175

limit. We must exhaust this lust to kill at the risk of total annihilation. We must be able to visualize the ultimate effect of murder before we can hope to eradicate the instinct. We must become the black magicians before we can become the white. We must possess power absolutely, not worship it merely, before we can understand the use of it.

There is an old story about a man who had committed fifty-two murders. It bears repeating . . .

As the story goes, it was after the fifty-second crime that the murderer became conscience-stricken and decided to seek out a holy man in order to mend his ways. He lived with the holy man a few years, doing everything that he was prescribed to do and striving with all his heart to get the better of his vicious nature. Then one day the holy man told him that he was free to resume his life in the world, that he need have no more fear of committing murder again. At first the man was overjoyed, but elation soon gave way to fear and doubt. How could he be certain he would sin no more? He begged the holy man for some sign, some tangible proof that he was really liberated. And so the holy man gave him a black cloth, telling him that when the cloth turned white he could be absolutely certain of his innocence. The man departed and resumed his life in the world. A dozen times a day he looked at the black cloth to see if it had turned white. He could think of nothing else— he was obsessed. Little by little he began to inquire of others what he could do to bring the miracle about. Each one suggested something else. He followed out every suggestion, but to no avail. The cloth remained black. Finally he made a long pilgrimage to the Ganges, having been told that the holy waters of that sacred river would surely make the black cloth white. But as with all his efforts this one too proved unsuccessful. Finally, in despair, he decided to return to the holy man and live out the rest of his days in his presence. At least, he thought, by living with the holy man he would be able to avoid temptation. So he set out on the long journey. As he was nearing his destination he came upon a man attacking a woman. The screams which the woman gave out were heart-rending. He caught hold of the man and implored him to desist. But the man paid no heed to him. On the contrary, he redoubled his blows. There was no doubt that he intended to kill the woman. Something had to be done, and quickly, if the woman was not to be murdered before his very eyes. In a flash the ancient murderer reviewed the situation. Fifty-two murders he had committed. One more could make no great difference. Since he would have to atone for the others he could just as well make it fifty-three. Even if he were to stay in hell forever he could not stand by and see this woman murdered. And so he set upon the man and killed him. When he came to the holy man he told him what had happened, whereupon the holy man smiled and said: "Have you looked at the black cloth I gave you?" He had forgotten all about the black cloth since the fifty-third murder. Trembling he took it out and gazed upon it. It had turned white . . .

There are murders and *murders* then. There is the kind that enslaves and the kind that liberates. But the final objective is to murder the murderer. The last act in the drama of "the ego and his own" is to murder one's own murderous self. The man who with the fifty-third murder renounces all hope of salvation is saved. To commit murder in full consciousness of the enormity of the crime is an act of liberation. It is heroic, and only those are capable of it who have purified their hearts of murder. Murder sanctioned by the Church, the State, or the community is murder just the same. Authority is the voice of confusion. The only authority is the in-

177

dividual conscience. To murder through fear, or love of country, is as bad as to murder from anger or greed. *To murder murder one has to have clean hands and a pure heart.*

If the Creator be all-powerful, all-wise, all beneficent why, it is often asked, does He permit us to murder one another? There are many answers to this conundrum, but the man who cherishes freedom realizes that the way to heaven is through hell. How can we eliminate what through lack of experience we do not understand? Murder is conflict on the lowest level, no more excusable when perpetrated en masse than when perpetrated by the individual. The man who attains to power and mastery, real power, real mastery, never makes use of his godhood for selfish reasons. The magician always breaks his magic wand eventually. Shakespeare understood that when he wrote *The Tempest*. Whitman demonstrated it when he elected to live the life of the common man. The Bodhisattva realizes it in renouncing the bliss of Nirvana. The whole world will understand and realize this simple truth eventually, slowly, one by one, through endless trial and error. The miraculous nature of power is made clear to us by those who renounced it. Power is in the being, not the having. Power is everywhere, in the tiniest atom as much as in the dynamo. Those who know the secret of it are those who realize that it is free and that it destroys those who would possess it and use it for their own glorification. Murder is the crudest manifestation of power. Murder is fear in the service of a ghost.

Since the democratic wars, which began with Napoleon, the passion for making war has dwindled. The manner in which America went to war in 1917 is significant. Never before in the history of the world had there been coined the slogan—*"a war to end war."* We failed in our high purpose because we were unwilling to accept the responsibility which this magnificent gesture entailed. We were *not* without selfish motives, as we pretended. Hand in hand with the desire to bring about the end of all war was the desire to "make the world safe for democracy." Not real democracy, but the American brand. We did not open the way to debate and experiment. We only enabled our allies, who were full of fear and greed, to reestablish dominion over the defeated. We stood by and watched them shackle and manacle their victims. We did everything possible to abort the one promising experiment which the war brought about.

Now the task has to be performed all over again, this time at greater cost, greater risk, greater sacrifice. During the twenty years of moral stagnation which followed upon the last war the great body of Americans became more than ever disillusioned about making war. We waited to be attacked. We knew we would be attacked. We invited it. It was the only way to salve our conscience. We gained nothing from the last war, not even the gratitude of those whom we saved from destruction. We start out even more confused this time, avowedly to save our own skins and rather shamefacedly to save the world. *We will not save the world*—let us admit that immediately. If God could not do it, by sending his only begotton Son, how can we, a people swollen with pride and self-satisfaction? It doesn't matter whether you believe in the Christ story or not. The legend is profound and tragically beautiful. It has truth in it. The Son of God came to awaken the world by his example. *How he lived* is the important thing, not how he died. We are all crucified, whether we know it or not.

Nations reflect the cowardice and selfishness of the peoples which constitute them. It may have been possible once to serve God and country simultaneously. That is no longer true. The peoples of the earth have a great and compelling urge to unite. The boundaries established by nationalism are no longer valid. People are now murdering one another in a confused effort to break down these boundaries. Those who realize the true nature of the issue are at peace, even though they wield the sword.

Freedom without self-mastery is a snare and a delusion. Do we want power over others, or do we want liberation? The true liberators want to establish a world in which there is neither master nor slave, the democracy which Lincoln advocated. The warrior of the future will murder freely, without orders from above. He will murder whatever is murderous in human nature. He will not be an avenger but a liberator. He will not fight to destroy an "ism" but to destroy the destroyers, *whoever* they be and *wherever* they be. He will go on fighting even after peace is declared. He will make war until war becomes the lifeless thing which at heart it is.

*Murder, murder!* It's a fascinating subject. No end to it, seemingly. You know what it's like to kill a spider, an ant, a fly, a mosquito. You do it automatically, without the least compunction. Somehow it's not so easy to adopt that attitude with regard to human beings, even when the latter are annoying or dangerous, as the case may be. In a war such as the present one human beings are being polished off like fleas. To imagine the possibilities ahead, should we really discover that human Flit I spoke of, is almost unthinkable. Right now, at this point in the game, it is difficult to say whether the discoverer would be hailed as a saviour or an enemy to human society. If he springs from *our* side of the fence he will probably be looked upon as the saviour of mankind; if from the other side then as the Devil incarnate. *Is that so, or isn't it?* It's a moral dilemma of the first water. The so-called honest citizen who, in casting his vote for Tweedledum or Tweedledee feels that he has done his duty by the State, will of course refuse to occupy his mind with such a moral problem. It's too fantastic, too remote. He went to the polls last election, both sides promising to keep him out of the war, and he cast a mighty vote. Then the dirty Japs came and stabbed us in the back. Of course neither Tweedledum nor Tweedledee had expected such a dénouement. They were aghast, both of them, at such perfidy. And so war was solemnly declared. We were attacked by a treacherous enemy, our honor was violated. Just yesterday I saw Roosevelt and Churchill posing for the photographers. They were sitting side by side, and Roosevelt was beaming all over. Churchill looked a ringer for Schweik the good soldier. These are the heavenly twins who are going to save the world for us. Angelic creatures, I must say. Mind you, there'll be a bit of hard sledding first. We may have to sacrifice twenty-five or thirty million men, to say nothing of the enemy's losses. But when it's over there'll be an end of Hitler and Mussolini—and perhaps of that feeble-minded yellow-bellied Emperor Hirohito. It'll be worth it, what! A year from now, or two years or five or ten or twenty, we may have the pleasure of again seeing our two leaders arm in arm—when it comes time to inspect the graves of the dead. They will have to go places to bless all the dead this time. But with new inventions coming along they will probably be able to visit all the graves in jig time. If any one reading these lines imagines for one moment that it wasn't necessary to sacrifice all these lives I advise him to keep his mouth closed. There *was* no other way out, you understand. Over 200,000,000 people, hypnotized by their insane leaders, refused to see that the democratic way of life is the best. Somehow, possibly because of the bad example we gave them, they remained unconvinced. Or perhaps they were just lazy-minded and decided that, if they had to fight, they might as well fight for their own way of life. That's a possibility too. Anyway, under the divine tutelage of Roosevelt and Churchill, we are now going to convince them—by extirpating them. Stalin will have something to say about it too, don't forget, because for the moment he's a democrat too. Good old Stalin! Only a few months ago he was an assassin, a fiend who was putting to death a helpless little country like Finland.[1] Some say that Stalin is even more democratic than Roosevelt or Churchill, believe it or not. They say he doesn't trust his democratic partners completely. I don't know why, because our hands are clean, we always act above board, as they say. We never help the little countries unless they're on the right side of the fence. *Strictly neutral*—until we're attacked and our own rights placed in jeopardy! Spain, Greece, Holland, Denmark, Belgium, Norway— we've always given them fine words of encouragement, haven't we? Gentleman-like, you know. Even with a big country like China we were behaving strictly according to Hoyle—until the Pearl Harbor fiasco. No more scrap-iron now for the dirty Japs—we're through with them. China, you will be rescued too—just wait a bit! *And India?* Well now, that's a horse of another color. Don't be so impatient, dear India. You will be freed, in time. Roosevelt and Churchill will arrange everything—when the proper moment comes. First we must get Hitler—he's the one who's responsible for this terrible mess. Impossible even to think straight until he's eliminated. You see how it is, don't you? *Be reasonable!*

Suppose we win the war, as we undoubtedly will, because we *must*, don't you know. Every one will get a square deal, including Hitler, Mussolini and Hirohito the feeble-minded yellow-belly. Austria will become Austrian again; Czechoslovakia Czechoslovakian; Poland Polish; Denmark Danish; France French; Hungary Hungarian; Greece Greek; China Chinese; Finland Finnish; Latvia Latvian; Spain Spanish. Et cetera, et cetera, et cetera. Everything will be put in place again, just as it was before Hitler. It will be a new A. D. for the world, only this time everybody will have to

[1] Now he's putting her to death again, but this time it's O.K.—she deserved to

182

be satisfied. We won't stand for any grousing. Wilhelmina must be put back on her throne. Haakon must be put back on *his* throne. (That is, if they're still alive and hankering for the job.) Hirohito of course must die, and so must Hitler and Mussolini. We've had enough of these bastards—they damned near ruined the world. And when we polish these maniacs off we don't want any revolution to spring up either. None of that nonsense this time. Revolutions are not democratic—they're disturbing, that's what. The Russian revolution, of course, was different. They made a good job of it, as we see now twenty years later. There *are* exceptions, naturally. But all that is in the past. Russia has been doing magnificently recently—just like any other democratic country. In fact, almost too good. We want her to act discreetly when this affair is over. Stalin, no monkey business! Yes, we've got to go cautiously when it comes to re-arranging the world. A little country like Bosnia or Croatia—an "enclave," we call it—can cause a lot of trouble. And then there's France, don't forget. Now she's half Vichy and half Pluto. We've got to fuse or weld the irreconcilables—gently, skillfully, of course. With an acetylene torch, if necessary. Can't allow France to slip back into a monarchical form of government. That would be disastrous. The monarchy is all right for Norway, Belgium, Holland and such like—or for England. But not for France. Why? Well *because* . . .

You see, there are going to be little problems coming up. We must be patient and willing to cooperate. That is, *they* must, the other fellows. We wouldn't be sacrificing the lives and fortunes of our good honest citizens did we not know what we were about. We honestly avoided the issue as long as possible, did we not? We had been worried about the world, what it was coming to, ever since Hitler began his crazy antics. But it wasn't our place to interfere—until we were ourselves attacked and dishonored—and by a half-witted yellow-belly of all things. That really was unforgivable. And yet, if he hadn't spat in our face, who knows—perhaps we wouldn't yet be ready to assume the task of putting the world in order. We have nothing to gain from this conflict. That's clear to every one, I hope. All we want is to see the restoration of the old status quo. We've kept all the maps of the ancient world; we know just what belongs to whom, and we're going to see to it that what's his name gets his what not. And this time, dear fellow-Europeans, dear Chinese, dear Hindus, dear Patagonians, dear Eskimos, dear Zulus, dear Zombies, we want to be spared the humiliation of receiving a kick in the slats for our pains. Though we had to wait until we were treacherously attacked by that degenerate son of the Sun, we do not intend to stop fighting once we have driven the invader from our colonial outposts. We took a terrible slap in the face, but it was good for us, it enabled us to get properly worked up about the plight of the world. To be "the arsenal of the world" was all right as political propaganda—because at bottom, you know, we just loathe and abhor war—but now that we can use the arsenal ourselves we feel better. War is a nasty thing to watch, but once you're in it you feel differently about it. If you want to see an all-out war, boy, just keep your eye on us! We'll fry them alive, every man, woman and child that opposes us. Yes sir, no holding us back once we get our dander up. Nagasaki will look like a flaming rum omelette once we concentrate our attention on it. Berlin too, I'm telling you. And if it weren't for the Pope and his dear Vatican, I'd say the same for Rome. But that's a ticklish proposition, the Vatican. We don't want to blow up his Holiness the Pope accidentally. That's understandable, is it not? The Pope stands for peace—almost at any price. We all do, as a matter of fact—it's only in this matter of the price that we differ from one another. Even the Crusaders were peaceable souls. But they wanted Christ's bones to be left untouched, to lie in Christian soil. And so they fought tooth and nail to destroy the infidels. Some of them returned with the most amazing booty—but that's another story. I was almost on the point of saying that the civilization of Europe began with the return of the victorious Crusaders—you know, Chartres, Amiens, Beauvais, Notre Dame. It would be strange now, wouldn't it, if our Crusaders came back from Moscow and Leningrad, after signing the Peace Treaty, and found themselves afire with the spirit of collective government. That *would* give a queer twist to the situation. Let's hope that the good democratic spirit will survive all temptation. After all, it's a Christian world that we want to save, isn't it? To-morrow is Christmas day and we Christians all over the world will unite in prayer, as we have been doing for nigh on to two thousand years. It seems a little discouraging, perhaps, that after two thousand years we are praying for peace in full uniform, but that's not our fault. If it hadn't been for Hitler and that yellow-faced pagan Hirohito, we'd probably be at peace, isn't that so? It's amazing how, just when we get set for the millennium, some warmonger comes along and upsets our equilibrium. Fortunately we have our own dialectic. That instructs us how to build a permanent peace while being realistically on the alert to make war whenever and wherever necessary. We know what the goal is, which is more, I suppose, than one can say for Hitler and his satellites. The goal is Peace—but to get there you would be a damned fool if you didn't keep a revolver, or at least a hand grenade, in your hip pocket. There have always been, and there still are apparently, two kinds of people in the world: those who want peace and those who want war. Logic dictates that the peaceable ones must extinguish the war-like ones. That is to say, in order to be peaceful you must be a better fighter than the warrior. It sounds like a conundrum at first, but then the history of the world has demonstrated that it is very clear and simple. Wars are getting less and less frequent. We've had about six or eight wars in my life-time, but that's nothing compared to years ago. Before Napoleon's day only professional armies waged war. Nowadays everybody fights—to bring about peace. The last fight will be a splendid one, I'm sure of it. We've only begun to fight, as the saying goes. You see, the more peaceful we get the better we fight. If we were just fighting to fight we might grow slack, because even fighting can grow dull and monotonous if you think only of fighting. But to fight for peace—that's marvelous. That puts iron in you. When the millennium comes we'll all be tough as steel. We'll know how to enjoy peace, just as a murderer learns to enjoy the electric chair. In his zeal to kill, the murderer forgets about the electric chair—but it's always there, always waiting for him. That's his bliss, and when he sizzles and fries he realizes it and thanks the Creator for having made him a murderer. So it is with us. In our zeal to destroy the enemies of peace we forget that war brings about the death and destruction of all that is human and sacred. Peace awaits us, yes—but it is the peace of the grave. The only peace we seem capable of understanding is the peace of death. We make one grand crusade after another in order to rescue the tomb of Christ from the hands of the infidel. We preserve the dead Christ, never the living one. Merry Christmas, I say, and peace on earth! I will not step into St. Patrick's Cathedral to offer up a prayer. I will not appeal to an impotent God to stop the carnage. I will not stand like a savage before the altar of superstition with a javelin in my hand and a mumbo-jumbo incantation on my lips. I will not ask the Creator to bless America without including Japan, Germany, Italy, Roumania, Bulgaria, Hungary and the other countries of the world. I cannot consider myself as innocent and the other fellow guilty. I am not a hypocrite, neither am I an ignoramus, though the society in which I was reared has done its best to make me behave like both. I say that peace can be brought about any time—*when we want it!* We have found the cunning and the ingenuity to invent the most diabolical weapons of destruction. We are versed in the art of war as no people before us has ever been. War is what we wanted—not peace! And now we have it, I say once again: "Merry Christmas! And a happy New Year!"

The above is scarcely off the typewriter when, on my way to lunch (it is the day before Christmas), I pick up the N. Y. *Post*. At the Italian restaurant, where I usually eat, I spread it open and lo! I come upon the following:

## "CHRISTMAS IN MOSCOW"

### by

### A. T. Steele

It's not about Christmas at all because, as the correspondent explains in his special radio to *The Post*, December 25th will be just another working day to the Russian people. Christmas will come on January 7th in Moscow. No, it's about the failure of the Germans to celebrate Christmas in Moscow this year. There are two items in this message which have a little of the Christmas spirit in them. The first is this:

"I keep thinking of that callow boy with silky growth of down on his cheeks who lay under a snow-burdened fir tree on the battlefield at Klin, which I visited the other day. He was one of many German dead, but I noticed him especially because of his youth, the bandage half wrapped around his head and the way his frozen eyes looked unseeingly upward. He had apparently been wounded and had died of cold.

"Young Otto Seiter is probably listed on Hitler's casualty rolls

187

as 'missing.' But I know he is dead. He won't be home this Christmas or any other Christmas. There are a lot like him."

He goes on to speak of the letters which he retrieved from the battlefield, letters of German wives and mothers to their men and boys. "They make appropriate reading for Christmas Eve," he cables, "because they remind you of something you are prone to forget in the heat of the war—that enemy soldiers are not beasts or monsters but human beings who have been hypnotized into blind allegiance to the mad idea of a half-mad leader. Scarcely any of these letters mentioned politics and only one of them closed with the salutation 'Heil Hitler' . . . In all the letters I examined . . . I found no words of bitterness against the Russians."

Yes, I agree—it sure does make appropriate reading for Christmas Eve. It's rather edifying, if I may say so. *Read it again, please.*

On the front page of this same journal the Pope gives his Five Points for Peace. Also very edifying. The trouble is nobody pays a damned bit of attention to the Pope. He's just a symbol of spiritual power. Anyway, among the other things he says: "True respect for treaties must be observed, and the principles of freedom and equality of rights for all people must underlie the new day." It's obvious that His Holiness is also a forward looker. There's such a gentle, passive, civilized note to his plea—might have been written by Woodrow Wilson himself. I'm making a note to have the Viking Press send him a copy of *The Bertrand Russell Case.* In praying for peace so assiduously this little drama of spiritual sabotage by the good Catholics of America may have escaped his attention.

*If some one should give us Germany and Japan this minute, we would be so embarrassed we would hardly know what to do or say . . . We do not have the smallest notion of what we are going to do when we win. We are hopelessly unprepared for victory . . . We must face the truth. The hardest blow that could strike us at*

188

*the moment would be victory. We would pass it from hand to hand as if it were hot, and would not know where to set it down. Our Congress once did conduct some rather magnificent debates as to what to do with new territories as they came into the democratic system. We even discussed whether there should be slavery or freedom in the new States. Both houses now sit tight, with nothing to say. Not to be able to put into specific, hard words the things the Colin Kellys are dying for is a confession of ineptness.*

These are not my words, dear, gentle reader. These come to you through the courtesy of the N. Y. *Post* on Christmas Eve. They were written by Samuel Grafton in his column called "I'd Rather Be Right." And most of the time, to do him justice, he is right. Sometimes he's so damned right that it almost sounds treasonable. But everybody knows that Sam is on the right side; he can get away with murder.

I wish I had a little joke to tell now. It's such a solemn moment, and we've been through so many like it before. "Now is the time," as Dorothy Thompson says, "for the United States to wage the most brilliant psychological warfare against Germany and Italy and amongst the people of Europe." (Why leave out the Japs, I wonder?) "But," she adds, "no strategy of psychological warfare has been developed, and no command and staff capable of waging it have been created."

Yes, as Dorothy says—"it is a negligence which will prolong the war, and it should be remedied immediately." But then, if you follow Sam Grafton's reasoning, on the same page, you will see that we need a little time—because we haven't the least idea yet what our victory program should be. It's a bit confusing, to say the least.

A little joke, as I was saying a minute ago. Yes, Lincoln had his little joke just before reading the Emancipation Proclamation. In-

189

cidentally, you would think, if you were not a student of history, that the Emancipation Proclamation came first, and then the attack on Fort Sumter. But no, it was the other way round. It's like the Pope again. He talks about good, honest to God peace treaties, about non-persecution of the Church et cetera, before he knows what the outcome of the war will be. Anyway, the story goes that Lincoln had called his cabinet members together on a very important matter. The war was on some time already and the dead were rather numerous, to say nothing of the halt, the blind, the maimed, the mutilated. Lincoln has a book in front of him—by Artemas Ward. He reads a passage aloud to the assembled scarecrows and he laughs heartily in doing so. Nobody else laughs. So he tries it again. And again he laughs fit to burst his sides. But the gravediggers look askance. They are at a loss to understand this ill-timed hilarity. Has he gone off his nut, they wonder? Lincoln feels sorry for them—for their lack of humor. It's a good book, he tells them, and you ought to sit down and read it. It would do you a world of good. Something like that. Then he quietly reaches into the tail pocket of his flap-doodle walking coat and, extracting the Emancipation Proclamation, he reads it to them quietly and solemnly . . . Whether it be true or not, it's a damned good story. Lincoln had his feet on the ground, as we would say. But his head was in the clouds. He had a quiet, sure confidence that right would prevail—in the end. He was ready to sacrifice any number of lives, his own included, to bring about that end. "As I would not be a *slave*, so I would not be a *master*. This expresses my idea of democracy. Whatever differs from this, to the extent of the difference, is no democracy." Those are Lincoln's words. It's a pity we never gave heed to them. We freed the black slaves, or we thought we had, but we forgot to free the white slaves. We freed the Filipinos and the Cubans and the Porto Ricans, but we didn't free ourselves. We rescued France and Belgium from the heels of the German military clique but then we put the Germans in the clink. So now, while Russia deals the death-blow to the Germans, we're getting ready to wipe out Hitlerism and all the other isms, as well as that degenerate yellow-bellied Hirohito.

Nobody can deny that we're the most philanthropic-minded people in the world. A few months ago there were eight or nine million people unemployed in this wonder-working land. Now it's down to about a million, an irreducible minimum, I believe it's called. We work fast, I'll say. And all because that half-witted Hirohito stabbed us in the back. Some say we had no right to be taken by surprise—criminal negligence they call it. Others seem pleased that it turned out so—it proved that we were angels, that we had no intention of going to war with Japan, that our fleet and our fortifications were created only to *frighten* the enemy away. It's six one way and a half dozen the other. I was always of the opinion that if you make cannon you've got to use them some time or other. I'm never surprised when a gun goes off unexpectedly. I expect the unexpected. What does surprise me is that people who believe in making cannon should be aggrieved to see them used so effectively. "In time of peace prepare for war," said the Father of this beloved country. He was a realist, just as Stalin is to-day. He didn't get himself elected a third time by promising to keep his people out of war. He was no half-wit. No sir, he was an aristocrat, a great land-holder with slaves and port and sherry in the cellar. The people were so grateful to him for making this country a democracy that they almost made him a king. About seventy years later there appeared in the State of Massachusetts, noted even then for its hypocrisy, repression and iniquity, a troublesome character who sensed that all was not well with the government of these United States. What's more, he had the courage to say so. He wrote a paper called "Civil Dis-

191

obedience" which we look upon to-day as a monument to the democratic spirit. Here is a citation from this beautifully embalmed document:

"The progress from an absolute to a limited monarchy, from a limited monarchy to a democracy, is a progress towards a true respect for the individual. Even the Chinese philosopher was wise enough to regard the individual as the basis of the empire. Is a democracy, such as we know it, the last improvement possible in government? Is it not possible to take a step further towards recognizing and organizing the rights of man? There will never be a really free and enlightened State until the State comes to recognize the individual as a higher and independent power, from which all its own power and authority are derived, and treats him accordingly. I please myself with imagining a State at last which can afford to be just to all men, and to treat the individual with respect as a neighbor; which even would not think it inconsistent with its own repose if a few were to live aloof from it, not meddling with it, nor embraced by it, who fulfilled all the duties of neighbors and fellow-men. A State which bore this kind of fruit, and suffered it to drop off as fast as it ripened, would prepare the way for a still more perfect and glorious State, which also I have imagined, but not yet anywhere seen."

That was Henry David Thoreau, author of *Walden* and defender of John Brown, speaking. No doubt the only excuse we can make to-day for such a treasonable anarchistic utterance is to palm him off as a half-witted graduate of the then Transcendentalist School of Philosophy. About the only person I can think of who would have dared to defend him, in our time, had he openly expressed his desire to live a life apart from the most holy and sacrosanct State, is the recently defunct Justice of the Supreme Court, Louis D. Brandeis. In the case of Whitney versus the State of California,

Brandeis, whose vote was overruled, wrote a brief in which there appeared these words:

"Those who won our independence by revolution were not cowards. They did not fear political change. They did not exalt order at the cost of liberty. To courageous, self-reliant men, with confidence in the power of free and fearless reasoning applied through the processes of popular government, no danger flowing from speech can be deemed clear and present, unless the incidence of evil apprehended is so imminent that it may befall before there is opportunity for full discussion. If there be time to expose through discussion the falsehood and fallacies, to avert the evil by the processes of education, the remedy to be applied is more speech, not enforced silence. Only an emergency can justify repression. Such must be the rule if authority is to be reconciled with freedom. Such, in my opinion, is the command of the Constitution. It is, therefore, always open to Americans to challenge a law abridging free speech and assembly by showing that there was no emergency justifying it."

Nevertheless, when the good shoe-maker and the poor fish-peddler found themselves at the bar of justice in the benighted State of Massachusetts some few years ago, they were unable to get a fair, honest hearing. Despite all the noble words handed down by the upstanding members of the judiciary, and they are the wordiest people on God's green earth, Sacco and Vanzetti were foully murdered. But just before he went to the chair Vanzetti gave birth to a few lines which are destined to be as immortal as any of Lincoln's or Jefferson's . . .

"If it had not been for these thing, I might have live out my life talking at street corners to scorning men. I might have died, unmarked, unknown, a failure. Now we are not a failure. This is our career and our triumph. Never in our full life could we hope to do such work for tolerance, for joostice, for man's understanding of man as now we do by accident. Our words—our lives—our pains—nothing! The taking of our lives—lives of a good shoemaker and a poor fish-peddler—all! That last moment belongs to us—that agony is our triumph."

A few days ago, moved by the President's declaration of war the newspapers gave some space to the remarks made by John Haynes Holmes, Minister of the Community Church, N. Y., in tendering his resignation. He had just finished a sermon, it seems, on the 150th anniversary of the Bill of Rights. Mr. Holmes is quoted as saying that "neither as clergyman nor as citizen would he participate in the war," adding however that "neither would he oppose, obstruct or interfere with officials, soldiers or citizens in the performance of what they regard as their patriotic duty."

Then he threw this bombshell:

"I will be loyal and obedient to my government, and loyal and obedient to my God; and when these loyalties conflict, I will choose, as did the Apostles, to 'obey God rather than men.'"

I wait to see if Mr. Holmes will be condemned to prison. In the last world war there were three great figures who, because they openly announced their opposition to war, suffered dire persecution. They were Romain Rolland, Bertrand Russell and Eugene V. Debs. Unimpeachable characters, all three. I'm going to give you Debs' speech on being condemned to prison, but before I do so I want to mention the Very Reverend Dean Inge's statement about a German theologian named Harnack. "War," writes the gloomy Dean, "is a very horrible thing, an unmixed evil, a reversion to barbarism no less than cannibalism, human sacrifice and judicial torture. Most of us think that we were obliged to resist German agression, which threatens to extinguish liberty, and with liberty all that makes life worth living, over the whole continent of Europe. But no good can ever come out of war. It is a flat negation of Christianity. Even Harnack, a Prussian and the most learned theologian in Europe, said that it is futile to deny that Christ condemned war absolutely." He adds that the Quakers believe they are the only consistent Christians. And what is the history of the Quaker movement? According to recent authority on the subject, the Quaker movement was met with terrific persecution, first from mob violence and later from organized legal procedure. George Fox himself endured eight imprisonments, and more than fifteen thousand Quakers were imprisoned in England before the period of toleration, of whom three hundred and sixty-six died under their sufferings. Four Quakers were hanged on Boston Common and a great number in the American Colonies endured beatings and mutilation.

To-day the Quakers are exempt from military service, in these United States. But what a battle! A man who is not a Quaker, like Eugene V. Debs for example, gets it in the neck. Yet no Quaker could have made a more simple, honest, dignified statement of his views than did Eugene V. Debs. Here are his beautiful, moving words:

"Gentleman of the Jury, I am accused of having obstructed the war. I admit it. Gentlemen, I abhor war. I would oppose the war if I stood alone. When I think of a cold, glittering steel bayonet being plunged in the white, quivering flesh of a human being, I recoil with horror.

"Men talk about holy wars. There are none. War is the trade of unholy savages and barbarians . . .

"Gentlemen of the Jury, I am accused of being unpatriotic. I object to that accusation. It is not true. I believe in patriotism. I have never uttered a word against the flag. I love the flag as a symbol of freedom . . .

"I believe, however, in a wider patriotism. Thomas Paine said, 'My country is the world. To do good is my religion.' That is the sort of patriotism I believe in. I am an Internationalist. I believe that nations have been pitted against nations long enough in hatred, in strife, in warfare. I believe there ought to be a bond of unity between all of these nations. I believe that the human race consists of one great family. I love the people of this country, but I don't hate a human being because he happens to be born in some other country. Why should I? Like myself, he is the image of his Creator. I would infinitely rather serve him and love him than to hate him and kill him . . .

"Yes, I am opposed to killing him. I am opposed to war. I am perfectly willing on that account to be branded as a traitor. And if it is a crime under the American law to be opposed to human bloodshed, I am perfectly willing to be branded as a criminal and to end my days in a prison cell . . .

"And now, Gentlemen of the Jury, I am prepared for the sentence. I will accept your verdict. What you will do to me does not matter much. Years ago I recognized my kinship with all living beings, and I made up my mind that I was not one whit better than the meanest of earth. I said then, and I say now, that while there is a lower class, I am in it; while there is a criminal element, I am of it; while there is a soul in prison, I am not free."


"Unless from us the future takes place, we are death only," said D. H. Lawrence. A monumental statement. Meanwhile death is piling up all around us. The political and military leaders, if they do not actually make light of it, discount it as they would a promptly paid bill. The bill is victory, they say, and they are willing to pay in advance no matter how many millions of lives it costs. They are even ready to sacrifice their own lives, but fortunately for them most of them are so placed that the risk is slight. When the war is ended the victory will be theirs, no gainsaying it. The dead won't count, nor the millions of maimed and mutilated ones who will go on living until death robs them of the fruits of victory.

Death, especially on a wholesale scale, can raise an awful stench. On the battle-fronts now and then a truce is declared to give the opposing forces an opportunity to bury their dead. It has never occurred to the political and military cliques that it might be an excellent innovation to incorporate among the polite rules of civilized warfare a clause stipulating that every thirty or sixty days a truce shall be declared (for twenty-four hours, let us say) to reconsider the supposed basis of the erstwhile conflict. What would happen, I wonder, if the armies waging war all over the earth, and the friends and relatives supporting these armies, could pause every so often in the process of blood-letting and honestly examine their conscience? Supposing further—and now we get really fantastic—that during these let-ups a vote could be taken on both sides of the fence to see whether the fight should be continued or not. It is not altogether impossible to imagine that perhaps only the higher officers of the armies and navies, together with the congressmen and of course the various dictators, would be in favor of continuing with the slaughter. The great body of men and women, the ones of whom the great sacrifice is being demanded, would most likely yell for peace. Perhaps even "peace at any price"! *If they were given an honest chance!*

The stench of death . . . One day we read that 4,000 Germans were killed on the Russian front. Another day it may be 16,000 or 23,000. Fine! *Progress*, we say. Or, if we wipe out a nest of dirty Japs, still better . . . *bully!* According to this logic, the most magnificent step forward that we could make would be to annihilate them utterly. (Let's get busy and trot out that human Flit I was talking about earlier!) Now the military man will tell you, and utterly sincerely too, that annihilation of the enemy is not the goal at all. The objective, according to the military expert, is merely to render *hors de combat* the enemy's army or navy, as the case may be. That accomplished, the war is won. If it can be done without loss of life, so much the better. The most brilliant defeat that could be inflicted, from the standpoint of these experts, would be a bloodless one. That would indeed be something to record in the annals of history! That would make war look quite jolly, for a change. It would be most superlatively magnificent: a super-duper sort of victory, if you get what I mean. Some people credit Hitler with having had some such idea. He had it all figured out—it was to be a push-over, as we say.

However, to get back to war as we know it, nothing like this is going to happen in our time. War now means just as it did in the past, "blood, sweat and tears"—oodles of it. Not blood, sweat and tears for those who launch it, but for those who have to go through with it. And that means practically everybody, except, as I said before, the favored few who direct the show. The latter are just as eager to give their lives as the little fellows, don't make any mistake about that. Only, because of the peculiar set-up involved in these fracases, they are somehow never privileged to enjoy this supreme sacrifice. They must be protected in order that the others can be most efficiently sacrificed. You can understand what anguish this causes the political and military leaders of any war. (Yet few of them ever pine away because of it. On the contrary, they seem to grow tough as steel.) However, if it were possible to take them by surprise, assure them that nothing they said would be held against them, it's just possible you'd discover that they were fed up with it too. A moment later, to be sure, they would be ready to deny such weak sentiments. "What would the people think?"

they'd say. Always that to fall back on. *The people!* It was the people who wanted the war. Of course. Yes, when they're stabbed in the back the people may cry for war, *but*—how does it happen that they get stabbed in the back, and at just the right moment? And so, right or wrong, willing or unwilling, "the war must be fought to a just and victorious conclusion!" From time immemorial every leader has proclaimed that high and mighty truth. That's why the future is always so full of death. Right or wrong, the war must be continued, always. No looking back. No looking forward. *Head down and charge!* That's the order of the day. Victory? Just around the corner. And if not victory, death. Death, death, death. Always death. Or, if you're lucky, your old job back in the mines. The future? It never begins. You had your future yesterday, don't you remember? There is only the present, and the present is never pleasant. Only the future is bright. But then, the future never takes place. The future always recedes, that's the law. When the original Fascists have been vanquished, or exterminated, we'll all be Fascists —that's what the future, if there is to be any future, promises. And that means more death, more blood, sweat and tears, more Churchills, more Roosevelts, more Hitlers, more Stalins. There won't be any more Mussolinis, probably, because he for one has been thoroughly exploded. But there may be another Hirohito, and mark my words, he'll be a yellow-belly too.

It's going to be a lovely world to-morrow, when everything is properly organized and running smoothly. It may take a hundred years, but what's that (Man lives in the eternal—*when he lives.*) There may even be another war—or several—between times, but that shouldn't disturb us any. We got through this one, didn't we? You see the logic . . . it runs as smooth as tooth-paste from an old-fashioned tube. Incidentally, you won't have to worry about tooth-paste when the New Day is ushered in; we'll all be fitted with

199

Dr. Cowen's beautiful light-weight platinum teeth. Only cows will chew with their own teeth in the future. Everything's going to be under control, you'll see. Should a new enemy arise (though it's hard to see why he should, with Utopia just in the offing), we'll know how to deal with him. Nothing must or shall hinder our plans for the world-wide improvement of the human race. The human race, of course, will not be understood to include such inferior peoples as the Zulus and the Hottentots, for example. No sir, let's not fall into that sublime error. Only people walking around in pants, with Bibles in their hands and platinum teeth in their mouths, and preferably only those speaking the English language, will be regarded as belonging to the human race.

Utopia, then, will be a world in which the white race (half Slav, half Anglo-Saxon) will know no enemies and will have as neighbors such harmless peoples as the Javanese, the Hindus, the Malays, and perhaps the Arabs too—if they behave. On the fringe of our tremendous colonial possessions there will be the not-quite-human species, who are no longer a menace . . . in other words, the primitives. These will gradually be absorbed into the blood-stream by the process of higher education. They will be "our little brown brothers," so to speak, and will work for us (willingly, of course) like bees and ants. For how otherwise will they be able to make themselves fit to enjoy the fruits of civilization?

There will be only two languages to begin with: Russian and English. After a time the Russians will give up their mother tongue and speak English only. What the Chinese and Hindus will speak will hardly concern us since, though numerically superior, perhaps even morally and spiritually superior, they will be of no consequence in the management of a Utopian world. As for the primitives, they have survived these last fifty to a hundred thousand years without the knowledge of English, so why worry?

There will be no money, of course. Not even the hat money of the Penangs. As it used to say on the silver dollar: *e pluribus unum!* The bookkeeper will be eliminated, and the breed of lawyers too, since most litigation arises over money transactions. The absence of money will also solve the debt problem which arises after every war to end war. No money, no debts! *All for one and one for all,* just like it said once on the silver dollar. The New Deal will go into effect throughout the whole pluralistic universe. Naturally there will have to be a new flag: the flag of Utopia. I should imagine it will be pure white, signifying "peace, purity, and forgiveness of sins." No emblem will be needed, not even the hammer and sickle . . . not even a *plastic* hammer and sickle. Nothing but a white piece of cloth—of the finest material. Under this banner, for the first time in the history of mankind, everybody will get a break, perhaps even the Zulus and the Hottentots. War will be a thing of the past; all our enemies will be dead or incapacitated. Should any new ones threaten to arise, get out the Flit! Simple, what! No need for standing armies any longer. Just oodles of Flit—and a big squirt gun. To be sure, it may be necessary to do a bit of wholesale murdering—clean house, so to speak—before all the enemy are eliminated. It may take ten to twenty years to eradicate the last Jap, German, Bulgarian, Roumanian, Hungarian, Finn or other human pest, but we'll do it, we'll weed them out like vipers. The problem will be what to do with those of mixed blood. It will take a Solomon to decide that issue. However, with the education and training heretofore wasted in turning out admirals, generals and field marshals, we shall undoubtedly pave the way for the emergence of several Solomons. If necessary we can import a few from India or China.

With war eliminated and money eliminated, with the breed of lawyers and bookkeepers wiped out, with politics converted to management, with Solomons sitting in judgment upon all grave matters of dispute, can any intelligent person visualize even the possibility of a miscarriage? Under the slogan "all for one and one for all" the earth will slowly but surely be transformed into a Paradise. There will be no more struggle, except to surpass one another in virtue. There will be no more pain, except that which doctors and dentists impose. We will love one another to death.

Truly, if people would only realize what a glorious future is about to unroll, would they not this instant get down on their knees and devoutly offer up thanks to those great benefactors—Stalin, Churchill, Roosevelt and Madame Chiang Kai-shek? If they were to think about the matter profoundly, would they not also bless Hitler and Mussolini, and above all that yellow-bellied Hirohito, because, if these angelic monsters had not unleashed this grim catastrophe, we would never have thought to usher in the millennium. How true the saying: "It's an ill wind that blows no one some good!" In glory and significance all other wars pale before this one. That Ireland, Sweden, Spain, Portugal, Switzerland, India, Argentina have not evinced the spirit of the crusader is regrettable, but they will doubtless see the wisdom of this heroic strife when we make life more comfortable for them. With the Utopia to follow upon the close of this war the neutral countries will enjoy the same privileges and advantages as the ones that went to war.

The question may arise: what will become of the instinct to kill, which is so deep-rooted in the human being? Can an instinct be wholly extirpated? The answer is Yes and No, which is the answer to all fundamental questions. Men will still kill animals, birds of the air, and ground birds too, as well as insects, snakes and microbes. By the time a hundred years have rolled around there will be new, more intangible, still more invisible, creatures—if we may call them such—to kill. Don't worry, there are more millennia to come before killing is killed off altogether. But, if we stop killing one another, that is a big step forward. And that is all we are concerned about on the threshold of this Utopia. Just to stop killing one another en masse. It's taken us a long time to reach this point. Cannibalism has died out, at least among the civilized peoples of the earth. That took quite a long time to disappear, but it disappeared. Incest is no longer in vogue either, nor the practice of suttee, thanks to the humane conquerors of India. No, we should never despair. Every two or three hundred thousand years we make a real step forward. The point is not to take one step forward and three steps backward, which is what human beings usually do. With the facilities offered us by the higher education and all that rigamarole, however, there appears to be little danger that we shall go on repeating our old habit patterns.

If we were there now in that Utopia we all long to establish, and which none of us now living shall ever see, if we were there for just one moment, could take one swift backward glance at that old murderous self which made history so exciting, how odd everything would look to us! See, there stands a man with a javelin in his hand, ready to plunge it into the breast of a fellow man. There is another, with a hand grenade which he is making ready to hurl; when it hits the mark it will explode, and another fellow being, an "enemy," will be blown to bits. Why are they carrying on this way? Because they believe that by killing their fellow men they will make the world a better place to live in. And why are they so afraid of one another, why do they hate each other so? Because they all believe in a god of love. Do they not sense the inconsistent in their behavior? Yes, but they have a logic which accounts for all inconsistencies. By this logic they prove to themselves that to usher in the new life, to bring about the kingdom of heaven on earth, it is first necessary to slaughter all the enemies of mankind. And who are the enemy? You, me, anybody, according to how the wind blows . . .

If we could see it from over the line, this period of ten to twenty thousand years, which has been called civilization, would seem like a night of utter confusion. By comparison the savage lived in clear daylight. Civilization, compared with other periods the human race has lived through, will be like a parenthesis in the preamble to a new way of life. For there *will* be a new way of life, no matter how many wars have to be fought, no matter how many lives are destroyed.

With the conclusion of this war it is not even probable that we shall see the dissolution of national boundaries. To eliminate race prejudice no one can say how many more wars it will require. There are thousands of problems for which men will find no solution but war. No system of government now in vogue offers the slightest hope of a future free of war. The remedy for dissent is still, as it was in the past, subjugation or extirpation. The government has never existed which recognizes the freedom and equality of all men. As for freedom of thought, freedom to express one's ideas—not to speak of living them out—where is the government which ever permitted this? Conformity is the rule, and conformity will be the rule as long as men believe in governing one another.

Men of good-will need no government to regulate their affairs. In every age there is a very small minority which lives without thought of, or desire for, government. These men never brought about a war. So long as civilization lasts it is quite possible that this minority will never be substantially increased. Such men are not the products of our religious organizations or our educational systems; they live outside the cultural pattern of the times. The most we can say, in explanation of their appearance and existence, is that they are evolved beings. And here we must needs touch on the draw-back to all schemes, Utopian or otherwise, for the improvement of human society: the failure inherent in all of them to recognize that the human race does not evolve at the same speed nor with the same rhythm. Where there is dream and wish fulfillment merely—and what else can there be if one focuses on society instead of the indi-vidual?—there is confusion and disillusionment. Even with red-hot bayonets up their rear, men cannot be prodded all at the same time into Paradise. It is this fact, of course, which the so-called real-ists, who are always defeatists, seize upon with grim relish in order to excuse and perpetuate the business of murder. With each war they pretend that they are preserving society from a dire fate, or that they are protecting the weak and the helpless. The men of wisdom, who are really the men of good-will, and who are found in every stratum of society and not in any particular class, never make such pretences. They are often accused of being aloof, re-mote, out of touch with the world. Yet it is to them that all men turn for comfort and guidance in their hour of need. For, even the clod seems to sense that genuine disinterestedness is a source of strength.

If any particular set of men were destined to rule the world it would seem logical that it should be ruled by the men of wisdom. But that is not the case, and there is good reason for it. No one man, no set of men, is capable of ruling the world. The world is ruled by its own inner, mysterious laws. It evolves according to a logic which defies our man-made logic. The higher the type of man, moreover, the less inclined he feels to rule others; he lives in har-mony with the world despite the fact that he is in total disagree-ment with the vast majority, as well as with the leaders of the world. Were there good reason to kill, he could find a thousand justifications to the ordinary man's one. The principal reason, however, for his failure to become embroiled in world conflicts is his absence of fear. Accustomed as he is to live habitually in the world of ideas, he is not frightened when he learns that his neighbor thinks differently from him. Indeed, he might really become alarmed if he found that his neighbors were in agreement with him. The average man, on the contrary, is more frightened of alien ideas than of cold steel or flame throwers. He has spent most of his empty life getting adjusted to the few simple ideas which were thrust on him by his elders or superiors. Anything which menaces this precarious adjustment, which he calls his liberty, throws him into a panic. Let an alien idea become active, and the transition from fear to hate proceeds like clock-work. Trot out the word "enemy," and the whole bloody race behaves as if it had the blind staggers. The nit-wits who never showed the least ability to govern themselves suddenly get the idea that their last mission on earth is to teach the enemy good government. It makes no difference whether this nit-wit be a Communist, Fascist, or Democrat: the reaction is always the same. Just tell him that the other fellow is threatening his liberty, and he reaches for his gun—*automatically*.

And what is the little bundle of ideas around which this precious notion of liberty is formed? Private property, the sanctity of the home, the church he belongs to, the preservation of the political party, or the system, which gives him the privilege of being a drudge all his life. If he could but take one sweeping view of the planet, see what different things the same words mean everywhere, see how all men, including the primitives, believe that whatever they believe is right and just, and of course supremely intelligent, would he be so quick to reach for the sword or the gun? Yes, he would, because he has been educated to understand with his head but not with the rest of his being. As a civilized creature, a man can study and know the ways and customs of a thousand different peoples, yet insist on defending the ways of his own, even though he knows them to be stupid, inadequate or wrong. He will describe with irony and subtle discrimination the reasons why other peoples make war, but he will go to war himself when the time comes, even though he does not believe in killing. He will kill rather than be humiliated by his own people.

In how many wars have people killed who had no desire to kill? Many who killed one another had more in common than with their own compatriots. Were men to seek their real enemies they would have only to turn round and examine the ranks behind them. If men were to realize who their true enemies were, what a scrimmage would ensue! But again, one of the disadvantages of living under civilized rule is that only those may be considered as enemies, and therefore killed or enslaved, whom the governments designate as such. To kill your commanding officer, for example, even though he be the bitterest enemy you have, is strictly taboo. So it goes . . . scholars killing scholars, poets killing poets, workers killing workers, teachers killing teachers, and no one killing the munitions makers, the politicians, the priests, the military idiots or any of the other criminals who sanction war and egg one on to kill one another off.

Just to take one element, the munitions makers, for example: who could be more international-minded than they? Come war and they will sell to any side that has the money to buy. Strictly neutral, these birds, until they see which way the wind blows. No amount of taxation impoverishes them; the longer the war lasts, the more the dead pile up, the fatter they grow. Imagine the colossal absurdity of supporting a body of men whose mission in life it is to supply us with the means of self-destruction. (Whereas it is a crime to attempt to take one's own life by one's own means, no matter how unbearable life becomes!) Nobody considers the munitions maker —not even the Communist, mind you—as an enemy. Yet he is the greatest enemy man has. He sits like a vulture and waits and prays for the day to come when we shall lose our reason and beg him to furnish us with his most expensive lethal products. Instead of being looked upon as a leper he is given a place of honor in human society; often he is knighted for his indubitably dubious services. On the other hand, Monsieur le Paris, who really performs a service for society, albeit a most disagreeable one, is shunned like a pariah. Strange paradox. If there is any logic to it it is thus: the man who by our own sanction justly removes a murderer from the ranks of society is a worthless wretch, whereas the man who provides the means of killing en masse, for no matter what reason good or bad, deserves a place of honor in our midst. Corollary logic: murder on a wholesale scale is always justifiable, as well as profitable and honorable, but ordinary murder, whether for passion or greed, is so disgraceful that even the man whose duty it is to make way with the culprit appears to us as tainted.

And what of all the plans fond parents make for their children's sake? Why bother to make plans when we know for a certainty that in each generation there will be one or more wars? Why not plan to make no plans at all, to just vegetate until the bugle calls? What a waste of time, money and effort to prepare your son for the ministry or the law, or any other pursuit, when you know that the army or navy will get him, and if not the army or navy, then the marines. Why think of training your boy to go into business when the only important business of every new generation is to make war? Talk about common sense . . . what sense is there in pretending that one will engage in peaceful pursuits when the only pursuit we ever enter whole-heartedly, and with vim and vigor, is the pursuit of war? Why not train your son from the beginning to be a killer, an expert killer? Why delude yourself and him too? Sooner or later your boy must learn to kill; the quicker he learns the less pain and disillusionment he will suffer. Don't teach him how to live, teach him how to die! Prepare him not for the pleasures of this world, for the chances are he will never taste them; prepare him for the pleasures of the afterworld. If you find that he is hypersensitive, kill him while he is still young. Better to kill him with your own hands than to let him die at the hands of a ruthless enemy. Kill off all the males, if possible, and let only the females survive. And if the females begin warring with one another, kill them off at birth too. In any case, believe no one who promises you peace and prosperity unless all the munitions makers have been killed off and the machines they employ destroyed.

If the idea that your son must become a killer as well as a provider is abhorrent to you, if you believe that death-dealing weapons should not continue to be manufactured, even if never used, then make a new world in which killing will be unnecessary. Concentrate all your energies upon that, and that alone. If you had a home which you were fond of, and it were suddenly invaded by rats, would you not set everything aside to eliminate the pest? War is the greatest plague that civilized man has had to contend with. And what has he done in all these thousands of years to grapple with the problem? Nothing, really. With the passage of time he has devoted increasing effort, ingenuity and money towards aggrandizing the horrors of war, as though pretending to himself that if war became too horrible it might cease of itself. The greatest nations have ruined themselves in preparing for and making war. Nevertheless the whole civilized world deludes itself into believing (by what amazing self-hypnosis!) that men are becoming better, more humane, more intelligent, more considerate of one another. The truth is that the farther along the path of civilization we go the more diabolical men seem to become. The torture inflicted upon one another by savages is nothing compared to the torture which civilized beings inflict upon one another. (This is true even in times of peace.) Add to this, that in taking over the so-called inferior peoples of the earth, in adapting them to our ways, the price we demand of them is that they become good auxiliary fighters. When there is a particularly dirty job of butchering to be done, we throw in the colonial troops. Progress! Progress!

Moreover, and above all, and to add to the illogical, the inconsistent and the paradoxical—does any serious-minded person believe for one moment that a victorious China, Russia, America, England will not become more militant, more ready and prepared for war, more suited to find fresh problems to quarrel over? Germany and Japan *may* be put out of harm's way. Agreed. But what then? Are they the only enemies man will ever have or could have? Since when have Big Powers agreed with one another, or laid down their arms and become as lambs? Since when have the Big Powers treated Little Powers with equal tact and consideration? And what of the Little Powers, when we have liberated them by our victorious but ruinous campaigns? Will they be grateful and ready to fall in line with our way of life when their people return to the desolate, ruined lands which we turned into a stupendous proving ground? Will they perhaps differ with us as to how life and liberty is to be maintained in the future?

Who will rule the coming world? The strong ones. And who are the strong? America, Russia, England, China. (We have not yet finished with Japan. It remains to be seen if she will be thoroughly subjugated and castrated, or if one of the present Big Powers will form an unholy alliance with her, in order to be better prepared for the next conflict, which already impends.) England, we know, will not give up her Empire willingly. France will demand the restoration of her colonies. So will Holland. Perhaps Italy too. Germany of course will never be allowed to have anything but the air to breathe. As for America, she will relinquish everything, that goes without question. The one great Empire which will remain, and which should long ago have fallen to pieces, is the British Empire. This is only fair and just, because the Four Freedoms, being an Anglo-Saxon conception of justice, does not exclude Empires. France will be allowed to grow strong again, because France is a freedom-loving nation, though also an Empire. But France mustn't grow too strong, for then she might become a menace to England's freedom and security, which is based upon a greed for possessions almost unheard of. Everything will have to be maintained in an equilibrium as delicate as the workings of a Swiss watch. The master minds of the new Entente Cordiale, however, will solve all these intricate problems with ease and dispatch. There is no danger of their quarreling among themselves. Oh no, not the slightest! Russia will remain Communist, England an Empire, America a benevolent Democracy (with Roosevelt at the helm until death), and France Republican. China, of course, will remain a complete chaos, as always. The directors of the great show will see eye to eye on all future major problems; as for the minor problems, the future will take care of these.

The great question, to be sure, which will come up as soon as the war ends, is: who will buy whose goods and how? As for the debt problem, that is easily solved. The people will pay off the debts. The people always pay. Though the people never start a war, nor even a revolution, the government somehow always convinces the people that they must pay for these adventures, both before and after. A war is fought for the benefit of the people. By the time the war is over, however, there are no benefits, just debts, death and desolation. All of which has to be paid for.

This time the peoples who make up the victorious nations won't mind the cost because they will have the Four Freedoms. They will also have all sorts of new machines, new labor-saving devices, which will make work a pleasure. (And the harder they work the faster the debts will be paid off; the more ready they will be, too, for the next war.) Yes, there will be all sorts of new inventions, which, if they are not used destructively, will bring untold bliss. There will be, among other things, new airplanes capable of taking us back and forth to China in twenty-four hours—and for a song! Week-ends the workers of the world will be flying around the globe greeting their fellow-workers in Java, Borneo, Mozambique, Saskatchewan, Tierra del Fuego and such places. No need to go to Coney Island any more, or Deauville, or Brighton—there will be far more interesting places at which to spend the week-end. There will be television, too, don't forget. If you don't care to fly around the world in your spare time you can sit quietly by the hearth and watch the Eskimos climbing up and down the slippery icebergs, or look at the primitive peoples in the jungle busy gathering rice, ivory, coffee, tea, rubber, chicle and other useful commodities for our delectation. Every one will be working blissfully, even the Chinese coolies. For, by that time the vast and all-powerful Chiang Kai-shek dynasty will be operating with the smoothness of a high-powered dynamo. The opium traffic will be wiped out, and the heretofore ignorant coolies will be able to understand and appreciate American movies, which are an excellent substitute for opium. We will probably make special Grade D pictures for them at a figure so absurd that even the lowest coolie will be able to afford the price of admission. We will have Grade K or J pictures for "our little brown brothers" too. We will make chewing gum in greater quantities, and Eskimo pies, and malted milk shakes, to say nothing of can openers and other gadgets, so that the little people everywhere may enjoy some of the luxuries of our economic millennium.

The thing to guard against, however, is that the little peoples of the world should not be infected with Communism. Russia will have to be content to communize Siberia, Mongolia, and possibly Japan. But not China! And not the Malay archipelago, nor Africa, nor South America. South America will be somewhat of a problem, especially as miscegenation assumes increasing proportions. It won't do for the peoples of North America, "the melting pot," to begin intermarrying with the black, brown and yellow races. Marrying red-skins is quite another matter; the Indian, it seems, is a hundred percent American, and we don't mind any more if they have a touch of color. But don't let any one think, especially south of the Mason-Dixon line, that the Four Freedoms means freedom for blacks and whites to intermarry! That belongs to the fifth or sixth freedom, and will probably demand another war.

With a plethora of new labor-saving devices flooding the market there will no longer be any question of who is to do the dirty work of the world. *The machine will do it!* No one will need to soil his hands. The machines will work with such efficiency, in fact, that there may be danger of the workers growing bored. Unless the master minds introduce new forms of creative activity. It is quite possible that in the next few hundred years we shall see everybody turning artist. An hour or two at the machine each day, and the rest of the day for art! Perhaps that will be the new order in the world to come. How glorious! *The joy of creation:* something man has never known before, at least not the civilized races. Suddenly, thanks to the ubiquity and the domination of the machine, we will become again as the primitives, only wiser, happier, conscious at last of our blessedness. Everybody dancing, singing, painting, carving, fiddling, drumming, strumming . . . so marvelous! All due to the machine. How simple!

Finally, when every one has become a genius, when genius becomes the norm, there will be no room for envy or rivalry. Art will be truly universal. There will be no need for critics or interpreters; the dealers and middle men will perish, and with them the publishers and editors, the lawyers, the bookkeepers, the politicians, perhaps even the police. Every one will have the kind of home he chooses to live in, and with it a frigidaire, a radio, a telephone, a vacuum cleaner, a washing machine, an automobile, an airplane, a parachute, *and*—a full set of Dr. Cowen's light-weight platinum teeth. The cripples will all have the most wonderful, the most extraordinary, light-weight artificial limbs, which will enable them to run, skip, dance, jump or walk with perfect ease. The insane will have better lunatic asylums, and more humane, more intelligent keepers. The prisons will be more spacious, more sanitary, more comfortable in every way. There will be hospitals in abundance, on every street, and ambulances fitted up like Pullmans. There will be such a variety of pain removers that no one need ever suffer any more, not even the throes of death. Add to this, that when all the world learns English, which will happen inevitably, there won't be the least possibility of a misunderstanding any more. One language, one flag, one way of life. The machine doing all the dirty work, the master minds doing all the thinking: an Entente Cordiale with a vengeance.

That's how it looks for the next five hundred years or so. *Or doesn't it?* Anyway, that's how it *could* look, you must admit. And what's to hinder? Well, we don't know yet, but undoubtedly there will arise some idiot, some fanatic, who will have a better idea to foist upon us. And that will cause trouble. Trouble always starts with "a better idea." It's too soon to predict the nature of the monkey wrench which will wreck the Utopian machine we have just described, but that there will be such a joy-killer we have no doubt. It's in the cards.

So, just to play safe, hold on to your battle-ships and battle wagons, your tanks, your flame-throwers, your bombing machines and everything super-duper in the way of destructive devices—we may have need for them again. One day, out of a clear sky—always a clear sky, mind you!—some fanatic will make an issue of some unforeseeable little incident, magnify it to the proportions of a calamity, and then a fresh catastrophe will be at our door. But if we are armed to the teeth, if we are better prepared than we were this last time, perhaps we shall get it over with more quickly. We must never relinquish the Four Freedoms, remember that! If possible, we must pave the way for a fifth and sixth freedom. Because, the more freedoms we pile up, the nearer we will be to freedom in the abstract.

Each new freedom, to be sure, will entail a few million deaths, as well as the destruction of our principal cities. But, if we achieve ten or twelve freedoms, we won't mind how many millions of lives are sacrificed, nor will we care how many cities are destroyed. After all, we can always make babies, and we can always build new cities— better babies, better cities. If we were able to discover a way to homogenize and irradiate cow's milk we surely will find the way to homogenize and irradiate the minds of our children. If we have to destroy everything now standing, including the Vatican, it will be worth it. What we want is a world in which war will be unthinkable. And, by God, if we have to wipe out the human race in order to achieve it, we will. *Mieux vaut revenir en fantôme que jamais*, as the French say.

So, until that blessed day looms upon the horizon, do please go on murdering one another. Murder as you have never murdered before. Murder the murderers, murder murder, but murder! murder! murder! Murder for God and country! Murder for peace! Murder for sweet murder's sake! Don't stop murdering ever! Murder! Murder! Murder! Murder your mother! Murder your brother! Mur-

215

der the animals of the field, murder the insects, the birds, the flowers, the grass! Murder the microbes! Murder the molecule and the atom! Murder the electron! Murder the stars, and the sun and moon, if you can get at them! Murder everything off, so that we shall have at last a bright, pure, clean world in which to live in peace, bliss and security until the end of time!

THE HONEYMOONERS (Watercolor) *by Henry Miller*

# ASTROLOGICAL FRICASSEE

I MET Gerald in the lobby of a theatre during the intermission. I had hardly been presented to him when he asked me what my birth date was.

"December 26th, 1891 . . . 12.30 noon . . . New York City . . . Conjunction of Mars, Uranus and the Moon in the 8th house. Does that help?"

He was delighted. "Then you know something about astrology," he said, beaming at me as if I were a devoted disciple.

Just then a dashing young woman came up and greeted Gerald warmly. Gerald quickly presented us to one another. "December

26th, meet April 4th . . . Capricorn—Aries . . . You should get along beautifully together."

I never got the dashing young woman's name nor she mine. That was utterly unimportant to Gerald. People existed merely to corroborate his celestial theorems. He knew in advance what every one was like—quintessentially, that is. In a way, he was like an X-ray specialist. He looked immediately at your astral skeleton. Where the unobserving saw only a Milky Way, Gerald saw constellations, planets, asteroids, shooting stars, nebulae and so on.

"Don't make any important plans the next few days," he would say. "Just lay low for a while. Your Mars is squared with your Mercury. It won't do any good to make decisions now. Wait till the moon is full . . . You're inclined to be rather impulsive, aren't you?" And he'd give his victim a sly, inquisitive look, as though to say: "You can't fool me, you know. I see right through you."

There was a lot of handshaking going on in the lobby during that intermission. Every one was introduced by his celestial monniker. There seemed to be a preponderance of Pisces individuals about— tepid, kindly, milk-and-water creatures who were inclined to be pop-eyed and lymphatic. I kept a weather eye open for Scorpios and Leos, especially of the female variety. The Aquarians I gave a wide berth.

In the restaurant later that evening Gerald and I got down to brass tacks. I don't remember what he said he was—perhaps Gemini or Virgo—but in any case he was damned slippery. There was something androgynous about him too. He seemed to be wound up about Libra, Leo and Sagittarius. Now and then he made some periphrastic remarks about Capricorn—cautiously, guardedly, as if he were sprinkling salt on a bird's tail.

He talked a lot about the various bodily organs, as well as the joints, muscles, mucous membranes and other parts of the body. He

218

advised his host, who had recently been run over by a truck, to be careful of his knee-caps next month. The young lady on my left was to watch her kidneys—some nefarious influence was just entering one of the houses which had to do with the kidneys and the ductless glands. I wondered to myself just what sort of astral set-up it was which had given him such a liverish complexion, and why he hadn't done anything about it, perhaps with the aid of the local pharmacist.

By the time I had had three champagne cocktails I was thoroughly confused. I couldn't remember whether he had said the coming week was to be a good one financially or full of broken bones. What's more I didn't give a damn. Any Saturnian influences revealed by my horoscope are more than offset by a benevolent and beneficent Jupiter. Never once did he mention Venus, I noticed. It was as though he didn't give a shit about one's love life. His forte was accidents, raises in salary, and voyages. The conversation was beginning to taste like a dish of cold scrambled eggs at the Hospital for Joint Diseases. I tried to draw him out about Pluto, because Pluto and her mysterious ways intrigued me more than the other planets, but the subject seemed unpalatable to him; he grew glum, almost morose. What he liked were more mundane queries, such as— "Do you think spaghetti agrees with one of my temperament?" or, "Is exercise good for me at this time?" Or, "What about that job in San Francisco—is this the moment to make a move?" To such questions he always had a ready answer. It was amazing what confidence he possessed. Sometimes, just to make his reply more dramatic, he would close his eyes for a moment to make a rapid survey of the celestial map. He could read the future backwards, yet, in some strange way, like everybody else in this world, he had to buy the morning paper to find out what had happened (during our conversation) on the Russian front. Had the stock

219

market crashed during the night I am certain he would have been none the wiser. When the moon went into eclipse a few weeks later he was on the look-out for quakes and tremblors; fortunately, in some forlorn outpost it was recorded seismographically that there had been a disturbance some five or six thousand miles out in the Pacific. No one suffered, except the monsters of the deep . . .

A week or so later Gerald called me up to invite me to a house-warming. He had promised that I would meet a beautiful Sagittarian with red apple breasts and lips like crushed raspberries. "You're going to be very active soon," said Gerald, as a parting shot. The way he confided this bit of news to me sounded very promising—over the telephone. On reflection, however, I realized that activity in and by itself is meaningless. Ants and bees are active, perpetually active, but where does it get them? Besides, I resented the idea of activity. I was at peace with myself and I wanted to remain that way, at least a little while longer.

It was late afternoon when we drove up to Gerald's house. I had brought two friends along, a Libra and a Sagittarius. Both sides of the street, for the entire length of the block, were filled with cars, mostly limousines, all sleek and shiny, and guarded over by liveried chauffeurs who had already begun to fraternize. Seeing us step out of our Ford coupe they looked us up and down with a critical eye.

It was a rather pleasant little house Gerald had chosen for his new abode. Pleasantly neutral, I should say. It could have been the home of a successful palmist or a 'cellist. The living room was crowded with people—standing, talking, sitting, sipping tea, munching biscuits. As we entered, Gerald dashed forward and began presenting us: Libra—Gemini . . . Sagittarius—Aquarius . . . Leo—Capricorn, and so on. It was all a bit like Alice in Wonderland and Gerald, now that I saw him at close range, was a ringer for the Red Queen.

When the introductions were finished I stood apart, at the bay window, and surveyed the scene. I was wondering who would fasten on me first. I didn't have long to wait.

"Are you interested in astrology?" said a pale, sunken individual who had with difficulty extricated himself from the sofa where he had been crushed between two dowdy females with oatmeal complexions.

"Only mildly," I said, smiling and shaking his limp hand.

"We're all so fond of Gerald. He's really a wizard, you know. I don't know what we'd do without him."

An awkward pause, since I had made no response. He continued: "You're living in Hollywood, I suppose, Mr. . . . What was your name again? Mine is Helblinger . . . Julius Helblinger."

I put out my hand again and said, "Glad to know you, Mr. Helblinger. No I'm not living here, I'm just visiting."

"You're a lawyer, aren't you?"

"No, I'm a writer."

"A writer—how interesting! Indeed, and what sort of books do you write, may I ask?"

At this point I was rescued by Gerald, who had been eavesdropping, and who now joined us all a-flutter.

"You mustn't look at this man's books," said Gerald, holding his arm up with wrist loose and fingers dangling like broken splinters. "He's got a very naughty mind, haven't you December 26th?"

Just then one of the monsters on the sofa tried to rise to her feet with the aid of a thin, gold-knobbed cane. I saw her fall back like a dead fish and hastened to her side to offer my support. As I did so I noticed her legs which were like two splints. Obviously she had never walked any farther than from her car to the door-step. Her eyes, set in a pasty white face, were like two bird seeds. There wasn't a spark of light in them, unless it was the glint of greed

221

and rapacity. She might have been the twin sister of Carrie Nation done by Grant Wood in a moment of satanic illumination. I could see her on the lawn at Pasadena, where she lived, watering the chrysanthemums with a leaky flower pot. She probably went from the hair-dresser to the numerologist and from the numerologist to the palmist and from the palmist to the tea room where, after the second cup of tea, she probably felt a slight stirring in her bowels and congratulated herself that she no longer needed a laxative every day. For her the supreme joy in life was to be able to have a clean stool, no doubt about it. As I gently yanked her to her feet I could hear her dirty heart ticking away like a rusty Ingersoll.

"You're so kind," she said, trying to wreathe her cast-iron face into a beatific smile. "Dear me, my poor legs seem to be giving way on me. Gerald says it's my Mars in opposition with Saturn. That's my cross, I suppose. What are you—an Aries? No, let me think a minute . . . you're a Gemini, aren't you?"

"Yes," I said, "I'm a Gemini . . . and so is my mother, my sister, too. Curious, isn't it?"

"I should think so," she said, wheezing now from the effort of controlling her giddiness. The blood was running through her veins like mucilage soaking through blotting paper.

"Gerald says I worry too much . . . but what are you going to do when the government eats up all your income? Of course I believe we've got to win the war, but dear me, what will be left for us when it's all over? I'm not getting any younger, that's a certainty. We've only got one car now, and God only knows when they'll take that from us. What do *you* think about the war, young man? Isn't it terrible, all this slaughter that's going on? Heavens only knows if we're safe here. I wouldn't be surprised at all if the Japs invaded California and took the coast right under our nose. What do *you* think? You're a very patient listener, I see. You must forgive me if I prattle on like this. I'm not a young woman any more. *Well?*"

I didn't say a word. I just smiled at her—perhaps a bit sadly.

"You're not an alien, are you?" she said, suddenly looking a bit panic-stricken.

"No," I said, "just an American."

"Where are you from—the Middle West?"

"No, New York. That is, I was born there."

"But you don't live there, is that it? I don't blame you. I think it's a horrid place to live . . . all those foreigners. I've been out here thirty years. I'd never go back . . . *Oh*, Lady Astenbroke! . . . well, it's *so* good to see you again. When did you arrive? I didn't know that you were here in California."

I was left holding the crutch, as it were. The old bitch seemed to have forgotten me completely, though I was still at her side ready to give support to her tottering frame the moment she should reel or crumple up. Finally, observing Lady Astenbroke's somewhat embarrassed glances in my direction, she moved her rusty hinges and wheeled about an eighth of an inch, just sufficient to make me aware that she was cognizant of my presence.

"Lady Astenbroke, allow me to present Mr. . . . I'm so sorry, what did you tell me your name was again?"

"I never told you," I said flatly. I allowed a due pause and added: "Himmelweiss . . . August Himmelweiss."

Lady Astenbroke winced visibly at the mention of this horrendous Teutonic name. She held up two icy fingers which I crunched gleefully with a most unseemly hale and hearty handshake. What annoyed Lady Astenbroke more than the disgustingly effusive handshake was the insolent way in which I allowed my eyes to fasten on the three cherries which were dangling over the brim of her incredible hat. Only a madwoman of the British upper

223

class could have discovered such a creation. She stood there like a tipsy Gainsborough to which Marc Chagall had put the finishing touches. All that was needed to consolidate the feeling of Empire was a bunch of asparagus stuck between her deflated leathery breasts. Her breasts! Automatically my eyes roved to the place where the breasts should have been. I had a suspicion that she had stuffed some excelsior there at the last moment, perhaps when squeezing the last drop of perfume out of her atomizer. I'm sure she never looked at her private parts, as they say. So disgusting! Always had been . . . If only one didn't have to make water now and then one could forget about it entirely . . .

"Lady Astenbroke is the author of the Winnie Wimple books," the old Pasadena derelict hastened to inform me. I knew I was supposed to look *au courant* at this juncture but somehow I just didn't give a damn whether Lady Astenbroke was a celebrated writer or a champion croquet player. So I said quite calmly and cold-bloodedly:

"I'm sorry to say I never heard of the Winnie Wimple books."

That fell like a bomb.

"Now please, Mr. . . ."

"Mr. Himmelweiss," I mumbled.

"Please, Mr. Himmelweiss, don't tell us you've never heard of Winnie Wimple. Why, everybody's read the Winnie Wimple books. Where have you been all these years? Dear me, I never heard anything like it."

Said Lady Astenbroke condescendingly: "Mr. Himmelweiss probably reads Thomas Mann and Croce and Unamuno. I don't blame him. I write because I'm bored. I can scarcely read them myself, you know. They're really shockingly simple."

"My dear Lady Astenbroke—how can you say such a thing! Why

224

they're fascinating, your books! Last winter, when I had the gout, I read them all over again . . . every one of them. Such whimsy as you have! Such fantasy! I don't know what we'd do without your Winnie Wimples, really I don't . . . *Oh*, there's Baron Hufnagel. I *must* say a word to him. You'll excuse me, won't you, Lady Astenbroke?" She hobbled off towards the other end of the room, screaming hysterically: "Baron Hufnagel! Baron Hufnagel!"

Lady Astenbroke lowered herself onto the sofa—as if she had a glass ass. I offered to bring her some tea and biscuits but apparently she didn't hear me. She was staring with glassy eyes at a photograph of a lascivious blonde, rather scantily clad, which stood on a little table near her elbow. I edged away from her to find myself rubbing bottoms with a faded actress. I was about to excuse myself when I heard a shrill little laugh, like mica cracking.

"It's only me . . . don't bother," she gurgled. "The Eskimos rub noses . . ." Another little peal of laughter, à la Galli Curci falling downstairs. And then: "I'm November 12th, what are you?"

"December 26th," I said, "all goat and a pair of horns."

"How darling! I don't know what I am—a snake or a centipede. A little of the devil in me and a lot of sex." She gave a lascivious wink with her pale china blue eyes. "I say," and she snuggled up closer, "you don't think you could find me a drink, do you? I've been waiting for that bird" (indicating Gerald) "to offer me something, but I don't think he ever will, do you? Listen, what's going on here? Is some one going to throw a fit, or what? My name's Peggy, by the way. And yours?"

I gave her my real name. "Officially," I said, "I'm known as Himmelweiss." I gave her the horsewink.

"*Officially!*" she echoed. "I don't get it. Officially *what?*"

"Gaga," I said. "You know," and I tapped my head.

"Oh, that's it? You mean they're all screw-balls? I thought as much. Listen, who *is* this guy . . . the guy that runs the joint? What's his game?"

"Horoscopes."

"You mean astrology? Listen, I'm not such a dumb cluck. But what's the racket? What did he round them up for? Is he getting ready to shake 'em down? If he tries to rustle me he's going to get a big surprise."

"I don't think he'll bother you any," I said. "Not that way anyway." I gave her another slippery horsewink.

"I get you. So that's his game!" She made a cool survey of the guests. "Not much competition that way, I'll say. Maybe they're just a blind." She gave a supercilious nod intended to embrace the old hags who surrounded us.

"What's *your* game?" she asked suddenly.

"*My game?* Oh, I write."

"Go on . . . do you mean it? What sort of stuff? History, biology . . . ?"

"Naughty books," I said, trying to blush deeply.

"What kind of naughty books? Naughty-naughty—or just dirt?"

"Just dirt, I guess."

"You mean—Lady Chatterby, or Chattersley, or whatever the hell it is? Not that swill you don't mean, do you?"

I laughed. "No, not that sort . . . just straight obscenity. You know—duck, chit, kiss, trick, punt, . . ."

"*Not so loud!* Where do you think you are?" She gave a quick look over her shoulder. "Say, listen, why don't we sit down somewhere and talk this over? What else do you know? This sounds promising. What did you say you were—a goat? What's that— Sagittarius?"

"Capricorn."

226

*Capricorn!* Well, now we're getting somewhere. What did you say your date was? I want to remember that . . . Are all Capricorns like that? Jesus, I thought I was sexy, but maybe I'm going to learn things. Listen, come over here, where nobody can hear you. Now, what did you say you wrote again? Straight what?"

"Straight duck, chit, kiss, trick, punt, . . ."

She looked up at me as though she were going to bless me. She held out her mitt. "*Shake*, partner! You're talking my language. I say, can you embroider that a little—from where you left off? Those were good clean words, the coin of the realm. Can't you reel off a few fancy ones? Go on, try it. I'm beginning to wet my pants. Cripes, imagine finding *you* here. And what's about a little drink, eh? Don't bring me any stale horse-piss. Some Bourbon, if you can find it . . . Wait a minute, don't run just yet. Tell me some more before you go. Begin with duck, you know—like you did before. Only ring some fancy ones in. Maybe you and I'll go places before the night's over. You don't just say the words, do you? That'd be cruel. Come here, I want to whisper something in your ear."

As I bent over I saw Gerald heading straight towards us.

"Shoo this guy away, will you," she whispered. "He looks like a dose of crabs to me."

"What are you two whispering about?" said Gerald, beaming like the heavenly twins.

"Brother, you'd never guess . . . would he?" She gave a dirty laugh—just a little too loud, I gathered from the expression on Gerald's face.

Gerald bent over, using a *sotto voce:* "It wasn't about sex, was it?"

The woman looked up at him in amazement, almost frightened. "Say, you *are* a mind-reader, aren't you? How the hell did *you* know? You don't read lips, do you?"

"I could read *your* lips even in the dark," said Gerald, giving her a withering glance.

"You're not trying to insult me, I hope? Listen, I know a few tricks myself. Maybe I don't know nothing about astrology, but I've got *your* number."

"Shhhhh!" Gerald put his fingers to his lips. "Not here, my dear. You wouldn't give me away before all these people, would you?"

"Not if you can dig up a drink, I won't. Where do you keep it? I'll get it myself. Just tell me. You weren't brought up on lemonade."

Gerald was just about to whisper in her ear when a ravishing beauty who had just made her entrance pulled him by the coat tails.

"Diana! *You* here? How lovely! I never dreamed that you'd come." He waltzed her off to another corner of the room without bothering to introduce her. Probably congratulating himself on a lucky escape.

"He's a dirty cheap skate," muttered the blonde between her teeth. "He could have told us where he kept it, couldn't he? Pretending to be all wrapped up in Diana. Huh! He'd faint if any one showed him a—you know!—with hair on it."

It was the sort of place you couldn't sit long in without being molested. While Peggy went to the pantry to search for liquor, a Norwegian spinster who was serving tea in the next room advanced on me, leading by the hand a celebrated analyst. He was an Aquarian whose Venus was unaspected. He looked like a dentist who had degenerated into a desert rat. His false teeth shone with a blue flame beneath a ridge of rubber gums. He wore a perpetual smile which by turns indicated satisfaction, dubiety, ecstasy and disgust. The Norwegian woman, who was psychic, watched him reverently, giving significance even to his sighs and grunts. She was a Piscean, it developed, and her veins were filled with the milk of compassion.

228

She wanted all who were suffering to come unto Dr. Blunderbuss. He was really unique, she informed me, after he had taken leave. She compared him first to Paracelsus, then to Pythagoras, and finally to Hermes Trismegistus. That brought us round to the subject of reincarnation. She said she could remember three previous incarnations—in one of them she had been a man. That was during the time of the Pharaohs, before the temple priests had corrupted the ancient wisdom. She was working out her Karma slowly, confident that in another million years or so she would escape from the wheel of birth and death.

"Time is nothing," she murmured, with eyes half-closed. "There is so much to be done . . . so much. Won't you try one of our delicious cookies? I made them myself."

She took me by the hand and led me into the adjoining room where an aged Daughter of the Revolution was pouring tea.

"Mrs. Farquahar," she said, still holding me by the hand, "this gentleman would like to try one of the cookies. We've just had a grand talk with Dr. Blunderbuss, haven't we?" She looked into my eyes with the touching humility of a trained poodle.

"Mrs. Farquahar is terribly psychic," she continued, handing me a delicious cookie and a cup of tea. "She was a great friend of Madame Blavatsky. You've read *The Secret Doctrine*, of course? Of course you have . . . you're one of us, I know."

I noticed that Mrs. Farquahar was looking at me strangely. She wasn't looking into my eyes, either, but sort of slant-wise, from the roots of my hair upward. I thought perhaps Lady Astenbroke might be standing behind me—and the three cherries dangling above my head.

Suddenly Mrs. Farquahar opened her mouth. "What a beautiful aura! *Violet* . . . with a touch of magenta. *Look!*" and she pulled the Norwegian woman to her, made her bend her knees and look at a spot on the wall about three inches above my thinning locks. "Do you see it, Norma? Just squint one eye. Now . . . *there!*"

Norma bent her knees a little more, squinted for all she was worth, but had to confess she could see nothing.

"Why it's as plain as can be. Any one can see it! Keep looking. It'll come . . ."

By now several old hens were crooking their knees and trying for all they were worth to see the halo which enveloped my cranium. One of them swore she saw it very distinctly—but it turned out that she saw green and black instead of violet and magenta. That irritated Mrs. Farquahar. She began to pour tea furiously, finally spilling a cupful over her lavender dress. Norma was terribly upset by this. She fussed over Mrs. Farquahar like a wet hen.

When Mrs. Farquahar stood up there was a tremendous stain visible. It looked as if she had become excited beyond control. I stood there looking at the stain and instinctively put one hand above my head to bathe it in the violet light of my aura.

Just then a clean-shaven, portly, interior decorator type of homosexual gave me a knowing smile and remarked in a suave, silken tone of voice that my aura was perfectly stunning. "I haven't seen one like it for years," he exclaimed, reaching nonchalantly for a handful of home-made cookies. "Mine is just too disgusting for words . . . at least so they tell me. You must have a beautiful character. My only distinction is that I'm clairaudient. I would so love to be clairvoyant too, wouldn't you—or *are* you? I suppose you *are* . . . it's silly of me to ask. Any one with *your* aura . . ." He made a charming little moue and wagged his hips. I thought he was going to wave his hand and shout Yoo-hoo! But he didn't.

"You're an artist, I suppose," I ventured, after this flirtatious exchange.

"I suppose I am," he replied, dropping his eyelashes coyly. "I

230

love to handle beautiful things. And I just loathe figures and all that sort of thing. Of course I've lived abroad most of my life—that helps, don't you think? Have you ever lived in Florence—or Ravenna? Isn't Florence just a darling of a place? I don't know why we had to have a war, do you? It's so messy. I do hope the English will spare Ravenna. Those horrible bombs! Ugh! It makes me shudder to think of it . . ."

A woman who had been standing beside us now spoke up. She said luck had been against her the last seven years, ever since she had had her palm read in Majorca. Fortunately she had put aside a little nest egg for a rainy day—a cool million, it was—she said it without batting an eyelash. Now that she had become an agent things were going a little better. She had just made a place for some one at three thousand a week. A few more like that and she wouldn't have to starve to death. Yes, it was rather pleasant work. After all, one had to have something to do, something to occupy one's mind. It was lots better than sitting home and worrying about what the government would do with your money.

I asked if she were a Seventh Day Adventist by any chance. She smiled with her gold teeth. "No, not any more. I guess I'm just a believer."

"And how did you meet Gerald?" I asked.

"Oh, *Gerald* . . ." and she gave a thrilly-dilly little laugh. "I met him at a boxing match one night. He was sitting with a Hindu nabob or something and I asked him for a light. He asked me if I wasn't a Libra and I told him I didn't know what he was talking about. Then he said— 'Weren't you born between the first and the fifth of October?' I told him I was born October first. 'That makes you a Libra,' he said. I was so dumbfounded that I had him do my horoscope. Since then things have been looking up. It seems I was under an eclipse or something. I don't understand it all yet . . .

do you? Anyway, it's fascinating, don't you think? Imagine asking some one for a light and being told when you were born! He's terribly brilliant, Gerald. I wouldn't make a move without consulting him first."

"I wonder if you could get me a job in the movies," I said. "This is a good period for me, so Gerald says."

"Are you an actor?" She looked rather surprised.

"No, I'm just a writer. I'd make a good hack if I were given a fair break."

"Are you good at dialogue?"

"That's my middle name. Do you want a sample? Look . . . two men are walking down the street. They're walking away from an accident. It's dark and they've lost their way. One of them is over-excited. Dialogue . . .

Excited man: Where do you suppose I could have put those papers?

Calm man: Suppositions are often like random shots on a billiard table without cloth.

Excited man: What? Anyway, if they fall into the wrong hands I'm done for.

Calm man: You're done for anyway . . . I thought we covered all that ages ago.

Excited man: Do you suppose some one could have picked my pockets while we were standing there? Why didn't they take my watch and chain also? How do you explain it?

Calm man: I don't. I neither suppose nor explain. I merely observe.

Excited man: Do you think I ought to phone the police? God, man, we've got to do something.

Calm man: You mean *you* have to do something. I have only to go home and go to sleep. Well, here's where we part. Good-night!

232

Excited man: You're not going to leave me now, are you? You mean you're going to walk out on me . . . Just like that?

Calm man: I always say exactly what I mean. Good-night and sleep tight!

"I could carry on like that for a half hour. How was it? Pretty bad? All impromptu, of course. If I were putting it down on paper it would sound quite different. I'll give you another sample, if you like . . . Two women, this time. They're waiting for a bus. It's raining and they have no umbrellas . . ."

"Excuse me," said La Libra, "but I've got to go. It was so nice meeting you. I'm sure you'll have no trouble finding a place for yourself in Hollywood."

I was left standing there like a wet umbrella. I wondered if my aura was still showing or if it had become extinguished. Nobody seemed to take a bit of notice any more.

Now that the old ones had bathed their intestines with luke-warm tea they were thinking about getting home for dinner. One by one they gingerly raised themselves from their seats and hobbled slowly towards the door, availing themselves of canes, crutches, umbrellas and golf clubs. Lady Astenbroke was remaining, it appeared. She had fallen into a fascinating conversation with a fat Cuban woman who was dressed in a Butterick pattern of the mutton chop epoch. They were speaking several languages at once, Lady Astenbroke being an accomplished linguist. I was standing behind a rubber plant about two feet away from them, trying to decode this amazing lingo. As the departing ones approached to bid her good-bye, Lady Astenbroke bent forward like a broken hinge and extended her clammy paw which scintillated with jeweled rings. The chauffeurs were crowded round the doorway, ready to proffer an arm to their aged charges. Gerald escorted his patrons in turn to their respective cars. He looked like a distinguished bonesetter who had just pocketed a handsome fee. When the last of the derelicts had vanished he stood on the door-step mopping his brow, took a silver cigarette case from his hip pocket, lit a cork-tipped cigarette and exhaled a thin cloud of smoke through his nostrils. A thin crescent moon was visible low above the horizon. Gerald gazed at it a few moments, took another puff or two, then flung the cigarette away. As he re-entered the house he looked about searchingly. A shade of disappointment was visible in his countenance; apparently the one he was looking for had not arrived. He chewed his lips absent-mindedly. "Oh, foodle!" he seemed to say, and then he made a dash for the kitchen where he probably took a quiet nip all by himself.

Lady Astenbroke was now talking French to the Cuban woman. She was gushing about Juan les Pins, Cannes, Pau and other famous resorts. Evidently she had spent considerable time in the south of France, as well as in Italy, Turkey, Jugoslavia and North Africa. The Cuban woman listened imperturbably, fanning herself the while with a diminutive, ivory-studded fan which could only have been stolen from a museum. The perspiration fell in little drops onto her bosom. Now and then she swabbed the huge crack between her tightly squashed teats with a tiny silk handkerchief. She did it quite casually, never once lowering her eyes. Lady Astenbroke pretended not to notice these unseemly gestures. If she had paused to reflect she would have been horrified. Lady Astenbroke had probably never touched her own breasts since the day they shriveled up.

The Cuban woman was very fat and the chair she was sitting on was very uncomfortable. For one thing, her ass was hanging over the seat of the chair like a piece of limp liver. Occasionally, when Lady Astenbroke's eyes roved wildly about the room, she discreetly scratched her ass with the handle of her little fan. Once she put it down her back, not realizing my proximity, and vigorously poked it up and down. It was obvious that she had lost interest in Lady Astenbroke's disconnected remarks. Her one desire was to get home as soon as possible, rip off her corset, and scratch herself like a mangy dog.

I was amazed, when a dapper little man approached, to hear her present him as her husband. Somehow I had not expected her to own a husband, but there he was in flesh and blood, a monocle in one eye and a pair of butter-colored gloves in his hand. He was an Italian count, so I gathered from the introductions, and his profession was architecture. There was something tremendously alert and pertinacious about him, something of the bird of prey and something of the dandy. Something of the poet also, the kind that walks upside down on the ceiling or swings from the chandelier while pondering a phrase or a cadence. He would have looked more natural in doublet and hose with a big heart pasted over his chest.

With infinite patience, not untinged with malice, he stood behind his wife's chair and waited for her to conclude her séance with Lady Astenbroke. An undefinable asperity gave him the air of a Neapolitan barber waiting for an opportune moment to quietly slit his wife's throat. There was no doubt about it, once they were seated in the car he would pinch her until she was black and blue.

Only about a dozen people were left in the big room now. Mostly Virgos and Geminis, it seemed to me. A torpor had come over them, a gentle torpor induced by the sultry heat and the drone of insects. Gerald was in the bedroom, where the photos of his favorite stars—his clients undoubtedly—were conspicuously displayed. A rather attractive young woman was seated beside him at the writing table. They were going over a horoscope together. I recalled that she had arrived with a handsome young man, who was either

235

her lover or her husband, and that they had separated almost immediately

The young man, who turned out to be an actor—he was doing Western parts at Universal—had the attractiveness of a man who is just about to go insane. He roved about nervously, flitting from group to group, always hovering on the fringe, listening a few moments, then breaking away like a colt. He was dying to speak to some one, I could see that. But no one gave him a chance. Finally he flung himself on the sofa beside an ugly little woman whom he completely ignored. He looked about disconsolately, ready to explode at the slightest provocation.

Presently a woman with flaming red hair and violet eyes made her entrance; in her wake came a towering young aviator with shoulders like Atlas and the sharp, beak-like features of the air-man. "Hello everybody!" she said, assuming that everybody knew at once who she was. "I'm here, you see . . . Couldn't believe it possible, could you? Well, get busy, hand out the compliments . . . I'm all ears," she seemed to say, meanwhile perching herself on the edge of a rickety chair, her back straight as a ramrod, her eyes flashing, her toes quivering with impatience. She had an impeccable English accent which belied the mobility of her features. She might have been Conchita Montenegro—or Loulou Hegoroboru. Anything but a flower of the British Empire. I inquired discreetly who she was. A Brazilian dancer, I was told, who had just burst into the pictures.

A Brazilian peacock would have been more accurate. Vanity, vanity! It was written all over her. She had moved her chair into the very center of the room—to make certain that no one else should monopolize the attention of the torpid assemblage.

"Yes, we took a plane from Rio," she was saying. "I always travel

236

by plane. I suppose it's extravagant, but I'm too impatient. I had to leave the dog with the maid. I think it's stupid, all these silly regulations. I . . ."

I . . . I . . . I . . . I . . . She never seemed to use the second or third person. Even when she referred to the weather she used the first person. She was like a glittering iceberg, the Id completely submerged and about as useful to her as Jonah was to the whale. Her toes twinkled as she spoke. Elegant, polished toes, capable of executing the most intricate figures. The sort of toes that would make one swoon to lick.

What surprised me was the rigidity of her body. Only her head and toes were alive—the rest of her was anaesthetized. It was from the diaphragm of this immobile torso that she threw her voice, a voice which was at once seductive and grating. She said nothing which she had not already said a hundred or a thousand times. She sat there like a rat-catcher, always whistling the same tune, looking bright, gay and alert, but secretly bored to tears, suffocated with ennui. She saw nothing and heard nothing, her mind blank and flawless as stainless steel.

"Yes, I'm a Gemini too," I heard her say, implying by the tone of her voice that the gods had indeed blessed her. "Yes, I'm very dual." I . . . I . . . I . . . I . . . Even in her duality she was just a capital I.

Suddenly Gerald came from the bedroom. "Lolita!" he exclaimed, putting an extra rapturous thrill into his falsetto voice. "How sweet of you! How *gorgeous* you look!" He held her with outstretched arms by the tips of his fingers, as in the ballet, and with fluttering orbs he ravished her from head to foot.

As he was going through this little farce my eye happened to rove and alight upon the woman at the writing table in the bedroom.

237

She had taken a handkerchief from her bag and was drying her eyes. I saw her clasp her hands feverishly and glance imploringly at the ceiling. She seemed utterly distraught.

"My dear Lolita, it was so good of you to come. You came by plane, I suppose? How ducky! You extravagant creature, you! And that lovely hat . . . where *did* you buy it? In Rio, I suppose? You're not running away yet, I hope? I've such wonderful things to tell you. Your Venus is magnificent now."

Lolita didn't seem to be at all surprised by this announcement. She probably knew more about the position of her Venus than Gerald and all the psychopomps of the underworld. Her Venus was right between her legs—and what's more, it was always under control. The only time her love life ever suffered an eclipse was when she had the curse. Even then there were a lot of things one could do without opening or closing the legs.

Now that she was on her feet her body had more animation. There was an effulgence about the hips which was unnoticeable when she was sitting. She used them very much like a flirt uses her eyebrows. She arched them coyly, first one then the other. It was a sort of veiled masturbation, such as boarding-school girls resort to when their hands are otherwise occupied.

She made a few steps towards the bedroom with the sprightliness of an icicle just beginning to thaw. Her voice had a different resonance now. It seemed to come from the girdle of Venus; it was lush and curdled, like radishes floating in sour cream.

"When you're through," she said, glancing over his shoulder at the figure in the bedroom, "I'd like to have a word with you."

What it sounded like was: "Get rid of that weepy wretch in there and I'll tell you about my oojie-woojie love life."

"Oh we'll be through in no time," said Gerald, turning his head stiffly in the direction of the bedroom.

238

"You'd better make it snappy," said Lolita. "I'm going soon." She gave her left hip an imperceptible jerk, as though to say— "I'm warning you. Make it snappy!"

Just then the Brazilian flyer appeared, laden with a tray of sandwiches and some sherry. Lolita pounced on the food rapaciously. The cowboy with the maniacal look in his eye had jumped to his feet and was helping himself manfully. Lady Astenbroke sat in her corner, waiting disdainfully for some one to pass her the platter. Suddenly it seemed as though every one were on the qui vive. The insects stopped buzzing, the heat abated. The general torpor seemed to be evaporating.

It was the moment the cowboy had been waiting for. He had a chance to spout now and he did, in a deep, booming voice which, despite the note of hysteria, had something ingratiating about it. He was one of those neurotic he-men created by the movie studios who loathe their false masculinity. He wanted to tell us about his fears, of which he had a good skinful. He didn't know quite how to begin, that was obvious, but he was determined to make us listen somehow. So, quite as if that had been the subject of conversation all afternoon, he began talking about shrapnel wounds. He wanted to let us know how it felt to be all cut up and bleeding, particularly under a foreign sky, and no hope of being rescued. He was sick of riding wild horses in the chaparral at a hundred and fifty dollars a week. He had been an actor once, back East, and though he hadn't become a celebrity he had at least done without a horse. One felt that he was trying to precipitate a dramatic situation in which he could display his true histrionic powers. One also felt that he was hungry, that perhaps the reason why his wife was closeted with Gerald in the bedroom was to find out when they would eat again. One had the suspicion that the hundred and fifty dollars a week meant every fifth or sixth week, and that between times they chewed

239

horse-leather. Perhaps too his wife had closeted herself with Gerald to learn what had become of her husband's missing virility. A lot of things were dangling in the air, above and beyond those brutal, hair-raising descriptions of shrapnel wounds.

He was a most determined, wild-eyed young man—positively Scorpionic. He seemed to be begging our permission to writhe on the carpet, to gnaw Lolita's ankles, to hurl the sherry glass through the window-pane. Something only remotely connected with his profession was eating him up. Probably his status in the draft. Probably the fact that his wife had become pregnant too soon. Probably a lot of things connected with the general catastrophe. Anyway, he was in the dead center of it, whatever it was, and the more he thrashed about the more obfuscated he became. If only some one would gainsay him! If only some one would take exception to his wild, random remarks! But no, no one opened his lips. They sat there, quiet as sheep, and watched him go through his contortions.

At first it was rather difficult to know just where he had oriented himself—amidst the flying shrapnel. He had already mentioned nine different countries without pausing to catch his breath. He had been routed out of Warsaw, bombed out of Rotterdam, driven to the sea at Dunkirk, fallen at Thermopylae, flown to Crete and been rescued by a fishing boat, and now, finally, he was somewhere in the wilds of Australia, grubbing a bite of food from the cannibals of the high plateaus. One couldn't say whether he had actually participated in these bloody disasters or whether he was rehearsing a part for a new radio program. He used all the pronouns, personal, reflexive, possessive, indiscriminately. Sometimes he was piloting a plane, sometimes he was merely a straggler and free-booter in the wake of a defeated army. At one moment he was living on mice and herrings, at another he was swilling champagne like Eric von Stroheim. Under all circumstances, no matter what the time or place,

240

he was miserable. Words can't describe how miserable he wanted us to believe he felt.

It was in the midst of this fever and agony that I decided to get up and take a stroll about the grounds. In the driveway leading to the garden I met my Sagittarian friend, Humberto, who had just sneaked away from the clutches of a hunch-backed woman with eczema. We walked back to the garden, where we found a ping-pong table. A young couple, who introduced themselves as brother and sister, invited us to join them in a game of doubles. We had hardly begun to play when the cow-boy made his appearance on the back porch; he watched us in glum silence for a few minutes, then disappeared inside. Presently a very sun-tanned woman, full of vim and bounce, came out and watched us hungrily. She was like a bull in female clothes, her nostrils breathing fire, her breasts heaving like ripe cantaloupes. The first ball she took a swat at broke in two; the second went over the fence; the third ball caught my friend Humberto square in the eye. With this she retired in disgust, saying that she preferred Badminton.

In a few moments Gerald came out to ask us to stay for dinner. The interior decorator friend had promised to make spaghetti for us, he informed us. "Now don't you run away," he said, pointing his finger at us mockingly.

We of course said we wouldn't think of staying. (Couldn't he see that we were bored stiff?)

"Oh, so you don't like spaghetti? It's not good enough for you, is that it?" said Gerald, putting on the pouting hussy act.

"Can we get some wine?" I asked, hoping that he would take the hint and tell us that cocktails were being prepared.

"Now don't go worrying about those things," said Gerald. "You Capricorns are so damned practical. Yes, we'll have something to drink for you."

"What sort of drink?" said Humberto, whose lips had been parched all afternoon.

"Oh, shush!" said Gerald. "Concentrate on the ping-pong. Haven't you any manners?"

"I'm thirsty," Humberto persisted.

"Then come inside and I'll give you a glass of cold water. That'll do you good. You're getting too excited. Besides, you should watch your liver. Wine is poison for you."

"Offer me something else then," said Humberto, determined to wheedle something alcoholic out of him.

"Now listen, Sagittarius . . . you've got to behave like a gentleman. This isn't John Barrymore's tenement house. Run along now and play your ping-pong. I'm going to send a charming little girl out to play with you." He turned his back on us and slid inside.

"Can you beat that?" said Humberto, throwing his racket aside and pulling on his jacket. "I'm going to get myself a drink." He looked around, waiting for some one to join him. The brother of the beautiful-looking Leo agreed to go along.

"Don't stay too long!" said Humberto's wife.

Humberto suddenly remembered he had forgotten something. He went up to his wife and asked her where her bag was. "I need some change," he said. He fished around in the bag and extracted a couple of bills.

"That means we won't see Humberto for a few hours," said his wife.

They had hardly left when the "charming" young girl came out. She was about sixteen, gawky, with carroty red hair and pimples. Gerald stuck his head out to give an approving nod. Suddenly no one wanted to play any more. The girl was almost on the verge of tears. At this moment, however, the bull-dyker reappeared, rushed to the table and grabbed a racket. "I'll play with you," she said to the gawky one, and with that she whizzed a fast one just over the girl's head. "I've got too much energy," she muttered. She slapped her thighs with the racket while the young gawk crawled on hands and knees among the rose-bushes in search of the ball.

We sat on the stoop and watched them a few minutes. Sister Leo, with the golden spots in her eyes, was talking about the dunes of Indiana. She confided that she had come to California to be near her brother, who was in an army camp nearby. She had found herself a job in a department store, selling candies. "I hope Rodney doesn't get drunk," she murmured. "He can't stand very much. You don't think Humberto will get him drunk, do you?"

We assured her that her brother was in good hands.

"I don't want him to get into trouble," she continued. "When he drinks he's apt to pick up with any one. There's so much disease around here . . . you know what I mean. That's why I like to be near him. I don't mind if he finds a nice, clean girl . . . but these other women . . . I understand all the boys get infected some time or other. Rodney never did run around very much at home. We were always good pals together . . ." She looked at me suddenly and exclaimed: "You're smiling. Did I say something foolish?"

"Oh no," I said, "on the contrary, I thought it was very touching."

"Touching? What do you mean? You don't think Rodney's a sissy, do you?"

"I wasn't thinking of Rodney."

"You think there's something wrong with *me?*"

"No, I don't think there's anything wrong . . ."

"You think I'm in love with him?" She laughed gaily. "Well, if you want to know the truth, I *am* in love with him. If he weren't my brother I'd marry him. Wouldn't you?"

"I don't know," I said, "I never was a sister."

A woman came out on the back porch to put some garbage in the can. She didn't look like a charwoman—there was something "spiritual" about her.

"Don't catch cold sitting out here," said the old lady. "The nights are treacherous, you know. We'll be having dinner for you shortly." She gave us a motherly smile, stood a moment with hands clasped over her fallen womb, and disappeared inside.

"Who is she?" I asked.

"That's my mother," said Miss Leo. "Isn't she sweet?"

"Why yes," I said, somewhat surprised that her mother should be doing Gerald's dirty work.

"She's a Quaker," said the girl. "By the way, you can call me Carol if you like. That's my name. Mother doesn't believe in astrology, but she likes Gerald. She thinks he's helpless."

"Are you a Quaker too?"

"Oh no, I haven't any religion. I'm just a plain country girl. I guess I'm sort of dumb."

"I don't think you're so very dumb," I said.

"Maybe not so very . . . but dumb just the same," she responded.

"How do you know? What gives you that idea?"

"By listening to other people talk. I can tell what I sound like when I open my mouth. You see, I just have simple, ordinary thoughts. Most people are too complicated for me. I listen, but I don't know what they're talking about."

"That sounds most intelligent to me," I confessed. "Tell me, do you dream much?"

She seemed startled by this. "What makes you ask that? How do you know I dream?"

"Why, everybody dreams, don't you know that?"

"Yes, I've heard say they do . . . but you didn't mean it that way. Most people forget their dreams, don't they?"

I nodded.

"Well, I don't," said Carol, brightening suddenly. "I remember everything, every detail. I have wonderful dreams. Maybe that's why I don't use my mind more. I dream all day long, as well as at night. It's easier, I suppose. Anyway, I'd rather dream than think . . . you know what I mean?"

I pretended to look puzzled.

"Oh, you know what I mean," she continued. "You can think and think and not get anywhere. But when you dream it's always there—whatever you want, just as you want it. It's like a short cut. Maybe that makes your brain soft, but I don't care. I wouldn't change even if I could . . ."

"Listen, Carol," I interrupted, "could you give me an idea what your dreams are like? Can you remember the one you had last night —or the night before, for instance?"

Carol smiled benignly. "Of course I can tell you," she said. "I'll tell you one I dream over and over . . . Of course, putting it into words spoils it. I can't describe the gorgeous colors I see, or the music I hear. Even if I were a writer, I don't think I could capture it. At least I've never read in a book anything like what I experience. Of course, writers don't go in much for dreams, do they? They're always describing life—or what goes on in people's heads. Maybe they don't dream the way I do. I dream about things that never happen . . . things that *couldn't* happen, I suppose . . . though I don't see why, either. Things happen the way we want them to happen, don't you think? I live so much in my imagination, that's why nothing ever happens to me, I guess. There's nothing I want very much—except to live . . . to go on living forever. That sounds a little foolish, maybe, but I mean it. I don't see any reason

**245**

why we should die. People die because they want to die—that's what I think. I read somewhere once that life was just a dream. That stuck in my head, because that's exactly what I thought myself. And the more I see of life the more I believe it's true. We're all living the life we dream . . ." She paused a moment to look at me earnestly. "You don't think I'm talking nonsense now, do you? I wouldn't talk to you this way unless I felt that you understood."

I assured her that I was listening most attentively, most sympathetically. Incidentally, she seemed to have grown a hundred times more beautiful. The irises of her eyes had become like veils studded with gold. She was anything but dumb, I reflected, as I waited for her to continue.

"I didn't tell you this, about my dreams, but maybe you've guessed it yourself . . . I often know what's going to happen to those around me. Last night, for instance, I dreamed that I was going to a party, a moonlight party, where I would meet a man who would tell me strange things about myself. There seemed to be a light around his head. He came from a foreign country, but he wasn't a foreigner. He spoke with a soft voice which was very soothing; he had a kind of drawl too—like you."

"What sort of things did you expect to hear about yourself, Carol?" I interrupted again. "What sort of strange things?"

She paused a moment, as if pondering her words. Then she said very frankly and innocently: "I'll tell you what I mean. It isn't about my love for my brother—that's very natural, I believe. Only people with dirty minds think that it's queer to love your own kith and kin . . . No, it wasn't that. It's about the music I hear and the colors I see. There is no earthly music like what I hear in my dreams, nor are the colors like those we see in the sky or in the fields. There is a music out of which all our music comes—and colors come from the same source. They were once one, that's what the man was telling me in my dream. But that was millions of years ago, he said. And when he said that, I knew that he must have understood too. I felt that we had known each other in some other world. But I also knew, from the way he spoke, that it was dangerous to admit such things in public. I had a sudden fear that if I were not careful people would consider me insane and then I would be put away and I would never dream again. I didn't fear that I would go insane—only that by putting me away they would murder this dream life. Then the man said something to me which frightened me. He said: *'But you are insane already, my dear girl. You have nothing to worry about.'* And then he disappeared. The next moment I saw everything in natural colors, only the colors were misplaced. The grass was violet instead of green; horses were blue; men and women were gray, ashen gray, like evil spirits; the sun was black, the moon was green. I knew then that I was out of my mind. I looked for my brother and when I found him he was staring at himself in a mirror. I looked over his shoulder, into the mirror, and I could no longer recognize him. He was a complete stranger. I called him by name, I shook him, but he continued to stare at his image in the mirror. At last I understood that he didn't recognize himself either. My God, I thought, we've both gone insane. The worst of it was, I didn't love him any more. I wanted to run away, but I couldn't. I was paralyzed with fear . . . Then I woke up."

"That's hardly what you'd call a beautiful dream, is it?" I said.

"No," said Carol, "yet it's beautiful to see things upside down some times. I'll never forget how wonderful the grass looked, nor how astonished I was to see the sun so black . . . Now that I think of it, the stars were shining. They were much closer to the earth than they usually are. Everything stood out brilliantly—much more clearly than in yellow sunlight. Did you ever notice how wonderful things look after a rain . . . especially in the late afternoon when the sun is setting? Supposing the stars were out—and twenty times bigger than we generally see them? Do you see what I mean? Maybe some day, when the earth wanders from its orbit, everything will look like that. Who knows? A million years ago the earth must have had a far different appearance, don't you think? The green was probably greener, and the red redder. Everything must have been magnified a thousand times—at least, that's what I imagine. Some people say that we don't see the real sun—only the lens of the sun, so to speak. The real sun is probably so bright that our poor human eyes can't see it. Our eyes are made to see very little really. It's funny but when you close your two eyes and start to dream, you see things so much better, so much clearer, so much lovelier. What eyes are those we see with then? *Where are they?* If one vision is real, why isn't the other also? Are we crazy when we dream? And if we're not crazy when we dream, why shouldn't we dream all the time? Or do you think that's crazy? You see, I told you I was a very simple person. I try to figure things out as best I can myself. But I don't get anywhere trying to think things out. I don't think anybody does."

At this point Humberto and Rodney returned, looking vague and roseate. Gerald was running about frantically, urging his guests to tackle the spaghetti. "It's vile," he whispered in my ear, "but the meat balls are good." We took our plates and sidled up to the Norwegian woman who was dishing it out. It was just like a canteen. The interior decorator went from one to another with a can of grated cheese and sprinkled the cheese over the fresh puke which passed for tomato sauce. He was infinitely pleased with himself, so much so that he forgot to eat. (Or perhaps he had eaten first.) Gerald was hopping about like a cherub, exclaiming: "Isn't it de-

248

licious? Did you get a meat ball?" As he passed behind me he nudged me gently and murmured under his breath: "I loathe spaghetti . . . it's vile."

Some newcomers had arrived during the interlude in the garden, youngsters mostly—probably starlets. The one called Claude, with blonde, wavy hair, had a lot of cheek. He seemed to know most every one present, especially the women, who treated him like a pet.

"I thought the party would be over by this time," he said, excusing himself for coming in his pajamas. Then, with a shrill bleat, he yelled across the room: "Gerald! Gerald! I say, Gerald!" (Gerald had just ducked into the kitchen to hide his mortification.) "Oh Gerald! When am I going to get a job? Do you hear me, Gerald? When am I going to work?"

Gerald came out with a frying pan in his hand. "If you don't shut your mouth," he said, going up to the dear brazen little Claude and swinging the frying pan over his head, "I'll crown you with this!"

"But you promised me that I'd have something before the month was up!" shrieked Claude, obviously enjoying Gerald's discomfiture.

"I promised no such thing," Gerald retorted. "I said the chances were good—*if you worked hard*. You're lazy . . . you expect things to come to you. Now be quiet and eat some spaghetti. You're making too much noise." He retreated to the kitchen once more.

Claude jumped to his feet and pursued him into the kitchen. I heard him say—"Oh Geraldine, did I say the wrong thing?" and then his voice was smothered, as if some one had laid a hand over his mouth.

Meanwhile the table in the dining room had been pushed back against the wall and a cute young couple began doing the jitterbug. They had the floor to themselves; every one stood and watched, gasping with admiration. The girl, who was tiny, cute, muscular, energetic, had a sort of Nell Brinkley face à la Clara Bow. Her legs twitched like a frog's under the scalpel. The young man, who couldn't have been more than nineteen, was just too beautiful for words. He was like a faun made of Dresden china, a typical California product destined to become either a crooner or an epicene Tarzan. Claude looked on with veiled contempt. Now and then he ran his fingers through his unruly locks and tossed his head back derisively.

To my astonishment Gerald now came forth and requested Humberto's wife to do a fling with him. He went at it with complete assurance, kicking his heels as if he were cock of the walk. What he lacked in finesse he made up for by his gymnastics. He had his own ideas about the jitterbug capers.

When he got a bit winded he stopped in front of Humberto and said: "Why don't you dance with your wife? She's a marvelous dancer." Now Humberto rarely ever danced with his wife—that was something which belonged to the past. But Gerald was insistent. "You *must* dance with her!" he exclaimed, making Humberto the center of all eyes.

Humberto wheeled off in desultory fashion, barely raising his feet from the ground. He was cursing Gerald for being such an idiot.

Lolita, whom nobody had asked for a dance, was furious. She sailed through the room, stomping her heels, and went straight up to the Brazilian flyer. "It's time to go," she hissed. "Will you take me home?" Not waiting for his assent, she took him by the hand and dragged him out of the room, saying in a loud, cheery voice which was full of ashes, "Good-night everybody! Good-night! Good-night!" (See, this is how I leave you, I, Lolita. I despise you. I'm bored to death. I, the dancer, I am leaving. I will dance only in public. When I dance I leave everybody gasping. I am Lolita. I am wasting time here . . .)

At the door, where Gerald was bidding her adieu, she paused to survey us, to observe if we were sufficiently impressed by her abrupt departure. Nobody was paying any attention to her. She had to do something, something dramatic, to call attention to herself. So she yelled, in her high, stagy, British voice: "Lady Astenbroke! Would you come here a moment, please? I have something to tell you . . ."

Lady Astenbroke, who seemed to be nailed to the armchair, had difficulty in getting to her feet. She had probably never been summoned like that before, but the thrill of hearing her name, the consciousness that all eyes were focused on her, overcame any resentment she may have felt. She moved like a ship in distress, her hat tilted at an absurd angle, her vigorous nose thrust forward like a vulture's beak.

"My dear Lady Astenbroke," Lolita was saying in a voice which seemed to be moderated but which she had thrown to the farthest corner of the house with the skill of a ventriloquist . . . "I do hope you will forgive me for running away so soon. You *will* come to the dress rehearsal, won't you? It's been such a pleasure seeing you again. You *will* come to see me in Rio, won't you? I'm flying back in a few days. Well, good-bye, then . . . good-bye! Good-bye everybody!" She gave a little toss of the head for our benefit, as though to say— "Now that you know who I am perhaps you'll behave more gallantly next time. You saw how Lady Astenbroke came trotting to my side. I have only to crook my little finger and the world comes running to me."

Her escort, whose chest was covered with medals, had come and gone without notice. His only chance for fame was to get killed in action. That would increase Lolita's publicity. One could easily visualize the item on the front page. "Daring Brazilian Flyer Killed

251

on the Libyan Front!" A few lines devoted to his exploits as an ace and then a long sob story about his "rumored" fiancée Lolita, the well-known dancer now starring in the big Mitso-Violet-Lufthansa film, "The Rose of the Desert." With photographs, to be sure, revealing Lolita's world-famous thighs. Perhaps in another part of the paper it would also be not too discreetly rumored that Lolita, heart-broken though she was at the news of the Brazilian's tragic death, had her eyes set on another dashing young officer, an artillery man this time. They had been seen together at this place and that during the Brazilian's absence. Lolita seemed to be attracted to tall, broad-shouldered young men who distinguished themselves in the gallant fight for freedom . . . And so on and so forth, until the publicity department of Mitso-Violet-Lufthansa thought the Brazilian's death had been properly exploited. For the next film there would of course be plenty to gossip about. If luck was with them, the artillery officer might also be killed in action. That would provide the opportunity for a double spread . . .

Absentmindedly I had taken a seat on the sofa, alongside a squat, garrulous creature whom I had been avoiding the whole afternoon.

"My name is Rubiol," she said, turning to me with disgustingly liquescent eyes. "*Mrs.* Rubiol . . ."

Instead of responding with "My name is Miller . . . *Henry* Miller," I said: "Rubiol . . . Rubiol . . . where have I heard that name before?"

Though it was obvious that there could only be one such name, one such monster in the whole United States, Mrs. Rubiol beamed with suffocating pleasure.

"Have you ever lived in Venice—or Carlsbad?" she cooed. "My husband and I always lived abroad—until the war. You probably heard of *him* . . . he's an inventor. You know, the triple-toothed bit for drilling . . . petroleum drills, of course . . ."

I smiled. "The only drills I know of are the ones that dentists use."

"You're not mechanical-minded, then, are you? Of course we love everything mechanical. This is the mechanical age."

"Yes," I replied, "I've heard it said before."

"You mean you don't believe it?"

"Oh yes, I believe it. Only I find it rather deplorable. I *loathe* everything mechanical."

"Not if you were living with us, you wouldn't. We never talk of anything else. You should have dinner with us some evening . . . our dinner parties are always a great success."

I let her rattle on.

"Everybody has to contribute something . . . some new idea, some fact of general interest . . ."

"How is the food?" I inquired. "Do you have a good cook? I don't care about the conversation as long as the food is good."

"What a funny man!" she giggled. "Of course the food is good."

"That's fine. That's all I ever worry about. What do you usually serve—fowl, steaks, roasts? I like a good roast beef, not too well done, and plenty of blood. And I like fresh fruit . . . not that canned stuff they give you in the restaurants. Can you make a good compôte? *Plums*—that's what I like . . . What did you say your husband was—an engineer?"

"No, an inventor."

"Oh yes, an inventor. That's a little better. What does he look like? Is he friendly?"

"You'd love him . . . he looks just like you . . . he even talks like you." She rattled on. "He's the most fascinating man when he begins talking about his inventions . . ."

"Do you ever have roast duckling—or pheasant?" I interrupted.

"Of course we do . . . What was I saying? Oh yes, about my

253

husband. When we were in London Churchill invited him to . . ."

"*Churchill?*" I looked dumb, as though I had never heard the name.

"Yes, Winston Churchill . . . the premier."

"Oh! Yes, I've heard of him."

"This war is going to be won in the air, that's what my husband says. We've got to build more planes. That's why Church . . ."

"I don't know a thing about planes . . . never use them," I interpolated.

"That doesn't matter," said Mrs. Rubiol. "I've only been up in the air three or four times myself. But if . . ."

"Now you take balloons . . . I like them ever so much better. Do you remember Santos Dumont? He took off in a balloon for Nova Scotia from the top of the Eiffel Tower. That must have been very exciting, don't you think? What were you saying about Churchill? Excuse me for interrupting you."

Mrs. Rubiol composed her mouth to make a long, impressive speech about her husband's tête-à-tête with Churchill.

"I'll tell you something," I said, just as she was about to open her mouth, "the dinners I like best are the ones where there's plenty to drink. You know, everybody gets a little drunk, and then there's an argument and somebody gets a crack in the jaw. It isn't good for the digestion to discuss serious things at the dinner table. By the way, do you have to wear a tuxedo at your dinner parties? I haven't got any . . . I just wanted to let you know."

"You can dress as you please . . . *naturally*," said Mrs. Rubiol, still impervious to my interruptions.

"Good! I have only one suit . . . the one I'm wearing. It doesn't look so bad, do you think?"

Mrs. Rubiol gave a gracious, approving smile. "You remind me of Somerset Maugham sometimes," she rattled on. "I met him on

254

the boat coming back from Italy. Such a charming, modest person! Nobody knew that he was Somerset Maugham except myself. He was traveling incognito . . ."

"Did you notice whether he had a club foot?" I asked.

"A club foot?" echoed Mrs. Rubiol, looking stupefactiously gaga.

"Yes, a club foot," I repeated. "Haven't you ever read his famous novel . . . *Of Human* . . ."

"*Of Human Passions!*" exclaimed Mrs. Rubiol, delighted to have guessed the wrong title. "No, but I saw the film. It was terribly morbid, don't you think?"

"Gruesome perhaps, but not morbid," I ventured. "Jolly gruesome."

"I didn't like Annabella so much in that film," said Mrs. Rubiol.

"Neither did I. But Bette Davis wasn't so bad, was she?"

"I don't remember," said Mrs. Rubiol. "What part did she play?"

"She was the switchman's daughter, don't you remember?"

"Why yes, of course I do!" exclaimed Mrs. Rubiol, trying desperately to remember something she had never seen.

"You remember when she fell headlong down the stairs with a tray full of dishes?"

"Yes, yes, of course I do! Yes, now I remember. She *was* wonderful, wasn't she? What a fall that was!"

"You were telling me about Churchill . . ."

"Yes, so I was . . . Now let me think . . . What was it I wanted to tell you . . . ?"

"Tell me first of all," I put in, "does he always have a cigar in his mouth? Some people say he goes to sleep with a cigar in his mouth. Anyway, that doesn't matter. I just wondered if he was as stupid in life as he is on the screen."

"*What!*" shrieked Mrs. Rubiol. "*Churchill stupid?* Whoever heard of such a thing? He's probably the most brilliant man in England."

"Next to Whitehead, you mean."

"*Whitehead?*"

"Yes, the man who rang the gong for Gertrude Stein. You know Gertrude Stein, of course? No? Well, then you must have heard of Ernest Hemingway?"

"Oh yes, now I know. She was his first wife, wasn't she?"

"Exactly," I said. "They were married in Pont-Aven and divorced in Avignon. Whitehead doesn't come into the picture yet. He was the guy who invented the phrase 'divine entropy' . . . or was it Eddington? I'm not sure now. Anyway, when Gertrude Stein wrote *Tender Buttons* around 1919, I should think—Hemingway was still sowing his wild oats. You probably recall the Staviski trial—when Loewenstein jumped out of the aeroplane and fell into the North Sea? A lot of water has passed under the bridge since then . . ."

"I must have been in Florence then," said Mrs. Rubiol.

"And I was in Luxembourg. I suppose you've been in Luxembourg, Mrs. Rubiol? No? A charming place. I'll never forget the luncheon I had with the Grand Duchess. Not exactly what you'd call a beauty, the Grand Duchess. A cross between Eleanor Roosevelt and Queen Wilhelmina—you know what I mean? She had the gout at the time . . . But I'm forgetting about Whitehead. Now what was it you were telling me about Churchill again?"

"I'm sure I don't remember any more," said Mrs. Rubiol. "We seem to flit from one thing to another. You're really a very strange conversationalist." She tried to compose her mouth again. "Now tell me a little more about yourself," she continued. "You haven't told me anything about yourself yet."

"Oh, that's easy," I replied. "What would you like to know? I've been married five times, I have three children, two of them normal, I earn about $375.00 a year, I travel a great deal, I never go fishing or hunting, I'm kind to animals, I believe in astrology, magic, telepathy, I take no exercise, I chew my food slowly, I like dirt and flies and disease, I hate aeroplanes and automobiles, I believe in long hours, and so on. Incidentally, I was born Dec. 26th, 1891. That makes me a Capricorn with a double hernia. I wore a truss until three years ago. You've heard of Lourdes, the city of miracles, haven't you? Well, it was in Lourdes that I threw away the truss. Not that any miracle happened . . . the damned thing just fell apart and I was too broke to buy another. You see, I was born a Lutheran and Lutherans don't believe in miracles. I saw a lot of crutches at the grotto of St. Bernadette—but no trusses. To tell you the truth, Mrs. Rubiol, hernia is not nearly as bad as people pretend. Especially a *double* hernia. The law of compensation, I suppose. I remember a friend of mine who suffered from hay fever. That's something to worry about. Of course you don't go to Lourdes to cure hay fever. As a matter of fact, there is no known cure for hay fever, did you know that?"

Mrs. Rubiol wagged her head in dismay and astonishment.

"It's much easier," I continued, rippling on like a brook, "to combat leprosy. I suppose you've never been to a leper colony, have you? I spent a day once with the lepers . . . somewhere off the island of Crete it was. I was going to Knossus to see the ruins when I happened to fall in with a doctor from Madagascar. He talked so interestingly about the leper colony that I decided to go along with him. We had a wonderful lunch there—with the lepers. Broiled octopus, if I remember rightly, with okra and onions. A marvelous wine they served there. Looked blue as ink. 'The Leper's Tears,' they called it. I discovered afterwards that there was a lot of cobalt in the soil. Magnesium and mica too. Some of the lepers were very wealthy . . . like the Indians of Oklahoma. Rather

257

cheerful people, too, on the whole, though you could never tell whether they were smiling or weeping, they were so disfigured. There was one American among them, a young fellow from Kalamazoo. His father owned a biscuit factory in Racine. He was a Phi Beta Kappa man—from Princeton. Interested in archaeology, I believe. His hands had rotted away rather quickly, it seems. But he managed pretty well with the stumps. Of course he had a good income and could make himself fairly comfortable. He had married a peasant girl . . . a leper like himself, or a *lepress* . . . I don't know how they call them. She was from Turkey, and didn't understand a word of English. But they were madly in love with one another just the same. They used a deaf and dumb language. All in all, it was a very pleasant day I spent there. The wine was excellent. I don't know whether you've ever tasted octopus. It seems a little rubbery at first, but you soon get used to it. Much better food there than at Atlanta, for instance. I had a meal once in the Penitentiary there . . . it nearly turned my stomach. Naturally the prisoners don't eat as well as the visitors . . . but just the same. No, Atlanta was foul. I think it was fried hominy they gave us— and pork drippings. Just to look at the stuff is enough to make you . . . I mean to turn your stomach. And the coffee! Simply incredible. I don't know how you feel about it, but I think that coffee, to be any good, must be black. It ought to look a little greasy too . . . oily like. Everything depends on the roasting, they say . . ."

At this point Mrs. Rubiol thought she would like to smoke another cigarette. It seemed to me that she was looking frantically about in search of some one else to talk to.

"My dear Mrs. Rubiol," I continued, lighting a cigarette for her and almost singeing her lips, "this has been a most delightful conversation. Have you any idea what time it is? I pawned my wrist watch just last week."

"I think it's time for me to go," said Mrs. Rubiol, glancing at her watch.

"Please don't go yet," I begged. "You have no idea how much I've enjoyed talking to you. What was it you were starting to tell me about Churchill when I so rudely interrupted you?"

Again Mrs. Rubiol, easily mollified, began composing her mouth.

"Before you begin," I said, agreeably surprised to see her twitch, "I must tell you one more thing. It's about Whitehead. You remember I mentioned his name a while ago. Well, it's about the theory of divine entropy. Entropy means running down . . . like a clock. The idea is that with time, or *in* time, as the physicists say, everything tends to run down. The question is—will the universe run down . . . and stop? I wonder if you've ever thought of that? Not such an impossible idea, is it? Of course, Spinoza had long ago formulated his own cosmological clock-work, so to speak. Given pantheism, it follows logically that one day everything must come to an end, God included. The Greeks had come to the same conclusion, circa 500 B. C. They had even formulated the idea of eternal recurrence, which is a step beyond Whitehead's theory. You undoubtedly must have run across the idea before. I think it appears in *The Case Against Wagner*. Or perhaps it's in another book. Anyway, Whitehead, being an Englishman of the ruling class, naturally looked with skepticism upon the romantic ideas current in the Nineteenth Century. His tenets, developed in the laboratory, followed *sui generis* upon those of Darwin and Huxley. Some say that, despite the rigorous traditions which hedged him in, there is traceable in his metaphysics the influence of Haeckel—not Hegel, mind you—who was at that time regarded as the Cromwell of morphology. I'm recapitulating all this rather briefly, you understand, merely to refresh your memory . . ." I gave Mrs. Rubiol a penetrating glance which had the effect of making her twitch anew.

In fact, I almost feared that she would go into a spasm. I didn't dare to think what I would say next, because I hadn't a thought in my head. I just opened my mouth and continued without a moment's reflection . . .

"There have always been two schools of thought, as you know, about the physical nature of the universe. I could take you back to the atomic theory of Empedocles, by way of corroboration, but that would only lead us afield. What I'm trying to tell you, Mrs. Rubiol, is just this: when Gertrude Stein heard the gong ring and declared Professor Albert Whitehead a genius, she inaugurated a controversy the consequences of which may not be fully felt until another thousand years have elapsed. To repeat, the question which Professor Whitehead posed was this: is the universe a machine which is running down, like an eight day clock, thus involving the inevitable extinction of life everywhere, and not only life but movement, even the movement of electrons—*or*, is this same universe imbued with the principle of regeneration? If the latter, then death has no meaning. And if death has no meaning, then all our metaphysical doctrines are eucharistic and eschatological. And by that I don't mean to embroil you in epistemological subtleties. The trend of the last thirty years is increasingly in the direction indicated by St. Thomas Aquinas. There are no more *pons asinorum* to be traversed, dialectically speaking. We have come out on firm ground . . . *terra firma*, according to Longinus. Hence the increasing interest in cyclical theories . . . witness the battles raging now over the Pluto-Neptune-Uranus transits. I don't wish to give you the impression that I am thoroughly conversant with all these developments . . . not at all! I merely point out that, by a curious spatial parallelism, theories developed in one field, such as astrophysics, for example, produce amazing reverberations in other fields, fields seemingly unrelated, as for example—geomancy and hydrodynamics. You were speaking of the aeroplane a little while ago, of its decisive importance in the ultimate phases of the present war. Quite so. And yet, without a more advanced knowledge of meteorological factors the Flying Fortress, to use a concrete illustration, will only become an impediment in the development of an efficient aerial armada. The Flying Fortress, to make it more clear, Mrs. Rubiol, stands in the same relation to the mechanical bird of the future as the dinosaur stands with regard to the human helicopter. The conquest of the stratosphere is only a step in the development of human aviation. We are merely imitating the birds at present. The birds of prey, to be more precise. We build aerial dinosaurs thinking to frighten the field mice. But one has only to think of the hoary ancestry of the cockroach, to give you an absurd example, to see how utterly ineffective was the dinosaur's maniacal development of the skeletal structure. The ant was never frightened out of existence—nor the grasshopper. They are with us to-day as they were with the *pithecanthropus erectus*. And where are the dinosaurs which once roamed the primeval veldt? Frozen deep in the Arctic tundras, as you know . . ."

Mrs. Rubiol, having heard me out to this point, suddenly began to twitch in earnest. Looking past her nose, which had become as blue as a cobra's belly, I saw in the dim light of the dining room what seemed like a bad dream. Dear precious Claude was sitting in Gerald's lap, pouring thimblefuls of some precious elixir down Gerald's parched throat. Gerald was running his fingers through Claude's golden locks. Mrs. Rubiol pretended not to be aware of this dénouement. She had taken out her little mirror and was sedulously powdering her nose.

From the adjoining room Humberto suddenly made his appearance. He had a whiskey bottle in one hand and an empty tumbler in the other. Rocking back and forth on his heels, he

261

looked at us benignly, as if we had requested the benediction.

"Who is that?" asked Mrs. Rubiol, at a loss to remember where she had seen him before.

"Why, don't you remember," I said, "we met at Professor Schoenberg's house last autumn. Humberto is the assistant gynaecologist at the Schizophrenic Sanitarium in New Caledonia."

"Would you like a drink?" said Humberto, staring at Mrs. Rubiol in utter bewilderment.

"Of course she would like a drink. Hand her the bottle!" With this I rose and, seizing the bottle, I pressed it to Mrs. Rubiol's lips. Too fluttered to know what to do, she swallowed a few spoonsful and began to gurgle. Then I put the bottle to my own lips and swallowed a good draught.

"It's getting interesting, don't you think?" I blurted out. "Now we can settle down to a real cosy intimate little chat, can't we?"

Humberto was listening with both ears cocked, the empty tumbler in one hand and the other grasping vainly for the missing bottle. He seemed unconscious of the fact that we had taken the bottle from him. He acted as though his fingers had grown numb; with his free hand he turned his coat collar up.

Spying a cute little vase on the table beside Mrs. Rubiol, I quickly disposed of the wilted flowers and poured a generous portion of whiskey into it. "We'll drink from this," I suggested, "it's much simpler."

"You're a Piscean, aren't you?" said Humberto, lurching violently towards Mrs. Rubiol. "I can tell by your eyes. You don't need to tell me when you were born, just give me the date."

"He means the *place* . . . latitude and longitude. Give him the azimuth too while you're at it; that makes it less complicated."

"Wait a minute," said Humberto, "you're making it embarrassing for her."

"*Embarrassing?* Nothing could embarrass Mrs. Rubiol. Isn't that so, Mrs. Rubiol?"

"Yes," she said meekly.

I lifted the vase to her lips and decanted a half cup of whiskey. In the dining room Gerald and Claude were still playing chick-a-dee. They seemed oblivious of the world. In that eerie light, joined together like the Siamese twins, they reminded me vividly of a water color I had made recently—the one called The Honeymooners.

"You were about to say . . . ?" I chirped, looking fixedly at Humberto who had wheeled round and was staring with ice-cold fascination at the Honeymooners.

"Y-e-es," said Humberto, pivoting slowly around, but without taking his eyes from the forbidden sight, "I wanted to ask you if I might have a drink."

"I just poured you one," I said.

"Where?" he asked, looking in the far corner of the room (as if there were a nice clean spittoon there with a cool drink hidden away in it.)

"I was just wondering," he continued, "where my wife disappeared to. I hope she didn't take the car." He held out his free hand expectantly, as though certain the bottle would return to its original position without effort on his part. Like a slow motion picture of a man juggling Indian clubs.

"Your wife left long ago," I said. "She went off with the aviator."

"*To South America?* She must be crazy." By now he had made a few steps forward in the direction of the bottle.

"Don't you think you ought to ask Mrs. Rubiol to have a drink, too?" I said.

He stopped dead. "A *drink?*" he shouted. "She's had half a gallon already. Or am I seeing things again?"

"My dear fellow, she hasn't had as much as a thimbleful yet. She's been sniffing it, that's all. Here, give me your glass. Let her taste it, at least."

Mechanically he proffered the glass. Just as I was about to grasp it he dropped it and, turning on his heel, staggered towards the kitchen. "There must be more glasses in this house," he muttered thickly, weaving through the dining room as if it were enveloped in a thick fog.

"Naughty, naughty!" came Gerald's voice. "Sagittarius has a perpetual thirst." Pause. Then sharply, like a weary, demented old cluck: "Don't you make a mess in that kitchen, you cute little blunderbuss! The glasses are on the top shelf, left-hand side, towards the back. *Silly archer*. These Sagittarians are always stirring up trouble . . ." Another moment of silence. "In case you want to know, it's now 2.30. The party was over at midnight. Cinderella isn't going to appear to-night."

"What's that?" said Humberto, making his appearance in the doorway with a tray full of glasses.

"I said the party ended hours ago. But you're such an exclusive package we're making an exception for you—and your friends in the next room. That dirty writer friend of yours particularly. He's the queerest Capricorn I've ever met. If he wasn't human I'd say he was a leech."

Mrs. Rubiol looked at me in consternation. "Do you suppose he's going to throw us out?" said her eyes.

"My dear Mrs. Rubiol," I said, putting a judicious tincture of benzoin into my voice, "he doesn't dare to throw us out—it would jeopardize the reputation of the establishment." Then, putting a little edge to the words, "You don't mean to tell me you've finished off that vase?"

I could feel her flustering as she staggered to her feet. "Sit down,"

264

said Humberto, pushing her none too gently back onto the couch. He reached for the bottle, or where he thought the bottle was, and began to pour as if it were really in his hand. "You must have a little drink first," he said, almost with a purr.

There were five glasses on the tray, all empty.

"Where are the others?" I said.

"How many do you want? Isn't that enough?" He was groping blindly under the couch for the bottle.

"How many what?" I said. "I'm talking about people."

"And I'm trying to find the bottle," said Humberto. "The other glasses are on the shelf."

"Don't mind us!" shouted Claude from the dining room.

"Why don't you go home?" shouted Gerald.

"I think," said Mrs. Rubiol, "that we really ought to be going, don't you?" She made no effort to rise.

Humberto was now half-way under the couch. The bottle was standing on the floor beside Mrs. Rubiol.

"What do you suppose he's looking for?" she said. Absent-mindedly she took another sip from the vase.

"Turn out the lights when you go," shouted Gerald. "And be sure to take Sagittarius with you. I won't be responsible for him."

Humberto was now trying to raise himself to a standing position —with the couch on his back and Mrs. Rubiol on the couch. In the commotion Mrs. Rubiol spilled some whiskey on the seat of Humberto's trousers.

"Who's peeing on me?" he yelled, making still more frantic gestures to free himself of the couch.

"If anybody's peeing," shouted Gerald, "it must be that Capricorn goat."

Mrs. Rubiol was now holding on to the back of the couch like a shipwrecked mariner.

265

"Lie flat, Humberto," I urged, "and I'll drag you out."

"What fell on me?" he mumbled forlornly. "This is a hell of a mess." He put his hand on his rear end, wondering, I suppose, if he had dreamed that it was wet. "As long as I didn't make caca . . . Haha! Caca! Wonderful!" he chuckled.

Mrs. Rubiol, who had now righted herself, thought this last was quite funny. She gave a few cackles and then began to choke.

"If you would go to sleep, the lot of you, I wouldn't mind," shouted Gerald. "Don't you have any sense of privacy?"

Humberto had disengaged himself; he was resting on hands and knees and blowing like a whale. Suddenly he spied the bottle. He flattened out like magic and reached for it with two arms, exactly as if he were struggling for a life-saving belt. In doing so he brushed Mrs. Rubiol's shins. "*Please!*" she murmured, her eyes twittering like two desynchronized song birds.

"Please *shit!*" said Humberto. "This is *my* turn."

"Be careful of that rug!" shouted Gerald. "I hope it's not the goat who's in trouble. The toilet is upstairs."

"Really," said Mrs. Rubiol, "this has gone far enough. I'm not accustomed to this language." She paused, as if quite distraught. Looking straight at me, she said: "Won't some one take me home, please?"

"Of course," I responded, "Humberto will drive you home."

"But can he drive—in his condition?"

"He can drive in any condition, as long as there's a steering wheel."

"I wonder," said Mrs. Rubiol, "if it wouldn't be safer if you drove me?"

"I don't drive. I could learn, though," I added quickly, "if you'd show me how the damned thing works."

"Why don't you drive yourself home?" said Humberto, pouring himself another tumblerful.

"I'd have done that long ago," said Mrs. Rubiol, "if I didn't have an artificial leg."

"*What?*" shouted Humberto. "You mean . . . ?"

Mrs. Rubiol didn't have a chance to explain what she meant. "Call the police!" boomed Gerald's voice. "They'll drive you for nothing."

"Fine. Call the police!" echoed Humberto.

"That's an *idea*," I thought to myself. I was just about to ask where the telephone was when Gerald forestalled me.

"It's in the bedroom, dearies . . . See that you don't knock the lamp over." His voice sounded weary.

"You don't think they'll arrest us?" I heard Mrs. Rubiol saying as I stepped into the next room.

As I lifted the receiver off the hook I suddenly wondered how you ask for the police. "How do you call the police?" I shouted.

"Just yell POLICE!" said Humberto. "They'll hear you."

I called the operator and asked for the police station.

"Is anything wrong?" she asked.

"No, I just want to talk to the lieutenant at the desk."

In a moment I heard a gruff, sleepy voice yelling—*Well?*

"Hello," I said.

There was no answer.

"Hello, hello . . . do you hear me?" I shouted.

After a long silence the same gruff voice replied: "Well, what's on your mind? Anybody dead?"

"No, nobody's dead."

"Speak up! What's the matter, are you frightened stiff?"

"No, I'm all right."

"Well, come on then, get it off your chest. What is it, an accident?"

"No, everything's fine. It's just that . . ."

"What do you mean, everything's fine. What are you calling *me* for? What is this?"

"Just a minute. If you'll let me explain . . ."

"All right, all right. Go ahead and explain. But make it snappy. We can't sit on the telephone all night."

"It's like this," I began.

"Listen, cut the preliminaries! What is it? Who's hurt? Did somebody break in?"

"No, no. Nothing like that. Listen, we just wanted to know . . ."

"Oh, I see . . . Wise guy, eh? Just wanted to know what time it is, is that it?"

"No, honest, nothing like that. I'm not kidding you. I'm serious."

"Well, spit it out, then. If you can't talk I'll send the wagon down."

"The wagon? No, don't send the wagon, please. Couldn't you send a car . . . you know, a regular police car . . . with a radio and all that?"

"And soft seats, I suppose? I get you. Sure we can send a nice little car along. What would you like—a Packard or a Rolls Royce?"

"Listen, Chief . . ."

"Don't chief me! Now *you* listen for a change. Shut your trap, do you hear me? Now listen! How many of you are there?"

"There's just three of us, Chief. We thought . . ."

"Three of you, eh? Now ain't that nice? And I suppose one of you's a lady too. She sprained her ankle, ain't that it? Now listen to me! You want to sleep to-night, don't you? And you don't want any bracelets on your wrists, do you? Well listen! Just go to the bathroom . . . put a nice soft pillow in the bath tub . . . and don't forget the blankets! Then get in the bath tub, the three of you—do you hear me?—and don't let me hear another squawk out of you! Hello! And listen to this . . . when you get nicely settled

268

in the tub, open the cold water faucet and drown yourselves!"
Bang!

"Well," yelled Gerald, when I had hung up, "are they coming?"

"I don't think so. They want us to sleep in the bath tub and then fill it with water."

"Have you ever thought of *walking* home? I think a brisk walk would be just the thing for you. Capricorns are usually very nimble on their feet." With this he advanced out of the darkness.

"But Mrs. Rubiol has an artificial leg," I pleaded.

"Let her hop home then."

Mrs. Rubiol was now deeply insulted. She rose to her feet with a surprising alacrity and made straight for the door.

"Don't let her go," said Humberto. "I'll see her home."

"That's right," shouted Gerald, "you see her home like a good boy and then fry yourself a kidney steak. Take the goat along with you." He glared at me in really menacing fashion. Claude now sidled up in his pajama top. Mrs. Rubiol turned her head away.

I had the presentiment then and there that we were going to get the bum's rush.

"Just a minute," said Humberto, still holding the bottle. He glanced towards Mrs. Rubiol disconsolately.

"Well, what now?" snapped Gerald, drawing still closer.

"But Mrs. Rubiol . . ." stammered Humberto, and he looked with pain and bewilderment at her lower limbs.

"I was just thinking," he continued, not knowing just how to phrase it, "I was wondering, since we're going to walk, if she shouldn't take off . . . well, I mean we could sort of carry her along." He made a helpless gesture with his two hands. The bottle slipped to the floor.

Being on the floor, and not knowing how to express his solicitude in words, Humberto impulsively began to crawl towards Mrs.

Rubiol. Suddenly, when within reach of her, he grasped both her legs by the ankles.

"Excuse me," he mumbled, "I just wanted to know which one . . ."

Mrs. Rubiol raised her good leg and shoved him off. Humberto rolled against the leg of a rickety stand, dislodging a marble statuette. Fortunately it fell on the rug; only an arm was broken, at the elbow.

"Get him out of here before the house tumbles down!" hissed Gerald. With this he bent over Humberto's prostrate figure and with the aid of Claude raised him to a semi-standing position. "My God, he's made of rubber." He was almost whimpering with rage now.

Humberto slipped to the floor.

"He needs a drink," I said quietly.

"Give him his bottle then and bundle him out of here. This isn't a distillery."

Now the three of us struggled to raise Humberto to his feet. Mrs. Rubiol graciously rescued the bottle and raised it to Humberto's lips.

"I'm hungry," he murmured faintly.

"He wants a sandwich, I guess," I said in a gentle voice.

"And a cigarette," whispered Humberto. "Just a little puff."

"Oh, dragon's britches!" said Claude. "I'll warm the spaghetti."

"No, no spaghetti!" Humberto protested. "Just a meat ball."

"You'll take spaghetti," said Gerald. "I said it wasn't a distillery. It's not a cafeteria either. It *could be* a menagerie, though."

"It must be getting late," said Humberto. "If only Mrs. Rubiol . . ."

"Just forget about Mrs. Rubiol," snapped Gerald. "I'll take Mrs. Rubiol home."

270

"That's good of you," muttered Humberto. He reflected a moment. "Why the hell didn't you say so in the first place?"

"O, shush! Button your lips! You Sagittarians are just little children."

Suddenly the door-bell rang. The police, undoubtedly.

Gerald suddenly became an electric eel. In a jiffy he had hoisted Humberto to a sitting position on the couch. The bottle he kicked under the couch. "Now listen, Capricorn," he said, grabbing me by the lapels, "think fast! This is *your* house and *your* party. You're me, understand? Everything's under control. Some one did telephone, but he left. I'll take care of Claude. Now answer the bell," and he whisked off like a flash.

I opened the door to find a plain clothes man standing there. He seemed in no hurry to rush in and fingerprint us.

"Come in," I said, trying to act as if it were my home and only four in the afternoon.

"Where's the body?" That was the first question out of him.

"There ain't any body," I answered. "We're all alive."

"So I see," he said.

"Let me explain . . ." I stammered feebly.

"Don't bother," he said quietly. "Everything's O. K. I'll sit down, if you don't mind."

As he bent over I suddenly got a whiff of his breath.

"Is that your brother?" he asked, nodding in Humberto's direction.

"No, he's just a roomer."

"A rumor? That's a good name for it. Well, don't I get a drink? I saw the lights and I thought . . ."

"Give him a drink," said Humberto. "And give me one too. I don't want any spaghetti."

"*Spaghetti?*" said the man. "I just want a drink."

"Did you bring a car?" asked Humberto.

"No," said the man. After a pause, in a respectful tone: "Is the body upstairs?"

"There is no body."

"That's funny," said the man. "I was told to fetch the body." He seemed to be in dead earnest.

"Who are you?" I asked. "Who sent you?"

"Didn't you phone for us?" said the man.

"Nobody phoned for you," I said.

"I must have the wrong house. Are you sure nobody died—about an hour ago?"

"Give him a drink," said Humberto, stumbling to his feet. "I want to hear what he has to say."

"*Who* asked you to come here?" I put in. "Who are you?"

"Give me a drink, like he says, and I'll tell you. We always get a drink first."

"What's this 'we' business?" said Humberto, growing more and more lucid. "Listen, somebody give him a drink, please. And don't forget me."

"Well," said the man, "you're an astrologer, aren't you?"

"Y-e-s," I said, wondering what next.

"People tell you when they were born, don't they? But nobody can tell you when you're going to die, *right?*"

"Nobody's dying here," said Humberto, his hands twitching for a glass.

"All right," said the man, "I believe you. Anyway, we don't come till they're cold."

"There's that 'we' again. Why don't you tell us? What's your game?" Humberto was almost shouting now.

"I dress 'em," said the man, throwing a bland smile.

"And the others, what do they do?"

272

"They just sit around and look cheerful."

"Doing what?" I asked.

"Waiting for trade, what do you think?"

Mrs. Rubiol had at last unearthed the bottle. I thought I might as well introduce her. "This is Mrs. Rubiol," I said. "Another body . . . still warm."

"Are you a detective?" said Mrs. Rubiol, extending her hand.

"A detective? What ever gave you that idea?"

Pause.

"Lady, I'm just a plain mortician," said the man. "Somebody phoned and said you wanted us. So I put on my hat and came over. We're just two blocks away, you know." He got out his wallet and handed her a card. "McAllister & Co. That's us. No frills, no fuss."

"Jesus!" said Humberto. "A mortician, no less. Now I must have a meat ball." He stumbled a few feet towards the dining room. "Hey!" he yelled, "what became of the soubrettes?"

I went to the kitchen. No sign of either of them. I opened the back door and looked out. Everything quiet.

"They've vamoosed," I said. "Now let's see what's left in the larder. I could go some ham and eggs."

"So could I," said Humberto. "Ham and eggs. That's more like it." He paused a moment, as if puzzling something out. "You don't suppose," he whispered, "that we might find another bottle somewhere?"

"Sure, we might," said I. "Turn the place upside down. There must be a gold mine here. Ask the undertaker to help you."

# OBSCENITY AND THE LAW OF
REFLECTION

To DISCUSS the nature and meaning of obscenity is almost as difficult as to talk about God. Until I began delving into the literature
which has grown up about the subject I never realized what a morass
I was wading into. If one begins with etymology one is immediately
aware that lexicographers are bamboozlers every bit as much as
jurists, moralists and politicians. To begin with, those who have
seriously attempted to track down the meaning of the term are
obliged to confess that they have arrived nowhere. In their book,
*To the Pure,* Ernst and Seagle state that "no two persons agree on

the definitions of the six deadly adjectives: obscene, lewd, lascivious, filthy, indecent, disgusting." The League of Nations was also stumped when it attempted to define what constituted obscenity. D. H. Lawrence was probably right when he said that "nobody knows what the word obscene means." As for Theodore Schroeder, who has devoted his whole life to fighting for freedom of speech [1] his opinion is that "obscenity does not exist in any book or picture, but is wholly a quality of the reading or viewing mind." "No argument for the suppression of obscene literature," he states, "has ever been offered which by unavoidable implications will not justify, and which has not already justified, every other limitation that has ever been put upon mental freedom."

As someone has well said, to name all the masterpieces which have been labeled obscene would make a tedious catalogue. Most of our choice writers, from Plato to Havelock Ellis, from Aristophanes to Shaw, from Catullus and Ovid to Shakespeare, Shelley and Swinburne, together with the Bible, to be sure, have been the target of those who are forever in search of what is impure, indecent and immoral. In an article called *"Freedom of Expression in Literature,"* [2] Huntington Cairns, one of the most broadminded and clear-sighted of all the censors, stresses the need for the re-education of officials charged with law enforcement. "In general," he states, "such men have had little or no contact with science or art, have had no knowledge of the liberty of expression tacitly granted to men of letters since the beginnings of English literature, and have been, from the point of view of expert opinion, altogether incompetent to handle the subject. Administrative officials, not the populace who in the main have only a negligible contact with art, stand first in need of re-education."

[1] See his A *Challenge to Sex Censors* and other works.
[2] From the *Annals of the American Academy of Political and Social Science,* Philadelphia, November, 1938.

Perhaps it should be noted here, in passing, that though our Federal government exercises no censorship over works of art originating in the country, it does permit the Treasury Department to pass judgments upon importations from abroad. In 1930, the Tariff Act was revised to permit the Secretary of the Treasury, in his discretion, to admit the classics or books of recognized and established literary or scientific merit, even if obscene. What is meant by "books of recognized and established literary merit?" Mr. Cairns gives us the following interpretation: "books which have behind them a substantial and reputable body of American critical opinion indicating that the works are of meritorious quality." This would seem to represent a fairly liberal attitude, but when it comes to a test, when a book or other work of art is capable of creating a furore, this seeming liberality collapses. It has been said with regard to the Sonnets of Aretino that they were condemned for four hundred years. How long we shall have to wait for the ban to be lifted on certain famous contemporary works no one can predict. In the article alluded to above, Mr. Cairns admits that "there is no likelihood whatever that the present obscenity statutes will be repealed." "None of the statutes," he goes on to say, "defines the word 'obscenity' and there is thus a wide latitude of discretion in the meaning to be attributed to the term." Those who imagine that the *Ulysses* decision established a precedent should realize by now that they were over-optimistic. Nothing has been established where books of a disturbing nature are concerned. After years of wrestling with prudes, bigots and other psychopaths who determine what we may or may not read, Theodore Schroeder is of the opinion that "it is not the inherent quality of the book which counts, but its hypothetical influence upon some hypothetical person, who at some problematical time in the future may hypothetically read the book."

276

In his book called *A Challenge to the Sex Censors*, Mr. Schroeder quotes an anonymous clergyman of a century ago to the effect that "obscenity exists only in the minds that discover it and charge others with it." This obscure work contains most illuminating passages; in it the author attempts to show that, by a law of reflection in nature, everyone is the performer of acts similar to those he attributes to others; that self-preservation is self-destruction, etc. This wholesome and enlightened viewpoint, attainable, it would seem, only by the rare few, comes nearer to dissipating the fogs which envelop the subject than all the learned treatises of educators, moralists, scholars and jurists combined. In Romans XIV: 14 we have it presented to us axiomatically for all time: "I know and am persuaded by the Lord Jesus that there is nothing unclean of itself, but to him that esteemeth anything to be unclean, to him it is unclean." How far one would get in the courts with this attitude, or what the postal authorities would make of it, surely no sane individual has any doubts about.

A totally different point of view, and one which deserves attention, since it is not only honest and forthright but expressive of the innate conviction of many, is that voiced by Havelock Ellis, that obscenity is a "permanent element of human social life and corresponds to a deep need of the human mind." [1] Ellis indeed goes so far as to say that "adults need obscene literature, as much as children need fairy tales, as a relief from the oppressive force of convention." This is the attitude of a cultured individual whose purity and wisdom has been acknowledged by eminent critics everywhere. It is the worldly view which we profess to admire in the Mediterranean peoples. Ellis, being an Englishman, was of course persecuted for his opinions and ideas upon the subject of sex. From the nineteenth century on all English authors who dared to treat the

[1] *More Essays of Love and Virtue.*

277

subject honestly and realistically have been persecuted and humiliated. The prevalent attitude of the English people is, I believe, fairly well presented in such a piece of polished inanity as Viscount Brentford's righteous self-defense—"*Do We Need a Censor?*" Viscount Brentford is the gentleman who tried to protect the English public from such iniquitous works as *Ulysses* and *The Well of Loneliness*. He is the type, so rampant in the Anglo-Saxon world, to which the words of Dr. Ernest Jones would seem to apply: "It is the people with secret attractions to various temptations who busy themselves with removing these temptations from other people; really they are defending themselves under the pretext of defending others, because at heart they fear their own weakness.

As one accused of employing obscene language more freely and abundantly than any other living writer in the English language, it may be of interest to present my own views on the subject. Since the *Tropic of Cancer* first appeared in Paris, in 1934, I have received many hundreds of letters from readers all over the world; they are from men and women of all ages and all walks of life, and in the main they are congratulatory messages. Many of those who denounced the book because of its gutter language professed admiration for it otherwise; very, very few ever remarked that it was a dull book, or badly written. The book continues to sell steadily "under the counter" and is still written about at intervals although it made its appearance thirteen years ago and was promptly banned in all the Anglo-Saxon countries. The only effect which censorship has had upon its circulation is to drive it underground, thus limiting the sales but at the same time insuring for it the best of all publicity—word of mouth recommendation. It is to be found in the libraries of nearly all our important colleges, is often recommended to students by their professors, and has gradually come

278

to take its place beside other celebrated literary works which, once similarly banned and suppressed, are now accepted as classics. It is a book which appeals especially to young people and which, from all that I gather directly and indirectly, not only does not ruin their lives, but increases their morale. The book is a living proof that censorship defeats itself. It also proves once again that the only ones who may be said to be protected by censorship are the censors themselves, and this only because of a law of nature known to all who over-indulge. In this connection I feel impelled to mention a curious fact often brought to my attention by booksellers, namely, that the two classes of books which enjoy a steady and ever-increasing sale are the so-called pornographic, or obscene, and the occult. This would seem to corroborate Havelock Ellis's view which I mentioned earlier. Certainly all attempts to regulate the traffic in obscene books, just as all attempts to regulate the traffic in drugs or prostitution, is doomed to failure wherever civilization rears its head. Whether these things are a definite evil or not, whether or not they are definite and ineradicable elements of our social life, it seems indisputable that they are synonymous with what is called civilization. Despite all that has been said and written for and against, it is evident that with regard to these factors of social life men have never come to that agreement which they have about slavery. It is possible, of course, that one day these things may disappear, but it is also possible, despite the now seemingly universal disapproval of it, that slavery may once again be practiced by human beings.

The most insistent question put to the writer of "obscene" literature is: why did you have to use such language? The implication is, of course, that with conventional terms or means the same effect might have been obtained. Nothing, of course, could be further from the truth. Whatever the language employed, no matter how objectionable—I am here thinking of the most extreme examples—one may be certain that there was no other idiom possible. Effects are bound up with intentions, and these in turn are governed by laws of compulsion as rigid as nature's own. That is something which non-creative individuals seldom ever understand. Someone has said that "the literary artist, having attained understanding, communicates that understanding to his readers. That understanding, whether of sexual or other matters, is certain to come into conflict with popular beliefs, fears and taboos, because these are, for the most part, based on error." Whatever extenuating reasons are adduced for the erroneous opinions of the populace, such as lack of education, lack of contact with the arts, and so on, the fact is that there will always be a gulf between the creative artist and the public because the latter is immune to the mystery inherent in and surrounding all creation. The struggle which the artist wages, consciously or unconsciously, with the public, centers almost exclusively about the problem of a necessitous choice. Putting to one side all questions of ego and temperament, and taking the broadest view of the creative process, which makes of the artist nothing more than an instrument, we are nevertheless forced to conclude that the spirit of an age is the crucible in which, through one means or another, certain vital and mysterious forces seek expression. If there is something mysterious about the manifestation of deep and unsuspected forces, which find expression in disturbing movements and ideas from one period to another, there is nevertheless nothing accidental or bizarre about it. The laws governing the spirit are just as readable as those governing nature. But the readings must come from those who are steeped in the mysteries. The very depth of these interpretations naturally make them unpalatable and unacceptable to the vast body which constitutes the unthinking public.

280

Parenthetically it is curious to observe that painters, however unapproachable their work may be, are seldom subjected to the same meddling interference as writers. Language, because it also serves as a means of communication, tends to bring about weird obfuscations. Men of high intelligence often display execrable taste when it comes to the arts. Yet even these freaks whom we all recognize, because we are always amazed by their obtuseness, seldom have the cheek to say what elements of a picture had been better left out or what substitutions might have been effected. Take, for example, the early works of George Grosz. Compare the reactions of the intelligent public in his case to the reactions provoked by Joyce when his *Ulysses* appeared. Compare these again with the reactions which Schoenberg's later music inspired. In the case of all three the revulsion which their work first induced was equally strong, but in the case of Joyce the public was more articulate, more voluble, more arrogant in its pseudo-certitude. With books even the butcher and the plumber seem to feel that they have a right to an opinion, especially if the book happens to be what is called a filthy or disgusting one.

I have noticed, moreover, that the attitude of the public alters perceptibly when it is the work of primitive peoples which they must grapple with. Here for some obscure reason the element of the "obscene" is treated with more deference. People who would be revolted by the drawings in *Ecce Homo* will gaze unblushingly at African pottery or sculpture no matter how much their taste or morals may be offended. In the same spirit they are inclined to be more tolerant of the obscene works of ancient authors. Why? Because even the dullest are capable of admitting to themselves that other epochs might, justifiably or not, have enjoyed other customs, other morals. As for the creative spirits of their own epoch, however, freedom of expression is always interpreted as license. The artist must conform to the current and usually hypocritical, attitude of the majority. He must be original, courageous, inspiring and all that—but never too disturbing. He must say Yes while saying No. The larger the art public, the more tyrannical, complex and perverse does this irrational pressure become. There are always exceptions, to be sure, and Picasso is one of them, one of the few artists in our time table to command the respect and attention of a bewildered and largely hostile public. It is the greatest tribute that could be made to his genius.

---

The chances are that during this transition period of global wars, lasting perhaps a century or two, art will become less and less important. A world torn by indescribable upheavals, a world preoccupied with social and political transformations, will have less time and energy to spare for the creation and appreciation of works of art. The politician, the soldier, the industrialist, the technician, all those in short who cater to immediate needs, to creature comforts, to transitory and illusory passions and prejudices, will take precedence over the artist. The most poetic inventions will be those capable of serving the most destructive ends. Poetry itself will be expressed in terms of block-busters and lethal gases. The obscene will find expression in the most unthinkable techniques of self-destruction which the inventive genius of man will be forced to adopt. The revolt and disgust which the prophetic spirits in the realm of art have inspired, through their vision of a world in the making will find justification in the years to come as these dreams are acted out.

The growing void between art and life, art becoming ever more sensational and unintelligible, life becoming more dull and hopeless, has been commented on almost ad nauseum. The war, colossal and portentous as it is, has failed to arouse a passion commensurate with its scope or significance. The fervor of the Greeks and the Spaniards was something which astounded the modern world. The admiration and the horror which their ferocious struggles evoked was revelatory. We regarded them as mad and heroic, and we had almost been on the point of believing that such madness, such heroism, no longer existed. But what strikes one as "obscene" and insane rather than mad is the stupendous machine-like character of the war which the big nations are carrying on. It is a war of materiel, a war of statistical preponderance, a war in which victory is coldly and patiently calculated on the basis of bigger and better resources. In the war which the Spaniards and the Greeks waged there was not only a hopelessness about the immediate outcome but a hopelessness as to the eternal outcome, so to speak. Yet they fought, and with tooth and nail, and they will fight again and again, always hopelessly and always gloriously because always passionately. As for the big powers now locked in a death struggle, one feels that they are only grooming themselves for another chance at it, for a chance to win here and now in a victory that will be everlasting, which is an utter delusion. Whatever the outcome, one senses that life will not be altered radically but to a degree which will only make it more like what it was before the conflict started. This war has all the masturbative qualities of a combat between hopeless recidivists.

If I stress the obscene aspect of modern warfare it is not simply because I am against war but because there is something about the ambivalent emotions it inspires which enables me better to grapple with the nature of the obscene. Nothing would be regarded as obscene, I feel, if men were living out their inmost desires. What man dreads most is to be faced with the manifestation, in word or deed, of that which he has refused to live out, that which he has throttled or stifled, buried, as we say now, in his subconscious mind. The sordid qualities imputed to the enemy are always those which we recognize as our own and therefore rise to slay, because only through projection do we realize the enormity and horror of them. Man tries as in a dream to kill the enemy in himself. This enemy, both within and without, is just as, but no more, real than the phantoms in his dreams. When awake he is apathetic about this dream self, but asleep he is filled with terror. I say "when awake," but the question is, *when is he awake, if ever?* To those who no longer need to kill, the man who indulges in murder is a sleep walker. He is a man trying to kill himself in his dreams. He is a man who comes face to face with himself *only in the dream.* This man is the man of the modern world, everyman, as much a myth and a legend as the Everyman of the allegory. Our life to-day is what we dreamed it would be aeons ago. Always it has a double thread running through it, just as in the age-old dream. Always fear and wish, fear and wish. Never the pure fountain of desire. And so we have and we have not, we are and we are not.

In the realm of sex there is a similar kind of sleepwalking and self-delusion at work; here the bifurcation of pure desire into fear and wish has resulted in the creation of a phantasmagorical world in which love plays the role of a chameleon-like scapegoat. Passion is conspicuous by its absence or by monstrous deformations which render it practically unrecognizable. To trace the history of man's attitude towards sex is like threading a labyrinth whose heart is situated in an unknown planet. There has been so much distortion and suppression, even among primitive peoples, that to-day it is virtually impossible to say what constitutes a free and healthy attitude. Certainly the glorification of sex, in pagan times, represented no solution of the problem. And, though Christianity ushered in a conception of love superior to any known before, it did

284

not succeed in freeing man sexually. Perhaps we might say that the tyranny of sex was broken through sublimation in love, but the nature of this greater love has been understood and experienced only by a rare few.

Only where strict bodily discipline is observed, for the purpose of union or communion with God, has the subject of sex ever been faced squarely. Those who have achieved emancipation by this route have, of course, not only liberated themselves from the tyranny of sex but from all other tyrannies of the flesh. With such individuals, the whole body of desire has become so transfigured that the results obtained have had practically no meaning for the man of the world. Spiritual triumphs, even though they effect the man in the street immediately, concern him little, if at all. He is seeking for a solution of life's problems on the plane of mirage and delusion; his notions of reality have nothing to do with ultimate effects; he is blind to the permanent changes which take place above and beneath his level of understanding. If we take such a type of being as the Yogi, whose sole concern is with reality, as opposed to the world of illusion, we are bound to concede that he has faced every human problem with the utmost courage and lucidity. Whether he incorporates the sexual or transmutes it to the point of transcendence and obliteration, he is at least one who has attained to the vast open spaces of love. If he does not reproduce his kind, he at least gives new meaning to the word birth. In lieu of copulating he creates; in the circle of his influence conflict is stilled and the harmony of a profound peace established. He is able to love not only individuals of the opposite sex but all individuals, everything that breathes, in fact. This quiet sort of triumph strikes a chill in the heart of the ordinary man, for not only does it make him visualize the loss of his meagre sex life but the loss of passion itself, passion as he knows it. This sort of liberation, which

285

smashes his thermometrical gauge of feeling, represents itself to him as a living death. The attainment of a love which is boundless and unfettered terrifies him for the very good reason that means the dissolution of his ego. He does not want to be freed for service, dedication and devotion to all mankind; he wants comfort, assurance and security, the enjoyment of his very limited powers. Incapable of surrender, he can never know the healing power of faith; and lacking faith he can never begin to know the meaning of love. He seeks release but not liberation, which is like saying that he prefers death instead of life.

As civilization progresses it becomes more and more apparent that war is the greatest release which life offers the ordinary man. Here he can let go to his heart's content for here crime no longer has any meaning. Guilt is abolished when the whole planet swims in blood. The lulls of peacetime seem only to permit him to sink deeper into the bogs of the sadistic-masochistic complex which has fastened itself into the heart of our civilized life like a cancer. Fear, guilt and murder—these constitute the real triumvirate which rules our lives. *What is obscene then?* The whole fabric of life as we know it to-day. To speak only of what is indecent, foul, lewd, filthy, disgusting, etc., in connection with sex, is to deny ourselves the luxury of the great gamut of revulsion-repulsion which modern life puts at our service. Every department of life is vitiated and corroded with what is so unthinkingly labeled "obscene." One wonders if perhaps the insane could not invent a more fitting, more inclusive term for the polluting elements of life which we create and shun and never identify with our behavior. We think of the insane as inhabiting a world completely divorced from reality, but our own everyday behavior, whether in war or peace, if examined from only a slightly higher standpoint, bears all the earmarks of insanity. "I have said," writes a well-known psychologist, "that this is a mad world, that man is most of the time mad; and I believe that in a way what we call morality is merely a form of madness, which happens to be a working adaptation to existing circumstances."

---

When obscenity crops out in art, in literature more particularly, it usually functions as a technical device; the element of the deliberate which is there has nothing to do with sexual excitation, as in pornography. If there is an ulterior motive at work it is one which goes far beyond sex. Its purpose is to awaken, to usher in a sense of reality. In a sense, its use by the artist may be compared to the use of the miraculous by the Masters. This last minute quality, so closely allied to desperation, has been the subject of endless debate. Nothing connected with Christ's life, for example, has been exposed to such withering scrutiny as the miracles attributed to him. The great question is: should the Master indulge himself or should he refrain from employing his extraordinary powers? Of the great Zen masters it has been observed that they never hesitate to resort to any means in order to awaken their disciples; they will even perform what we would call sacrilegious acts. And, according to some familiar interpretations of the Flood, it has been acknowledged that even God grows desperate at times and wipes the slate clean in order to continue the human experiment on another level.

It should be recognized, however, with regard to these questionable displays of power, that only a Master may hazard them. As a matter of fact, the element of risk exists only in the eyes of the uninitiated. The Master is always certain of the result; he never plays his trump card, as it were, except at the psychological moment. His behavior, in such instances, might be compared to that of the chemist pouring a last tiny drop into a prepared solution in

287

order to precipitate certain salts. If it is a push it is also a supreme exhortation which the Master indulges in. Once the moment is passed, moreover, the witness is altered forever. In another sense, the situation might be described as the transition from belief to faith. Once faith has been established, there is no regression; whereas with belief everything is in suspense and capable of fluctuation.

It should also be recognized that those who have real power have no need to demonstrate it for themselves; it is never in their own interests, or for their own glorification, that these performances are made. In fact, there is nothing miraculous, in the vulgar sense, about these acts, unless it be the ability to raise the consciousness of the onlooker to that mysterious level of illumination which is natural to the Master. Men who are ignorant of the source of their powers, on the other hand, men who are regarded as the powers that move the world, usually come to a disastrous end. Of their efforts it is truly said that all comes to nought. On the worldly level nothing endures, because on this level, which is the level of dream and delusion, all is fear and wish vainly cemented by will.

To revert to the artist again . . . Once he has made use of his extraordinary powers, and I am thinking of the use of obscenity in just such magical terms, he is inevitably caught up in the stream of forces beyond him. He may have begun by assuming that he could awaken his readers, but in the end he himself passes into another dimension of reality wherein he no longer feels the need of forcing an awakening. His rebellion over the prevalent inertia about him becomes transmuted, as his vision increases, into an acceptance and understanding of an order and harmony which is beyond man's conception and approachable only through faith. His vision expands with the growth of his own powers, because creation has its roots in vision and admits of only one realm, the realm of imagination. Ultimately, then, he stands among his own

288

obscene objurgations like the conqueror midst the ruins of a devastated city. He realizes that the real nature of the obscene resides in the lust to convert. He knocked to awaken, but it was himself he awakened. And once awake, he is no longer concerned with the world of sleep; he walks in the light and, like a mirror, reflects his illumination in every act.

Once this vantage point is reached, how trifling and remote seem the accusations of moralists! How senseless the debate as to whether the work in question was of high literary merit or not! How absurd the wrangling over the moral or immoral nature of his creation! Concerning every bold act one may raise the reproach of vulgarity. Everything dramatic is in the nature of an appeal, a frantic appeal for communion. Violence, whether in deed or speech, is an inverted sort of prayer. Initiation itself is a violent process of purification and union. Whatever demands radical treatment demands God, and always through some form of death or annihilation. Whenever the obscene crops out one can smell the imminent death of a form. Those who possess the highest clue are not impatient, even in the presence of death; the artist in words, however, is not of this order, he is only at the vestibule, as it were, of the palace of wisdom. Dealing with the spirit, he nevertheless has recourse to forms. When he fully understands his role as creator he substitutes his own being for the medium of words. But in that process there comes the "dark night of the soul" when, exalted by his vision of things to come and not yet fully conscious of his powers, he resorts to violence. He becomes desperate over his inability to transmit his vision. He resorts to any and every means in his power; this agony, in which creation itself is parodied, prepares him for the solution of his dilemma, but a solution wholly unforeseen and mysterious as creation itself.

All violent manifestations of radiant power have an obscene

glow when visualized through the refractive lens of the ego. All conversions occur in the speed of a split second. Liberation implies the sloughing off of chains, the bursting of the cocoon. What is obscene are the preliminary or anticipatory movements of birth, the preconscious writhing in the face of a life to be. It is in the agony of death that the nature of birth is apprehended. For in what consists the struggle if it is not between form and being, between that which was and that which is about to be? In such moments creation itself is at the bar; whoever seeks to unveil the mystery becomes himself a part of the mystery and thus helps to perpetuate it. Thus the lifting of the veil may be interpreted as the ultimate expression of the obscene. It is an attempt to spy on the secret processes of the universe. In this sense the guilt attaching to Prometheus symbolizes the guilt of man-the-creator, of man-the-arrogant-one who ventures to create before being crowned with wisdom.

The pangs of birth relate not to the body but to the spirit. It was demanded of us to know love, experience union and communion, and thus achieve liberation from the wheel of life and death. But we have chosen to remain this side of Paradise and to create through art the illusory substance of our dreams. In a profound sense we are forever delaying the act. We flirt with destiny and lull ourselves to sleep with myth. We die in the throes of our own tragic legends, like spiders caught in their own webs. If there is anything which deserves to be called "obscene" it is this oblique, glancing confrontation with the mysteries, this walking up to the edge of the abyss, enjoying all the ecstasies of vertigo and yet refusing to yield to the spell of the unknown. The obscene has all the qualities of the hidden interval. It is as vast as the Unconscious itself and as amorphous and fluid as the very stuff of the Unconscious. It is what comes to the surface as strange, intoxicating and forbidden, and which therefore arrests and paralyzes, when in the form of Narcissus we bend over our own image in the mirror of our own iniquity. Acknowledged by all, it is nevertheless despised and rejected, wherefore it is constantly emerging in Protean guise at the most unexpected moments. When it is recognized and accepted, whether as a figment of the imagination or as an integral part of human reality, it inspires no more dread or revulsion than could be ascribed to the flowering lotus which sends its roots down into the mud of the stream on which it is borne.

# REMEMBER TO REMEMBER

We cling to memory in order to preserve an identity which, if we but realized it, can never be lost. When we discover this truth, which is an act of remembrance, we forget everything else. "God himself," wrote de Nerval, "cannot turn death into annihilation."

292

IT BEGAN last night when I was lying face down on the floor beside Minerva, showing her on the map of Paris the neighborhoods I once lived in. It was a large Metro map and I became excited merely repeating aloud the names of the stations. Finally, with my index finger I began to walk rapidly from one quarter to another, stopping now and then when I came to a street which I thought I had forgotten, a street like the rue de Cotentin, for example. The street I had last lived on I couldn't find; it was an impasse between the rue de l'Aude and the rue Ste. Yves. But I found the Place Dupleix and the Place Lucien Herr and the rue Mouffetard (blessed name!) and the Quai de Jemmapes. There I crossed one of the wooden bridges which span the canal and got lost in the jam at the Gare de l'Est. When I came to my senses I was on the rue St. Maur. From there I headed due Northeast—towards Belleville and Menilmontant. At the Porte des Lilas I suffered a complete trauma.

A little later we were studying the *départements* of France. Such beautiful evocative names! So many rivers to traverse, so many cheeses to nibble at—and drinks of all kinds. Cheese, wine, birds, rivers, mountains, forests, gulches, chasms, cascades. Think of a region being called the Ile de France. Or the Roussillon. It was in my proofreading days that I first came upon the Roussillon, and always I connected it with *rossignol* which in English is nightingale. I never heard the nightingale until I came to visit the sleepy village of Louveciennes where Madame du Barry as well as Turgenev once lived. Returning one night to "the house of incest," where Anais Nin lived, it seemed to me that I heard the most miraculous song coming from the honeysuckle vine which draped the garden wall. It was the *rossignol*, which in English is nightingale.

Anyway, there in the garden I struck up a friendship with a dog, the third dog I had come to know intimately. But I am running ahead of myself. The dog comes later . . . when I am in the restaurant waiting for Miss Steloff to bring me a brochure called *The Meaning and the Use of Pain.* We were still on the floor, Minerva and I, studying the names of the *départements.* Minerva is asking if I ever visited Les Baux. She describes how she came upon it late one afternoon by bicycle.

"But that's exactly how I came upon it!" I shouted. "Do you remember those worn steps leading to the summit? And that weird pre-human landscape all about, as of Arizona or New Mexico?"

Minerva seemed to remember everything. It had been her first and only visit to France, just about the time of the Munich affair. At that moment I was probably sitting on a bench in the Allées de Tourny at Bordeaux. There were always pigeons waiting to be fed. And there was Hitler of course, only he demanded bigger mouthfuls.

From Les Baux I had cycled to Tarascon. It was noon when I arrived there and the town seemed absolutely deserted. I remember so vividly the broad street and the large *terrasses* set well back from the curb. At once I understood why Daudet had embarked on those wild adventures in the Africa of the mind. A little later, talking to the chef at the Hotel de la Poste, I realized that Tartarin had also visited the Waldorf-Astoria in New York. Still later, on the island of Spetsai, I came upon a replica of the inner court of the Hotel de la Poste . . . everything exactly the same, even down to the bird cages. The only difference was that the chef had become a Byzantine monk with a harem of dark-eyed nuns.

All this is preliminary to the real trance which came over me when I caught sight of the railway posters in the French restaurant. In the interval I swallowed at one gulp a book called *The Renegade* by my friend Alfred Perlès. It was like swallowing the

294

Door of an old building in Sarlat, France.

river of remembrance. I am not going to speak of the book here except to say that it has a peculiar anthroposophical flavor, thanks to the beloved Edgar Voicy and his master, Rudolf Steiner. There is an interlude of three pages, entirely in French, the gist of which might be divined from the phrase—*"l'orgasme est l'ennemi de l'amour."*

There is however another, more important, phrase which is repeated two or three times: "The mission of man on earth is to remember. . . ." It is one of those phrases like "the end justifies the means." It speaks only to those who are waiting for the cue.

Now I am sitting in the restaurant. The cooking is abominable, *Bordelais* supposedly, but actually, from the gastronomical standpoint, of no epoch, no region, which a gourmet could recognize. Even the pies are counterfeits. The hall-mark is dyspepsia.

It must have been the year 1942 when I was licking up this abominable food. With my eyes I was devouring the familiar railway posters—Le Corrèze, Quimper, Lourdes, Le Puy . . . I had been over a good part of America and I was hungry and thirsty for I knew not what. It was as if I had just returned from Timbuctoo, the first white man to get out alive, except that I had nothing to tell of but monotony, sterility and ennui. I had eaten in this restaurant before, had seen these same railway posters many times, and the food, though bad, was no worse than it had been. Suddenly everything was altered. They were no longer railway posters but deep, penetrative visions of a land I knew and loved, *souvenirs* of a home I had found and lost again. Suddenly my hunger and thirst were assuaged. Suddenly I realized that I had traveled twenty thousand miles in the wrong direction.

My gaze turned ever deeper inward; everything was bathed in the golden shaft of memory. Le Roussillon, which I had never visited, became the voice of Alex Small seated at the Brasserie Lipp,

Boulevard St. Germain. Like Matisse, he had been to Collioure, and he had brought back with him the feel, the smell, the color of the place. At that time I was about to make my first departure from Paris—by bicycle. Zadkine had drawn on the marble table top a rough sketch of the route which my wife and I were to follow in order to reach the Italian border. There were certain towns he insisted we must not overlook; Vezelay was one, I remember. But had he mentioned Vienne? That I can't recall. Vienne stands out vividly, shrouded in dusk, the sound of a rushing stream still pounding my ear drums. The Annamites must have been quartered there; they were the first I saw in France. What a strange army the French army was to me in those days! It seemed as though there were only the Colonials. Their uniforms captivated me, particularly those of the officers.

I am following an Annamite down the dark street. We have eaten and are looking for a quiet café. We enter one of those high-ceilinged cafés such as one comes upon in the provinces. There is sawdust on the floor and the sour smell of wine is strong. In the center of the room is a billiard table; two electric bulbs suspended from the ceiling by long strings are shining down on the green cloth. Two soldiers are bent over the table, one in a Colonial outfit. The whole atmosphere of the place is reminiscent of Van Gogh's work. There is even the pot-bellied stove with the long bent smoke-stack disappearing through the center of the ceiling. It is France in one of her homeliest aspects, a tiny morsel perhaps, but even if tucked away in an old vest one that never loses its savor.

There are always soldiers in France and they usually look forlorn and bedraggled. It is always evening when I notice them; they are either just leaving the barracks or just returning. They have the air of absent-minded ghosts. Sometimes they pause in front of a monument and stare at it blankly while picking their noses or scratching their behinds. One would never believe what a powerful army they make when all together. Separate and alone, they inspire pity: it is unseemly, unnatural, undignified for a Frenchman to be wandering about in uniform—unless he is an officer. Then he is a peacock. But he is also a man. Usually a very intelligent man, even if he is nothing more than a general.

At Perigueux one evening, thinking of the softness of Maryland, I notice the vacant lot which seems always to surround a barracks, and across it, as if he were making for the Sudan, lumbers a corporal with an unlit cigarette dangling from the corner of his mouth. He is absolutely dejected, his fly unbuttoned, his shoe laces coming undone. He is heading straight for the nearest *bistrot*. I am heading nowhere. I am full of the enameled blue sky, one foot in Maryland, one foot in the Perigord. The misery of the poor conscript is soothing to me; it is just another already familiar aspect of the France I adore. No dirt, no stench, no ugliness can mar my serenity. I am having a last look at France and whatever is is glorious.

Maybe it was an hour later, sitting outdoors before a delicious drink, that I thought of the soldier and then of the war of 1914 . . . *and then of Luneville.* A frail German girl with a deep, husky voice is telling me of the cellar she inhabited during those harrowing days and nights. It might as well have been the story of an escaped rat. There are no human traces in it, nothing but horror and deprivation. She has been starved, raped and tortured so many times that there is nothing left of her but a cracked voice. A few nights ago I said good-bye to her in Paris. I escorted her to the door of the Club where she sings for the Lesbian clientèle. The next war is already over-due. Her last words are of Lunéville, of the lurid night bombardments, the pillaging, the manhandling. She trembles from head to foot as if struck by the ague. Inside some one is humming *"Wien, Wien, nur du allein."*

The train rolls Eastward, towards Luxembourg. Soon we shall be passing through Sedan, that ominous spot whose name spells defeat and humiliation. Nearby is Charleville but we are too drunk to recall the exploits of the youthful Rimbaud. (What would I now give to stop that train and descend!) A bit Northward are Maubeuge, Mons, Charleroi, Namur, dread names with iron rings in their nostrils. War, war. The land of fortresses and the invasions which they invite. The iron ring draws tighter. The eagles scream.

In traveling one is always accompanied by the retinue of Death or by his batman. The quiet village where the river flows so peacefully, the very spot you choose to dream in, is usually the seat of ancient carnage. What stirs one to reverie is the blood that was spilled more copiously than wine. At Orange, so tranquil, so full of lost grandeur, the historical recitative whistles through the whitened bones of somnolent ruins. The Arc de Triomphe squats with mute eloquence in blinding sun-lit isolation. Through a doorway, over a jug glistening with cold sweat, the past leaps out. One sees through the arch into the Midi. On flows the Rhone with a thousand furious mouths to expire in the Gulf of the Lion. *"Départ dans l'affection et le bruit neuf."*

Somewhere between Vienne and Orange, somewhere in a village without name, we pulled up beside a curving street where there was a spacious, shady *terrasse*. A low hedge which followed the arc of the street and almost completely surrounded it. There, in a state of pleasant exhaustion, I gave way to a sense of absolute disorientation. I no longer knew where I was, why I had come, when or whither I would go. The delicious feeling of being an alien in an alien world filled me and drugged me. I was adrift and without memory. The street had no face. Church bells sounded, but as if from another world. It was the sheer bliss of detachment.

Heard enough, seen enough. Had come and gone again. Still here. Was flying and it seemed I heard the angels weep. No tongue wags. Beer cold, collar still floating. Was good.

"*Rumeurs des villes, le soir, et au soleil, et toujours.*"

Yes, and always. Always yes. Am here, was gone, and always, yes always, same man, same spot, same hour, same everything. Always same. Same France. *Same as what France?* Same as France.

Then I knew, without words, without thoughts, without *cadre, genre,* frame or reference, or frame of reference, that France was what it always is. Balance. Pivot. Fulcrum. This at-one-ment.

"*Assez connu. Les arrêts de la vie.*"

Ticking away in the heart of a watch that will never stop. The arc that never closes. The hum of traffic in a world without wheels. No name for it, no identification marks. Not even a trace of the vandal's hoofs.

———————

*The mission of man on earth is to remember* . . . Why did we laugh so uproariously when this phrase fell out of his mouth? Was it the way he looked when he uttered it, his mouth half full and the fork poised in mid-air like a prolonged forefinger? Was it too sententious for that quiet rainy day, for that sordid, inconspicuous restaurant on the edge of the 13th arrondissement?

To remember, to forget, to decide which it shall be. We have no choice, we remember everything. But to forget in order the better to remember, ah! To pass from town to town, from woman to woman, from dream to dream, caring neither to remember nor to forget, but remembering always, yet not remembering to remember. (Flash: Le Cours Mirabeau, Aix-en-Provence. Two giant Atlases, their feet buried in the sidewalk, holding the weight of the

299

upper stories of a house on their bulging shoulders.) At night in a lonely Western town (Nevada, Oklahoma, Wyoming) flinging myself on the bed and deliberately willing to remember something beautiful, something promising out of the past. And then, for no reason, out of sheer Saturnian perversity alone, my ears are afflicted by a heart-rending scream. "Murder! Murder! O God, help me, help me!" By the time I get to the street the cab has disappeared. Only the echo of the woman's screams animates the deserted street.

Sometimes I have only to touch the pillow and the most enchanting scenes re-emerge. Like cobwebs they form behind the retina. From cellar to ceiling I am one glittering web of visual enchantment. Closing my eyes I allow myself to be strangled by veritable festoons of memory. I take them below to be rearranged by the tyrannical psychopomp called Metamorphosis. In this fashion I came to see Carcassonne invested by the lions of Mycenae. Thus I met Richard the Lion-hearted at the Ham and Iron Fair. *Sur un chaland qui passe* I spotted *le jongleur de Notre Dâme.*

The mission of man on earth is to remember. To remember to remember. To taste everything in eternity as once in time. All happens only once, but that is forever. *A toujours.* Memory is the talisman of the sleepwalker on the floor of eternity. If nothing is lost neither is anything gained. There is only what endures. I AM. That covers all experience, all wisdom, all truth. What falls away when memory opens the doors and windows is what never existed save in fear and anguish.

One night, listening to the rain drumming on the tin roof of our shack, I suddenly recalled the name of the village to which I had made my first excursion: *Ecoute s'il Pleut.* Who would believe that a town could have such an enchanting name? Or that there could be one called *Marne-la-Coquette* or *Lamalou-les-Bains* or *Prats de Mollo?* But there are a thousand such endearing names

300

throughout France. The French have a genius for place names. That is why their wines too have such unforgettable names—Château d'Yquem, Vosne Romanée, Châteauneuf du Pape, Gevrey-Chambertin, Nuits St. George, Vouvray, Meursault, and so on. Before me is the label I salvaged from a bottle we finished the other night at Lucia, chez Norman Mini. It was a Latricières-Chambertin from the Caves des Ducs de Bourgogne, Etablissements Jobard Jeune & Bernard, Beaune (Côte d'Or), maison fondée en 1795. What recollections that empty bottle calls up! Especially of my friend Renaud who had been a *pion* at the Lycée Carnot, Dijon, and of his visit to Paris with two precious bottles of Beaune under his arm. "What a horrible French they speak here in Paris!" was the first thing he exclaimed. Together we explored Paris, from the Abattoirs de la Villette to Montrouge, from Bagnolet to the Bois de Boulogne. How wonderful to see Paris through the eyes of a Frenchman beholding it for the first time! How exotic to be an American showing a Frenchman his own great city! Renaud was one of those Frenchmen who loves to sing. He also loved the German language, which is even more rare for a Frenchman. But he loved best his own language and spoke it with perfection. To understand the nature of that perfection I had to wait until I heard him converse with Jeanne of Poitou and again with Mademoiselle Claude of the Touraine country. Finally it was with Nys of the Pyrenees. Nys of Gavarnie.

Gavarnie! Who gets to see Gavarnie? Perpignan, yes. Chamonix, yes. But *le cirque de Gavarnie?* It is small, France, but crowded with wonders. At Montpellier one dreams of Le Puy; at Dômme of Rouen; at Arcachon of Amiens; at Troyes of Amboise; at Beaucaire of Quimper; in the Ardennes of the Vendée; in the Vosges of Vaucluse; in Lorraine of Morbihan. It makes you feverish to move from place to place; everything is interconnected, perfumed with the past and alive with the future. You hesitate to take a train because while you doze you may miss a bewitching little area you may never have the chance to see again. Even the dull spots are exciting. Is there not always an Amer Picon to greet you, or a Cinzano, or a Rhum d'Inca? Wherever you see the letters of the French alphabet there is good food, drink and conversation. Even when it looks grim, sombre, forbidding, there is a chance you will meet some one who will enliven the scene with talk. It may not be that cultured looking old gentleman with the walking stick, it may be the butcher or the *femme de chambre*. Go towards the little fellow always, towards *les quelconques*. It is the little flowers which make the most ingratiating bouquets. The precious things in France are usually little things. What is adorable is what is *mignon*. The cathedrals and chateaux are grand; they demand prostration, veneration. But the true Frenchman loves what he can hold in his two hands, what he can walk around, what he can encompass with a sweep of the eye. You do not have to crook your neck to see the wonders of France.

I was speaking of Monsieur Renaud's exquisite French. Just as to enjoy the bouquet of certain rare wines one must have the proper ambiance, so to hear French at its best one needs the atmosphere which only the *jeune fille* of the provinces knows how to create. In every land it is the beautiful woman who creates the illusion of speaking the language best. In France there are certain regions where the spoken language achieves the maximum of beauty and enchantment. Claude was a prostitute and so was Nys, but they spoke like angels. They used the clear, silvery speech of the men who fashioned the French language and made it immortal. With Claude there were reflections as pure as the images which float in the Loire.

If the memory of certain *femmes de joie*, as they are justly called, is precious to me it is because at their breasts I drank again those strong draughts of mother's milk in which language, landscape and myth are blended. They were all so gentle, tolerant and wise, employing the diction of queens and the soothing charms of houris. There was purity in their gestures as there was in their speech, at least to me it seemed so. I was not prepared for the subtle graces they exhibited, knowing only the crude, awkward, over-assertive mannerisms of the American woman. To me they were the little queens of France, the unrecognized daughters of the Republic, spreading light and joy in return for abuse and mortification. What would France be without these self-appointed ambassadors of goodwill? If they fraternize with the foreigner, or even with the enemy, are they therefore to be regarded as the lepers of society? I hear that France is now cleaning house, that she intends to do away with her houses of prostitution. Absurd though it be (in a civilization such as ours), perhaps this "reform" will produce unexpected results. Perhaps these unfortunate victims of society will now infect the hypocritical members of the upper strata, imbue the pale sisters of the bourgeoisie with spice, wit and tang, with a greater love of freedom, a deeper sense of equality.

It is so common, so hackneyed, to see in the films a drab, narrow street in which the pathetic figure of a prostitute stands waiting like a vulture in a fog or drizzle of rain in order to pounce upon the forlorn hero. One is never given the sequel to this pathetic scene; one is left to suppose that the miserable hero is immediately shorn of his lucre, infected with a dread disease, and abandoned on a verminous bed in the small hours of the night. They do not tell us how many desperate souls are rescued by these rapacious sisters of mercy; they do not indicate what led this "leprous vulture" to follow such a calling. They do not compare this direct, honest pursuit of a livelihood with the slimy, deadening tactics

303

of the women of the upper classes. They do not dwell on the desperate courage, the thousand and one little braveries—quotidian acts of heroism—which the prostitute must enact in order to survive. They portray these women as a breed apart, *infect*, to use the native word for it. But what is truly *infect* is the money sweated from their hides which goes to support the churches and war machines, filthy little sums sieved through pimps and politicians (who are one and the same) which finally becomes a golden dung-hill used to buttress a decayed and tottering society of misfits.

---

When I look at the map of France, at the names of the old provinces particularly, there is evoked a veritable galaxy of celebrated females, some noted for their sanctity, others for their easy virtue, or their heroism, their wit, their charm, their high intelligence, but all illustrious, all equally dear to the French heart. One has only to reel off such names as Bourgogne, Provence, Languedoc, Gascogne, Saintonge, Orléannais, Limousin, to recall the role of woman in French history, French culture. One has only to think of the names of familiar French writers, the poets in particular, to recall the indispensable part played by the women they loved: women of the court, women of the stage, women of the street, sometimes women of stone or wood, sometimes a mere wraith or a name to which they became attached, obsessed, inspired to perform miraculous feats of creation. The aura which surrounds so many of these names is part of a greater aura: service. Service to God, service to Love, service to Creation, service to Deed . . . service even to Memory. No movement of consequence was ever initiated that did not include the person of some magnetic, devoted woman. Everywhere you go in France there is the inner story of feminine inspiration, feminine guidance. The men of France can accomplish nothing heroic, nothing of permanent value in whatever realm, without the love and the loyalty of their womenfolk.

In visiting the famous chateaux of the Loire, or the formidable bastides of the Dordogne, it was not of the warriors, the princes, the dignitaries of the Church that I thought, but of the women. All these strongholds, imposing, stately, elegant, gracious, awesome, as the case may be, were but shells to harbor and protect the flower of the spirit. The women of France were the palpable symbol of that flowering spirit; they were not merely idolized, eulogized, worshiped in verse, stone and music, they were enthroned in the flesh. These vast musical cages, immune to everything but treachery, vibrated with feminine ardor, feminine resistance, feminine devotion. They were courts of love and scenes of valor; all the dualities modulated through their ribs and vaults. The flowers, the animals, the birds, the arts, the mysteries, all were permeated by the marriage of the male and female principles. It is not strange that the country which is so gloriously feminine, *la belle France,* is at the same time the one in which the spirit, which is masculine, has flowered most. If proof were needed, France is the living proof that to exalt the spirit both halves of the psyche must be harmoniously developed. The rational aspect of the French *esprit* (always magnified by the foreigner) is a secondary attribute and a much distorted one. France is essentially mobile, plastic, fluid and intuitive. These are neither feminine nor masculine qualities exclusively; they are the attributes of maturity, reflecting poise and integration. That sense of equilibrium which the world so much admires in the French is the outcome of inner, spiritual growth, of continuous meditation upon and devotion to what is *human.* Nowhere in the Western world does man, as creature and being, loom so large, so full, so promising. But nowhere else in the Western world has the spiritual aspect of man been so thoroughly recognized, so generously developed. This exaltation of man as man, of man as arbiter of his fate, is the very seed of the revolutionary spirit of France. To this we owe that strong sense of reality which is always experienced in their midst. It is what ennobles them in defeat and makes them unpredictable in crises. The courage and the resources of the French are always best displayed by the individual. The nation as a whole may go to pot, the individual never. As long as one Frenchman survives all France will remain visible and recognizable. It does not matter what her position, as a world power, may be; it matters only that this molecular-spiritual product known as a Frenchman should not perish.

I never worry about France. It would be like worrying about the earth. What is French is imperishable. France has transcended her own physical being. And by that I do not mean just recently, as the result of defeat and humiliation, or by passing from a first to a second-rate power. The transcendence I speak of began from the day France was born, when she became conscious, as it were, that she had something to give the world. The mistake which foreigners so often make, in judging France, is to confound the spirit of conservation with miserliness or niggardliness. The French are not prodigal with their physical possessions; they do not give readily of the things which nourish the body. They give the fruits of their creation, which is much more important. The source they jealously guard. This is wisdom, the wisdom of a people who love the earth and who identify themselves with it. Americans are the very opposite. They are lavish with that which does not belong to them, with riches they have not earned. They exploit the earth and their fellow-men. They would plunder Paradise, if they knew how. Impoverished at the source, their bounty avails not. The Frenchman protects the vessel which contains the spirit; it makes him seem hard and self-concerned to the easy-going ones. But it is only the story of the wise and the foolish virgins. Eventually, when what now seems a menace becomes reality, it is to the French we shall be obliged to turn for sustenance and inspiration. Unless the French too, which I doubt, succumb to the modern spirit.

Almost forty years ago Péguy pointed out the danger. "THE MODERN WORLD DEBASES," he shouted. "This is its specialty. I would almost say that this is its calling, if the beautiful word calling were not above all to be respected." He returns to the theme again and again. He explains how and why this is so. And then, in one paragraph, he sums it up definitively, passes judgment on this world which since his time has moved with alarming rapidity towards its own annihilation. This is the epitaph he engraved in letters of fire:

"The modern world debases. It debases the state; it debases man. It debases love; it debases woman. It debases the race; it debases the child. It debases the nation; it debases the family. It even debases (always our limitations), it has succeeded in debasing what is perhaps most difficult in the world to debase, because this is something which has in itself, as in its texture, a particular kind of dignity, like a singular incapacity for degradation: it debases death."

Despite the truth of his words, despite the terrible experience through which the French people have just passed, despite the fact that everything is going from bad to worse and that France is no more immune than any other country in the world, despite all this there are Frenchmen to-day who refuse to surrender to the ignominious debacle taking place on all fronts. There are Frenchmen so anchored in reality, so certain even to-day of the indomitable spirit of man, that they stand before the world as the chosen survivors, I might almost say, of a planet already doomed to extinction. They have envisaged everything which is likely to happen, every dire calamity which indeed most probably will happen, but

307

they remain resolute and undaunted, determined to carry on, *as men*, to the end of time. They realize that the example which France gave the world has been dishonored and disfigured; they are aware that the power to shape the world to their liking has been deprived them. They go on living, nevertheless, as though none of this mattered. They go on like forces which, wound up and put in motion, cannot cease exerting influence until thoroughly dispersed. They do not rely on government, nationhood, culture or tradition, but on the spirit which is in them. They have abandoned the props, burned the scripts. On the naked stage of the world they improvise their lines according to an inner dictation, acting without directors, spurning rehearsals, costumes, stage sets, taking no cues from the wings, observing no concern for the temper of the audience, obsessed with only one idea—to act out the drama which is in them. This is the desperate drama of identification, the drama in which the barrier between actor and audience and actor and author, too, is dissolved. The actor is no longer the agent of a vehicle created for him; he is the means and the end at the same time. The world is his stage, the play is his own, the audience is his fellow-men. The idea which the name France once evoked *magically* now becomes a living element of reality which, to be accepted, must be played out. The whole French past has now become a theatre so magnified that it embraces the world. In it the Chinese have their part, as do the Russians and the Hindus, the Americans, the Germans, the English. This is the last act in the drama of nations. If it is the end of France it will be the end of all other countries too. That mobility, that plasticity of the French will assert itself even more eloquently in the moment of dissolution.

In an article called "The End of the War," written for *Les Temps Modernes*, Jean-Paul Sartre writes: "And if we pledge ourselves to life, we pledge this also for our friends, for ourself personally, and for France. We undertake the endeavor to integrate ourselves into this strong, ruthless world, into this humanity under peril of death. We must also make a pledge for this earth, even though it may shortly crumble away. We must do this simple because we *are*." [1]

That France had become for me mother, mistress, home and muse I did not realize for a long time. I was so desperately hungry not only for the physical and the sensual, for human warmth and understanding, but also for inspiration and illumination. During the dark years in Paris all these needs were answered. I was never lonely, no matter how miserable my condition. To be a prisoner of the streets, as I was for a long time, was a perpetual recreation. I did not need an address as long as the streets were there free to be roamed. There are scarcely any streets in Paris I did not get to know. On every one of them I could erect a tablet commemorating in letters of gold some rich new experience, some deep realization, some moment of illumination. All those individuals without name whom I encountered in moments of anxiety or desperation remain permanently engraved in my memory. I identify them with the streets on which I met them. Theirs, like mine, was a world without passports, visas or calling cards. A common need brought us together. Only the desperate ones can understand this sort of communion, evaluate it truly. And always, on these same immemorial streets, it was chance which saved me. To go into the street was like entering a gambling hall: always all or nothing. To-day millions of people once respectable, once comfortably situated, once secure, as they thought, have been obliged to adopt the same attitude. "Only get desperate enough," I used to say, "and everything will turn out well." No one elects voluntarily to become desperate. No one believes, until he has experienced it for himself, how salu-

[1] From the translation in *Portfolio 3*, Washington, D. C.

tary this condition can be. The revolutionaries do not subscribe to this view of things. They expect men and women to affirm the right principles without having been through the fire. They want heroes and saints without giving them the opportunity to suffer, to pass through the ordeal. They want a transition from a bad state of affairs to a good one without the *dépouillement* which alone will make them surrender their old habits, their old and out-worn view of things. The man who has not been stripped to the bone will never appreciate a so-called good state of affairs. The man who has not been forced to help others (in order to save himself) can never become a revolutionary force in society. He has not been cemented, he can never be cemented, into the new order; he has simply been glued to it. He will come undone the moment the heat is applied.

One may wonder, since I had been through the ordeal before (in America), why I had to go through it again. Let me explain. In America, when I went under, it was to touch a false bottom. The real bottom, *chez nous*, is a quicksand from which there is no emerging. I could never muster hope. There was no to-morrow, only the endless prospect of a deadly gray sameness. I could never escape the feeling that I was in a vacuum, bound in a straitjacket. To free myself was to rejoin a world whose air I could not breathe. I was the bull in the bull ring, and the end was certain death. A death without hope of resurrection, moreover. For not only do we make sure in America that the body is dead, we make certain that the soul too is killed.

In France I not only found the things I mentioned but I found also a new will to live. I found a father too, several in fact. The first was my old French teacher from the Midi, dear old Lantelme, dead now I suppose. He spent his summers on the Ile d'Oleron.

My visits seemed to gladden his heart. Our talk was always of the old France, of Provence particularly. He gave me the illusion that I had once been part of it, that I was closer in spirit to the men of the Midi than to my own countrymen or to the barbarians of Paris. Between us there were no barriers which had first to be broken down. We understood and accepted one another from the very beginning—despite my horrendous French. Through his offices my mind was made ready to perceive the ripe wisdom of the French, their native courtesy, their tolerance, their sense of discrimination, their keen ability to evaluate the essential and the significant. Through him I became aware of a new kind of love: the love for the humblest things. Everything with which he surrounded himself was cherished. I who all my life had parted so lightly with everything now began to view the most trifling objects, the most insignificant events, with a new eye. In his home I began to understand for the first time the true meaning of man's creation. I saw that it was a reflection of the divine. I saw that we must begin at home, with what is nearest to hand, with what is despised and overlooked because so familiar. Slowly, slowly, as if veils were being removed from my eyes—and they were indeed!—I began to realize that I was living in a treasure garden, the garden of France at which the whole world casts loving, yearning glances. I understood why the Germans, above all others in Europe, had need of this garden, why they never ceased to cast covetous glances in its direction. I understood why they would trample on it if they could not possess it for their own. I understood also why my own countrymen would continue to make it a refuge though they had (supposedly) everything in the world at their disposal. I could understand why in moments of envy or bitterness, or out of a perverse nostalgia, they would one day refer to this paradise as an asylum for the aged and the feeble. I could foresee that the very land which offered them freedom and ease they would one day renounce, or denounce, as a bed of corruption.

*La France vivante!* Why does that phrase continue to ring in my ears? Because it is the one which communicates the signal fact about France. Even putrescent, France is always alive, alive to the finger-tips. How many times since the war's end have I heard from the lips of Americans—"But France is finished!" I am tired of giving the lie to these glib defeatists. France finished? *Jamais.* The very thought is inconceivable. That France was defeated, that she was sorely humiliated, that she has assumed a guilt incommensurate with the crime (*crime,* what crime? I ask), all this is undeniable. That she is finished, *ausgespielt, foutu,* no, never. It does not matter to me if the hyenas have taken over; it does not matter ultimately if the element which has won out is not representative of the best. All that matters is that France is still *vivante,* that the spark has not been extinguished. What do we expect of a country which has been under the heel of the conqueror for five long years? Do we expect her citizens to turn somersaults in the streets? (Think how the people of our own South reacted when the War between the States was terminated. Think how they feel and act even to-day eighty years after they surrendered to the North.) What do we expect of France? That her citizens should rise from their graves as did the saints on the day of the Crucifixion? What the blithe, insensitive spirits of the New World fail to understand is that the French as a whole have yet to be convinced that the agony is over. For us the war may be over, but not for France, not for any country in Europe. When with our cute little bomb, one of those Christmas packages which only America knows how to prepare, we "saved the world" again we forgot to include the recipe for eternal peace. We jealously guard the power to anni-

312

hilate the world at one stroke but we have nothing to offer in the way of hope and enthusiasm.

Europe is always the disrupter of the peace. We (of course) only make war to stop the Europeans from fighting. After each war Europe is supposed to be finished. "It will never be the same again," we croak. And of course it never is, not *quite* the same. It is only here in America that everything always remains the same. The most profound, agonizing cataclysms leave us exactly where we were before, in spirit, at least. Europe changes inwardly as well as outwardly with each crisis she undergoes. Not only is the heart affected, but the mind and soul. The ravages of war leave ineradicable traces. America always remains safe and secure. We continue as always to produce bumper crops, new and better machines, and babies too. Occasionally there are shortages, not because of any lack but because of greed and mismanagement. While we set about to democratize the world our own rigid caste system is left intact.[1] Nothing from above seeps below, and vice versa. America's 140,-000,000 people continue to live, as before, in strait-jackets, comfortable strait-jackets, perhaps, because of the illusion cleverly fostered that they enjoy free speech, free press, free trade, free air.

In another section of the paper General Eisenhower, who ought to know what he's talking about, is quoted as saying: "War is not only destructive, it is sterile of positive result." This is the military man's usual way, of course, of urging us to be prepared. Prepared for what? Prepared to make war again—i. e., *if necessary*. Has any one ever heard of a war that was not necessary at the time? Put an end to war, but don't ever stop for one minute thinking up newer

[1] A news dispatch from Detroit the other day had as caption: "U. S. NEGROES TAKE APPEAL TO THE U. N." The item begins thus: "In a demand for 'full freedom and absolute equality', the National Negro Congress to-day (June 2, 1946) petitioned the United Nations to bring 'relief from oppression' to 13,000,000 members of the race in the United States."

and more devastating instruments of destruction! This is military thinking.

There is about as much chance for revolution here in America as there is for Buddhism to take hold. With the Declaration of Independence we dreamed that we became a free people. We are still in the dream, only now it has become a nightmare. What was to be a crucible for all the desperate ones in search of freedom has now become a prison. A nation which makes no effort to attune itself to the rhythm of the times is doomed. A nation that wishes to remain for ever the same has ceased to live. The thought of reaching a dead planet such as the moon inspires much more emotion than the thought of communicating with our fellow-men throughout the globe. We are not interested in saving the world nor even in saving ourselves: we are interested in fleeing this planet. We have drained the earth until the promise it contained is lost. We face neither backwards nor forwards, but outwards, outward towards the cold dead realms of space—where there is eternal atomistic bliss.

I prefer the corrupt world of Europe. I prefer the maggots which crawl. I prefer the song of the flesh, even though that flesh be rotting. While there is still a body there will be spirit. Where there is no body there can be nothing, not even spirit. Not even spirit, I say, as though spirit were not the all! But there has been so little evidence of the spirit here in America that one grows accustomed to thinking of it in terms of negation. All is goods, weights, facts, measurements, prices—*and bargains*, of course. We know that Europe is alive because it demands food, clothing, medicine. We know that Europe is alive because every now and then she erupts and we are dragged into the maelstrom. But the living spirit of Europe seems beyond our grasp and comprehension. A skin disease were better understood, better treated. Why do they clamor so over there? Because they are ill, because they are filthy, because they are dying like cattle. Well then, throw them food, clothing, medicines! Drown the agony with a flood of materials! We will give you anything you want, only please stop that infernal racket! Don't infect us with your distress! Please, for God's sake, we beg you, don't start another revolution! Let us rot in peace, we implore you! The old song: Peace and Prosperity. We are still singing it. Peace and Prosperity! The peace of the grave, the prosperity of nit-wits. Die out, old Europe, so that we may take over the earth! Back up, Russia, we are moving in! Pipe down, you Hindus, it is not time yet to ask for independence! Stop fighting, China, you are hindering the advance of free trade! Quiet, quiet! We are making ready the bomb which will soon set the whole world free.

---

To find in the midst of corruption something perpetually new, something perpetually blossoming, something perpetually alluring and enticing, that perhaps is the chief attraction which Europe holds for a man of the New World. *Here* nothing surprises or astonishes me. Nothing, absolutely nothing. I know what waits for me around the corner just as I know what awaits me a thousand miles hence. The familiar has no endearing qualities, not for me, at least.

I have been told that I am an "old soul." Perhaps. But it does not therefore follow that I am indifferent, bored, satiated. If I am an old soul I am also an enthusiast. Some would like to dispose of me by calling me a romantic. But these soon discover that my realism is shocking. Some pretend that I am in love with the dung-heap. Others say it is the womb I am trying to crawl back into. Yes, I admit that I am interested in the womb, the womb as seat of creation. I am interested in birth, or better—in "birthing."

Creation is my obsession. Whatever is not giving birth is for me dead.

I do not see Europe standing still. I do not see France rotting away with inertia. I do not adore her because she is a cold statue eternally fixed in a garden surrounded by a high wall. What impresses me is the intense cultivation going on in that garden spot of the world. There the spirit of man is nurtured, there it flowers and scatters its seeds. A man is known by his fruits, a people likewise. Examine the spiritual products of France, compare them with those of America or Russia.

For myself I have only to think back to any ordinary day of those ten glorious years in France. I have only to think of what greeted me when I stepped outdoors in the morning. I shan't talk now of the cathedrals, the palaces, the royal gardens, the museums and libraries. I talk of little things, homely, every-day things. I talk of the street, to begin with, of the look it had at eight in the morning. It is a sleepy look and the gray sky does not improve its complexion. The façades of the houses are worn and faded but they are not intimidating. In the concierge's loge the canaries are already singing or taking a bath. The sidewalks are lined with trees and the birds are chirping madly. The aroma of fresh-baked bread greets the nostrils, the stalls are full of fruit, the butcher has set out his most attractive cuts. People are carrying their groceries home in their two arms. The stationer is selling the morning papers. It is a quiet humdrum routine, soothing to the nerves. The day does not begin with a bang; it sneaks in like a young girl who has been up all night. I go from shop to shop selecting what I need. I do this for each meal. Occasionally I have lunch at a nearby restaurant. On the way home I stop sometimes to pay my respects to the stationer; I buy a book which he recommends just for the pleasure of chatting with him a little longer. At the corner I sit down to have a black coffee with a dash of rum. At the tobacconist's I stop to buy a pack of cigarettes and have another drink. No hurrying. The day is interminable.

Back in my studio I listen to a gramophone playing next door. The sculptor across the street is hacking away at a statue in his garden. The whole street is given up to quiet, joyous work. Every house contains a writer, painter, musician, sculptor, dancer, or actor. It is such a quiet street and yet there is such activity going on, silently, becomingly, should I not say reverently too? This is how it is on my street, but there are hundreds of such streets in Paris. There is a constant army of artists at work, the largest of any city in the world. This is what makes Paris, this vast group of men and women devoted to the things of the spirit. This is what animates the city, makes it the magnet of the cultural world.

How can I ever forget the ill-concealed joy of the New Yorker when he learned that Paris had fallen. "Now our city shall be the art center of the world!" That is what people were saying to one another. With every artist who took refuge there their pride, greed and envy swelled. "We shall have them all here soon!" They were so certain that once here, once inoculated with the American virus, these artists would never return to their homelands. "We will give them dollars, millions of dollars!" As if that were certain to hold them. "Paris is finished. Europe is dead!" How they chuckled, how they gloated over their good fortune. Never have I witnessed anything more disgraceful.

But we are not holding them. Despite the threat of famine and pestilence, the European artists are returning home. There is a veritable exodus from America. There would be a greater one if we had the facilities to meet the demand.

All our powers of seduction proved futile. The Europeans are returning to their ruins. They are not remaining here to make a

317

new life for themselves. They prefer their own way of life even if it entails poverty, bitterness, defeat. Dollars do not inspire artists, nor do they sustain them. It takes something more, something infinitely better, something which quite obviously we are not able to offer. What that something is you feel every minute of the day in Europe. If it is an intangible something, it is nevertheless very real. You partake of it with the bread you swallow, with the coffee which you drink on the sidewalk. It is not only in the air, it is in the very stones, in the soil itself. *And it is not vitamins!*

I remember those armchairs in the cheap hotels which I was forced to occupy in the early days and which later I came to love. What decrepitude in those chairs! Held together by wires, leather straps and nails, they were the very symbol of conservation. The Surrealists adored such objects, and rightly. They belong to the paraphernalia of the soul's most intimate longings and memories. They are enshrined in the very walls of one's identity. In departing this world it is these object-images which constitute the furnishings of one's special place in limbo.

As with the armchairs so with everything you made use of: all became part of you, the phantasmal impedimenta which you dragged about in moving from hell to purgatory to paradise. Looking about me in my American home I see not one object to which I feel attached. Nothing has endeared itself to me. Everything is replaceable without effort and without sentiment. I can almost speak in the same way of the people I know. Almost. There are a few, a very few, whom I shall never forget. But the rest—I shall leave them behind with the furniture, the knick-knacks, the bric-à-brac, the facts, the figures, the vast and incredible junk which constitutes the mental and physical furniture of America.

"But you had such a happy childhood!" remonstrates one of my friends when I talk this way. Yes, it is true, I did enjoy a happy childhood. I was happy until I became conscious of the sort of world I was living in. By the age of sixteen I was wretchedly morbid. I turned inward, seeking an escape from the ugliness and villainy which hemmed me in. The first ray of hope that there might exist another world, brighter, richer, more alive, came when I met on the street one day an old friend who had just returned from Europe. That chance meeting decided my fate. From then on my gaze was fixed. It took several years before I could make the break. It meant that I had to write a book under someone else's name, see the manuscript destroyed, play the roles of clown, thief, beggar, pimp. But I made the boat! What a sigh of relief I heaved when the American shore faded out. I could scarcely believe my eyes. One year in Europe had been vouchsafed me. One year only. But it was like a promise of Paradise.

I saw many countries on that trip, and I enjoyed them all. I could have gone on traveling for the rest of my life, so wonderful it was to be away from my native land. Was I ever homesick? Never. Not once. I missed nothing, no one. My only hope was that by some miracle I would be able to remain permanently in Europe.

That was in 1928. I was then thirty-six years old. I had waited a long time for my chance. In 1930 I was able to return and stay ten years. When the American Minister at Athens forced me to return I was heartbroken. I had used every argument to induce him to allow me to go somewhere else, anywhere, only not back to America. But he was adamant. It was for my own protection, he explained. "And if I don't want your protection?" I asked. For answer he gave me a shrug of the shoulders.

The day the American boat left the port of Piraeus was one of the blackest days in my life. It seemed as if all my efforts to make a new life for myself had come to nought. Back in the rat-trap, that was how I saw it. And back I was, no doubt about it. Back on

319

that same hideous street—"the street of early sorrows"—where nothing had happened since I left, nothing of the least consequence. This or that one had been married, this or that one had gone insane, this or that one had died. Nothing of any consequence to me. The street itself looked exactly the same, that sameness of the bad dream which is more terrifying than the plunge into Orcus. To make it worse, the war had cut off all communication with those I had left behind in Europe. The one place with which I had a living, vital connection was blotted out. For six years now I have been trying to reconstitute the image of the world I knew and loved. Day after day I keep wondering how it will look when next I set eyes on it. Some of my friends write that I will not recognize it; others say it is just the same, only worn, battered. I know what it is to be separated from one you love, to look forward day after day, year in and year out, for the eventual meeting. I know what it is to preserve from deterioration an image which you know in your heart no longer has existence in reality. I have steeled myself to the most terrible disillusionments, to the most cruel deceptions. Like all the desperate faithful ones I have said to myself a thousand times: "But it won't matter what she looks like, if only I can see her once again!"

It is with this same sort of fever and anxiety that I wait anew for my chance. Once it was a world of promise which awaited me; now it is a world admittedly in ruins. It is as though, while waiting to rejoin the beloved, you read each day of how she was raped, starved, beaten, tortured. You know that when you see her again you will recognize nothing in her except perhaps that glow in the eyes. Even that may be extinguished. Perhaps she will come forward to meet you on two stumps, her teeth gone, her hair white, her eyes sightless, her body a mass of ulcerous wounds. The thought of it sends an involuntary shudder through my limbs. *"That is her?"*

320

you say? O God, no, not that! Please, *not that!*" Sometimes that is how the beloved is returned to you. These are the special horrors reserved for the faithful. I know, I know. I have studied not only the history of Europe, I have studied man himself. I know the perfidies he is capable of. I know that of all the desecrators of life he is the worst, the most ignominious. Only he, of all God's creatures, is capable of destroying what he loves. Only he is capable of destroying his own image.

The letters I receive now from my friends back there are heartrending. They do not speak of their physical discomforts, of the food and clothes they lack. No, they speak of the emptiness of the future. They speak of the absence of something which they once thought imperative, that intangible something which came from nowhere and everywhere, which sustained them in the darkest hours, which sustained them even in defeat. That is gone now, it appears. "It appears," I say. I still do not believe them utterly. I must see with my own eyes, experience it in my own soul. Before I can admit this monstrous truth I too must succumb to this terrible despair, this harrowing sense of futility. Europe has survived so much, so much. Is it possible that it has drained the last drop of courage, the last ounce of hope? Is this really the end?

For my friends over there perhaps it *is* the end. But it is not *the* end, not "the end of all men." I refuse to believe it. *Présence de la mort, oui. Mais pas la fin.* Man knows no end, no more than he knows a beginning. Man is. He is as imperishable as the stars.

"Yes," some of these friends agree, "man will go on, he will continue to exist. *But what kind of man?* We have seen the face of the monster. We want no traffic with this new breed. We would rather perish."

Naturally they are not referring to the enemy. The enemy is already forgotten. They are talking of the new spawn in their own

321

midst. They are talking of the men whom a year ago, a week ago, yesterday in fact, they regarded as comrades, brothers, friends. They are talking of the great change which has come about, of an unnatural schism, as if man had suddenly split into two separate beings, each determined to murder the other. They recognize the division as taking place not only between man and man, friend and friend, brother and brother, comrade and comrade, but as taking place in the soul of every individual. The eternal conflict between monster and angel now manifests itself openly. That is how they see it. That is what paralyzes them. "The Time of the Assassins" has come. And with it the great split. The world is no longer able to contain its anguish. Fear, nameless and uncontrollable, has broken loose. The world egg totters on its precarious balance. Do we face a period of total chaos? Or will the gods come forth again in all their splendor through the shell of the egg?

———————

When I think of the illustrious names which stud the pages of that open book called Europe I think of the atmosphere which surrounds each one. For every great accomplishment, whether in the realm of science, religion, art or politics, the ambiance was such that each act of creation called for an agony comparable only to the agony of birth or of death. Despite all the grand words about culture and civilization, the men of genius who made Europe what it is had to pay with their life's blood for the contributions they made. Seldom indeed was it made easy for these great leaders of mankind to pursue their goals. For them the time was always out of joint. Looking back on these epochs, these crucial periods of the past, it is easy for us to understand the emergence of these figures and the roles they played. But to them it was often like being born in darkness. Not only did there exist the ever imminent threat of persecution or death, but the security of the nation itself was ever in jeopardy. Wars, revolutions, schisms of all sorts were constantly rife. Never was the condition of the masses anything but precarious and degrading. Ignorance, bigotry, superstition always held sway, no matter what the age. It is a black picture Europe presents when the long glance is flung down the corridor of time. It is like entering the darkness of outdoors after being in a brilliantly illuminated room. There is an interval in which the brilliance of the heavens is dimmed. But when the eye becomes adjusted to the soft illumination of distant suns a sense of grandeur, of infinitude and of eternality is awakened. One realizes that the vast reaches of space in which our little planet swims is flooded with inexhaustible light. One forgets the vulgar glare of that single sun which rules the day; one is dazzled and awed by the splendor of those sparkling worlds which speak to us from remote distances, which never cease to bathe us in their radiance. In the silence of night the light of the stars sustains us in a manner beyond words. In such moments we become the link between past and future, we go out of ourselves to become one with the cosmos. In the face of their eternal duration nothing matters, we feel. Nothing we do will alter anything, that too we deeply suspect. We have but to shine with the light of our own being, like the stars, each one a sun.

Often I have thought that the vulgar glare which illumines the American scene is the effect of our refusal to accept anything but a day-time world. Our countenances are fixed with the stare of the hypnotic obeying the dictates of an invisible presence. We refuse to look facts in the face, or rather to look behind the facts for the reality which animates them. We are a people who regard sleep as a waste of time. We turn night into day, like children who are afraid of the dark. For us the dark world is the world over which we reluctantly admit we have no control. It wounds us to admit that there are domains beyond our ken, beyond our control or usurpation. Artificially illumined, we carry with us everywhere our crude and vulgar daylight world.

By comparison Europe seems a Stygian underworld. It is the realm where mysterious and unpredictable events occur, usually of an unpleasant nature. It is in a state of perpetual upheaval, perpetual torment. It seems to thrive on death. A benighted world, truly, which in moments of lassitude we permit ourselves to sink down into and indulge the senses. A world of sin and corruption, yielding soft pleasures and vomiting forth demons of unsuspected power and seduction.

Europe is the crucible, not America. There everything is tried out, at the expense of the world. All the strange phenomena which characterize our time have as their focal center Europe. A bomb thrown in Sarajevo sets the world on fire. A dreamer in a tiny European village creates reverberations which endure for centuries. The vibrations which emanate from Europe affect the world almost instantaneously. She is the center and vortex of this ever changing world. America, destined seemingly to play the role of shock-absorber, merely responds; no movements are engendered or initiated here which upset or restore the equilibrium of the world. Great movements, great events, are engendered in the dark, in the secret places of the blood.

Despite the chaos which dominates the European theatre at the moment, the idea that everything taken together constitutes "a body" of things, a vital organism, still persists. Europe is centrifugal in spirit; it gathers in the world forces. If America is the power-house of the world Europe may well be called its solar plexus. Every European is aware of the presence of this invisible dynamo, this smothered sun, so to speak. It is what keeps him alive, dangerously alive. As for the European man of genius, he is a parti-

cularly disturbing force. He is always revolutionizing, always seeking to transform the world from within out. There can be no peace
in Europe, never, not in the sense in which we Americans employ
the term. For Europe peace would mean death: it would mean
that the dynamo had ceased to revolve. No, Europe does not seek
the return of broad daylight in which everything is viewed with
equanimity. It does not want to establish a day-time world. Europe
knows that her role is that of fecundator.

------

*La Mort et Resurrection d'Amour:* this is the title which a celebrated queen in the time of Rabelais chose for one of her books.
The French Renaissance was then dawning. The Americas had just
appeared on the horizon. It is then almost five hundred years since
Abélard stirred the world, and Héloise even more. In the next five
hundred years Europe moves towards extinction. Even Nostra-
damus cannot see much beyond the end of the century. In this
millennium Europe has given to the world a galaxy of geniuses which
will continue to shed a glow over the entire world even though
darkness falls over all the land. Many of them arose in France, or
made their home in France, or found refuge there. In passing
through the château country you are reminded that da Vinci spent
the last years of his life there; in the Midi you are reminded that
Dante received an inspiration (at Les Baux) which was to affect
his description of the Inferno. In the Vaucluse it is Petrarch. What
countless examples one could give of the importance and the influence of France throughout the last ten centuries!

Walking the streets of Paris the book shops and art galleries
never cease to remind one of the heritage of the past and the fever
of the present. A random jaunt through one little quarter is sufficient often to create such a glut of emotions that one is paralyzed
with conflicting impulses and desires. One needs no artificial stimu-

325

lation, in Paris, to create. The atmosphere is saturated with creation. One has to make an effort to avoid being over-stimulated. After a day's work one can always find recreation. It costs almost nothing, the price of a coffee merely. Just to sit and watch the passing throng, this is a form of recreation almost unknown in America.

*La Mort et Resurrection d'Amour:* the title alone has great significance. It implies that there once existed a world of love. And by love I mean love with a capital L. Yes, once passion reigned, the passion of the head and the passion of the heart. And passion means suffering, symbolized by the story of the Cross. Love, Passion, Suffering: this is the trinity which epitomizes the moving spirit of Europe. Only in the name of this trinity can we interpret the great discoveries, the great inventions, the great pilgrimages, the great deeds, the great philosophies of the Western world. Nothing came easy to the men of Europe. The most gifted ones were usually the ones who experienced the greatest agony.

The resurrection of love! I think that is what I felt more than anything during my sojourn abroad. Coming from a world in which everything pertaining to the soul had been killed, even a cheap postcard had in it something to arouse my emotions. I was always conscious of the trees and the care expended in preserving them. I treasured the little menus written out by hand each day. I liked the waitresses even though they were slatternly often and bad tempered. To see the bicycle cops patrolling in pairs at night always gave me a thrill. I adored the patches in the old carpets which covered the worn stairs in the cheap hotels. The way the street cleaner went about his task fascinated me. The faces of the people in the Metro never ceased to intrigue me, as did also their gestures, their conversation. The order which reigned in the bars, the faithful way in which the menials performed their duties, the dexterity and endurance of the *garçons* in the cafés, the disorder and confusion in the post office, the atmosphere of *la salle des pas perdus* in the railway stations, the exasperating red tape in bureaucratic quarters, the cheap paper on which the most extraordinary books were printed, the beautiful stationery served gratis in the cafés, the exotic names of writers and artists of all genres, the way the vegetables were piled up in the streets, the fairs and carnivals constantly rotating, the fetid odor of the neighborhood cinema in winter, the air of elegance about first-class trains, the look of the dining car at evening on one of the grand trunk lines, the almost too civilized aspect of city parks, the feel of small change and the beauty of a thousand francs note (which you could change most anywhere) these and a thousand similar details of daily life form a rich body of souvenirs. No matter what I touched, what I looked at, my interest and curiosity were aroused. Nothing grew stale, not even the vegetables in the stalls.

Whenever I think of Paris I think of bad weather. It seems now as though it were always raining, or threatening to rain. One could be miserably cold on rainy days in fall, spring or winter, even when there was a pretense of heating. But the cafés exuded a delicious warmth in which there was mingled the odor of coffee, tobacco, wines and the aroma of perfumed and inviting bodies. At meal time there were also the appetizing odors issuing from the kitchen. But the strongest odor was that which emanated from the personality of those who comprised the clientèle. Each individual was a distinct character, you felt. Each one had a history, a genesis, a background, in short a reason for being what he was. There was never that nondescript quality about them which is so annihilating here in America. Even the *garçons* looked interesting, each one unique and individual. The cashiers, of course, were highly interesting, belonging as most of them did to that breed of human vulture which has created a universal type. More interesting still, because more pathetic perhaps, was the woman condemned to the *lavabo*. Always courteous and affable she was when you left your little tip in the saucer; always ready to perform an extra little service for you if you were not sparing of the change. And what amazing little services she could render!

To the "Sanforized" citizen, whether Fascist, Plutocrat or Communist, there is something about this picture which inspires disgust, contempt or pity. It is too small, too homely, too drab. It has all the elements of that stinking bourgeois world which is so repulsive to the forward-looking man. No denying it. When looked at from a certain angle this ingratiating little tableau is tepid and moth-eaten. Above all it is petty. People addicted to this routine are not inclined to fly into a passion about putting the world in order. They are obsessed with their little comforts, their silly little rituals, their sordid cares and anxieties. They can dismiss injustice with a shrug of the shoulders. They will raise a clamor about a few sous and listen with equanimity, or with feigned distress, to the horrors of famine and flood in India or China. No grand passion ever stirs their blood. They believe fervidly in nothing, show no ardor, make no spontaneous, generous or unexpected moves. Their whole wisdom consists in leaving you be, only with them it is not fair to call it wisdom but rather an insurance policy. The practise of tolerance thus insures them against the gratuitous, the spectacular, the extraordinary, the sensational. Never disturb the smooth monotony of the daily grind. Otherwise, do as you please. *Quant à moi, je m'en fiche!*

It is that way, no denying it. Or it *was*. That is the *mesquin* view of the situation. Admitting it, I could always say however: "*Tout de même, il y avait là quelque chose qui* . . ." Yes, I could always find something to compensate for that niggardliness which is so loathsome when we detect it in others. I could stand this pettiness because it was not the all. If the beverage is excellent we do not examine the dregs at the bottom of the cup. One does not think of lees and dregs with each draught one swallows. When I felt like grousing I could find in everything the smear of lees and dregs. "*C'est emmerdant!*" one hears frequently over there. The equivalent, in English, is not used so freely in this country. "It's lousy," we say, though what we often mean is that it's shitty. We indulge in this sort of language only when drunk. The Frenchman, however, can use any language that suits his mood, when he's in the mood. Nobody is going to arrest him for using foul speech. It may be in very bad taste, such language, and he may be made to feel it, but he won't be shunned like a leper and he won't be accused of being a copraphagic monster.

However *emmerdant* the situation, I always had the secure and delightful feeling that I could extricate myself. I don't mean by running away to another country, or by taking refuge in my status as an American. I mean that it was relatively easy to break the spell. It needed only a good book (and there were hundreds of them available), an excursion to the country (or simply to the suburbs), a meal with a friend in some quite ordinary restaurant, a visit to the studio of a painter, or a chance encounter with a woman of the streets. One was not in it up to the neck. Sometimes a mere stroll into another *quartier* was sufficient to dissipate the fog of ennui.

"*J'ai le cafard!*" How often one heard that in Paris! It was a mood to be respected. The *cafard* wasn't just boredom or ennui, it was something more, something deeper than that. It was what the French word so eloquently expresses. It was something which attacks one most poignantly precisely in a city like Paris. You could not have the *cafard* in Oklahoma City or Butte, Montana, not even if you were a Parisian. It is a peculiar form of spiritual paralysis

329

which descends only upon those who are highly aware of the unlimited possibilities which surround them. If it is to be compared
with anything, it should be with the lassitude which invades the
anchorite. It is what.assails you when the mind becomes empty,
when it ceases to think *what* or *how* it should see. It is the fatigue
which overcomes the inner eye.

We have nothing analogous to this that I know of. The feeling
of emptiness which the American knows, and which is always mir-
rored by an all too real outer emptiness, produces nothing less than
a state of black despair. There are no exits. There is the escape
through alcoholism, but that only leads to deeper, blacker despair.

The other night, in a state of mild despair, I chose a book which
I thought would deepen the mood and thus rout me out of it. I
chose it because of the title: *Le Désespéré*, by Léon Bloy. The
opening page was in the right key: the color was black, no mistake
about it. But it did not augment the blackness in me. On the contrary, to my disgust I was suddenly aware that I was becoming gay.
I attribute this phenomenon to the spell of Bloy's language; it had
a rich, velvety texture, it was generous and exalted, however bitter
and macabre. So extreme, so poisonous was it, that it was almost
un-French. Ah, I thought, what a treat! Here is a deep, rich *noir*
. . . revel in it! And I gave myself up to the book in the manner
that one gives way to grief sometimes. Those loaded adjectives and
adverbs, those frightening new nouns, those tirades, those acid-
bitten portraits . . . *quel soulagement!* It was like being outside
a cathedral when the cortège pulls up and all that fanfarole which
the French adore in the performance of their obsequies is made
to reverberate. *Le désespéré, c'était bien moi. Un cadavre roulant,
oui, et comment! Rien de mignon, rien de mesquin, rien de menu.
Tout était sombre, solennel. J'ai assisté à l'enterrement de mon
âme, avec tout ce qu'il y avait de vide et de triste. Je n'avais rien*

*perdu que l'illusion de ma souffrance. On m'avait libéré de mon sort . . . Que de nouveau je parlai français, c'était cela qui m'avait fait du bien!*

---

Everything which evokes raptures from me, in connection with France, springs from the recognition of her Catholicity. A man from a Protestant world suffers from morbidity: he is uneasy in his soul. Something is eating him away, something which leaves him, to put it in one word, joyless. Even Catholics, if they are born in such a world, assume the cold, inhibited qualities of their Protestant neighbors. The American Catholic is totally unlike the Catholic of France, Italy or Spain. There is nothing in the least Catholic about his spirit. He is just as Puritanical, just as intolerant, just as hidebound as the Protestant American. Try to think of a Catholic American writer who has the verve, the amplitude, the sensuality of men like Claudel and Mauriac. They are non-existent.

The virtue of France is that she made her Catholics catholic. She made even her atheists catholic, and that is saying a good deal. To make whole, universal, to include everything, that is the pristine sense of catholic. It is the attitude which the healer adopts. This larger meaning of the word is something which the French as a people understand par excellence. In a catholic world the small and the great exist side by side, as do the sane and the insane, the sick and the well, the criminal-minded and the law-abiding, the strong and the weak. It is only in such a world that true individuality can assert itself. Think of the great diversity of types in France among the literary figures alone, now or in any epoch of the past. There is nothing to match it that I know of. There is actually a greater difference between one French writer and another than between a German and a French writer. One could say that there is more in common between Dostoievski and Proust than between

331

Céline and Breton or between Gide and Jules Romains. Yet there is a thread, a tough and unbroken one, which connects such unique men of letters as Villon, Abélard, Rabelais, Pascal, Rousseau, Bossuet, Racine, Baudelaire, Hugo, Balzac, Montaigne, Lautréamont, Rimbaud, de Nerval, Dujardin, Mallarmé, Proust, Mauriac, Verlaine, Jules Laforgue, Roger Martin du Gard, Duhamel, Breton, Gide, Stendhal, Voltaire, de Sade, Léon Daudet, Paul Eluard, Blaise Cendrars, Joseph Delteil, Péguy, Giraudoux, Paul Valéry, Francis Jammes, Elie Faure, Céline, Giono, Francis Carco, Jules Romains, Maritain, Léon Bloy, Supervieille, St. Exupéry, Jean-Paul Sartre, to name but a few.

The homogeneity of French art is due not to the uniformity of thought or environment but to the infinite variety of soil, climate, scenery, speech, customs, blood. Every province of France has contributed to the creation of her culture. What unites the French more than anything is love of the soil. Jacob Wassermann, in *My Life as German and Jew,* has emphasized the relation between a writer's style and the landscape of his birthplace or the place he chose to make his home. "Any landscape," he writes, "which somehow becomes part of our destiny generates a definite rhythm within us, an emotional rhythm and a rhythm of thought of which we usually remain entirely unconscious and which hence is all the more decisive. It should be possible to recognize from the cadences of a writer's prose the landscape it covers as a fruit covers its kernel. . . . The landscape in which a person lives does not merely frame the picture; it enters into his very being and becomes a part of him. This can, of course, be seen much more clearly among savages than within the range of civilization. That is why rivers, deserts, oases and groves play so important a role in the formation of myths, which often represent only the scenic experience of a long succession of generations . . . Personality is engendered at the point where the inner and outer landscapes are contiguous, where the mythical and the permanent flow into limited time. And every literary work, every deed, every achievement is the result of an amalgamation of the tangible and the intangible, of the inner vision and the actual picture, of the idea and the factual situation, of conception and form. The outer landscape of the world no longer needs to be discovered, though its influence and effect on the soul are not yet fully known. But the inner landscape of man largely remains *terra incognita*, and when it comes to illuminating this unknown region our so-called psychology is but a pale little lamp."

In the case of a writer like Alain Fournier, author of *Le Grand Meaulnes*,[1] the accuracy of Wassermann's observation is made strikingly apparent. The enchantment which this book continues to create stems from the successful fusion of inner and outer landscapes. The aura of mystery which envelops it and which gives it its charm and austerity, issues from the marriage of dream and reality. The region of the Sologne, where the author was born and spent the better part of his young life, is the setting through which he leads us as in a dream. It is a region known for its gentle, harmonious, discreet aspect, a region that has been "humanized for centuries," as one French writer puts it. How eminently suited therefore to evoke dream and nostalgia!

Widely accepted since the day of its publication, the repercussion of this little classic has been slight here in America. Yet it is precisely the sort of book which should be popularized among Americans. It is thoroughly French, but in a way that foreigners often do not appreciate. In a letter to his friend Jacques Rivière, written in 1906, the author intimates the nature of the aesthetic problem with which he was then wrestling and the solution of which he so admirably found in writing *Le Grand Meaulnes*. "Mon crédo

---

[1] Published by New Directions in translation under the title of *The Wanderer*.

en art et en littérature est l'ENFANCE. Arriver à là rendre sans aucune puérilité, avec sa profondeur qui touche les mystères. Mon livre futur sera peut-être un perpetuel va-et-vient insensible du rêve à la réalité; 'Rêve' entendu comme l'immense et imprécise vie enfantine planant au-dessus de l'autre et sans cesse mise en rumeur par les échos de l'autre."

Alain-Fournier is not, to be sure, one of the great French writers, but he is one who despite the passage of time endears himself more and more to the French heart. He is one of those, like Péguy again, who makes us realize what is truly French. In him the spirit of France speaks strong and clear. It is "*la doulce France*" once more, the gentle, wise, tolerant France which is revealed only to those who have been permitted to live on terms of intimacy with her.

It is a common saying that in France the young are born old. The violence and gaiety of youth are short-lived. Responsibilities are shouldered before one has had time to have his fling. The result is the cultivation of the spirit of play. The child is adored, the sage is venerated, the dead are worshiped. As for art, it invades every domain of life, from the temple to the kitchen. To penetrate the spirit of France one has to examine her art; it is there she reveals herself absolutely.

Hardly was the war terminated and communication restored, than we learned of the courageous pertinacity of her artists. Almost the first thing France demanded of the outside world was books, books and paper with which to print. Throughout the war her great painters had continued with their work. The older ones revealed a continuous development and a surprising evolution considering their isolation. The agonies of war had deepened, not annihilated, the spirit of the artist. Both those who fled and those who remained had something new and vigorous to show for the years of defeat and humiliation. Is not this the sign of an invincible spirit? The enemies of France would, no doubt, have preferred to see her artists die to the last man. To them this picture of quiet, persistent devotion to one's art smacks of cowardice or resignation. How can a man go on painting flowers or monsters when his country is under the heel of the conqueror, they ask. The question answers itself. They were not painting "flowers or monsters"! They were painting the experiences registered in their souls. They were transforming pain and brutality into symbols of beauty and truth. They were rendering, or restoring, if you like, the faithful picture of life which the absurdities and horrors of war obscure and nullify. Whereas the Maginot Line proved to be but an illusory defense against the invader, the spirit of the French artists revealed something more durable. The obsession for beauty, for order, for clarity —why should I not add *for charity*?—that is what underlies the spirit of creation, which is the true seat of resistance. It was the men who were poor in spirit who conceived the idea of a Maginot Line. The artists are not of that stripe. They are, as we have been told so often, the eternally young. They ally themselves with all that endures, with that which triumphs even over defeat. The artist does not resist the time spirit, he is of it. The artist is not a revolutionary, he is a rebel. The artist does not crave experience for its own sake, but only as it serves his imagination. The artist does not dedicate himself to the preservation of his country, but to the preservation of what is human. He is the link between the man of to-day and the man of the future. He is the bridge over which humanity as a whole must pass before it can enter the kingdom of heaven. Are we to say of him who holds the passport to paradise that he is of no use unless he too offers himself up to be slain? Where shall we find our refuge and our strength if not in those who dedicate their lives to the unfoldment of Beauty, Truth, and Love?

335

Those patriotic avengers who are so thirsty and ravenous for the annihilation of every last man, on what foundation do they hope to build? On blood and sand? Each generation stands amidst fresh ruins, ruins smoking with blood. Each generation seeks to establish order, to work in peace, to create music out of agony. Some pretend to see an abstract historical evolution in these repeated dramas of failure and frustration. They ask us not to measure the blood which has been spilled. They urge us to stop our ears when the cries of the wounded and the mutilated make us squirm in anguish. They read progress and evolution in the bloody wake of Moloch. They sanctify the sacrifices incessantly demanded by this insatiable god of history. They bellow with indignation when one calls this view of life a superstitious one. We know what constitutes reality, they say. We have the finger on life's pulse. It is thus and so because it *must* be thus and so. Logic. The logic of the earthworm.

No, I am happy to say this is not the view of the creative spirits. The defendants of life have no such clear-cut logic to marshal. They are not the victims of thought, they are the inspirers of wisdom and of justice. They do not talk peace and continue to prepare new and more devastating weapons of destruction. They go about their appointed rounds "irregardless" of the state of the world.

Perhaps we can come nearer to understanding what these adherents of life stand for when we re-read the simple words of young Fournier who, weary of the struggle, offered himself up as a sacrifice on the battlefield: "Je dis que la sagesse est de renoncer à sa pensée, aux chateaux de cartes de sa pensée, et de s'abandonner à la vie. La vie est contradictoire, ondoyante—*pourtant énivrante—et pourtant là où elle nous mène est le vrai.*"

———————————

This morning I awoke in the midst of a dream landscape. I heard the conductor yelling Châtellerault, or was it Châteauroux? That meant that I was on my way south again. Came the sound of the little trumpet and then a voice bellowing: *"En voitures! En voitures!"* Soon the frail coach is rattling and swaying on the narrow gauge line. It is a *rapide*, which does not mean an express train. But in the night it flies like the wind. On a French train I always have the sensation that it is the fastest thing on wheels.

Traveling southward my mind flies north, east and west. All the places I intended to visit at one time or another leap to mind. Now it is Provins I am dreaming of. (Was it not Balzac who said that Provins was the nearest to Paradise of any place he had seen?) I had gone to the Bibliothèque Nationale one day, shortly after my arrival in Paris, and I had demanded in my lame French if I might examine the wonderful chess pieces from the time of Charlemagne. After a charming conversation with one of the directors the man inquired if I had ever visited Provins. "Go as soon as you can," he urged, "you will never regret it." And now I am heading for Toulouse of Toulouse-Lautrec. In a moment I shall be reconstructing Albi, Agen, Tarbes, Cahors, Cordès, all places which I had skipped on previous excursions south. Around each name there are woven stories related me by fellow travelers, to say nothing of the tangled strands of history and legend.

Musing thus I find myself back in Paris, at the Place Dancourt. I am taking my old French teacher to see *Dommage Qu'elle Soit Putain!* I have already seen it twice at this same Thêatre de l'Atélier. I am going again because it will be a treat for Lantelme who seldom gets anywhere these days. I am going especially, however, to feast my eyes. The actress who plays the leading role has bewitched me. Never have I heard a voice like hers. It is the voice of a thrush from the Pripet marshes. (How is it I forget her name, once as fa-

337

miliar to my lips as that of Edwige Feuillère or Marcel Chantal?) She is not only beautiful, she is lovely. Lovely and beautiful. She should have become one of the great actresses of France. Perhaps she has. (I keep trying to recall her name. All I can drag up from the depths are: Levallois-Perret and Draguignan.) [1] What I shall never forget about her performance is the way she allowed herself to be dragged back and forth across the stage. By the hair, no less! Back and forth, the entire length of the stage. And those beautiful golden locks streaming down her tear-streaked face . . .

Whoever has read *Nadja* must surely recall those marvelous corridors of memory which Breton unlocks as he slowly opens his narrative. Who can forget that absolutely insane performance which he goes into at length in describing his visit to the Thêatre des Deux Masques? The play is *Les Détraquées*. One of the characters is a Mademoiselle Solange. Opposite page 58, in one of the strangest little books produced in our era, is a photograph (a bad one too!) by Henri Manuel. Beneath it is the following: *"L'enfant de toute à l'heure entre sans dire mot."* This line, together with other shoddy photographs (deliberately employed, no doubt) and reproductions of Nadja's sketches, accompany me on my journey southward. (One of the most disturbing, the most haunting, of these black and white reproductions which vie with a text as erratic as the trail of a comet, is the one called *La Profanation de l'Hostie*. Never was Uccello in such weird company.)

Just as I remember for fifteen years the suggestion of the man at the Bibliothèque Nationale, perhaps because it was my first prolonged conversation in French, so I recall at intervals this most amazing, most fantastic description of Blanche Derval's performance in *Les Détraquées*. Why? Because the first piece I ever sub-

[1] The name is Lucienne Lemarchand.

mitted to an editor was a wild, abortive, thoroughly incomprehensible description of a moment when, entering a vaudeville theatre just as the curtain was rising, I caught sight of a woman ascending a broad staircase with a marble balustrade. In that moment I was split and saw with two different eyes, the inner vision matching the outer and blending with it in a harmony and logic unbelievable. To my astonishment the piece brought a letter of encouragement from the editor, Francis Hackett. It was a brief, cordial note which sustained me throughout ten years of dismal failure . . . And now I am in France, reading a book by a man whose poetic gift I shall always admire, and the description of his visit to Le Théâtre des Deux Masques seems startlingly similar to this first piece I submitted for publication. Breton's is, of course, infinitely better. But what would have happened to *Nadja*, is what I wonder, if Breton had had to submit it to an American editor?

*Landscape.* Inner and outer landscape. What is it, I often wonder, which drew me to France and enabled me to match inner with outer? In America there was only one landscape, if it could be called that, which lodged in the depths of me: the 14th Ward, Brooklyn, where I was raised. But there was no countryside attached to the 14th Ward, then my whole world. What drew me so warmly to the French provinces? What was it I found there which corresponded to my dreams? Archaic memories? Perhaps. Memories of childhood books? I don't remember reading anything about France as a child. My first remembrance of anything French is *The Wild Ass's Skin* loaned me by my Polish friend Stanley Borowski and snatched from my hands by my father because anything by a Frenchman, by Balzac particularly, was immoral. I was then sixteen. France didn't begin to penetrate my consciousness until almost ten years later when I struck up a friendship with a musician from Blue Earth,

Minnesota. I remember that he gave me a hand-written folio containing the translation he himself had made of a book called *Batouala*.

No, there is no landscape I can possibly recall which might have inspired the desire to wander through France. The instant I arrived, however, I felt at home. The first word in the language which registers on me, ironically, is *Défense*. It was plastered everywhere— on the doors and windows of the train, on the walls of buildings, on the sidewalk even. "*Défense de* . . ." The next thing I recall, because when it is translated for me it registers with a shock, are the words to be found in every French train: "these seats are reserved for *les mutilés de la guerre*." Suddenly the meaning of war (for the European) dawns on me. For us it was an adventure, so to speak. Something done with one hand tied behind the back. But France had been bled white. I shall never forget that train out of Le Havre, just as I shall never forget the look of Marseilles during the black-out when I touched there for the last time.

During the few years which preceded my arrival in France, years of feverish anticipation mingled with anxiety at the thought of being marooned for ever in New York, I would ask my friends who had been there the most idiotic questions. Were the streets still paved with cobblestone? Did every one dress in black? Could they describe for me *Le Rat Mort?* Was there a statue of Rabelais in the heart of Paris? How does one say, "I have lost my way"? And so on. Endless questions, which of course aroused endless gales of laughter. On visiting my parents I would take a French primer along and handing it to my father I would say: "Read me a few questions in English and see if I can answer them in French." And when I would answer, "*Oui, monsieur, je suis très content,*" my father would smile and say, "Why even I can understand that; it's just like English, only they use different words." Whereupon we would shake hands and say: *"Comment allez-vous aujourd'hui?"* We could mouth these little phrases perfectly, so I thought then. The moment, however, that I set foot on French soil I became panic-stricken. The simplest questions baffled me. All I could do by way of response was to grunt *"Oui, Madame,"* or *"Non, Monsieur."* I never forgot to include *"Madame"* and *"Monsieur."* The importance of this little politeness had been dinned into me before I left. This and *"s'il vous plaît."* It was like having your passport constantly available.

"What a world of red tape!" One of my first reflections. But then I had never been a foreigner in America. I knew from my friend Stanley how foreigners were treated at Ellis Island, and of course I had seen with my own eyes how we booted them around and saddled them with the dirty work. But to be a foreigner yourself is a horse of another color.

One of the first thrills I experienced was the greeting I received when a clerk, in fumbling through my passport, observed that I was an *écrivain.* At once a tone of respect crept into his voice. I was dumbfounded. So there was a place on earth where a writer was held in esteem? It was almost too good to be true. The clerk never asked me *what* I had written. I might have been the veriest hack for all he knew. It was the profession he was honoring. In America to mention that one is a writer is to arouse suspicion and hostility. Unless one bears a celebrated name the thought which immediately comes to the other person's mind, especially if he is a representative of officialdom, is that you are dishonest, irresponsible and probably an anarchist. If you are a newspaper man that is a different story. Reporters and correspondents are dangerous fellows; they can make or break you with a few words. But an ordinary writer, a writer of books, bah! he's a worthless fellow, on the same level as a toilet attendant.

Perhaps the first great surprise I got was when, after eating regularly for a few weeks in a little restaurant in the Rue des Canettes, I one day asked the *patronne* if she would extend me credit should I ever need it. "Why certainly, *Monsieur*, with pleasure. Willingly," she added. "What a country!" I thought. "They scarcely know me and here I am eating on credit." I tried to think of a restaurant keeper in New York who would have done the same for me. I could only recall those who spoke of washing dishes in return.

That was the first agreeable surprise. The second was even more agreeable. It was the knowledge that any time I needed a few francs I could have them of the *garçon* at a certain café at the end of the Boulevard St. Michel. We had had a few words now and then about Dostoievski as I sat drinking my *café noir*. These little exchanges were enough, evidently, for him to put full trust in me. Naturally I did not stop at a few francs; it was just as easy to borrow a few hundred from him. To top it off he would take me to dinner occasionally and to the theatre. When I left America, I must say here, I had not one friend who would lend me over a dollar. Often they handed me a dime or a quarter. It's true I had become a bad risk. It's true I had not proved to be a great writer. But we're talking about friends, many of them boyhood friends. They were all comfortably fixed. Remembering those days, remembering their cautiousness and niggardliness, I have made it a rule to be lavish and reckless, particularly if it is a stranger who asks me for help.

And now a word about the little ecstasies. One of these is connected with the toilet, I must warn my American reader. (Why do you jump so when the word toilet is mentioned?) It was like this . . . a sudden attack in the street and a dash for the nearest place, which happened to be a little hotel. It was not only a little hotel, it was a very old one to boot. The only available *cabinets* at the moment were on the third floor. I rushed up, squeezed my way in just in the nick of time and, while fumbling with my clothes, tried to get the door shut. The place was so tiny, so narrow, so awkwardly built, that it's a wonder I ever managed to get seated. It being daytime the light was off, of course. In the semi-darkness I gradually got the lay of the land. Some carefully torn pages from a newspaper were hanging on the hook. A cosy little place, when all was said and done, but why so cramped? As I stood up to rearrange my clothing my eye suddenly caught a view which took my breath away. From what was virtually an oubliette I was looking down on one of the oldest quarters of Paris. The vista was so sweepingly soft and intoxicating it brought tears to my eyes. What a blessed accident, I thought. If I had not been caught short I would never have known there was such a sight to be seen. I wanted to run below and fetch my wife, but then I realized that that might create a strange impression on the hotel-keeper. So I stood there dazed, lost in a deep trance. I stayed so long and the change which had come over my countenance was so great that when finally I rejoined my wife, who had been standing on the corner all the while, I found her in a vile mood. "Only a woman could have kept you that long!" she rasped. I reacted with such genuine bewilderment to this that she immediately changed tack. "Listen to me," I explained, "you must see it for yourself. Go up there, it's on the third floor. I'll wait for you here." She trotted off obediently, impressed by my earnestness. I took my stand on the corner, not caring how long I remained there. I was in a semi-comatose state, my eyes still glazed . . . Thereafter, whenever we were in the neighborhood of St. Severin, we would take time off to make pipi on the third floor back.

There were so many similar incidents, grotesque, whimsical, pathetic, absurd. Anything could happen to you in Paris, if you were

343

a stranger. How can I ever forget the utter amazement of a French gentleman who, being a stranger in Paris and stopping me for directions, finds himself being escorted to his destination, some blocks away, by a man who can barely talk the language. I can see that he is perplexed by my chivalrous attention. He is a little suspicious at first, but when he sees that I have nothing to ask of him he unlimbers quite gracefully. What would he have thought had I told him that the reason for going out of my way was simply for the pleasure of hearing him talk his own language! He would have thought I was mocking him, no doubt. How grateful he was for my solicitude! It was unusual nowadays, he made known to me in his roundabout fashion, to have a stranger show one such courtesy. Monsieur was an American? From New York, no less? *Tiens, tiens!* (*"Incroyable!"* he no doubt muttered to himself.) And Monsieur finds Paris interesting? *Vraiment?* Ah, there was something about Paris which always entices the stranger, *surtout les anglais.* The Americans too, of course. (An afterthought. Like saying: *"Les allemands? Ah oui, des boches!"*) As for him, the charms of Paris were wasted. He was only a *commerçant.* No time, alas, for the cabarets and the art galleries. *Pour les femmes non plus.* . . . Even a dullard like myself could follow this sort of monologue. It didn't matter in the least to me what he chose to talk about; what excited me was that I could get the drift of it.

He had of course taken me for a tourist. Never would he have suspected that in parting I was screwing up all my courage to hit him up for a few francs. I didn't, of course. I couldn't, what with the shower of thanks he bombarded me with. I had to carry on as the *chevaleresque flaneur* he credited me with being. I remember leaving him, my face wreathed in smiles, and heading straight for a bench where a workman was sitting with his lunch spread out and a bottle of wine beside him. "Now I'll sing a different tune!" I said to myself. I hadn't eaten for thirty-six hours . . .

---

The poem which gets me and which I find impossible to translate is Rimbaud's *Départ.* "*Assez vu. La vision s'est rencontrée à tous les airs.*" Put that opening line into English, the best English imaginable, and it will mean nothing. And how do I know it means something in French? To answer that I must relate another little anecdote out of those early days in France.

I am sitting in a cosy little restaurant in Avignon. A few feet away, at a table opposite me, a *commerçant* is having lunch all by himself. How we ever managed to strike up a conversation at that distance is a mystery to me, but we did. Stranger still is the fact that with my limited French I was making bold to describe to him a film I had seen just before leaving Paris: *L'Age d'Or* by Bunuel and Dali. I realized quickly enough that he was making sport of me, not because of my poor French—he was quite polite about that—but because of my admiration for such junk, as he put it. By one of those sudden transitions I am fond of making, when desperate to make myself understood, I began talking of Proust. "I beg pardon?" he said. "Proust," I repeated. "*Marcel Proust, celui qui a écrit A la Recherche du Temps Perdu.*" "Never heard of him," came the bland rejoinder, "but go on, I'm curious." That took the wind out of my sails. How was I to explain the work of an author such as Proust in my inadequate French to a man who obviously didn't give a damn what I told him? I knew he would give me his attention only until he had finished his meal and then politely excuse himself, leaving me suspended in the middle of a complicated sentence with a subjunctive on my hands. Fortunately, just as I was preparing the opening barrage, some students at a nearby table came to my rescue amid gales of laughter. For a moment I thought they were laughing at me, but no, they were directing their sallies at the *commerçant*. What! He had never heard of Marcel Proust? What was he, then, a pork vendor? Was he not ashamed of himself to have an American instruct him in his own literature? They ragged him unmercifully, throwing me sly winks all the while. The poor fellow did not wait to finish his meal; he fled precipitately.

He had hardly left when the students signaled me to join them. They would be honored if I would take a coffee and liqueur with them. "*Quel con celui-là!*" said one of them. "*Vous étiez épatant!*" said another. "Are you a writer perhaps?" another put in. Well, we sat there for an hour or more talking about everything under the sun. They were very curious about the Surrealist film. How had I come to read Proust? Had he been translated? What brought me to France, and how did New York compare with Paris? There were no more limitations of language. What I couldn't explain verbally I acted out. Sometimes I found myself saying the most complicated things in the most asinine way. But they understood. I knew they understood from the responses they made.

So it is with Rimbaud. I know from the response which I make to his lines that they have meaning. Even the meaningless lines. But it is especially in a poem such as *Départ* that I sense the correspondence between the unknown in myself and the unknown in another. It is no longer a question of landscape, inner or outer, but rather of levels, orders, hierarchies. Some one is speaking to me across the void. It is a mysterious language for which I have to employ another set of ears. Where will I find the right pair of ears? Why be so desperate? Could I not wait until I have attained a greater mastery of French? No! A thousand times No! I must get it now, at once. It is life or death.

If you were desperately in love with a woman who spoke an out-landish tongue you would find a means of understanding her, would you not? Perhaps the analogy is inept. To love Rimbaud it is first necessary to grasp the beauty of his language. I took to him on sight, like a moon-struck lover. I accepted him before I understood him. Is it necessary to explain such things? How can I convince the sceptic that I was ravished by Cendrars' *Moravagine* despite the fact that I had to consult the dictionary for almost every other word? How does one know *immediately* that a thing is after one's own heart? Why is it that despite the testimony of the finest critics I am still unable to read Stendhal or Sterne or even Homer? Why is it that I will try again and again to read the Marquis de Sade though I know each time I make the attempt I shall be bogged down? For some unaccountable reason I believe everything good that is said about de Sade. As I believe it about Francis Bacon, another one I find difficult to stomach. What I am trying to say is that some men compel you to accept them, compel you to under-stand, and finally, to adore.

With Rimbaud there is the instantaneous meeting or nothing. You meet in the sky or not at all. His is a language for which dic-tionaries are no avail. It is not French one needs to know but the forgotten tongue of the poet. Rimbaud is the last of the line and the first of a new order for which there is no name. Out of all the glittering constellations of French writers I am forced to choose him, a nova. That he was also a "*voyou*," what does that matter to me? Villon was a "gallows-bird," Baudelaire a "degenerate," de Sade a "monster." I choose Rimbaud because through him, through his break with the whole set-up, I understand France best. With his own youthful hands he created a monument as lasting as the great cathedrals. It is a work which defies all mishandling.

―――――

When I ran across Alfred Perlès on the Rue Delambre one rainy night a friendship was begun which was to color the entire period of my stay in France. In him I found the friend who was to sustain me through all my ups and downs. There was something of the *"voyou"* about him, let me say at once. My temptation, I must confess, is to exaggerate his failings. He had one virtue, however, which compensated for all his failings: he knew how to be a friend. Sometimes, indeed, it seemed to me that he knew nothing else. His whole life seemed centered about the cardinal fact that he was not just my friend, your friend, a friend, but *the* friend. He was capable of anything were it necessary to prove his friendship. I mean *anything*.

Fred was the sort of person I had been unconsciously looking for all my life. I had gravitated to Paris from Brooklyn and he from Vienna. We had been through the school of adversity long before reaching Paris. We were veterans of the street, on to all the tricks which keep a man afloat when all resources seem to be exhausted. Rogue, scallywag, buffoon that he was, he was nevertheless sensitive to the extreme. His delicacy, which manifested itself at incongruous moments, was extraordinary. He could be rude, impudent and cowardly without in the least diminishing himself. In fact, he deliberately cultivated a diminished state; it permitted him to indulge in all sorts of liberties. He pretended that all he wanted were the bare necessities of life, but he was an aristocrat in his tastes, and a spoiled darling to boot.

This potpourri of good and bad traits seemed to endear him to most every one. With women he would allow himself to be treated like a lap-dog, if that gave them pleasure. He would do anything they asked him so long as he could gain his end which, of course, was to get them to bed. If you were a friend he would share his women with you, in the same way that he would share his last crust

348

of bread. Some people found this hard to forgive in him, this ability to share *everything*. He expected others to act the same way, of course. If they refused he was ruthless. Once he took a dislike to a person nothing could win him over. He never changed his opinion of a person once he had made it. With Fred one was either a friend or an enemy. What he despised particularly were pretentiousness, ambitiousness and miserliness. He did not make friends easily, because of his shyness and timidity, but those with whom he became friends remained friends for life.

One of his irritating traits was his secretiveness. He delighted in holding things back, not so much out of inability to reveal himself but in order to always have a surprise up his sleeve. He always chose the right moment to let the cat out of the bag; he had an unerring instinct for disconcerting one at the most embarrassing moment. He delighted in leading one into a trap, particularly where it concerned his supposed ignorance or supposed vices. One could never pin him down about anything, least of all about himself.

By the time I caught up with him he seemed to have lived the proverbial nine lives of a cat. Knowing him superficially, one would be inclined to say he had wasted his life. He had written a few books in German, but whether they had been published or not no one knew. He was always vague about the past anyway, except when he was drunk, and then he would expand for a whole evening over a detail which he felt in the mood to embellish. He never threw out chunks of his life, just these unrelated details which he knew how to elaborate with the skill and cunning of a criminal lawyer. The truth is, he had led so many lives, had assumed so many identities, had acted so many parts, that to give any hint of totality would have meant reconstructing a jig-saw puzzle. He was as bewildering to himself, to be honest, as he was to others. His secret life was not his *private* life, for he had no private life. He lived continually *en marge*. He was *"limitrophe,"* one of his favorite words, to everything, but he was not *limitrophe* to himself. In the first book he wrote in French (*Sentiments Limitrophes*) there were microscopic revelations of his youth which verged on the hallucinatory. A passage which reveals how he came alive at the age of nine (on his native heath, the Schmelz) is a masterly piece of cortical dissection. One feels at this point in the narrative, which is an autobiography *aux faits divers*, that he was close to being endowed with a soul. But a few pages later he loses himself again and the soul remains in limbo.

Close association over a period of years with a man of his type has its rewards as well as its draw-backs. Looking back on those years with Fred I can think only of the good which resulted from our alliance. For it was an alliance even more than a friendship, if I may put it that way. We were allied to meet the future which every day presented its hydra-headed threat of annihilation. We got to believe, after a time, that there was no situation we could not meet and overcome. Often we must have seemed more like confederates than friends.

In everything he was the clown, even in making love. He could make me laugh when I was boiling with rage. I don't seem to recall a single day in which we did not laugh heartily, often until the tears came to our eyes. The three principal questions we put to each other every time we met were: 1.) Is there food? 2.) Was it a good lay? 3.) Are you writing? Everything centered around these three exigencies. It was the writing which concerned us most, but we always behaved as though the other two were more important. Writing was a constant, like the weather. But food and lays were quixotic: one could never be sure of either. Money, when we had it, we shared to the last penny. There was no question whom it belonged to. "Is there any dough?" we would ask, just as we would

350

ask, "Is there food?" It was or it wasn't, that was all there was to it. Our friendship began on this note and it remained thus till we separated. It's such a simple, efficacious way of living, I wonder it isn't tried out on a universal scale.

There were three possessions he clung to, despite all the pawning and liquidating of the dark days: his typewriter, his watch and his fountain pen. Each was of the finest make, and he took care of them as an engineer would take care of his locomotive. He said they were gifts, gifts from women he had loved. Maybe they were. I know he treasured them. The typewriter was the easiest thing for him to part with, temporarily, of course. For a time it seemed as though it were in the hock shop more than *chez nous*. It was a good thing, he used to say. It forced him to write with the pen. The pen was a Parker pen, the finest I had ever seen. If you asked to use it, he would unscrew the top before handing it to you. That was his little way of saying, "Be gentle with it!" The watch he seldom carried about with him. It hung on a nail over his work table. It kept perfect time.

When he sat down to work these three articles were always present. They were his talismen. He couldn't write with another machine or another pen. Later, when he acquired an alarm clock, he still wound his watch regularly. He always looked to *it* for the time, not to the alarm clock. When he changed residence, which was fairly frequent, he always disposed of some precious relic which he had been holding on to for years. He enjoyed being forced to move. It meant reducing his baggage, because all he allowed himself was one valise. Everything had to get in that valise or be discarded. The things he clung to were souvenirs—a post card from an old friend, a photo of an old love, a pen knife picked up at the flea market. Always the trifles. He would throw away a sweater or a pair of pants to make room for his favorite books. Of course I always rescued the things I knew he didn't want to get rid of. I would steal back to his room and make a bundle of them; a few days later I would show up and hand them to him. The expression on his face then was like that of a child recovering an old toy. He would actually weep with joy. To prove, though, that he really didn't need them he would dig out some precious object and make me a present of it. It was like saying, "All right, I'll keep the sweater (or the pants), since you insist on it, but here's my valuable camera. I really have no use for it any more." Whatever the gift, I was hardly likely to have any use for it either, but I would accept it as though it were a royal gift. In a sentimental mood he would sometimes offer me his fountain pen—the typewriter I couldn't use because it had a French keyboard. The watch I accepted several times.

Having a job on the newspaper, he had only a few hours in the afternoon to give to his writing. In order not to worry himself about how much or how little he was accomplishing, he made it a rule to write just two pages a day, no more. He would stop in the middle of a sentence if it were the bottom of that second page. He always seemed extremely cheerful to have accomplished this much. "Two pages a day, 365 days in the year, that makes 730," he would say. "If I can do 250 in a year I'll be satisfied. I'm not writing a *roman fleuve*." He had sense enough to know that, with the best intentions in the world, one seldom has the moral courage to write every day of the week. He made allowance for bad days: vile moods, hang-overs, fresh lays, unexpected visits, and so on. Even if the interruption lasted a week he would never try to write more than the two pages he had fixed as his stint. "It's good not to exhaust yourself," he would say chirpingly. "It leaves you fresh the next day." "But don't you feel like going on, don't you feel like writing six or seven pages sometimes?" I would ask. He would grin. "Sure I do, but I restrain myself." And then he would quote me a Chinese proverb about the master knowing how to *refrain* from working miracles. In his breast-pocket, of course, he always carried a note-book. At work he no doubt made notes with that flawless Parker pen of his, or continued where he had left off (bottom of page two).

It was characteristic of him to create the impression that everything was easy. Even writing. "Don't try too hard," that was his motto. In other words, "Easy does it." If you intruded upon him while he was at work he showed no irritation whatever. On the contrary, he would get up smiling, invite you to stay and chat with him. Always imperturbable, as though nothing could really interrupt what he was doing or thinking. At the same time he was discreet about intruding on the other person. Unless he was moody. Then he would burst in on me, or any one, and say: "You've got to drop what you're doing, I want to talk to you. Let's go somewhere and have a drink, eh? I can't work to-day. You shouldn't work either, it's too beautiful, life is too short." Or perhaps he had just taken a fancy to a girl and he needed some money. "You've got to help me find some dough," he would say. "I promised to meet her at 5.30 sharp. It's important." That meant I would have to go out and hit somebody up. I knew plenty of Americans, so he said, and Americans always had money hidden away. "Don't be shy about it," he would say. "Get a hundred francs while you're at it, or three hundred. Pay day will be here soon."

On pay day we were always most broke, it seemed. Everything went for debts. We would allow ourselves one good meal and trust in Providence to carry us through till the next pay day. We had to pay these little debts or there would be no more credit. But over a meal sometimes we would get a little high and decide to let it all ride. We would have our fling and wonder how to make up for it on the morrow. Often a stranger would turn up in the nick of time, one of those old friends from America who wanted to see the sights. We always handled the money for these visitors from America "so that they wouldn't be cheated." Thus, in addition to borrowing a bit, we would put aside a little extra on the sly.

Now and then an old friend of his would turn up, some one he had known in Italy, Jugoslavia, Prague, Berlin, Majorca, Morocco. Only then would one realize that the amazing tales he seemed to invent when drunk had a basis in fact. He was not one to boast of his travels or adventures. Usually he was shy and discreet about his personal experiences; only when drunk would he reveal choice morsels of the past. And then it was as though he were talking about some one else, some one he had known and identified himself with.

One day an Austrian friend turned up from God knows where. He was in a bad state morally and physically. Over a good meal he confessed that he was wanted by the police. We kept him in hiding for about two months, allowing him to go out of the house only at night when accompanied by Fred or myself. It was quite a wonderful period for the three of us. Not only did I get an insight into Fred's past but I got an insight into my own past. We were living then in Clichy, not very far from Céline's famous clinic. There was a cemetery a few blocks from the house to which we repaired in the evenings, always with one eye open for an *agent*.

After a time Erich, our guest, grew tired of reading and begged for something to do. I was at that time deep in Proust. I had marked off whole pages of *Albertine Disparue* which he eagerly agreed to copy for me on the typewriter. Every day there was a fresh pile of script lying on my work table. I can never forget how grateful he was for giving him this task to perform. Nearing the end, and observing that he had become thoroughly absorbed in the text, I invited him to give me his observations *viva voce*. I was so fascinated by his elaborate analyses of the passages selected that finally I persuaded him to go over the excerpts and make detailed annotations. At first he suspected that I was stringing him along, but when I had convinced him of the importance of his contribution his gratitude knew no bounds. He went to it like a ferret, pursuing every imaginable thread which would amplify the problem significantly. To see him work one would think he had received a commission from Gallimard. He worked more diligently and painstakingly than Proust himself, it seemed to me. All to prove that he really was capable of doing an honest day's work.

I can't remember any period of my life when the time flew more quickly than it did at Clichy. The acquisition of two bicycles worked a complete metamorphosis in our routine. Everything was planned so as not to interfere with our afternoon rides. At four on the dot Fred would have finished his two pages. I can see him now, in the courtyard, oiling and polishing his machine. He gave it the same loving care that he bestowed on his typewriter. He had every gadget that could be tacked on to it, including a speedometer. Sometimes he would sleep only three or four hours in order to take a long spin, to Versailles or St. Germain-en-Laye, for example. When the Tour de France was on we would go to the movies every night in order to follow the progress of the race. When the six day races came to the Vel d'Hiv we were there, ready to stay up all night.

Once in a while we dropped in at the Medrano. When my friend Renaud came up from Dijon we even ventured to go to the Bal Tabarin and the Moulin Rouge, places we loathed. The cinema was the principal source of relaxation, however. What I shall always remember about the cinema is the excellent meal we stowed away before entering the place. A meal and then a few leisurely moments at a bar, over a *café arrosé de rhum*. Then a quick hop to the nearest *pissotière* amidst the hum of traffic and the stir of idle throngs. During the entr'acte another dash to the *bistrot*, another visit to the urinal. Waiting for the curtain to go up we munched a peanut bar or lapped up an Eskimo. Simple pleasures, asinine, it seemed sometimes. On the way home a conversation begun in the street would often continue until dawn. Sometimes, just before dawn, we would cook ourselves a meal, polish off a couple of bottles of wine, and then, ready to hit the hay, would curse the birds for making such a racket.

Some of the more scabrous episodes belonging to this idyllic period I have recorded in *Quiet Days in Clichy* and *Mara-Marignan*, texts which are unfortunately unpublishable in England or America. It is strange that I always think of this period as "quiet days." They were anything but quiet, those days. Yet never did I accomplish more. I worked on three or four books at once. I was seething with ideas. The Avenue Anatole France on which we lived was anything but picturesque; it resembled a monotonous stretch of upper Park Avenue, New York. Perhaps our ebullience was due to the fact that for the first time in many a year we were enjoying what might be called a relative security. For the first time in ages I had a permanent address, for about a year.

When I moved to the Villa Seurat a wholly new atmosphere was created. Fred, after trying out a half dozen different quarters of the city, finally lodged himself nearby in the Impasse du Rouet. Here lived our mutual friends David Edgar and Hans Reichel. After a time Lawrence Durrell arrived from Greece. His appearance in our midst was truly sensational. He was electrifying. Fresh from the Mediterranean world, he was only too eager to throw himself into what he thought was the "decadent" life of Paris. Instead of debauches, however, he found a world of Rabelaisian jollity. If I had laughed long and heartily with Fred I laughed still more in Durrell's presence. It was only necessary for the three of us to meet in order to burst into guffaws. Everything about Fred, but particularly the clown and the mime, caused Durrell to go off into peals of laughter. He looked upon our life in the Villa Seurat as an endless three ring circus. Edgar, who was then in the worst phase of his neurotic career, was frequently with us; he acted as a sort of buffer, inveigling us against our will into the bogs of theosophy, astrology, anthroposophy and into other mephitic realms. Edgar seldom laughed. He went into long monologues in which he drew charts and diagrams explaining the evolution of man, his illnesses, and the glorious future which awaited him. We loved Edgar dearly, and when we were in difficulties it was to Edgar we turned, but unless we could rout him out of his obsessions, laugh him down, we were licked. Drink failed to relax him. Even if we carried him off to a night club, he was apt to go on analyzing, dissecting, construing. Sometimes on my way home of an evening—or it could be on my way home from lunch—I would run across him in a café, seated before an innocent glass of beer. It was impossible, ever, to get away from Edgar quickly, no matter how urgent the reason. If you insisted on leaving quickly he would accompany you home. He always seemed to have a book hidden away which he sprang on you just as you were getting fidgety. It was always a new book, one he had just finished reading, and which it was imperative for his friends to share with him. Sometimes, to give him credit, they were good books, stimulating, to say the least. The trouble was, however, that before he turned a book over to you, he had already read aloud to you the best passages—and with elaborate, hair-splitting exegeses delivered with passionate earnestness, all extemporaneous, to be sure. Often I would say "No! No, I refuse to read it! I'm not a damned bit interested, Edgar, I'm sorry." He wouldn't be offended by such outbursts, not Edgar. He would wait until you had cooled down, then slyly and insidiously work up to the point once again. When you had reached the phase of non-resistance, he would gently

357

put it in your pocket or under your arm. If you hadn't glanced at it by the time he saw you again he would pick it up and begin reading aloud once more. "But that's no way to seduce us," we would object. "You're a damned proselytizer, do you know it?" Edgar would smile blandly. "But seriously," he would begin, "once you get into it you will see . . ." "I can tell from the cover that it's no good," Fred would say. "The book smells bad." Edgar would be absolutely imperturbable. He would listen to you rant for twenty minutes, then go to work on you quietly, as if nothing had been said. In the end, of course, Edgar won out. In the end we were obliged to take over his language and incorporate it into our own. A stranger in our midst would have found our discussions absolutely unintelligible: we had achieved a code language almost as rarefied as the physicist's.

How I laugh when I read of the Villa Seurat *cult!* It was the English, of course, with their utter lack of humor, who began this talk of a cult or group. It is so strange that, separated only by the Channel, the English are able to make France seem like a distant realm. The then young English writers, who made occasional trips to the Continent, gave me the impression of being utterly unreal. Sometimes I would ask Durrell to translate for me what they had said, so complicated, so outlandish was their speech. What they were searching for I never understood. They always impressed me as nearsighted people shorn of their glasses. Durrell and Fred could imitate their mannerisms perfectly. Often, when they had left, we would put on a performance in which we pretended to stutter and stammer, to lisp, to perspire freely, to walk with a mincing gait, to ask ridiculous questions, to get deeply involved in abstruse problems, and so on. During these sessions even Edgar would laugh until the tears rolled down his face.

If there *was* a group in the Villa Seurat it was across the way, at the home of a foreign woman who held soirées once a week. There one could meet all the intellectual bores of Paris, people of every stripe and denomination. Now and then, when we were hungry, we would drop in. There was always plenty to eat and drink, and the sandwiches were extremely delicious. Sometimes there would be dancing. The "great minds" would go into a huddle and the others would disport themselves. The hostess seemed quite indifferent to what went on. All she demanded was that we enjoy ourselves. Her idea of enjoyment was rather simple. As long as you were active, either with the mouth or the feet, she believed you were enjoying yourself.

The real enjoyment came when, obliged to go abroad, she turned her flat over to Fred. There were no more soirées after that, just continuous festivities from morn to night. The cellar and the larder were soon exhausted, the furniture began to fall apart, precious vases filled up with cigarette and cigar stubs which gave off a vile odor, the plumbing got out of order, the piano needed tuning and repairing, the rugs had burnt holes in them, the dirty dishes were strewn all over the kitchen, and in general the place became an unholy mess. For two days and nights there was an extra piano standing outside the door, in the middle of the street. It had been delivered while we were in the midst of dinner one evening. For the pure hell of it, Fred had instructed the moving man to leave it outdoors, that we would haul it in ourselves when we were good and ready. In the midst of the meal the man and wife to whom the piano belonged arrived. They were shocked, of course, and almost on the verge of calling the police. But Fred had a smooth line of talk for them, plied them with strong drinks, insisted that they eat something, and finally cajoled them into believing that all was for the best. Then it began to rain. We went outside and put the lid of the piano down. It was a concert grand, and an excellent

make, if I remember well. Fortunately, the man, who was just recovering from an operation for hemorrhoids, had to hurry home.
Something had gone amiss; he could neither sit down nor stand
up for any length of time. Besides, the drinks had gone to his
head. We called a cab and bustled the two of them in it, promising
them most faithfully that we would get the piano indoors in jig
time. An hour later, both of us pie-eyed by this time, we sat down
in the middle of the street, the rain beating down on the keys, and
pretended to play a duet. The noise was horrific. Windows were
thrown up and threats and imprecations hurled at us from all directions. We then tried to find a few friends to help us get the
damned thing indoors. That took another hour or two. Finally
there were six of us struggling with might and main to squeeze it
through the doorway. It was no go. The piano was all legs, it seemed.
When we eventually desisted from this insane attempt the only
thing to do was to leave the piano where it was, upside down on the
sidewalk. There it remained for another thirty-six hours, during
which time we had several visits from the police . . .

My eye falls on *Le Quatuor en Ré Majeur* on the shelf by my
elbow. I open it at random, musing on this droll companion of
other days. In a few lines he gives a portrait of himself. It seems
extremely apposite after the above . . . "Je suis timide et d'humeur
inégale," the passage begins. "*Himmelhoch jauchzend, zu Tode be-
trübt.* De brusques accès de mélancolie et d'effrayants élans de joie
alternent en moi, sans transition aucune. Le cynisme n'est pas mon
fort. Si je m'en sers quand même, comme tout à l'heure, par exemple,
c'est précisément parceque je suis timide, parceque je crains le ridicule. Toujours prêt à fondre en larmes, j'éprouve le besoin de tour-
ner en dérision mes sentiments les plus nobles. Une espèce de ma-
sochisme, sans doute.

"Et puis, il y a autre chose aussi qui explique mes velléites d'ar-

360

rogance: je sais que tout à l'heure, je vais être obligé de me degonfler; alors, pour mieux me degonfler, je me gonfle d'abord; me gonfle de culot factice, de forfanterie, tellement ma couardise sentimentale et naturelle me dégoute de moi-même. Et comme ma sentimentalité porte surtout sur les femmes et sur l'amour, c'est sur ces sujets que ma hablerie artificielle s'acharne le plus furieusement."

"*Culot*" is the pass-word here. He calls it "*culot factice*," as though that helped matters. What a gall he had, when I think of it. Natural or artificial, inspired or trumped up, it took plenty of *culot* (and of course a bit of alcohol) to dash up to the open doorway of a police station and yell at the top of one's lungs: "*Merde à vous tous, espèces de cons!*" Twice I witnessed him do this, myself walking slowly along and him scurrying like mad around the corner. Meeting him at the appointed bar a few minutes later he would still be panting, still apoplectic with feigned rage. Since the evening had begun that way, he would continue in the same vein, insulting any one and every one with or without provocation. In such moments he seemed possessed by the desire to have his head bashed in. All his efforts proving futile, he would finally stand in the street, baring his chest or thrusting out his jaw, and yell: "You take a crack at me, Joey . . . go ahead . . . I want to see how it feels." If I gave him a good crack, as he requested, he would get angry and complain that I had taken advantage of him. But a minute later he would be laughing, perhaps opening his mouth very wide, to say *b-e-a-u*. He would repeat it a dozen times: *beau, beau, beau* . . . "It's so much more beautiful than beautiful," he'd say. "But you have to open your mouth wide, like this," and he would throw his head back to let me look down his gullet while he uttered the magic word. Then, stumbling along, rolling from side to side, he would invent phrase after phrase in which *beau* could be used effectively, always prolonging the O sound, resting on it as a rower rests on his oars. "Qu'il fait *beau* aujourd'hui!" "Qu'il fait *beau*, fait *beau*, fait *beau* . . ." This could go on from La Fourche to the Porte de Clichy and beyond. Everything was *beau*—always with the wide open mouth, as if he were gargling his throat. "That's the way to speak French, Joey. Move the muscles of your mouth. Make grimaces. Look idiotic. Never swallow your words. French is a musical language. You must open your mouth wide. Like this . . . B-E-A-U. Now say '*comédie*'! Not comedy . . . *comédie!* That's it." Here he might branch off into a disquisition on Paul Valéry's use of the French language, expatiating on his flair for that infallible resonance which makes French poetry conspicuously different from all other poetry.

During all these years of intimate association we were always fully conscious of the fact that we were enjoying life to the hilt. We knew there could not be anything better than what we were experiencing every day of our lives. We felicitated one another on it frequently. For the world in general I rather think that the ten years preceding the war were not particularly joyful times. The continuous succession of economic and political crises which characterized the decade proved nerve-racking to most people. But, as we often used to say: "Bad times are good times for us." Why that should be so I don't know, but it was true. Perhaps the artist, in following his own rhythm, is permanently out of step with the world. The threat of war only served to remind us that we had waged war with the world all our lives. "During a war money is plentiful," Fred used to say with a grin. "It's only before and after the war that things are bad. War time is a good time for guys like us. You'll see."

Fred had spent the closing years of the first World War in an insane asylum. Apparently it hadn't done him any great injury. He was out of harm's way, as we say. As soon as they opened the gates he sailed out, free as a bird, his tail set for Paris. He may have lived a while in Berlin and Prague before reaching Paris. I think he had also been in Copenhagen and Amsterdam. By the time we met in Paris his wanderings had become rather dim in his memory. Italy, Jugoslavia, North Africa, even these more recent adventures had lost their edge. What I remember distinctly about all these wanderings is that in every place he was hungry. He never seemed to forget the number of days on end he had gone without food in a certain place. Since my own wanderings had been colored by the same preoccupation, I relished the morbid accounts he gave me now and then. Usually these reminiscences were aroused when we were pulling our belts tight. I remember once at the Villa Seurat, not having had a morsel for forty-eight hours, how I flopped down on the couch, declaring that I would remain there until a miracle happened. "You can't do that," he said, a tone of unusual desperation in his voice. "That's what I did in Rome once. I nearly died. No one came for ten days." That started him off. He talked so much about prolonged and involuntary fasts that it goaded me into action. For some reason we had ceased to think in terms of credit. In the old days it was easy for me, because I was innocent and ignorant of the ways of the French. Somehow, the longer I lived in Paris the less courage I had to ask a restaurant keeper for credit. The war was getting closer and closer; people were getting more and more jittery. Finally, towards the end, knowing the war could not be staved off, they began to splurge. There was that last minute gaiety which means the jig is up.

Our gaiety, which had been constant, was the result of a deep conviction that the world would never be put to rights. Not for us, at least. We were going to live en marge, fattening on the crumbs which were dropped from the rich man's table. We tried to accommodate ourselves to doing without those essentials which keep the ordinary citizen ensnared. We wanted no possessions, no titles, no promises of better conditions in the future. "Day by day," that was our motto. To reach bottom we did not have to sink very far. Besides, we were resilient. There could be no very bad news in store for us; we had heard it all over and over, we were used to it. We were always on the alert for a windfall. Miracles did happen, not once or twice, but frequently. We relied on Providence in the way a gangster relies on his gat. In our hearts we honestly did believe that we were right with the world. We acted in good faith, even when to some patriotic souls it seemed like treason. It's curious, now that I mention this, to recall how, soon after war was declared, I wrote to Durrell and to Fred that I was certain they would emerge from it without a scratch. About Edgar I wasn't so certain. But he came out swimmingly too. The unpredictable thing about Edgar was—he enjoyed the war! I don't mean that he enjoyed the horrors of it; he enjoyed forgetting about himself and his neurosis.

Even Reichel, who seemed doomed, came out of it in good shape. All these men, and I say it not because they were my friends, all of them were clean, honest souls, *innocent,* if the word still has meaning. Despite all the buffetings of Fate, they were destined to lead charmed lives. Their problems were never the world's problems. Their problems went deeper, much deeper. With the exception of Durrell, who was decidedly gregarious, they were all lonely men. Reichel more than any of the others, I should say. Reichel was terrifyingly apart and alone. But that is what made him so wonderful when he entered a room full of people, or rather when he entered the company of a few chosen friends. His desire for companionship and communion was so great that sometimes it seemed, when he entered a gathering, that a bomb had gone off.

Never shall I forget one Christmas day we spent together, Reichel, Fred and myself. It was about noon when they turned up, expecting naturally that I would have food and wine on hand. I had nothing. Nothing but a hard crust of bread which I was too disgusted to bother nibbling. Oh yes, there was a drop of wine—about the fifth of a litre bottle. I remember that distinctly because what fascinated me later, after they had left, was the recollection of how long this meagre portion of wine had lasted. I remember too, most distinctly, that for a long time the crust of bread and the almost empty bottle stood untouched in the middle of the table. Perhaps because it *was* Christmas we all exhibited an unusual restraint about the absence of food. Perhaps too it was because our stomachs were light and the cigarettes short that the conversation proved much more exciting than filling our bellies would. The crust of bread lying there in full view all the time had started Reichel off on a story about his prison experiences. It was a long story about his awkwardness and stupidity, how he had been cuffed and cursed for being a hopeless idiot. There was a great to-do about right hand and left hand, his not remembering which was his right hand and which was his left hand. In telling a story Reichel always acted it out. There he was, walking up and down the studio, rehearsing his stupid past, his gestures so grotesque, so pathetic, that we laughed and cried at the same time. In the act of demonstrating a salute which "they" had finally succeeded in teaching him to do with éclat, he suddenly took notice of the crust of bread. Without interrupting his story he gently broke off a corner of it, poured himself a thimbleful of wine and leisurely dipped the bread in the wine. With this Fred and I automatically did the same. We were standing up, each with a tiny glass in one hand and a morsel of bread in the other. I remember that moment vividly: it was like taking communion, I thought to myself. As a matter of fact, it was really the first communion I ever participated in. I think we were all aware of this, though nothing was said about it. Anyhow, as the story progressed we marched back and forth, crossed and recrossed each other's path numerous times, sometimes bumping into one another and making quick apologies, but continuing to pace back and forth, to cross and recross one another's paths.

About five in the afternoon there was still a drop of wine in the bottle, still a tiny morsel of bread lying on the table. The three of us were as lucid, as bright, as gay as could be. We might have continued that way until midnight were it not for an unexpected visit from an Englishwoman and a young poet. The formalities concluded, I immediately inquired if they had any money on them, adding at once that we were in need of food. They were delighted to come to our rescue. We gave them a big basket and told them to gather whatever they could. In about a half hour they returned laden with food and wines. We sat down and fell to like hungry wolves. The cold chicken which they had bought disappeared like magic. The cheeses, the fruit, the bread we washed down with the most excellent wines. It was really criminal to toss those good wines off the way we did. Fred, of course, had become hilarious and uncontrollable during the feast. With each bottle that was opened he poured himself a good tumblerful and emptied it down his gullet in one draught. The veins were standing out at the temples, his eyes were popping, the saliva dribbled from his mouth. Reichel had disappeared, or perhaps we had locked him out. Our English friends took everything with composure and equanimity. Perhaps they looked upon it as the customary scene at the Villa Seurat which they had heard so much about.

That evening was fraught with strange consequences for Fred. Never did he reveal to any one what precisely had occurred that evening to alter him. That he *was* altered, definitely and for good, no one who had known him intimately could deny. It was a conversion. From then on the warring selves seemed to fall apart; little by little his true self asserted itself, gained the ascendancy over

366

the transient personalities which he used to assume like masks. The change-over had occurred in the dark, literally and figuratively. He had closeted himself in another room with the Englishwoman, for about an hour, I should say. In that time something occurred between them which decided the future course of his life. He predicted as much when we were alone together the next day. But even he did not realize at the time how truthfully he was speaking.

The outbreak of war was the crucial test. He was in England at the time and very much enamored of the English. I think he had already taken steps to become a citizen. To my amazement I received a letter one day saying that he had volunteered in the British Army. Any one who knew him in the past would have thought it impossible of him. He more than any one would have scoffed at the idea—before the conversion. "One war is enough in one's lifetime," he used to say. He used to brag about his inability to become a soldier. "I'm a physical coward," he would say. "Just to touch a gun makes me ill." In the space of a few months he was at home in the British Army. He took to it like a duck takes to water. He found everything enjoyable, even the food. Curiously enough, the thing he dreaded most—to kill some one in cold blood and at a distance—never proved necessary. But I remember him writing me that he was prepared even for that, that he would do it with zest if it were necessary. That was so typical of him. Whatever he did he did with good will, in the spirit of play. It may be a strain to think of a man killing joyously, but the more one thinks about it, the more one wonders if it isn't the best way. In this too his innocence asserted itself. He could not kill out of hatred, or greed or envy, nor because he was commanded to do it. He could kill only out of sheer exuberance. Sometimes I almost regret that he had not killed at least one man. I should like to have shaken hands with him after that, to have said: "Joey, my lad, fine work! I never thought it was in you." I can well imagine his response, can picture how he would have hung his head blushingly, not out of shame but out of embarrassment, grinning all the while and stammering out some absurd remark about it all being in the day's work, or pretending to brag about being an extraordinary marksman.

But let me not stop on this note. Let me go back in retrospect to that rainy day when Durrell, Nancy, Fred and myself were sitting in the little restaurant in the 13th arrondissement, somewhere in the vicinity of the rue de la Glacière. We are in high spirits as usual, Durrell laughing so uproariously over Fred's quips that the proprietor is irritated. (Often we were asked to leave the cinema because of Durrell's infectious laugh.) Suddenly, apropos of nothing at all, with his fork arrested in mid-air, Fred blurts out: *"The mission of man on earth is to remember . . ."* There was a brief pause, as if we had received a slap in the face, followed by peals of laughter. It was just inconceivable that Fred should have uttered this phrase at that particular moment. What was more inconceivable was that this time we could not put him off with our laughter. He began the sentence again, not once but several times . . . *"The mission of man on earth is to remember."* He could get no further with his thought; we simply drowned him in gales of laughter. Some one asked him if he had read it somewhere. No, he had made it up himself. He said this blushing, as if aware that he had given birth to something extremely significant. Whether he had thought it up himself or not, we all agreed that it was marvelous, more than that, memorable, that we would give him credit for it sometime, somewhere, somehow. But he didn't want any credit for it, he tried to let us know. He wanted us to listen. We couldn't listen. The phrase had electrified us. Another word tacked on to it and it would have been ruined. Especially an explanatory word.

368

It was Edgar who used to chew my ear off about the boon of memory—in Devachan. I used to fight him tooth and nail on this, I remember. I used to insist that memory must be killed off, that if the intervals between births have any purpose it must be to get rid of the baggage of memory. "But you can't do that before you have remembered everything," Edgar would argue. "You must rehearse every tiniest detail of your life over and over, until you have extracted the last significant juices from your experiences." Well, I could see the point of that clearly enough. "But in the end," I kept harping, "is it not true that you do lose all memory of things past?" I would say it to myself, not to Edgar. With Edgar, as you may imagine, it was more expedient to give in quickly. Not too quickly either, because then he would become suspicious.

But Fred's view of it was that it was here on earth man was to remember. That was what was novel and alarming at the same time. Novel because no one thinks of remembrance as "a mission," alarming because what then would one do in Devachan? Was he implying that Nirvana should be attained in *this* lifetime? Had he suddenly realized that, whatever or whoever he was, he now was once and for all, that all the pasts led to this endless present in which being and vision were one? Had he experienced his last death, and was it deathless that he uttered his innocent and sententious phrase? Of course these thoughts did not flit through my mind at the moment of utterance. They have come since, along with countless others, in moments of sudden recollection. But there is always something gratuitous which accompanies the remembrance of the phrase, something beyond his indescribable look and the indescribable shock which all of us experienced simultaneously. That something I cannot put my finger on. I can only give intimations, captured reverberations.

All this happened some seven years ago. One remembers lots of

369

strange, startling, inexplicable events and situations. One of them often stands out more vividly, more hauntingly than the others. Its unguessed significance increases with the passage of time. It seems to gather other phenomenal occurrences into its own magnetic field, to give them focus or a wholly new orientation. If it is remembered over and above everything else there must be a deep reason for it. Our ability to forget certain painful experiences is only matched by our ability to remember others. What is buried and what is kept alive seem to have equal importance. One works subterraneously, the other in etheric realms. But both are eternally operative.

In one of Fred's books (*The Renegade*), in which I notice he has resuscitated the phrase, attributing it to another person, he emphasizes that one has to forget much before one can remember. The passage towards the end of the book in which the subject of "remembrance" is dwelt on at some length is introduced by a most significant phrase. The narrator and the woman called Iris Day are having a farewell dinner. A wine is introduced which he says went to his head almost instantly, filling him with a sensation of great serenity and lucidity. "It's a wine," he is informed, "that was drunk long before Bacchus. It comes from the shores of the Eridanos where the water is purer and more limpid than anywhere else . . . They say (and this is the phrase I consider significant) *it makes the sick forget and the pure remember*."

Then says the narrator: "It's miraculous! What is it? There is a marvelous light in me, I can't describe it."

"You will see better when your eyes get used to it . . . Don't think it is the wine, it's you: you've merely found the key to the treasure that belongs to you."

"I don't remember, Iris."

"Don't worry, you will . . . *The mission of man on earth is to remember* . . . There's no science, no wisdom, not even love. In the end, everything boils down to one thing: *remembrance*."

When Iris Day proceeds to explain the sacrificial nature of renunciation (in which the "present" as a concept of time is eliminated) we learn that the purpose is "to rejoin the Source, which you do not as yet remember" . . . Then she adds: "Not till you have sacrificed everything you have acquired will remembrance come back to you . . . With every successive sacrifice you get nearer the Source."

The narrator here goes on to explain that the meeting with Iris Day was ordained. Had he not met her precisely when he did his life would have taken the wrong turn. "I've met you at the crossroads," he says.

This meeting, which the author places in London, corresponds with the Villa Seurat episode. Iris Day is unquestionably the woman who arrived that Christmas Day. Now then, though I had read *The Renegade* when it first came out (in 1943), I had completely forgotten that Fred had treated of all this in his book. It was only a few moments ago that I suddenly asked myself if my good friend Fred had not spoken of all this himself somewhere. What amazes me more, after reading the closing pages of the book, is to see how he himself explained his new attitude towards war. I think it is important to add a few excerpts from the discussion which follows upon the foregoing. I give merely the highlights, of course . . .

"Is war very wrong?" I asked.

"Not wrong, childish . . ." After a few remarks about the nature of the coming war (now finished), Iris Day adds: "I am happy to find you on the right side. From the point of view of the individual, it does not matter whether one is, by fate, on the right or the wrong side."

"How do you mean that, Iris?"

"You can still be right if destiny puts you in the wrong camp, but it is much more difficult, of course; it requires greater strength and greater sacrifices . . . It can be taken for granted that the vast majority of people who fight one another are convinced that they are on the right side. What makes their wars so sophomoric is that they believe it to be possible to enforce, by victory, the laws, order, dogmas, or ideas which they consider just; for in reality the only Law by which human beings can live at all has been laid down long before the earth was inhabited . . . Whether we are good or evil, we have to live by Right, Justice and Love; otherwise we perish in the long run. Hence it is unimportant (from the cosmic viewpoint) which side wins the war, for in the end he that stands for Right, Justice and Love is bound to be victorious. Simply because it is the Law."

"I daresay what you say is true, Iris, but it does not quite apply to us. I don't think we have a right to sit back and watch Destiny taking its long-winded course: man has got to fight for what he thinks is right."

"I am glad to hear you say that . . . There is nothing wrong if some one evades the war because he does not believe in its justice. I know you hate war, but I also know that deep down you sense that there is something great at stake—something that concerns the whole of humanity, and *ipso facto* yourself . . ."

After some lengthy remarks about England's role in the conflict, Iris Day returns to the heart of the subject. Her words assume a prophetic tone.

"Apart from the events that are being shaped in this conflict, in which you may be called upon to play but a small part, this war may have much to do in the moulding of your own personality. It may touch you in the quick. The very basis of your nature may be affected. *You have not yet begun living your own life, and it is im-portant to live one's own life.* Your past existence was merely the manifestation of something that was not essentially you . . . Not till you are bare and naked and all in ruins will you be able to clear the ground and start building your real house . . . This war, which may decide the future of mankind for many clock centuries, af-fords you the unique opportunity of atoning for the past. For you are involved in this war *personally*. It may sound cruel, and I dare-say it is not altogether your own fault, but the fact remains that you are personally responsible for the war to the extent that you have not lived your own life: the sum total of innumerable pasts like yours has to bear the responsibility of the catastrophe. It is no use pleading that you never hated anybody, that you had always kept clear of any direct activities that led up to the unavoidability of the war. That was not enough. Your great fault, which you share with the vast majority of men, was to lead a wrong life. It is that fault which you now have a chance to redeem. I know you will do it."

So this is the justification for participating in mass slaughter? you ask. By simply joining up with the "right" side your good friend Fred is going to redeem a wasted life? In the name of Peace and Justice he is going to kill, just like any other misguided individual, is that it? I know *all* the questions you are ready to hurl at me. And on top of it you are going to say, "What bilge! What self-decep-tion! What utter rot! We could have turned to the *Bhagavad Gita* and found it expressed more eloquently and convincingly."

Let us forget for a moment what justification he gave to his motives. Let us concentrate for a moment on what happened to him during the great catastrophe. How was it that he was not only spared, that he not only grew in stature morally and spiritually, but that he was never obliged to fire a shot; that moreover, instead

373

of killing his fellow-man, he was enabled to save a number from
death? Had he not participated directly and openly, in what way
would he have "participated," since we are all involved, like it or
not? Did he participate in slaughter or did he participate in a cause
which lies deeper than the war itself? I believe the latter. I know
that he had nothing personally to gain, as we say, by joining the
British Army. But he had everything to gain, as a human being,
by identifying himself with the plight of the world. He was renouncing the false security or immunity he enjoyed as a man living
*en marge*. He ceased being the "renegade" in order to be himself.
He made war not against his fellow-man, for he never had any
hatred of his fellow-man, but against what he considered were the
forces of evil. Evil in this instance—and is not this the true meaning of evil?—representing all that prevents one from leading his
own true life. He was ready to violate the commandment "Thou
Shalt Not Kill!", in which he had taken refuge out of weakness
(Don't kill me and I won't kill you!), because something bigger
than obedience to the Law seemed at stake. Actually, and I stress
this point once again, as events turned out he was never called upon
to break the Law. With those who retort that this was a mere accident, or that by serving in the Army he was helping others to
kill, I beg to differ. In no way were his services instrumental to
the furtherance of slaughter. Or, if they were, then the grocer who
supplied the able-bodied citizens of his country with food was also
collaborating in wholesale murder. As for its being accidental that
he did not kill any one, well, by what accident was it that instead
of being sent to the trenches he was employed in the Pioneer
Corps? Many of his comrades wanted desperately to go across and
wage active warfare; some of them had their wish and were killed.
Fred cheerfully accepted the dirty work, which meant dashing into
burning buildings on occasion and rescuing helpless men, women

374

and children. Some of his comrades met their death that way. They were spared none of the agonies which attend a heroic death on the battlefield. Fred, as I said earlier, led a charmed life. He was "saved," as we sometimes put it. Saved not *from* something, since he desired no protection, but *for* something. He emerged from the war with a sane, healthy, joyous outlook on life. He would have emerged from it in the same jubilant spirit even had he killed a few men. Besides, he would never have regarded himself as guiltless for those deaths: he would have considered himself thoroughly responsible—to God. He would have said, on the Day of Judgment, with a bit of the old *"culot factice,"* "I did it for *you*, O God. I acted according to the light that was in me."

Here we arrive at the contradiction which so deeply disturbs the ordinary mind. Neither the man who refuses to participate nor the man who does is of necessity guilty. The question of responsibility for mass slaughter cuts deeper than the matter of willingness or unwillingness to shed blood. Both he who kills and he who refrains from killing may be in the right, or they may just as well be in the wrong. The man who did not lift a finger may be more guilty than the man who proved himself responsible for thousands of deaths. Only a pacifist zealot would consider a man like General Eisenhower, for example, as "guilty." Only short-sighted beings can pin the guilt for the war on Hitler or Mussolini. War, like peace, involves us all.

There are always individuals who, though living in the very midst of catastrophe, remain untouched by it. I mean not just physically, but morally and spiritually. They are not only "above the fray," they are beyond the zone of fatality. They are out of all danger because, though they can not and would not remove themselves physically, in their heart of hearts they had elected from the beginning to stay out. *They have no heart in such things,* as the saying goes. The wine which they drank at the Source helps them to remember. It is only the pure who remember, only the pure who can remain aloof, and that not from choice but from necessity. With them the realm of accident is not a quixotic one but a deeply intelligible one. They are always conscious of direction just as they are always conscious of the real identity of those who confront them. They relegate nothing to chance; for them all proceeds according to law and all is therefore in order. They do not busy themselves putting things to right, neither do they occupy themselves with doing good. It is in the service of life that they are enrolled; they *elected* to serve, they were not conscripted. Consequently they are never called upon by fate "to take sides"; they are not crucified upon the horns of a tragic dilemma. The turbulent waves of conflict break before reaching them; they are never engulfed.

With such as my friend Fred, on the other hand, wars and revolutions provide an opportunity for them to "lose themselves." It is important for them to take sides, *not* to aid the right, *not* to become heroic instruments of justice, but to discover the meaning of sacrifice. Often through participation they achieve immunity. Immunity not so much from the hazards and dangers of involvement, but immunity from fear, immunity from the cowardly deceptions of the ego. They discover a deathless reality in which there can never again be the pain of separation. They have reached home, face to face with the Source, as much alive in the spirit world as in the flesh. Some of them, mourned as "lost," find freedom in death. Others, living the anonymous life of the little man, are privileged to manifest their freedom in life. These are the immortal spirits living in accordance with the Law who have discovered that victory and eternity are synonymous. To live one's own life, to lead it to the full, carries with it the reward of immortality. "That which now has life and is forever exempt from death," such is the definition of immortal. But the definition might also be stated thus: "That which has life is forever exempt from death." That is the meaning which the metamorphosis of mortal to immortal conveys. The immortal is the victorious one: he has conquered over time and death. He has triumphed over the "creature" by passing through the fires of sacrifice. Renouncing all claim to personal survival he becomes deathless. Remembering the road back, he "puts outside of himself" (*forgets*, in short) all the obstacles which he himself had put in his path. The snares and delusions of the world no longer exist: like a spider he realizes that he had spun the intricate, entangling web out of his own substance. Free of the world, he is free from Fate. He no longer postpones living. The past has been atoned for and thus obliterated; the future, robbed of its time track, has no meaning. The present dissolves in the all which has neither beginning nor end. *In the beginning was the Word and the Word was with God and the Word was God.* At the Source there is no separation either of God and creature or of spirit and time.

*The mission of man on earth is to remember . . .*

# BUFANO, THE MAN OF HARD MATERIALS

"I AM NOT interested in what we cannot do, only what we can do interests me . . . I know nothing in man's make up that is not possible and complete." This, in a nut-shell, is Bufano's philosophy. A philosophy of action, based on faith, courage, perseverance and inspiration.

In everything but physical stature Bufano is a giant. As a sculptor, he towers head and shoulders above our time. He thinks and acts in terms of the eternal. Everything he touches, everything he participates in, reflects permanence, duration, indestructibility. His realm is the NOW. He is never the critic, always the planner and builder. He never wastes a moment; he carries no impedimenta, is always fit and ready to enter the fray. In one being he combines dreamer, worker, athlete, gladiator, adventurer, monk, saint and statesman. He belongs to no particular place, his roots are everywhere. He is one of the most representative Americans and at the same time a man of all nations. He thinks in terms of the immediate, but in a way that unites him with all that is best in the past, all that is hopeful and promising in the future. He believes in man, man the potential being and man the actual being. Like Saint Francis of whom he is enamored, he does not stop there: he includes the creature world. For Bufano the world is completely alive, even that part of it which is called "inanimate." He anchors himself in the very plexus of this vital, breathing, ever-changing world.

Centuries from now he will be known as the man who challenged the hard materials. Centuries from now he will be hailed as a man of monumental vision. Bufano sees big, every one admits that. For most people he sees too big, that is the tragedy. Those who envy and malign him call him a swell head. They have never examined his heart. Little do they realize, these Lilliputians, that everything Bufano clamors for can be realized now in this living present. Looking at Bufano standing beside an enormous block of raw material which he is about to bite into, one is inclined to say *"Impossible!"* This little man, this overwhelmingly resistant material, this enormous inchoate mass—what patience, what effort, what fortitude is demanded! *What love!* It's true he works twice as many hours as the ordinary laborer. But that tells us almost nothing. It's true that in a single day he sometimes wears out a dozen implements. But that again tells us almost nothing. It is what he is seeking, what he is striving to bring to light, that matters. To put it briefly, his whole problem is one of creating forms which will express the utmost beauty, which will render truth and integrity in the simplest manner. In Bufano's aesthetic, simplicity represents that same perfect wholeness which monotheism did for the ancient Jews. It is not a child-like simplicity by any means, though children are often quicker to respond to his work than adults. It is a simplicity arrived at by ceaseless observation and vigilant discipline. It is the simplicity of the holy man, who is far from being a simple man. In the subtle manipulation of his forms, Bufano has been likened to Einstein. There *is* a connection between these two modern spirits, one a master of the abstract, the other a master of the concrete. Common to them both is the ability to open men's eyes. Speaking of Bufano's black granite statue of Saint Francis, which now reposes in a warehouse in Paris, Roger Fry described it as "the most significant piece of sculpture done within five hundred years." All his monumental pieces are revolutionary, as tonic and disturbing as the most abstruse theories of Einstein.

The work of a giant belongs in the open, commanding great vistas, in keeping with the spirit which animates them. Some of Bufano's pieces are imposing enough to dominate whole cities; some are eloquent enough to stand alone in the midst of a desert, there to commune eternally with the elements and the creatures of the air; around others there could well arise new communities, populated by men and women who look towards the future. Instead there is connected with his creations a shameful record of neglect, indifference, scorn and contempt, even theft and vandalism. With respect to some of his greatest works Bufano does not know what has happened, where they are, or in what condition. In certain cases the ownership is not clear. A legend of persecution and martyrdom hangs like an aura about this greatest of American sculptors. Bufano has become the nation's problem. Wherever he goes controversies arise, battles rage. He moves like a storm center.

Bufano himself is quiet, self-contained, thoroughly unosten-
tatious. He is a man of peace, a man striving with all his heart to
bring peace to the world. But being creative through and through,
being a man of direct action, a man who suits the gesture to the
word and the word to the deed, being a man of truth, incorruptible,
as unspoiled as a wild flower, he causes things to happen. There
is nothing enigmatic about Bufano, as some pretend. He is an
anomaly in our midst simply because he is a man of his word. He
believes in what he says, and he says what he thinks at any cost.
The moment you talk compromise or delay you automatically
separate yourself from the circle in which he moves. Bufano himself
does not reject or exclude. He is an all-inclusive man, a man whose
instinctive gesture is to embrace all things, all creatures, all points
of view. But he has his own way of seeing things, his own way
of getting things done, and it is the most commendable, efficient
way—*simply and directly*. He does not care to merely represent, he
wants to impersonate, embody, epitomize. If he has a political
flair, it is to eliminate politics. If he has a tendency to lead, it is
only to show the way, only to teach others how to lead themselves.
He is not a self-seeker, he is an activator. Unlike those generals in
modern warfare who direct the battle from a safe and remote distance, Bufano is always in the van, always up front, fully exposed,
ready to receive the first blow. Once upon a time he was regarded
as "a voice crying in the wilderness"; to-day he is rapidly becoming
a force to be reckoned with, not only in the domain of art but in
the realm of action. To him art and action are one. He labors to
empty the museums, not to fill them. His whole struggle with the
powers that be is to bring art out into the open, to have it participate, function, in daily life. This is his heresy, this is why he is
persecuted and condemned. Because he wants art to be a part of

life he is regarded with suspicion; because he wants the artist to reap the fruits of his labor, he is regarded as an agitator.

"The limitations of the hard stones and metals challenge the imagination," says Bufano. He has told how the use of these materials made possible his search for pure form. In a sense, Bufano himself has come to resemble these hard materials; in a sense, he has worked on himself just as valiantly as he has on his granites, porphyry and stainless steel. The inner and outer contours of the man follow simple, flowing lines, revealing a human form of striking purity. He is a figure polished by much rubbing against the world, a figure tempered by the fires of passion, a figure planted on a firm pedestal, capable of resisting all kinds of weather, all sorts of criticism. Everything he uses for his own needs is of the simplest: all his personal possessions could be put in a brown paper bag. For his work, on the other hand, he uses only the best materials, no matter how expensive. To accomplish his projects, which are usually on a generous scale, he has to make use of his wits, his courage, his imagination. Sometimes he strikes a snag. Bufano's battle with society is the old story of the rock and the web. The rock is massive, crushing, adamant; the web is cloying, binding, strangling. The rock is conscious of its strength: it is like crystallized will, so to speak. Whereas the web is listless, possessing no virtue but the dubious one of obstruction.

Aiming always for the heart and center of things, Bufano has the faculty of disturbing that delicate, invisible, intangible something which holds our rotten society together. When he gets into action, society quivers in all its parts—exactly like a jelly-fish. Like the jelly-fish, society always responds by wrapping its clinging, stinging tentacles about the intruder. The confusion and disturbance which follow in the wake of Bufano should be regarded as evidence of his aliveness. Most men, in trying to rectify matters, deal only with the periphery and circumference: they never touch the core. But Bufano, axe in hand, jumps immediately to the vital, aching center. Were our present society a delicate, sensitive mechanism, this image would be most unflattering. There is nothing, I must say, inherently crude, brutal or tactless about Bufano. Indeed, he has uncommon discrimination; no one can be more sensitive and alert, more tender, sympathetic and appreciative. But society, as it is constituted to-day, is anything but a delicate Swiss watch. Bufano knows this. He knows that if you would get anything done to-day you must ring the front door bell, and if there is no answer, then you must push the door in. He has not worked in hard materials all his life to be vanquished by a mere jelly-fish. When a conductor was needed for the People's Symphony Orchestra in San Francisco, he flew to London and brought back with him Sir Thomas Beecham. When the Open Air Show for San Francisco's artists was inaugurated, he rounded up 250,000 spectators, thereby enabling that city's artists to earn over $10,000.00, for all of which he received almost no credit and little thanks. When it was proposed to erect a fitting monument to the patron saint of San Francisco, a monument which would dwarf and nullify the hideous Coit Tower on Telegraph Hill, Bufano induced the city fathers to purchase a site for his statue at Twin Peaks. I was up there the other day with Bufano to take in the panorama. The land is there, the vista is there, the city lies below in all its sprawling magnificence —but where is the monument to the good Saint Francis? The rock and the web again. This time the web seems to be winning out. *Seems to be*, I say, because the battle is still on, because everything about the web is only seeming. Eventually the web will break; eventually the rock will emerge. Eventually Bufano will hatch his egg, hatch every egg he lays, whether it be of granite, stainless steel, Portland Cement or dynamite.

---

383

One would think that a city like San Francisco, a state like California, a nation like America, would be proud to call a man like Bufano its own; one would think that a great community would be proud to possess such a sculptor. One would think so because Bufano is precisely the sort of genius who thinks in terms of the community he belongs to, because he seeks ever to enrich, ennoble, glorify the community. He is the last man in the world to exist for himself alone. His choice of medium, his conception of the use of the medium, are in themselves indicative of his spirit. His work was never intended for the museum, to be admired solely by lovers of art. His statues were not meant to be stifled and asphyxiated by the fumes of culture. In other times Bufano would have had his patrons, men of taste and conviction like himself, men filled with grandiose dreams and capable of realizing them. In our day there are no such men directing affairs of state. America, the richest country on earth, has no Ministry of Fine Arts. Virtually nothing is done to nourish and protect the artist. Indeed, it seems as if everything possible were done to discourage and annihilate him. For years Bufano has been agitating for a Department of Fine Arts. Should he ever succeed in obtaining his wish, I here and now nominate him to be the first Minister of Fine Arts in America. I know that he would get things done. I know that he would enlist the support of the best talents in the country. As it is, Bufano's own precious talents are wasted, wasted in the accomplishment of things which might be left to lesser men. Actually, it is a crime to expect of Bufano that he give his energies in this direction. What we want of him is more monumental sculpture. Bufano should be endowed by the nation to execute his far-reaching plans for erecting in strategic places throughout the country statues which will reflect the glory of America and inspire its future citizens with those virtues of purity, simplicity, truthfulness and magnanimity which go to make the foundation of a great community. At present, as one of several members of the Art Commission for the City of San Francisco, he is crippled. He has been waging an almost hopeless fight to make the city restore those statues of his which were lost, mutilated and stolen while under the city's care. He has pleaded in vain with the city to return to the Federal government at Washington the statues which it loaned to the city. No one connected with the city government will acknowledge the least guilt or responsibility. He cannot get the slightest assurance that the same neglect and vandalism will not be employed with respect to the remaining statues of his now in the city's possession.

Where does the city keep Bufano's statues? it might be pertinent to ask here. Has it made a place for them in prominent, suitable surroundings? Do they greet the roving eye of the visitor as he enters the city by one of the leading thoroughfares? No, one has to search for them, they are hidden away. One of his finest pieces, originally intended for the entrance to the San Juan Battista Mission, is located at the Negro Housing Project. The colossal Peace statue, designed for the World's Fair, stands in a warehouse; it had been rejected because of the superb simplification employed in modeling the head. The stainless steel head of the Penguin, which stands at Aquatic Park, a deserted spot, is missing. The head of the Bach statue, intended for the village of Carmel famous for its Bach festivals, was decapitated the night before the unveiling of the statue, and to this day has not been found nor has any satisfactory explanation of this act of vandalism ever been vouchsafed by the police or the township. The statue of the Mother of the Races is missing, but the "Missing States Bureau" of the City of San Francisco would deny that it ever existed. Saint Francis, who has waited all these years to be honored by the City of San Francisco, was murdered in embryo, so to speak—perhaps with the

385

connivance of the city's own officials, who knows? All these works, and I have not given the complete list, took years and years to be executed, were made of the finest materials, were paid for by the various communities, and nothing, absolutely nothing, is being done to restore them, to make restitution of funds, to compensate the artist for his time and effort or make it possible for him to recommence his Gargantuan labors. The one statue which seems to have been given a fitting background, which seems to be cherished and properly preserved, is that of Sun Yat Sen in San Francisco's Chinatown. But then it is a well-known fact that the Chinese have been the faithful custodians of art for centuries.

This shameful record is the ironic answer to Bufano's own noble words: "Art is the people's one world—one color one race—it is the only universal language spoken—cherished by every people or race on earth it is the basic alphabet of human communication."

What a total lack of understanding of the spirit of an artist to insinuate, or openly allege, as has been done, that Bufano himself, perhaps with the aid of his colleagues, might have brought about the theft or mutilation of his own work! He might well have done this, it is asserted, in order to create more publicity for himself. What Bufano wants, however, is not more publicity but the restoration of his statues. But the City of San Francisco prefers to play the ostrich.

We know that when the Mayor of San Francisco appointed Bufano Art Commissioner, it took only a few hours to have him railroaded to jail. There Bufano, in characteristic fashion, caused a near riot. He refused to undress and sleep in the filthy bed provided for him; he refused to eat the filthy food which they served him; he refused to use the filthy toilets also. It was only a ten day sentence, but ten days of publicity such as Bufano gave the city fathers was too much for them. When his jailers endeavored to

386

make things more comfortable for him, Bufano insisted that they do the same for the other prisoners. "I'm no better than they are," he said. "If they are criminals, I'm a criminal too." He insisted that the food which had been sent him by his friends (and by guilty public officials) be distributed among his fellow prisoners; he insisted that their beds and bedding be made as clean as his. And so on. It was a most excellent way of beginning his career as Art Commissioner. He began by cleaning the Augean stables. He began at the bottom. He began with hands tied and feet shackled, symbolic of the role he had just been called upon to fulfill. He must often have thought, in those moments of humiliation, of those great figures with whom at different times he had been associated—Mahatma Gandhi and Sun Yat Sen, for example. He must have thought of his grandfather who was killed in the revolution with Garibaldi. He must have thought of Michelangelo and the persecution he suffered at the hands of the envious Aretino.

There is one definite fact about Bufano—he has no illusions about man. He goes into things with eyes wide open. However much he knows of man's frailty, man's ignorance, man's cruelty, he is never deterred by this knowledge. If there is something to be done, and it is his duty to do it, he goes forward like a true soldier. He sees things through. If he needs the help of a banker to execute a project, he will call on the banker; if he needs the help of the Governor of Oklahoma, he will call on the Governor of Oklahoma; if he needs the President of the United States to support his cause, he will see the President of the United States, no matter how many Secretaries are in the way. "I'm an artist," he says, "and artists have no time to waste." How true this simple statement! The great time wasters are the business men, the city administrators, the statesmen, the diplomats.

When one thinks of all that Bufano has already accomplished, both as an artist and as a man of action, it seems incredible. He is a man who shows no signs of age. He is always lean, fit, supple, girded for action. His wants are few, his tastes simple, his baggage nil. He has wandered to all the far corners of the earth, including Tibet, Siam, Bali, Easter Island, Japan, China, Africa. He knows many, many of the leading figures in all walks of life throughout the world. He is recognized and honored wherever he goes—except at the City Hall of San Francisco, one might say. And wherever he goes he leaves some precious bit of himself, a germ which grows with time into the tree of legend which is Bufano. People like to ridicule his quiet way of saying—"I've just come back from Moscow," or "I've just been to Chungking." But it's just like Bufano to be flitting back and forth from one end of the earth to the other, quietly, with wings of silver. He has a way of actualizing his desires which is characteristic of the man who has purified himself. He is a visionary who knows how to take flight with his whole being. He is always at the service of the imagination. Others are bogged down by impedimenta, sapped by spiritual inertia. Bufano is always free, always available. "A *votre service*," that is his motto.

There are legends to the effect that Bufano lived with Buddhist monks in India, that he himself became a monk, and that in this guise he penetrated Tibet, even the city of Lhasa. There are similar legends about his exploits and adventures in China, in the days of Sun Yat Sen. How much is legend and how much truth I do not know, nor do I care. From the very beginning of my acquaintance with Bufano I observed that there were elements in his character which seemed to derive from Oriental sources. One of the slighter, more amusing things I noticed about him, in this connection, was his way of not hearing, not answering silly questions. He had a way of continuing the conversation where he had left off, just as though there had been no awkward interruption. In such moments his eyes seemed to go dead; he no longer looked at one but through one. His eyes became the eyes of a statue, or of a man in a trance. "Hear no evil, see no evil, speak no evil." That is Bufano in his most Bufanoesque mood. I have remarked before that he does not indulge in criticism of his fellow artists. He has a way of looking at other men's work and saying not a word, good or bad; one feels that he sees and embraces what is good and quietly rejects what is bad. If you press him, he will give his honest opinion, but it would be better not to press him.

I remember him warning me once that if I were ever to visit the Navajos, about whom we had been talking, I should never ask them any questions. "They don't like Americans," he explained. "Americans ask too many questions." How refreshing, I often thought to myself on leaving Bufano, not to be plied with questions, not to be subjected to idle criticism of this and that. Bufano is a natural-born story teller. He prefers to impart his wisdom and experience in this manner rather than directly. For this reason, perhaps, he has sometimes been accused of evasiveness. For this reason, too, he has been accused of lying and exaggerating. Bufano is a fabulist, no doubt about it. But that is not to say that he is a liar, a distorter of truth. On the contrary, he comes much closer to the truth, even in his wildest inventions, than the man of facts. He speaks as a poet, as the poets of old, I might say, who created in the moment, spontaneously, through sheer verve and exuberance. Bufano takes the cold facts and restores to them the beautiful, discarded garments of symbol, myth and allegory in which they were originally clothed. He does this in consciousness of the fact that without their proper investiture facts have no significance whatever. He does it also in the knowledge that thus clothed they bring joy to the heart. This aspect of the man is a universal one which all ancient peoples had, which we observe even to-day in the Mediterranean peoples and in the Celtic races. Only among us Americans is this quality derided, made suspect. Put Bufano among the folk peoples of Europe, put him with the primitives of Africa or Australia, put him among the aesthetic Balinese, and you will find him at home in his role of story teller. Speaking of the Balinese, I think that of all the peoples on this earth Bufano loves them best. He loves them because, in one way or another, they are all artists. He loves them because they have innate grace, poise, tact, courtesy, reverence and artistic ability. Also, perhaps, because they are generous and hospitable. But above all, because they are jealous defenders of their natural rights.

A man with a predilection for such virtues is very likely to find himself ill at ease in our crass environment. Often I ask myself why he continues to stay here, why he does not set forth again, make a new life for himself amid happier, brighter conditions? I often wonder, for example, how he would feel were he, like Robinson Crusoe, to be cast up on the shores of Easter Island. Naturally he has been to Easter Island too. How could a sculptor of his proportions fail to visit the home of the most monumental sculpture in the world?

But I have digressed. I was speaking of his assimilation of certain Oriental qualities, particularly Taoist and Buddhist tendencies. Consider, for example, how well the following fits Bufano: "The true sage looks up to God (Heaven) but does not offer to aid. He perfects his virtue, but does not involve himself. He guides himself by Tao, but makes no plans. He identifies himself with charity, but does not rely on it. He extends his duty towards his neighbor, but does not store it up. He responds to ceremony, without tabooing it. He undertakes affairs, without declining them. He metes out law without confusion. He relies on his fellow-men and does not make light of them. He accommodates himself to matter, and does not ignore it."

In the statute of Sun Yat Sen, Bufano has, wittingly or unwittingly, raised the revolutionary to the stature of the sage. The position of the hands, for example, is eloquently expressive of the noble teacher. In the calm, dignified, utterly sure pose he has given this great revolutionary figure, Bufano has expressed a great deal of himself also. The head of Sun Yat Sen differs in line, contour and volume from other heads carved by Bufano. At first glance there is something anomalous about this head: it is so definitely a head, with distinct, naturalistic features, so to speak. A colossal head too, it seems at first, though entirely proportionate to the rest of the body, and not nearly as colossal as the head of his Peace statue, for example. This head which juts forth from its robe of stainless steel, this polished brown stone head is positively eloquent in its muteness. It is the head of Reason, the head of Wisdom, and it is Chinese reason, Chinese wisdom (so different from ours) which Bufano has expressed. At the same time, one has the feeling that it is a universal figure he has portrayed and not just an eminent Chinese revolutionary leader. The ability to capture these surface contradictions and resolve them in essence is typical of Bufano and a tribute to his psychological subtlety. In everything he seeks the underlying essence, the core of universal truth which pervades all life.

It gives me pleasure to dwell on this particular piece of work, to relive the moments of sheer joy, sheer admiration, which it inspires each time I gaze at it. Behind the figure, rising heavenward from a gentle knoll, is a row of poplars which bend and sway like graceful plumes above the great Emancipator. Behind the poplars is a row of rather shabby buildings painted in vivid colors—American buildings, but somehow redolent of China. Together, the trees and buildings form a curious background to the massive, stately statue of Sun Yat Sen. One has to walk around the statue, survey it from every angle, to receive the full effect of its beauty. From the rear it is just as impressive, just as imposing, as from the front. The austere, placid sweep of the figure is matchless. Inevitably, one is constrained to pause, to bow the head reverently, to mutter a prayer of thanks. Here, united in the spirit of the deepest Chinese tradition, is the embodiment of action and inaction. Here is peace, wisdom, compassion, gentle understanding, all epitomized in one being. Here is a monument to the evolution of man's consciousness expressing itself in a radical, revolutionary way acceptable to all time.

Strange as it may seem, another aspect of Bufano's Orientalism is his deep conviction that it is our life on earth which really counts. I say strange because at first blush this seems to be the very essence of the Western materialistic view of things. But when I say that for Bufano it is the life on earth which really counts, I mean it in a wholly different sense than that in which the phrase is usually taken. I mean, in the words of G. R. S. Mead,[1] that "it is the life on earth which really counts, for here is the meeting-place of the above and below, of the within and the without, the ground of really vital struggle, in which the world-process is most intensely engaged in realizing the world-purpose . . . It is said in one of the great myths of the soul, that the stature of the angel in heaven —the one who is elsewhere declared perpetually to behold the Face of the Father, that is, presumably, who is in the immediacy of the Divine Presence—grows with the struggles of its twin on earth, of the man who fights the good fight in the state of existence in time and space; until at last earth is raised to heaven and heaven

[1] See his *Quests Old and New*, G. Bell & Sons, London, 1913.

is brought down to earth, and necessity and freedom embrace in the consummation of the divine purpose." [2]

But let me continue with the citation, since it is in what follows that I detect a relation between Bufano's mute philosophy and this ancient doctrine of metempsychosis which the author is discussing . . .

"According to this high over-belief, the main lessons that life has to teach seem to be the essential non-separability of the life of the individual soul from the life of the whole, and therewith the power of the individual life to enjoy communion with the divine life. The soul's greater destiny includes both necessity and freedom. Freedom resides in the power of the soul to change its individual attitude with regard to the circumstances of life, which are the necessary expressions of the greater life of the whole. If instead of looking on circumstances as vexatious and inimical limitations, we regarded them as ever-fresh opportunities, and indeed the most immediate means of bringing us to ourselves, we might embrace them gladly as the ever-changing moods of our destined complement and fulfillment. For with this change of attitude our personal separative love and will would unite with the all-embracing will and love, and we should be at one with our own greater destiny and with that of the rest, and so find ourselves in conscious cooperation with the divine purpose."

This holistic conception of life, common to the ancient doctrines of the East, and one which underlies the science of astrology as well, expresses more adequately, richly and meaningfully man's relation to the universe than do our contemporary social, ethical or metaphysical views. I stress this for the reason that Bufano, who is so strongly an individual, Bufano, who has such a developed social consciousness, Bufano, who has so many seemingly antithetical

[2] How Marxian, except for the terminology, is this language!

traits, can only be understood from the vantage ground of a superior, more inclusive philosophy of life. To view him simply as a daring individualist—a fanatic or iconoclast—or to view him simply as a potential leader of men, or to view him simply as an artist who, through a superabundance of temperament and endowments, oscillates from one form of activity to another, is not to see him in his true light. Bufano has the qualities of the ancient man, for whom life was a whole, for whom life was meaningful. Like them, he has an understanding of reality which is at once immediate and transcendent. His active nature is one with his passive nature; the one is not the opposite of the other nor in conflict with the other. Bufano, it might be said, never sleeps. He is a man whose consciousness has been aroused to a point beyond that of the ordinary man, beyond that of even our exceptional men. His dreams are like neither those of the sleeper nor those of the waking man of to-day. His dreams are one with this all-pervading reality which is eternal and from which everything stems. If he does not affix his signature to his sculpture it is not out of false modesty but in full awareness of the divine nature of creation, in full awareness that he, Bufano, is but an instrument of creation, that it will not matter a thousand or two thousand years hence whether people know that it was he, Beniamino Bufano, who created them; what does matter, in his opinion, is that they should enjoy his creations and be inspired to further all creation. As for the present, who knows Bufano will always recognize his handiwork: his spirit is in every line, every contour, every flowing form. In every piece of sculpture he has given us may be found that delightful, often humorous, blend of opposites so characteristic of the poet and metaphysician, of dreamer and man of action, of iconoclast and traditionalist. Grave, eloquent and imposing as are his monumental pieces, the smaller ones, mostly of the animal kingdom, reveal a

394

roguish fantasy, a mathematician's wit and whimsy, which border on wizardry. Were he given support and encouragement, Bufano could create, in the remaining years that are left him, a veritable pantheon of figures which would express in essence the whole vital spirit of our age. It would be a creation as enduring and as intelligible to the men of the future as Egyptian, Aztec, Chinese or Indian sculpture is to the man of to-day.

The need for a man like Bufano in a country like ours, where everything in the domain of the aesthetic comes about haphazardly, is beyond dispute. Of all our sculptors, Bufano alone seems to have a vision which embraces the needs of the entire nation, a vision which regards the present in terms of the evolving future. Some of those marvelous anecdotes which he brings back from his trips around the world, those which reveal his true passion as well as the amplitude of his spirit, have to do with things architectural. His descriptions of the temples in India, Burma, Java, Siam, Cochin-China, remind one of the glowing pages of Elie Faure's *History of Art*. In listening to Bufano one lives again through great epochs of history, through periods of man's spiritual and aesthetic development in which everything seems super-dimensional. Only in the great cathedrals of Europe do we have anything which pretends to rival the wonders of antiquity. In America we have nothing to match this spirit of the East, neither in grandeur, sublimity of conception, nor in execution. Our skyscrapers are living tombs for soulless automatons, reflecting the ugly spirit which caused them to be. Nowhere do we find a city that was planned for beauty and reverence, unless it be Washington. But how does Washington look to-day? The statues and monuments which are strewn about the country should have been thrown on the junk heap long ago. A country alive and aware of its role would have all its great artists working simultaneously; it would have more work for all its artists than could be accomplished in their respective lifetimes. It would be planning now what could come to fruition only a hundred or five hundred years hence.

Bufano is the man who could mobilize all our potential artistic resources, who could plan the beginnings of such vast undertakings, who could rouse the consciousness of the public, inspire our legislators, defeat our inertia-ridden critics and authorities. He has something in him of da Vinci, of Michelangelo, of Lorenzo the Magnificent. Yet this singular figure, this man with all his talents and potentialities, is locked up, so to speak, in a room at the Press Club in San Francisco, emerging now and then to wage puny warfare with the pathetic powers that be. Here is a man whose fingers are itching to do big things, yet is obliged to twiddle his thumbs. Here is a man who can handle sixty foot monuments of the hardest materials but who, to keep his hand in, must sit in his little room and carve diminutive pieces of sculpture. Here is a man who can take a giant redwood and mould it into a dramatic figure of Saint Francis—but who will give him the redwood, who will grant him the site on which to erect his statue? Here is a man who has taken stainless steel and demonstrated to the manufacturers of it that with a wooden mallet, skill, and plenty of elbow grease he could accomplish things which the manufacturers said were impossible. Here is a man who, flying in the face of tradition, has taken the hardest granite *and* stainless steel and made of their alliance figures of eternal beauty, waiting on time to give approval to his daring.

Everywhere in America, and in every realm, it is the old story of profligate waste—waste of material resources, waste of manpower, waste of native genius. In the person of Bufano this wastage is strikingly revealed to us. It is not only that what he has done is hidden away, lost, neglected or misused; it is not only that he has received scorn, abuse and ridicule for his efforts; it is not only

396

that his forces have been dissipated in a vain struggle with the regressive elements in our midst; the great crime is that his potentialities are neither recognized nor utilized, that to-morrow there may be no Bufano with us. A Bufano is not born every day. True, we shall always have sculptors, but not of Bufano's stature. Bufano is of our size, our time, our spirit. No idea is too great, too humanitarian, no dream too grandiose, not to find in him a ready and eager response. He is never the one to say "Impossible!" He says "Yes!" He says, "Let's begin now!"

I remember well the day I spent with him at the City Hall in San Francisco, when he was trying to get a hearing in connection with the vandalism which had been perpetrated on his statues. How can I ever forget the atmosphere of vacillation, of tedium, of stupidity, indifference, red tape, confusion, delay, obfuscation which reigned? It does not take much imagination for me to visualize what it must be like whenever or wherever Bufano presents his case. The men who should be bending forward with neck strained and ears cocked quietly turn their backs and take a little snooze. One can witness this not only at the City Hall in San Francisco but at Washington, D.C., or at the Peace Conferences. Anything which has to do with the immediate and genuine relief or advancement of the world falls on deaf ears. The moment there is a cake to be cut it is another story, of course. Then every one is all attention, on his toes, awake even in his corns and bunions.

That day, observing the difference between Bufano's behavior and the behavior of the men he was appealing to, whom in fact he never had a chance to appeal to, I was convinced as I had never before been convinced that the chaos and injustice which reigns in the world is the result of a frantic effort to avoid doing what most obviously should be done, what even a child would have the intelligence to recognize should be done. More than ever I realized that the men to whom we have relegated our powers are, by virtue of their office, the very ones to defeat us, throttle us, stifle our dreams and visions. The man who talks common sense, the man who advocates simple, direct methods of procedure, the man who demands truth and honesty, the man who acts as if these ways of proceeding were right and natural, brings about a disturbance which permeates every layer of society. Of such a man it is certain to be said that he is a crack-pot, that he knows nothing about practical affairs, that he is a confused being, a meddler, that he is just a poet, which is to say an utter fool. But if we follow the doings of those other self-accredited experts, the wise-acres who have been leading the world by the nose from the beginnings of time, what do we see? Where is their order, their economy, their sense of beauty, their tolerance and forbearance, their humanitarian spirit? What has their domination brought about? And whither are they leading us now?

If I had ever heard one of them talk about municipal affairs, or national affairs, or world affairs, the way Bufano talks about sculpture, the technical difficulties involved, the stress and strain of materials, the use of the various implements, the relation of sculpture to architecture and landscape, its connections with traditional art in the past, and so on, I might have some respect for their ilk. Bufano talks a concrete language; they talk a smoke-screen language. Bufano has to have knowledge and skill or his statues would fall apart. Bufano has to think in long terms, for his creations are made to endure. These others, the so-called men of affairs, talk postponement and compromise, leaving the real work to be done by those who come after them. *They* seek the approval of the crowd; Bufano seeks the approval of the elect. *They* feather their nests; Bufano has no nest, his home is the world. *They* organize planned destruction, planned waste; Bufano speaks of creation, of plenitude for all. These men are right only because they know how to squash all opposition; from the very beginning of their careers they are trained in the arts of deception, duplicity, hypocrisy, frustration and obfuscation. They live by vote catching; they grow fat and powerful by lying and thieving; they have no one's welfare in mind but their own. *And every one knows it!* The greatest swindlers, the greatest crooks among them, get off scot-free, are often honored by the community, are sometimes sent abroad as emissaries of the very people whom they have disgraced and dishonored. These are the cold facts about these birds, no one will dispute them.

How it ever came about that men of this stripe should contemplate erecting a colossal monument to Saint Francis, how they ever linked in their minds a city of corruption with the gentle brother of all men is beyond me. Is it not strange that only recently the city of San Francisco has begun to think of erecting a monument to its patron saint? Who were the guiding spirits of the city in the past? Were they spirits or were they baser things, such as gold and opium? When was the spirit of the gentle saint invoked, if ever? How does that spirit manifest itself to-day in the behavior of its citizens? If Francis of Assisi were to appear to-morrow, in the flesh, at the City Hall, do you suppose he would be recognized? Would it not be precisely the moment to turn one's back and have a quiet little snooze?

It was when we were paying our respects to Bufano's little animals scattered throughout the "projects" that Saint Francis' name began to assume proportions in my mind. I thought of those glorious straightforward acts associated with his name, of how he stripped himself of his clothes in the court room and stood before his father clad only in a hair shirt; I thought of how he donned a coarse robe and, equipped only with a begging bowl, set about to open men's eyes to the truth; I thought of how natural it was that a lone man, armed with fervor, truth and simplicity, should convert thousands to the good cause, should be greeted everywhere with joy and benedictions, should bring peace and blessings to all men. I realized that this had happened not once in the history of mankind but numerous times, that it could happen again to-day, or to-morrow, whenever the spirit of a man became so great, so unassailable, that the world could not but give heed. All these figures who so moved the world were possessed of no material power; they had all stripped themselves bare, relying exclusively upon the divine spirit which animated them. Are these then the fools, the simpletons, the confused dreamers? Are we to impugn their simplicity, their love of truth, their straightforward acts? Are we to regard them as meddlers, fanatics, crack-pots?

Of such men we can only say that they were like rocks—gentle rocks, happy rocks, wise and compassionate rocks. They broke through the webs which threatened to strangle them. Their gestures were piercing and triumphant. Their deeds are like monuments which neither time nor the elements can destroy.

---

Taking them at their best, the celebrated sculptors of our time have given us works which, for the most part, belong in the salon, the morgue or the boudoir. They were meant, most of them, it would seem, to be enjoyed by other artists. They were not set down in the midst of life, not built to battle against the elements, nor even against public opinion: they are hidden away, protected, exposed only to the elite or the snobbish. The same is true of modern painting, to be sure. The cult of genius has brought about a thorough stalemate. The very arts which demand a profound public life, an exposed life, a life shared by all the people, the very arts which would enliven and rejuvenate the pallid, sickly atmosphere in which we live and move, are kept under cover. I am thinking not only of painting and sculpture but of the theatre, the dance, the art of costume and so on. In war-torn Europe to-day, in Europe which is in ruins, there is more evidence of cultural and artistic life than in prosperous America. We are a hundred years behind the rest of the world, when it comes to art. We have the means and the facilities to be on the spot, wherever anything vital and stirring is going on, in the twinkling of an eye. But we are never there. We arrive ten, twenty, fifty years too late, like visitors from a distant planet. If we have a dearth of genius, Europe has a plethora; we could import genius as we import wines and wools, if need be. We could import ideas too, if we are devoid of them. We could send our silver birds to the far corners of the earth and bring back the *élan vital* itself, sealed and bottled, if once we realized how desperate we were. We are more desperate than the boldest among us dares to imagine. We are dry and barren, joyless, sick at heart, sick in mind; we are being stifled and smothered by our own creature comforts, by our fear of change, our fear of adventure, but above all, by our fear of ideas. What we crave is a life of "gilt edge security." And we are getting it. We are embalming ourselves.

If this barren night is ever to end, if there is to come a dawn, then the first thing to do is to let down the bars, unbolt the locks, tear down the walls. What belongs under the sky, what belongs out in the open, in clear daylight, must be dragged out into the open, exposed to the elements, exposed to public view. If the purpose of art is to enrich, if the purpose of art is to increase man's joy and man's wonder, then art must be made public, made available for every one. If it is possible to move huge arsenals from place to place, if it is possible to transfer whole armies from one continent to another, if it is possible to spend in the building of one man of war more than was spent on the W.P.A. in the four years of its sway, then it should be possible to move the heaviest statues about—*or*, set other living sculptors to work to produce them by the hundreds. If some works of art, by reason of their disturbing nature, should be mutilated or destroyed, others could be created to replace them—bigger ones, bolder ones, more terrifying ones. *Or/and*, those who have a love of art commensurate with their love of country could volunteer to police these public monuments night and day; they could take turns standing guard, equipped with their own rifles or machine guns, their own tear gas equipment. There could be a special police to guard works of art as there is a special police to lure young girls into prostituting themselves. If one felt as keenly about the preservation of the art instinct as one hypocritically does about other people's morals, there would be no difficulty whatever, none, that I can see. If the city of San Francisco admits that it is unable to take proper care of the art work loaned it by the Federal government, and if that same Federal government is too indifferent to take measures of its own to preserve its works of art, then the private citizens, the private art lovers of America, could take the matter into their own hands. Surely the municipality, the State, the national government would not object if, of their own volition and at their own risk, the private citizens of this country took steps to protect public works of art. Is it necessary to press the subject further, to point out, for example, the absurdity and incongruity which permit a man caught defacing public property, property, incidentally, which often should be defaced or demolished, to be sentenced to a term in jail or a heavy fine, and which allow the mutilation or destruction of a great work of art without a finger being raised, without making the least apology, the least remuneration, to the artist in question?

I remember that day I spent with Bufano at the City Hall because it was a shameful day in which I heard nothing but timid counsel, suggestions of compromise, warnings to tread softly, go slowly, take it easy, and so on. One might have thought that it was Bufano who was the criminal, that the crime he was committing was to demand his rights. I can still hear that empty phrase repeated on all sides: "Don't worry, Ben, you know we're behind you." And I smile ruefully as I think of Bufano's retort to the Mayor when the latter, on a similar occasion, had said: "Don't worry, Ben, I'm right behind you." *"Just how far behind me are you, Mr. Mayor?"* was Ben's quick retort. Righto! Just how far behind are you all, you good, mealy-mouthed citizens who prate and prattle about the glory of your city? Where are you in this rat race? Have you drained yourselves of all power and spirit?

---

One of the quixotic stories about the good Saint Francis is his meeting with Orlando of Chiusi who owned great lands in Tuscany. It is said that the latter made Saint Francis the gift of a mountain, Alverno of the Apennines, where Saint Francis subsequently beheld the vision which so affected him. I mention this story because, when one wonders sometimes what one could give a certain individual who seems to require nothing, it is always possible to give him a mountain. A mountain is not a possession which you have to lug around with you—it stays put. Besides, mountains were never meant to be owned. And since Bufano is not an acquisitive type of individual, a mountain is just the sort of gift he would appreciate. Giving him a mountain to which he could retreat, work, meditate, pray, gather new strength, would be like giving him a piece of the divine essence. It would be a gift which he in turn could pass on to some one else when he no longer had need of it. Every inspired being has use for a mountain—and would never do the mountain harm.

I think strongly about mountains because I happen to have neighbors who own mountains. Orlando of Chiusi, however much he may have owned, could not have owned anything approaching the dominion of William Randolph Hearst, let us say. (I traveled recently for a whole day through just a portion of Mr. Hearst's former possessions.) It was not long ago either that Henry Miller, the Cattle King, boasted that one could walk from the Mexican border to the Canadian border without ever having to set foot outside his property. The State of California has set aside hundreds of thousands of square miles as national parks, as bird and game refuges. Around and about me at Big Sur is a territory at least forty miles square which is entirely devoid of human beings. Could you not, Mr. Governor, allot one little acre of your State's proud holdings to the greatest sculptor we have in this land? Could you not, in the name of Saint Francis, who loved all living creatures, permit him to chop down just one redwood in order to raise a monument to that great being? I know a spot on the Hunter Liggett Military Reservation where there is a tumble-down building which Bufano could convert into a huge studio, where he could live in peace and silence, undisturbed by any human presence. It is one of the most divine spots I have ever laid eyes on, situated in a golden bowl which is bathed in perpetual sunlight. Nobody but you, Mr. Governor, would ever know that Bufano was living there, so hidden from the public sight is it. We are no longer at war, the soldiers on that reservation have been withdrawn. Surely, Mr. Governor, if you cannot give Bufano a mountain, you could lease him this tumble-down house and the acre of land which surrounds it, could you not? I know that it is useless to appeal to the private landholder. I appeal to you, Mr. Governor, in the name of the people of this great State. You are taking excellent care of the wild animals, of the birds of the air, of the seals and otters, of the trout in the streams, the wild deer, the gophers, the chipmunks, the snails, the slugs, the rattle-snakes, the trees, the thorny cactus . . . could you not also take care of just one human being, one artist who wishes to convert your hard materials into symbols of joy and freedom? How long will it take you, Mr. Governor, to get behind us? How many centuries will we have to agitate this question before we get results? Mr. Governor, it is given to you to pardon a man whose life has been condemned. Can we not ask you to use your prerogative to do something in the name of creation?

When Bufano needed a conductor for his People's Symphony Orchestra he took a plane and flew to London. When Saint Francis desired to put an end to the Holy Wars he went straight to see the Sultan. When the people of Eureka Valley wished to quash the highway project which the City Fathers were trying to foist on them, they sent a rousing delegation right to the City Hall of San Francisco. Even if it doesn't work, there is something healthy and invigorating about direct action. Now and then one just has to see the Mayor, the Governor, or the President of the Republic. One has to buttonhole him and let him know how rotten things are. One has to do it even if he knows that the powers invested in such figures are nominal rather than real. Sometimes even a figure-head comes to life. Now and then even the worm turns.

And when all other measures fail, perhaps it would not be in vain to present a petition to the birds, animals, trees, snails, deer and slugs in the great public reserves, begging them in the name of forgotten, frustrated humanity to make room, just a tiny bit of room, for another living creature, a biped called man . . . Man, man, what a sorry spectacle you present! You set aside sacred haunts for the gentle creatures, allowing none of your own kind, however weary, homeless or despondent, to squat among them. You set aside thousands upon thousands of smiling acres for the

405

beautiful wild animals, so that once a year for a full thirty days you may go among them and slaughter them without let. But not for thirty minutes will you permit a serious artist, a man who has no desire to hunt, maim or slaughter, to live with the beautiful wild, gentle creatures of the great reserves . . . Man, man, you are of a strange race. When you hear an infant squawking in the night you are moved to the very bowels. Yet whole nations can roll in agony—if they happen to be "the enemy"—and you stand by and watch without moving a muscle. You feed the little fawns in the hills out of nursing bottles, and when they grow older you shoot them down in cold blood. You send packages of food and clothing to Europe to help the poor victims of the war, but you do nothing to prevent your elected representatives from starting another war. You move in power and glory when it comes to the kill, but you are even more helpless than the snail or the slug when it comes to creating peace and happiness.

It is quite possible that I am a fool to believe that man can ever be other than he now is. It is possible that my brother Beniamino is even more of a fool than I. It is even possible that Saint Francis was the greatest fool that ever lived. If believing in you, O Man, if praying for you, aiding you, abetting you, means being a fool, then I wish to remain a fool forever. I'd rather a thousand times be a fool than agree with those who shout *"Impossible!"* Nothing is impossible, I say. And what does my brother Beniamino say? Just this: "I know nothing in man's make-up that is not possible and complete." To which I say, "Amen! Amen, little brother, Amen!"

# ARTIST AND PUBLIC

THE gist of this speech, which lasted a good part of the journey, was to the effect that artists must learn to help one another. They must help one another if ever they are to help themselves. They can do this no matter what condition of society they find themselves in.

It was of present day America, however, that Rattner was talking, of the immense, undreamed of possibilities which confront the artist and the public alike. For the two are dependent on one another.

Curiously enough, he had begun this monologue by dwelling on the so-called failures, among which are always to be found the greatest names. What a heritage these failures bequeathed the world—just in wealth alone! Often the sale of *one* of their paintings was sufficient, had they been there to receive it, to have kept them all their lives. But in their lifetime no one dared speculate thus. (Yet in every other realm men speculate freely, daringly.) Pass over the fact that, had any of these painters been granted only a meagre tithe of what they had earned, they might have given us still greater treasures, still greater wealth. *We are talking only dollars and cents now,* to stress the point. The point is that art pays, believe it or not. *It does not pay the artist,* that is all. Not usually. With those who receive a fair share of what they produce in their lifetime we have no concern here. Our concern is for those who are denied, rejected, killed off. Our concern is with those who make others rich by their labor and who receive nothing but jeers and insults for their pains. The big question is: *Who suffers most, the artist who is denied or the public?* (To say nothing of art itself).

Well, then, let us add up the fabulous sums which the works of a Van Gogh, a Gauguin, a Modigliani, for example, have created. How much money does that make? Enough to keep Van Gogh all his life? Yes. Enough to keep Van Gogh *and* Gauguin? Yes. Enough to keep all three. Enough, in fact, to keep a dozen or more artists for a whole lifetime. Keep them not only in food, rent and clothes, in pigment, brushes and canvas, but enough to give them spending money, enough to permit them to travel, enough to permit them to enjoy themselves like other lesser creatures, like idiots in the insane asylum, for example.

But how would we know which artist to encourage?

This is the question which always stymies every discussion of the sort. It is like the question of giving India her freedom. The British government says: "When they agree among themselves." Similarly, when it comes to protecting the artist, people say: "When they prove that they are worth helping." But an artist needs to be helped before he can show his worth. It takes him time to develop.

How would you solve the problem, then?

Here I think every man reveals his true colors—on how he answers a question of this sort. The timid man gives a timid answer, the cautious man a cautious answer, the clever man a clever answer, and so on.

But isn't there one answer which would solve the whole question?

Yes, there is. It is to have faith, to give, and pray that the results will be good. Give to every artist, good or bad, deserving or undeserving. Every potential artist should have a chance. The man who is not an artist will tire of pretending to be one in due time. When he gives up, stop providing for him. But if he wishes to continue struggling until his 99th year, even if you can see no good in his work, give him the means to continue. Give it in the name of art, which includes good and bad works, successful and unsuccessful artists. *The first thing is to give.* After that you may inquire if it was worth while or not.

But who is to give and how much?

Let us answer the last first: by current standards, at least $2,500.00 a year. Those who want to live better than this can free lance it. We are thinking always only of those for whom a modest living is the essential; the real artist wants to produce, not to become rich. We are not concerned with the mediocre ones who pander to the public taste—the public will provide for them handsomely.

The principal problem is, how to get the ball rolling. Who is to sponsor this fund? Obviously, if we wait for the national, state or city governments to assume the burden they never will. (And if they do, they will botch it.) The thing is for all those artists who believe in the idea to band together and use their creative ingenuity to the utmost. There is no one way of solving the problem. It ought to be possible, however, to do this much . . . to present the case to the public in detail and then appeal to the community, or communities, to start a fund. In the city of New York, for example, perhaps enough could be raised to support *three* artists. Figuring that an artist has a possible fifty years in which to pursue his career, the amount required, to support one, would be $125,000.00. What a trivial sum! If the citizens of New York City could not raise three times this amount, then an appeal might be made to the State, and if that didn't work, to the whole country. Perhaps in the whole United States it would be possible to raise $375,000.00 for such an experiment: to support three artists from the beginning of their careers to the end. One has only to think for a moment of the huge sums wasted on unimportant things to see how plausible it would be to convince the hard-headed American business man that this is a good investment. What fortunes are thrown away on crack-brained projects! In America especially almost any sum can be raised for any purpose.

How would the first artists be chosen?

By those artists who believe in the plan and will work for it. One has to begin somewhere, somehow.

And if these are not the best artists?

What matter if the first chosen are not the most deserving? It may not be necessary to make appeal to the whole country, to begin with. It may be that the borough of the Bronx alone could raise $375,000.00. It may be that one borough, one county, one election district, will give support to a dozen artists. Once a beginning was made, competition and rivalry would create other nuclei elsewhere. New York could be pitted against Chicago, San Francisco against St. Louis, and so on. The State of New York could be made to vie with the State of Massachusetts. It would not be the borough, county, city or state, mind you, but the art lovers in these communities who would raise the funds.

Once it is clear that the paltry sum of $125,000—or let us say roughly, 100,000 dollars, since most artists will not enjoy fifty years of creativity—is all that is required to maintain an artist for life, the task should be simple. Think of the donations made by private individuals for libraries, museums, awards, etc. Much of this money is being squandered foolishly at present. (One has only to read the list of the Guggenheim awards each year to convince himself of this.) Besides, the artists themselves do not control the spending of it. Moreover, whatever accrues from the sale of the artists' work does not accrue to the foundations which offer the money. It should. According to this plan, whatever is earned by the sale of an art work goes back to the sinking fund until the $125,000.00 is written off. (The donators would then be paid off.) After that, a percentage would go to the artist, but the most of it to the fund. This surplus would take care of those artists who do not "pay," so to speak.

The important thing would be the management of affairs by the artists themselves. The art dealer would be eliminated, for one thing. Exhibits would be arranged by the artists, and in their own galleries. Traveling shows would be perpetual. The living artists would be featured, not the dead. Art would be brought to the public—it would belong to the public in a live way, and not to private collectors, museums, morgues and crematories. Instruction, if desired, would be given by artists—it would be part of the price they would pay for the privilege of protection and maintenance. The academies would thus be emptied in short order. The blind would no longer lead the blind.

What is said for the painter applies to the writer, the sculptor, the musician, the actor, the dancer. One need not wait for a Utopian form of government. Better always to avoid governmental supervision. Art should be kept free, as well as alive. No government on earth will permit freedom in art, as we know from experience. Neither will patrons. Nor will the public, probably, in the long run. What we are suggesting is merely a foothold, using the public—i. e. the art loving public—as a lever. In the course of time the artists themselves will secure control of the funds and there will then be no interference from without. There will, of course, be plenty of trouble from within. Disagreements? Certainly. Splits and schisms? Yes, in abundance. Artists do not get along with one another any better than other people do, probably less well. But they will have to learn to get along somehow, in some fashion, or perish. Never have they been in greater danger of being exterminated than to-day.

We were thinking of painters originally. There are the writers also. What weapons the writers control! What a power and an influence they could be, since their medium is words! Imagine the writers of America having their own press, their own means of distribution, their school for type-setting, printing, binding, etc. How long would it take them to become self-sufficient, self-supporting? Not very long. Add to this, that if each group of artists bent all their energies to the maintenance and furtherance of the idea, if they cooperated, if they armed themselves (figuratively) against their enemies, if they propagandized for themselves (instead of for editors, publishers, newspapers, etc.), what a force they could be! Who could combat the combined forces of all the artists in the world? In one decade they could bring about a revolution greater than any we have witnessed so far. What divides them is what divides men everywhere—the problem of earning a living. Scotch this and you begin to get somewhere. It is not necessary to be a Communist, a Socialist, or whatever you like (politically) to alter the situation radically. Work from within outwards. Begin with little, but begin! If only, as I said before, just three artists—a poet, a painter, a mu-

412

sician—could be assured of lifelong protection, it would be something. We are the richest people in the world. We feed the world and we save it when it is about to destroy itself. But we always wait till the last horn. Surely we can support three living artists, can we not? I feel certain the idea would spread like wild-fire. There would not be much opposition at first—merely ridicule, sneers, contempt. Swallow that! Once this country were maintaining a thousand artists, the effect would be overwhelming. Never have a thousand artists been subsidized simultaneously.

How many artists are there in America?

I do not know. I remember hearing it said that in Paris alone there were something like 50,000 artists of all kinds—dancers, actors, writers, painters, musicians, sculptors, etc. Perhaps America has 100,000. Who knows? One thing is certain—if she has 100,000 to-day she would under this plan have 500,000 a generation hence. What percentage of the entire population is 100,000 after all? Very little, isn't it? Think of the Periclean Age, of the great number of men of genius—*undisputed geniuses, attested by time*—who flourished in that epoch. To rival Greece of the Golden Age America would have to have at least a million artists!

And over and above this question of maintenance lies the greater one of making the public not only art-conscious but artists. Art has to be re-introduced, not via the gallery and museum, but via the individual home. There has to be reborn a desire to do things with the hands, to work from within out, to make the home itself a work of art, from the building which encloses it to the items which constitute it. People have to be encouraged to make things themselves, in their own fashion, according to their own limited aesthetic instincts. They must be taught again to believe that whatever they do themselves with their own hands is infinitely better than what is made for them by factory hands. (Better spiritually, better for the

413

morale!) They must not only design their own homes, but build them. They must learn the trades, the handicrafts, the humble arts —all forgotten now. They must start at the central hearth, which is merely the reflection of their own central fire. They must believe in themselves, in their own creative abilities. This is a revolution which can be begun any time and which needs no overthrow of governments. Nothing could stop this work of creation once the fever caught. By the same token the people could be their own financiers, if they were still foolish enough to believe in money. Why hand money over to bankers to squander? Why pay governments to build arsenals of destruction when all you wish is to live in peace? Why build battleships, bombers, etc. when you can build beautiful homes, create beautiful gardens, grow your own crops, handle your own money? Why go to work for a soulless corporation when you can work for yourself—without wages and without fear of being laid off?

Every Utopian community has proved to be a failure. What of it? Does that mean that the idea of self-government, of creative government, is false? It may require thousands of experiments before the light dawns. Christ was no failure, nor Buddha, nor Francis of Assisi. Their lives were certainly Utopian. No man is a failure who lives up to the best that is in him. That the world does not follow suit means nothing. The world never acts in concert. No Utopia is realizable which demands that every one think and act alike. A Utopia is in essence always a dream of harmony, if not perfection. What is demanded of a society, what gives it life, is the ability to inspire a greater measure of enthusiasm, a greater measure of freedom. It must inspire people *to live*, not to die, *to create*, not to destroy. The golden periods are when art flourishes, that is incontestable. But we must remember that however golden those periods now look to us, for the artists of those periods it was hell.

Art has come to be the province of the select few. Art has become a cult to which only the man of genius is admitted. But genius, if we really understood it, is the norm. The only tenable attitude towards art is to foster the artist in every human being, see to it that everything one handles, sees or hears is imbued with art. Art must penetrate through and through, from the humblest to the most exalted domain.

It would be impossible, and unwise, to attempt to outline the precise details for a program such as we discussed on that long train ride. That is the task of the artists themselves, acting in concert, when they are ready for it. But the main points should be clear. The foremost one is that the artist should be maintained for life; he should not be subsidized for a few years because he is in desperate need or because he looks as though he might lay a golden egg. The community must have faith in him, must realize that art, if it receives the support that other activities do, will yield as great, if not a greater return—*in dollars and cents*. We say, start with one artist rather than launch into chimerical attempts to solve the whole problem at once. (This method should not prevent those who prefer to give some artists a little help for a little while from continuing to do so.) The next important point is that the control and award of such funds, as well as the art products themselves, should be in the hands of the artists. The government, federal, state or municipal, should have no hand in the matter. It would be ideal if the program could be initiated by the artists themselves, i. e., by the help of the successful ones who, let us say, would donate of their own accord a tenth of their yearly earnings. But this is almost too much to be hoped for. The successful ones have no need of the plan and are apt to be indifferent, forgetting the struggles which they themselves went through in the beginning. The third major point is that all artists—poets, musicians, painters, and others—

should use their combined powers and resources to make themselves self-sufficient, self-supporting, to work as a unit against those destructive forces in the community which would exploit the artist. Once they have their own studios, schools, presses, propaganda bureaus, etc., they should be able to work directly with the public and eliminate agents, editors, publishers, dealers, galleries, etc. It is time America, like other countries in Europe, had hundreds of communities endowed with their own academies, galleries, theatres and so on. There could be many traveling galleries, traveling presses, traveling theatres, as well as fixed ones. The knotty problem is how to get artists to work together, work in their own interests, despite their very great differences of opinion on every subject under the sun. If *they* can do it, then, I suppose, the other members of society eventually will.

When one thinks of the astronomical sums spent each year by the various communities that make up America, to say nothing of the many governmental bodies, it makes one's head spin. That approximately only one hundred thousand dollars is all that is needed to support one artist for life is something to think about. It probably won't even require that much, for the majority of artists, since very few start in at twenty and live until seventy. The first few men elected may already be in their thirties or forties. On the other hand, they may be youths of fifteen or sixteen. The time to begin supporting an artist is the moment he shows signs of being one.

Should this idea ever be broadcast, look for an uproar. And mark whence it comes! The very men who are so willing and eager to squander our fortunes—our futures, indeed!—on pork barrel projects and on greater means of destruction—will be the first to talk about squandering the public's money. Fortunately, the present plan does not envisage taking money from the public by legislation; it is a purely voluntary form of offering we contemplate. Those who believe in it can give; those who don't can ridicule it. Once the money is donated, it can not be withdrawn. Thus, if only *one* artist should be maintained for a lifetime it will be something, an advance over the present dispensation. It is quite possible that that artist may prove a failure. (I should hate to be the first man in the world chosen for such an honor!) Are we to judge the validity of a plan by the work of one man? If by this method at least twenty painters, for example, could be supported, I think we would be able to judge better whether it pays or not to support the painters of America. That would require roughly $2,000,000.00. A paltry sum, truly. (I leave it to the Bureau of Propaganda to show how really less than nothing this is, when it comes to pissing away the public's money.)

To spike any malicious barbs, perhaps I ought to add that neither Rattner nor myself had thoughts of being included in such a provision. Rattner now has the best dealer in the world and I have a half-dozen publishers willing to publish me. After twenty-five years of struggle we are just beginning to see daylight. It is to prevent the wasted years of struggle, the bitterness it creates, that this plan is set forth. To those who fear that men will not create if they are not perpetually on the edge of starvation, I say that the true artist creates *despite* such conditions, not because of them. He is an artist because he feels the sufferings of humanity more than other men. His work is an incentive for men to recreate the world in terms of the imagination. He revolutionizes life not at the periphery but at the center.

One of the greatest advantages in protecting the artist economically, as I see it, is that it will kill off those who only imagine they are artists. If it is true, as the world in general believes, that economic security makes a man soft, kills his incentive, and so on, then what better way is there to find out than by this method? Speaking broadly, the way to get rid of drones is to give them a surfeit of luxury and idleness, let them kill themselves off. This idea was actually put into effect in a Belgian prison. It worked. The prisoner who did not want to work was given a luxurious cell, a man to wait on him, and anything in the way of food, drink, tobacco he demanded. After ten days of it, a man would beg to be allowed to work like the others.

The hypothesis supporting our plan is that the creative instinct is the dominant one, and that it exists to some degree in every one. The fact that the majority of great artists have continued to create even though they were not compensated for their labors seems to us a proof of the correctness of this hypothesis. Immediately I can hear some one saying: "Well, if *they* could do it, why can't the others?" The question is badly put. One could counter by saying: "If you derived joy and inspiration from the work of those who survived this cruel test, why shouldn't you look forward to increasing this joy and inspiration by aiding those who are not strong enough to meet the test?" Why do we wish to penalize those who provide us with blessings? Does this attitude not reveal an unconscious rivalry, a hatred for the man of talent?

There is, moreover, a very simple way of solving this dilemma. If it should turn out that some artists, after they had earned a good income from their work (over and above the stipend suggested), have become lazy and indifferent, support of these artists could be cut off. They could be maintained, in short, as long as they proved that they had the desire to create.

The principal thing, however, is *to awaken desire*. For every great soul who will continue to create, no matter what obstacles confront him, there are a thousand who give up before they have met the crucial test. The highest types require almost nothing in the way of material comforts: they are fortified by courage, vision, will. But the world is not made up of these types, neither in the realm of art

418

nor in any other realm. We believe in giving the child every possible advantage, including those we did not have ourselves. Why do we deny the grown man? Let each one take what he needs—but let there be something to take from! We know to-day beyond all argument that we can and do produce sufficient for every one, as far as basic needs are concerned. There is no question of a dearth; there is rather the question of a surplus. Our problem, in recent years, has been what to do with the surplus. The simplest solution, the most obvious one, would be to give it to those who need. But that is dangerous, in the opinion of those who have. Dangerous for whom? Only for those who want *more* than they need. The fear of growing soft is always voiced by those who are taking it easy, by those who have grown soft themselves. The hungry man, the desperate man, does not fear to grow soft.

We do not fear, as I said before, to give children every advantage. We do not take the food from their mouths for fear they will become soft or lazy. They are growing, we say. They need food. An adult is also a growing individual. He needs food too, richer, more complicated foods than a child. Aside from the privileged classes, most adults do not even get sufficient ordinary food, the kind that a child is fed. As for moral, intellectual and spiritual food, that is almost non-existent. This deprivation reveals itself in the realm of art primarily. The proportion of artists in a population such as ours is abysmally low. When I spoke earlier of a possible hundred thousand, I meant *potential* artists. It is impossible to mention over a dozen real artists in any one realm of art. But even if ninety-nine out of every hundred artists to be maintained by this plan were mediocre ones it would still be worth putting into effect. Art must be encouraged, not discouraged. We have to work with what we have. We can't demand, because we have suddenly grown conscious

419

of the problem, that our artists be the best in the world. We can't demand the impossible because we have at last decided to give our hard-earned money to the cause.

If you read the lives of great men, especially the lives of the great artists, you will discover that there was always some one who believed in them, some one who gave them the modicum of faith, of moral support, which they needed. How important an element in their lives this spiritual comfort was each one interprets in his own way. I have never met the artist who did not give it supreme importance. If this is a truth, one which even the hard-boiled materialist will not deny, then think what it would mean to the artist to have even the *moral* support of society! But there is a corollary to this. The person who gives his moral support is usually willing to give material support also. Those who believe in the virtues of poverty believe in it for themselves. They do not refuse aid to those who make appeal to them. It is precisely these beings who give freely, who can give their all. Those who give only their moral support give nothing really, as we well know. Morally and spiritually they are bankrupt. Such people, even when they give millions, give less than nothing. Society as a whole, in its relation to the artist, is in much this position. Whatever it gives, it gives grudgingly. It does not believe in the efficacy of giving. The artist to-day is made to feel that society is the enemy. He thinks of himself as an outsider, as a pariah often. What he portrays, therefore, is the death of society. He can think only of the preservation of the individual. But a real society is made up exclusively of individuals. It should be, at any rate. To-day, however, we speak of our "atomistic" society. Is it not curious that the most sensational discovery, or invention, of such a society should be the atomic bomb? Is it surprising that a society which kills off the individual should eventually discover the way of killing itself off?

420

We said earlier that the artist was never in greater danger of being exterminated than to-day, and we mean it. The beneficent power of the atom could have been uncovered in peace time and used for peaceful purposes, but it was not. It was the destructive urge which unleashed it, and it will be used destructively as long as men are indifferent to creation. It is easier to destroy this hell which we have made of the planet Earth than to convert it into a paradise. We have come to think of life on earth as a hell, no mistake about it. We want to *escape* punishment, not dispense with it. We punish ourselves, we punish one another, we punish the very earth. And to what end? That we may live in peace and comfort. But the ones we punish most abominably—in peace as well as in war—are the artists. He is the last one to be thought of in war times and the last one to be thought of in peace times. When we are at war we are too busy defending our lives; when we are not at war we are too busy trying to earn a living. There is never a time when we worry about the artist, as we do about the insane, the mental defective, the alcoholic, the criminal-minded, or about war veterans or unemployed. The perpetual condition of the artist is virtually that of a state of war. He has to make war on society in order to protect himself. He has to become a pan-handler, a pimp, a prostitute, a criminal, in order to survive. Sometimes he even has to pretend that he is an idiot or a madman. Anything to get a crust of bread! Do I exaggerate? Read the lives of these martyrs! Don't think that Van Gogh was an exception. Just think of your favorite painter, your favorite author, your favorite musician—then read their lives!

If those of you who have the means to foster a project such as the one outlined are still unmoved, still dubious, still sceptical, if you will not risk the experiment, then I have another proposal for you, and for this we do not have to appeal to you who have wealth but to all members of the community, rich or poor. It is this: give what

421

you can, what you no longer need, be it food, clothing, shelter or pennies. The saints were not ashamed to beg for food and shelter. Neither is a genuine artist. He will gladly accept the food you cannot swallow, the clothes you no longer wish to wear, the extra room you have no use for. He will, I say, provided you do not ask him to do what he does not want to do. If he wants to paint, you are not to ask him to clean out stables. You are to give what you don't want, or don't need, so that he may do what he wants to do. So that he may *create*. That is the only condition. Beware of the artist who is too proud to beg! The man who is too proud to beg is also too proud to give. We should expect the maximum of each other, not the minimum.

Americans, it has often been remarked, are the quickest to give, and the most generous when they do give. But they must be touched first, must be convinced there is a real need. They are a strange mixture of hard head and soft heart. What they fear, above everything, is to look ridiculous, "to be taken for a sucker." This fear that generosity may be interpreted as foolishness is unworthy of us. Generosity is never absurd, however extravagant it may be. Generosity is the only thing that pays, the only thing that draws dividends, so to speak.

Every great government in the world to-day is mortgaged to the hilt. The reason is—WAR. When its existence is threatened, a nation draws on its future potential. It does not think first—how much money is there in the treasury? It creates the wherewithal to carry on the fight. It puts its future generations into debt. Wartime is the one time when people and governments go all out. And what are the benefits of war? Death and ruin. It is for this that people make the supreme sacrifice.

This plan involves no such sacrifice. Nor does it promise death and ruin for reward. Thus far, it has been said, the war has cost us in America alone about three hundred billion dollars. That is only the visible, tangible cost. It has cost much more than that, be sure of it. No one can estimate the real cost of war—it is incalculable.

The minds of men are now turned to the task of rehabilitation. That will also cost an immense, a staggering sum. But in none of these rehabilitation plans have I heard a word about the artist. It is almost as though he were non-existent. The other day I met a Chinese artist. He told me that China had sent a number of artists abroad, during her fourteen years of war, so that they might be spared. We in America have done nothing to protect our artists in wartime. Will we do anything now that peace is here? It remains to be seen. It would be fatal, in my opinion, to wait until the government got ready to tackle the problem. It would be equally fatal to wait until the public got ready to tackle the problem. The artist is a stranger who stands outside the door, too timid to knock. At whatever door he stands he hears nothing but problems being discussed. The one word he never hears is "artist." He hangs his head in shame, he feels that he does not belong. But his problem is just as real, just as momentous, as that of the war victims in Europe. He too has no food, no home, no means of earning a livelihood. He too feels guilty, though he has no reason to. We have made him feel guilty because we have given him to believe that he is not a vital part of the community. But he committed no crime. He had no false or evil ideology, unless to practice one's art constitutes a crime. Why is he ignored, then? What is it he is guilty of?

If we could ask that question of every American we would get some pretty answers. "But what am *I* guilty of?" the man in the street will say. "I don't have enough to eat myself, nor enough clothes, nor enough this or enough that."

"But when you work you get paid for your work, do you not?"

To this he is obliged to answer in the affirmative. If and when he

423

works, he gets paid, there's no getting round that. But can the artist say that? Can he say when he will be paid, or how much? He has no certainty whatever of earning a livelihood, unless he deserts his calling. He can abandon his profession and become a roustabout. That choice is always open to him. He cannot abandon his calling and become overnight a lawyer, an engineer, a bricklayer or a plumber. But what we ask of him, in effect, is that like other men he should do some honest work, do something useful—then practise his art. Imagine asking a lawyer or a doctor to work all day at "something useful" and practise his calling in his spare time! I am ramming the point home as best I can. If I am unfair, I want to know in what way. I want to know why law, medicine, engineering and such like are considered useful professions, paying professions, and painting, literature, music and so on not. I want to know why it is that a good doctor, a good lawyer, a good engineer, fetches a good price for his labor, whereas the better an artist is the less remuneration he receives for his work. There are artists, to be sure, who receive big sums for their work. Unless they are well advanced in years, these artists are seldom the good artists. According to present standards, the worse the artist the more he receives for his labor. A good artist, only when he is near death—if he is that lucky!—begins to receive a fair sum for his work. If this is not true, then our whole argument falls. If it is true, then it is evident that there is a prejudice against the artist. The victim, however, is not the artist merely, but the public. The public to-day does not realize this fact. The public is being gulled by all sorts of pretty promises, chiefly of material benefits. It is being promised new automobiles, new vacuum cleaners, new refrigerators, new toasters even. As if these were the things of utmost importance! What statesman would be rash enough to promise the public a new artist? Can you imagine what a laughing stock he would be? Yet I can think of no greater gift to a war-weary world than a crop of new artists, so help me God.

# THE MOST LOVELY INANIMATE
# OBJECT IN EXISTENCE

(Fragment from *The Air-conditioned Nightmare*)

Coronado seeking the Seven Cities of Cibola found them not. No white man has found on this continent what he came in search of. The dreams of the acquisitive whites are like endless journeys through petrified forests. On the River of Mercy they were borne to their graves. On the Mountain that was God they saw the City of the Dead. Through the waters of the Prismatic Lake they stared at the Endless Caverns. They saw Mountains of Superstition and mountains of shiny, jet-black glass. The Virgin River brought them to Zion where all was lovely and inanimate, most lovely, most inanimate. From the Garden of the Gods they moved in a heavy armor to the Place of the Bird People and saw the City of the Sky. In the Fever River they saw the Sangre de Cristo. In the Echo River they heard the Desert of Hissing Sands. In the Dismal Swamp they came upon the passion flower, the fuzzy cholla, the snow-white blossoms of the yucca, the flaming orange of the trumpet-vine. Looking for the Fountain of Youth they came upon the Lake of the Holy Ghost wherein was reflected the Rainbow Forest. At Shiprock they were ship-wrecked; at Mackinac they were water-logged; at Schroon Lake they heard the loon and the wild antelope. The Gulf was lined with Cherokee roses, bougainvillea, hibiscus. They fell through Pluto's Chasm and awoke in Sleepy Hollow. They crossed the Great Divide (with Margaret Anglin) and came to soda canyons and borax fields. In the midst of the Thundering Waters, they stumbled on the Island of the Goat where Martha kept her vineyard. Through the clear waters they saw jungles of kelp and phosphorescent marines. Near Avalon they saw the abalone and other shellfish lying on the ocean floor. Looking for the Black Hills they came upon the Bad Lands. Calling upon Manitou they found a Turquoise Spring and when they drank of its waters they were turned into obsidian. Searching for the Green Table they came upon the Cliff Palace where the red man kept his Medicine Hat. Passing through the Valley of the Shenandoah they came upon the Hanging Gardens and were swallowed up by the Mammoth Cave. . . .

Endless was the trek and endless the search. As in a mirage the bright nuggets of gold lay always beyond them. They waded through poisonous swamps, they tunneled through mountains, they reeled through scorching sands, they built natural and unnatural bridges, they erected cities overnight, they compressed steam, harnessed water-falls, invented artificial light, exterminated invisible microbes, discovered how to juggle commodities without touching or moving them, created laws and codes in such number that to find your way among them is more difficult than for a mariner to count the stars. To what end, to what end? Ask the Indian who sits and watches, who waits and prays for our destruction.

The end is a cold, dead mystery, like Mesa Verde. We sit on the top of an Enchanted Mesa, but we forget how we got there, and what is worse, we do not know how to climb down any more. We are on top of the Mountain that was God and it is extinct—"the most lovely inanimate object in existence."

HENRY MILLER was born in Manhattan in 1891, and attended elementary and high school in Brooklyn where his family moved when he was one. The rest of his education has been informal, acquired through wide reading and through travel. His first published book, *Tropic of Cancer*, appeared in Paris in 1934, although he had written many stories and two novels before that time. He lived in France for ten years, returning to the United States at the beginning of World War II after he had made an eight months' trip through Greece which resulted in *The Colossus of Maroussi*. In the early 1940's with the American artist, Abe Rattner, Miller made a cross-country tour of the United States which is recorded in *The Air-Conditioned Nightmare* and *Remember to Remember*. Mr. Miller settled in Big Sur, California, in 1945, but now spends much time travelling throughout Europe. In 1958 he was elected to membership in the National Institute of Arts and Letters, and in 1961 was awarded a special citation of the Prix International des Editeurs on the occasion of the coming publication of *Tropic of Cancer* in the United States and Italy.

# BOOKS BY HENRY MILLER
## published by NEW DIRECTIONS

THE AIR CONDITIONED NIGHTMARE
An account of a three-year trip through the United States.
Paperbound.

BIG SUR AND THE ORANGES OF
   HIERONYMUS BOSCH
Henry Miller here describes the earthly paradise he has
found on the California coast and the devils, human and
natural, which have threatened it. Paperbound.

THE BOOKS IN MY LIFE
A candid and self-revealing journey back into memory, shar-
ing with the reader the thrills of new discovery that a lifetime of wide reading has brought to an original and questioning mind. Paperbound.

THE COLOSSUS OF MAROUSSI
A travel book about Greece. "It gives you a feeling of the
country and the people that I have never gotten from any
modern book." (Edmund Wilson.) Paperbound.

THE COSMOLOGICAL EYE
A miscellany of representative examples of Miller stories,
sketches, prose poems, philosophical and critical essays, surrealist fantasies, and autobiographical notes. Included are
several sections from *Black Spring*, together with the famous
story "Max." Hardbound and paperbound.

THE HENRY MILLER READER
A cross-section designed to show the whole range of Miller's
writing—stories, literary essays, "portraits" of people and
places—interlarded with new autobiographical comments by
Henry Miller. Edited, with an introduction, by Lawrence
Durrell. Paperbound.

**REMEMBER TO REMEMBER**
Miller continues his examination of the American scene, in essays and stories, and finds men capable of resisting the dehumanizing pressures of civilization. Hardbound and paperbound.

**STAND STILL LIKE THE HUMMINGBIRD**
A collection of stories and essays, many of which have appeared only in foreign magazines or in small limited editions now out of print, reflecting the incredible vitality and variety of interests of Henry Miller. Hardbound and paperbound.

**SUNDAY AFTER THE WAR**
Stories, essays, letters, long narratives, and other pieces, including three fragments from *The Rosy Crucifixion*, the story "Reunion in Brooklyn," an attack on Hollywood, and a study of the role of sex in the work of D. H. Lawrence. Hardbound.

**THE TIME OF THE ASSASSINS**
A study of Rimbaud that is as much a study of Miller and has throughout the electric quality of miraculous empathy. Paperbound.

**THE WISDOM OF THE HEART**
A rich collection of Miller's stories and philosophical pieces, including his studies of D. H. Lawrence and Balzac. Paperbound.

**HENRY MILLER ON WRITING**
Passages on the art and practice of writing chosen from all of Miller's books, brought together by Thomas H. Moore, co-founder of the Henry Miller Literary Society, with Miller's active collaboration. Paperbound.